Managing Human Resources in the Hospitality Industry

An Experiential Approach

Kathleen M. Iverson, Ph.D.

Roosevelt University

Prentice
Hall

UPPER SADDLE RIVER, NEW JERSEY 07458

Library of Congress Cataloging-in-Publication Data
Iverson, Kathleen M.
    Managing human resources in the hospitality industry: an experiential approach / by
  Kathleen M. Iverson.
        p. cm.
    Includes bibliographical references and index.
    ISBN 0-13-949181-3
    1. Hotels—Personnel management.   2. Food service—Personnel management.   I. Title.
TX911.P4 I94 2001
647.94'068'3—dc21

                                                                              00-064966

Executive Editor: Vernon R. Anthony
Production Editor: Marianne Hutchinson, Pine Tree Composition
Production Liaison: Barbara Marttine Cappuccio
Director of Production and Manufacturing : Bruce Johnson
Managing Editor: Mary Carnis
Manufacturing Manager: Ed O'Dougherty
Art Director: Marianne Frasco
Cover Design Coordinator: Miguel Ortiz
Cover Designer: Maureen Eide
Cover Image: David Tillinghast/SIS/images.com
Marketing Manager: Ryan DeGrote
Editorial Assistant: Susan Kegler
Interior Design: Pine Tree Composition
Printing and Binding: Courier Westford

Prentice-Hall International (UK) Limited, *London*
Prentice-Hall of Australia Pty. Limited, *Sydney*
Prentice-Hall Canada Inc., *Toronto*
Prentice-Hall Hispanoamericana, S.A., *Mexico*
Prentice-Hall of India Private Limited, *New Delhi*
Prentice-Hall of Japan, Inc., *Tokyo*
Prentice-Hall Singapore Pte. Ltd.
Editora Prentice-Hall do Brasil, Ltda., *Rio de Janeiro*

10   9   8   7   6   5   4   3   2   1
ISBN 0-13-949181-3

To my wonderful family,
Bruce, Eric, Dana & Kristen
for their love and support

C O N T E N T S

9 Protecting Employee Rights

PART III   A NEW ERA OF MANAGEMENT

10 Labor Relations

11 Evolution of Management Theory

Success in the hospitality industry is tied directly to employee performance. Workers can only provide outstanding service when they feel that managers and supervisors are on their side. Effective leaders in our industry realize that a dissatisfied employee often makes for a dissatisfied guest. Companies that put people first, not only customers but also employees, will thrive despite high levels of competition. Due to the continued labor intensity of the hospitality industry, the manager of the future will be first and foremost a people manager, involved in leading, motivating, counseling and rewarding employees. Supervisors in the hospitality industry must be prepared to take on new roles in the reengineered, highly participative organizations that are emerging.

Managing Human Resources in the Hospitality Industry will help you develop the knowledge, skills, and abilities needed to put people first. You will study cutting-edge management principles so that you can select, train, appraise, and motivate your employees for exceptional performance. Diversity, self-managed teams, coaching, the learning organization, personal mastery, career modeling, and behavioral interviewing, are just a few of the important new developments in the field of human resource management that are addressed in your text.

This text is also a high-quality learning instrument designed to allow you to participate in your education, take chances, be challenged, and to ultimately become an outstanding supervisor. Each chapter is filled with real-life examples, stories, cases, and thought-provoking exercises to help you and your classmates master the material in a fun and engaging manner. As a student of hospitality management, you will be introduced to the newest approaches, concepts, and techniques in leadership and supervision. The experiential components allow you to not only read the text, but also apply concepts in situations similar to those you will encounter in the industry.

Part 1 is a management development component focusing on essential skill sets of supervisors including communication, problem solving, decision-making, and professional development. Part 2 addresses topics significant to managing human resources including selection, appraisal, counseling, discipline, and training. Finally, Part 3 provides an overview of organizational principles of the past and future including important contemporary topics such as organizational culture and change, diversity management, teams, learning organizations, and the quality movement. Students who use this text will be well versed in theory, human resource practice, and contemporary approach to service management.

OUTSTANDING FEATURES

This text contains full chapters addressing important, contemporary topics in hospitality management such as performance management, diversity, and quality. It has many significant features that promote its readability and facilitate your comprehension of important concepts. Designed to provide a number of learning experiences, it contains numerous real-life examples, experiential exercises, and skill testing opportunities that will keep you involved.

Each chapter will open with an Advanced Organizer to encourage students to cognitively connect the material that follows to their future career. Summary boxes called "Best Practices," "Insights," and "Research Links" will be located throughout the text to link the theoretical material to actual situations in the hospitality industry. At the end of each chapter are case studies, review questions, critical thinking exercises, an on-line exercise, and a portfolio building exercise designed to create opportunities to apply the concepts you have studied. Here is a brief description of the supporting materials found in each chapter.

Advanced Organizer: A brief mini-case designed to help students to relate the chapter topic to their future careers.

Behavior Objectives: Clear objectives will be stated at the beginning of each chapter. These objectives are based on both the topics addressed in the chapter and the learning outcomes that occur when you complete the case studies and exercises.

Insights: Each chapter will contain one or more examples from recent publications highlighting real-life application of the principles discussed.

Best Practices: Chapters will contain several brief examples of best practices in action in the hospitality industry.

Running Case Application: Each chapter will contain a running case study featuring the experiences of two new hospitality supervisors. Readers will act as mentors and advise the new managers on problem solving strategies.

End of Chapter Exercises: A series of questions designed to reinforce learning will be included at the end of each chapter. Then can be assigned as homework or used by students for test review.

Critical Thinking Exercises: To foster the analysis and application of chapter materials, this section requires students to use their knowledge in new and unique situations by employing critical thinking skills.

On-Line Link: Each chapter will contain an exercise that requires students to utilize the Internet as a research tool.

Portfolio Exercise: Students may complete exercises designed to help them build a professional portfolio that they can then use to promote their skills as a supervisor when they seek employment or promotion.

Web Site Support: Additional supporting materials for both instructors and students will be located at the Prentice-Hall web site. Included will be group exercises and additional web-based learning experiences that will be updated regularly to provide current information and application of the material.

Leadership 2000

ADVANCED ORGANIZER

As the job of managing hospitality establishments grows in complexity, the pool of qualified candidates steadily shrinks. Today there is a bidding war for management talent. The Bureau of Labor Statistics predicts a 44 percent increase in the number of foodservice and lodging management positions by the year 2005.[1] If you are seeking excellent job opportunities, job security, the opportunity for rapid advancement, and exciting work, you have certainly chosen the right field. Careers in hospitality management offer many advantages.

Imagine that a good friend asks you, "Why did you choose a career in hospitality management?" What would you answer? What do you hope to get from your career in this field? In all likelihood, one of your answers would be that you want to have the opportunity to lead and manage others. This is a big part of any career in our industry. This chapter introduces you to the important topic of leadership in the hospitality industry.

BEHAVIORAL OBJECTIVES

- Describe the four benefits of outstanding service.
- Explain the steps companies take to put people first.
- Specify the key behaviors of effective leaders.
- Define the relationship between internal and external customers.
- Compare the characteristics of great hospitality industry leaders.

The Ritz-Carlton Naples. © 1992 The Ritz-Carlton Hotel Company. All rights reserved. Reprinted with the permission of The Ritz-Carlton Hotel Company, L.L.C. The Ritz-Carlton© is a federally registered trademark of The Ritz-Carlton Hotel Company, L.L.C.

LEARNING TO LEAD

This book will help you develop valuable management skills. It provides the knowledge and tools you will need to put people first in your organization and to manage your human resources effectively. It is a mix of theory and practical application that will develop your knowledge of management principles and teach you to implement them. You will learn to select, train, appraise, and motivate your employees for exceptional performance. In addition, you will examine cutting-edge management philosophy that can be readily applied to the hospitality industry. Quality management, self-managed teams, diversity, the learning organization, and technology are just a few of the important developments in the field of human resource management that you will study.

This text is also a high-quality learning instrument designed to allow you to participate in your education, take chances, be challenged, and to ultimately become an outstanding supervisor. Each chapter is filled with real-life examples, stories, cases, and thought-provoking exercises to help you and your classmates master the material in a fun and engaging manner. This book is based on the principles of **experiential learning** or learning by doing. To learn new management techniques, you must practice them over and over again, or you won't remember them for long.[2] This orientation to learning, first proposed by John Dewey back in 1916, makes sense. Think about a child learning to ride a bicycle. Reading books about bicycle riding and listening to parents explaining the process may provide initial direction, but the child could never master the skill without drill and practice. The child must attempt to ride the bike, receive feedback in the form of a successful ride or a bumpy fall, and then try again. The same principles apply to becoming an outstanding leader. Until you practice, get feedback, and try again, you will not internalize management principles. Learning by doing in an educational setting minimizes the pain of failure. Managers who first begin practicing their skills on real employees may experience some particularly bumpy falls in the form of disgruntled workers, high turnover, and even litigation. This text allows you to study and practice leadership skills in a controlled environment and gain valuable experience that will reduce the number of management mishaps you encounter on the job.

> *You can dream, create, design, and build the most beautiful place in the world, but it requires people to make it a reality.*
>
> —Walt Disney

Walt Disney, perhaps one of the greatest innovators of all times, spoke these words shortly before his death; they are illustrative of his realization that creative genius alone does not make a successful organization. Even Walt Disney, skilled at making dreams a reality, understood that the driving force behind his success was his employees. The most elaborate hotel or the most exquisite restaurant are simply cold structures without the warmth brought by the people who work there. Success comes to companies that have the best people, not just the best facilities or the best location. The hard assets of a service business contribute far less to the value of its ultimate product than do the abilities of its people, the effectiveness of its managers, and the quality of its leadership. What would the Disney experience be like without all those wonderful, kind, warm, caring employees to guide you through the maze of confusion?

VALUING HUMAN CAPITAL

We often think of employees in terms of payroll or cost, but what is their value? If a server earns $20,000 per year, how does this compare with what he or she delivers in revenue for a restaurant? Perhaps if the server is outstanding, responsible for lots of repeat customers, he or she may bring in gross income of $1,000 per night for the restaurant or $300,000 per year! What if that individual left your company and joined a competitor—could you recoup the loss? Corporate stars are high-risk commodities. If a group of outstanding servers and cooks leave an existing restaurant to take a job at a newly opened, competing restaurant because they offer better pay, benefits, or working conditions, your business is going to feel the blow and have a difficult time recovering. Hospitality organizations must recognize the added value that their human capital, or people, bring to their businesses. Your job as a supervisor is to take good care of your employees and give them the tools they need to do their best. When Casey Stengel was asked, "What has made you the best baseball coach in the world?" He replied, "I don't trip my players on the way out of the dugout."[3] Some managers actually create roadblocks that make it harder for employees to serve guests. Instead great leaders do all they can to facilitate their employees' ability to "wow" their customers.

INSIGHT **1.1**

When hotels calculate their value, they must not only assess their land, structure, and profits, they must also appraise their human assets. This process often occurs when a hotel is in the process of being bought or sold. Human asset appraisals typically take two to three days. The following information must be collected:*

- The background of each member of the executive committee, for example, their training, education, and career path.

- An assessment of the executive committee's style of leadership. Does the committee work well together? Do they support each other? Who is uncooperative? Do they support their managers?

- What is the general manager's leadership style? Does he or she get everyone involved? Is the general manager supportive and motivating?

- What is the balance between customer service and cost control?

- Is employee morale high?

- What type of training do employees receive?

- Are performance reviews a positive tool for reinforcement?

- What is the quality of the foodservice operations? How are menus set? How are costs controlled?

- What are the results of customer satisfaction surveys? What do customers complain about?

By the end of the human assets appraisal, the hotel will have a clearer understanding of the strengths and weaknesses of their management system. If human assets are underutilized, this may effect the purchase price of the hotel. It can also highlight differences in the existing management philosophy and those of the company purchasing the hotel.

*B. Dungman. "Human Asset Assessment Provide Property Appraisal Tool." *Hotel & Motel Management* 218, no. 10. (June 1, 1998). 10.

EXCELLENT SERVICE IS OUR MISSION

The primary focus of any hospitality-related business is providing top-notch service to our customers. Those who choose this career path are engaged in one of the finest pursuits possible—serving others. As a service manager, your job is to coach, facilitate, and advise your work group in their effort to make each guest's experience with your organization positive and memorable. See Figure 1.1 for a short refresher on the strategy of service

The core principles of service management include:

- **Listening precedes action.** Ask customers what they really need from your organization. Great managers actually walk around and talk to guests, asking them about their satisfaction with the service and products.
- **Reliability is the core of service quality.** Customers lose confidence when frequent mistakes are made. Get employees involved in both identifying and solving guest problems.
- **Service customers just want the basics.** Customers do not have extravagant expectations. Most customers want a quality meal, served in a reasonable amount of time, or a quiet, comfortable guest room. Extras are great, but first make sure you are doing a great job in delivering the basic product.
- **Poor quality is a design, not a people problem.** To improve service quality, look to the system for breakdowns. Equipment and physical environment must be appropriate to facilitate excellent service. Itemize each step in the service process and note where problems arise. If food delivery is too slow, decide whether the problem lies in the kitchen or front of the house. Before pointing fingers, make sure equipment and supplies are adequate and not slowing things down.
- **Good service recovery can save delivery.** Dissatisfied customers can be salvaged if recovery is accomplished successfully. When server problems occur, guests want an apology, and also some sort of compensation for their inconvenience. When handled properly disgruntled customers can be transformed into lifelong guests.
- **Surprising customers pays off.** Ask, What is the "wow" factor in our product or service? Find out how you can deliver it. Customers in hotels are "wowed" when employees remember their names and recall special requests from previous visits. Find a way to record and save this information so your employees will be able to anticipate guest needs.
- **Teamwork promotes excellence.** Coworkers who support each other can offset burnout. Encourage your employees to work together. When one person is swamped, others should come in and help. Consider establishing "service pairs" where employees have a partner with whom they regularly work. Foster an atmosphere of cooperation.
- **Employee research is important to improvement.** Employees know what conditions reduce service quality. Asking their opinion can provide an early warning system. Carefully analyze this information and follow up by letting employees know the actions you will take based on their feedback.
- **Leadership service.** Managers must inspire and enable service workers to achieve. They must view their role as setting direction and standards while giving people the tools and freedom to perform. Yours is a service job and your customers include both guests and employees.

Figure 1.1 A Service Quality Refresher

quality. In the past you may have held guest service positions where you were responsible for meeting customer needs face-to-face. As a manager you will have a different role in the organization. You are no longer directly responsible for serving guests, but must instead work through others as you lead and motivate your employees to provide a level of service that consistently exceeds guest expectations.

In a sense you and your employees must form a strategic alliance with each guest that enters your establishment. You must enter into a partnership with them, helping them to achieve their goals. They may need to clench an important business deal, hold a key meeting, or merely impress their in-laws. Great food, great service, and impeccable facilities lead to success. Poor food, inattentive service, and poorly maintained facilities can sour your clients' deals, make their meeting a disaster, and cause their in-laws to wish Jenny had married that nice boy from Poughkeepsie instead of your customer's son, Bill.

You can only achieve strategic alliances through your human resources, the people who work for you in the service industry. The individuals that prepare the food, clean the guest rooms, and answer the phones create winning partnerships and are your most important business asset. Thus learning how to manage people is perhaps the most important lesson you will master as a supervisor in the hospitality industry.

INSIGHT 1.2

There are many incorrect assumptions about the labor market in hospitality management. Here are just a few erroneous attitudes about employment in our industry:*

- *There is an abundant supply of cheap labor to draw from.* Perhaps this may have been true during the 1970s and 1980s when unemployment rates were high and there were large numbers of baby boomers available as cheap labor. Today unemployment rates are at an all time low and the number of sixteen to twenty-four-year-olds available to work has declined and will continue to decline.

- *Employee turnover is inevitable, so employers should minimize both selection and training costs.* Turnover is very high in our industry with rates from 60 percent to 300 percent.† Companies that seek to increase their profits by spending large sums of money on marketing, but little on employee development, may bring in more customers, but unless service quality is improved, they won't keep them. Well-trained employees are your best marketers. Don't ask, "What happens if I train employees and they leave?" Instead ask, "What happens if I don't train them and they stay?"

- *Technology will eliminate many routine tasks.* Personalized service is more important to customers than ever. Although technology can certainly streamline some of our practices, we will always need a large staff of human service providers to deliver products and services. It is unlikely that technology will eliminate a large number of jobs in our industry.

*B. C. Mill, "How to Treat Your Employees Like Customers," *Nation's Restaurant News* 30, no. 11 (March 18, 1996): 56–57.
†B. Worcester, "The People Problem: Management Companies Struggle to Attract, Train, and Retain Employees," *Hotel and Motel Management* 214: 4 (March 1, 1999) 38–40.

THE HIGH COST OF POOR SERVICE

The management of service workers is like a newly discovered, still uncharted ocean with few knowing exactly how to navigate it smoothly. Perils in the form of poor service or just disinterested service can have tremendously damaging effects on an organization. Customers are more demanding than ever before. In a recent Zagat survey, customer awareness of service has increased in the last decade.[4] At the same time, the American Customer Satisfaction Index announced that customer satisfaction fell to new lows in 1997, with a full one-third of American customers dissatisfied with the service they receive. According to the results of a research project conducted by Forum:[5]

- 15 percent of customers chose not to do business with companies because of technical quality.
- 15 percent left due to price.
- 20 percent left because of too little contact and attention.
- A whopping 49 percent left because their contact with people was poor in quality.

When we look at the service statistics cumulatively, their effect is even more dramatic. A total of 69 percent of customers were lost because of poor or disinterested service. Not only does bad service cause the direct loss of customers, but indirectly it can also poison future success through negative word of mouth.

On the other hand, providing outstanding customer service delivers dividends in the form of customer retention and increased profits. Companies rated high on the quality of their customer service have the following things in common:[6]

- They keep customers longer—as high as 50 percent longer or more.
- They have lower sales and marketing costs—20 percent to 40 percent lower.
- They experience higher return on sales—7 percent to 12 percent higher.
- They have better net profits—7 percent to 17 percent better.

Research also indicates that companies offering superior service achieve higher than normal market share growth; they also realize increased profitability by charging more than their competitors for similar products.[7] In addition organizations that improve customer loyalty by just 5 percent, improve profits by 25 percent to 85 percent.[8] An investment in service quality does pay off in increased market share, premium prices, and overall profitability.

It is obvious from these statistics that guests aren't buying rooms or facilities when they stay in a hotel, or simply good food when they dine in a restaurant, they are buying service. They are buying lots and lots of service in a nice setting. Thus our primary mission in the hospitality industry is to provide outstanding service, and your primary job as a leader in this industry is to facilitate its delivery.

It is difficult to find an aspect of our industry that has not become compulsively concerned about service. Take a typical Chicago diner for example. Lou Mitchell's Restaurant looks like lots of other coffee shops in Chicago, but it's not. It has distinguished itself with a reputation for fantastic food and even more fantastic service, which begins with a personal greeting by the owner and a complimentary newspaper and box of Milk Duds. Customers feel that they are getting much more than their money's worth, and they flock to the restaurant, waiting in long lines for great food and great service.

ORCHESTRATING GREAT SERVICE

How do you make certain that the guest's entire experience from initial contact to the final good-bye not only meets their expectations but also exceeds them? Managing a group of service employees is like orchestrating a symphony. If the dinner is to be successful, if the stay is to be memorable, each component must work in synchrony with the others. If one instrument (person) is out of tune, the entire performance could be a disaster. Mediocre managers are satisfied with mediocre service in their organizations while outstanding managers strive to consistently deliver stellar service to all guests all the time.

To make service work, managers at all levels within the organization must be role models of doing things the right way—from dealing with customers to interacting with fellow workers.[9] Workers learn more from observation than conversation. Employees will try no harder and will feel no more committed to serving customers than their manager reflects in his behavior, attitude, commitment, and enthusiasm. If you want great service employees, be a great service role model. See Research Brief 1.1 for more on what makes great hospitality managers.

YOUR INTERNAL CUSTOMERS

> *A happy employee is the most important amenity a hotel can offer.*
>
> —Keith Hensley, Executive Assistant Manager
> Adams Mark, Philadelphia

Learning to successfully lead the people that serve your guests is perhaps the most important skill you must have today. There is nothing magical about it. When your employees enjoy their jobs and feel passionate about their

RESEARCH BRIEF 1.1

PERSONALITY TRAITS OF SUCCESSFUL MANAGERS

What personality traits make managers successful in the hospitality industry? In a study designed to test the perceptions held by human resource executives and recruiters concerning the personality traits of successful hospitality managers, it was found that successful managers were viewed as energetic, sociable, trustworthy, friendly, stable, disciplined, confident, and objective.* Of these the personality factors that were most important were energy level and trustworthiness. Managers can use this information to identify and develop leaders within their organizations, reduce turnover, and encourage educators to write and implement curriculum that includes these specific traits.

*N. Graves, "Personality Traits of Successful Managers as Perceived by Food and Beverage Human Resource Executives and Recruiters," *Journal of Hospitality and Tourism Research* 20, no. 2, 95–112.

work, it shows. Customers will want to do business with your company over and over again. But, if you want your employees to provide outstanding guest service, you first have to provide the same type of attention and appreciation to your **internal customers,** your employees. You can't expect your employees to selflessly serve your guests when they feel that they are not well served by their employer. Before you can meet the needs of your external customers, you must first meet the needs of your internal customers. When employees are rewarded, recognized, and given opportunities to achieve great things, they feel proud to be part of their organization. This attitude is communicated in the service provided to guests. The purpose of this text is to help you to develop the knowledge, skills, and abilities you will need to accept the challenge of managing human assets in the hospitality industry and to provide excellent service to your internal customers so they will do the same for your external customers.

Excellent customer service begins with excellent employee service. Great leaders in our industry realize that you cannot expect employees to provide top notch service to your customers if you do not treat them well. In the next century, the effective management of people will distinguish the most successful hospitality companies from those who fail.[10] Managing human assets is the biggest problem facing the service industry today.[11] In dealing with future challenges, leaders must consider an array of concerns regarding the people side of the business. In particular leaders must examine the ways they recruit, train, and develop employees and their approach to dealing with high turnover, low levels of employee satisfaction, and the image of our industry.

When you view employees as intelligent, motivated, trustworthy people who are the resources upon which your success rests, they feel valued and will in turn value your customers. Good management is about caring for your employees. Good managers seek out employees' opinions and learn to keep their "big fat egos" out of the way.

PUTTING PEOPLE FIRST

If service organizations are to achieve competitive advantage, they must put their people first. Customer service is like a baseball game. To get home runs, you must have a great team. Advertising and marketing will get you to first base, good products will get to second base, a knowledgeable staff will send you to third base, but to bring it home and win that return guest, you must wow your customers by bringing service to a higher level. You can only achieve this by putting people first. Service organizations must turn their attention toward their employees if they want to please customers. When we think of the millions of dollars that hotels and restaurants spend on advertising, only to lose customers to poor service experiences, the need to focus on our service workers is obvious.

What does it really mean to put people first? It means publicly announcing your commitment to your employees. And it means letting them know that they are critical to the success of your department and your organization. It also means letting employees know you are available to them and that you are willing to meet with them or talk with them about their concerns and ideas. This action tells people that they are important and taken seriously by you and your organization.

Putting people first also means making training a priority. There are several ways that organizations might accomplish this. Larger companies may

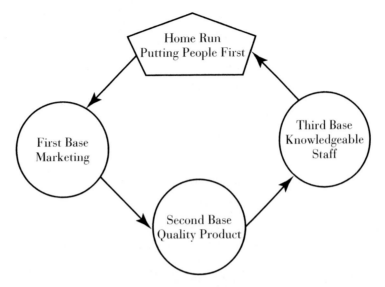

Figure 1.2 Putting People First Earns Home Runs

have a corporate training staff that will conduct on-site educational programs in such areas as diversity management, guest service, prevention of sexual harassment, and interpersonal communication. Other companies that cannot support a large corporate training staff may look to the human resources manager or individual department supervisors to conduct training programs on key job-related issues. Managers who really value employees will make their development a priority and show this by their commitment and active involvement in the orientation and training process.

Finally putting people first means communicating effectively with your work group. This involves skill in listening, sincerely expressing your views and ideas, and giving and soliciting feedback from others.

Organizations that put people first follow many of the practices listed in Figure 1.3. These basic people management practices create a high-performance management system that provides competitive advantage to the organization. These practices make organizations more profitable because they decrease turnover, increase customer satisfaction, increase innovation, increase productivity, increase employee satisfaction, and create a more flexible organization that can readily adapt to new competition and threat.

- Select employees carefully.
- Create a team-based work environment.
- Provide extensive training.
- Share information openly.
- Managers and supervisor are readily available.
- Solicit employee input and ideas.
- Compensate fairly and adequately.
- Reduce status differences between management and employees.

Figure 1.3 A Human Asset Based Strategy

REINVENTING THE ORGANIZATION

Many corporations, large and small, have adopted or are in the process of transitioning into a new set of values and practices. This change in values is reflected in the more "humane" or "respectful" job titles that are emerging. Superiors, subordinates, bosses, hourlies, and, sometimes, even employees, are words that are being eliminated from organizational vocabulary. They are being replaced with coach, team leader, associate, and, at Disney, cast member.

Organizational change is not limited to titles. Many corporations are adopting practices that reinvent the way they deal with employees and customers. For example, the Ritz-Carlton Hotels gave their employees complete responsibility for their work process by developing self-directed work teams. Employees do their own scheduling, payroll, performance reviews, and purchasing, thereby freeing managers' time up to do more planning and leading. You'll read more about this practice in Chapter 14.

Below are several other major transitions organizations are experiencing:

- *Flattened Organizational Structure.* To eliminate bureaucracy and make it easier for those who directly serve guests to achieve quick results, organizations are restructuring by flattening or reducing layers of management. The layers of bureaucracy are reduced, or perhaps even done away with completely, shifting greater responsibility to those in front-line positions.
- *Empowerment.* A common outcome of removing layers of authority in organizations is to empower employees to participate in decision making and take responsibility for solving problems. In most "flattened" organizations, employees are empowered to take responsibility for solving guest problems. This may involve the ability to award extra amenities or gifts to unhappy guests, or, as is the case with Ritz-Carlton Hotels, to go as far as to spend up to $2,000 to make guests happy. In an empowered organization, employees have the ability to respond quickly to guests' needs.
- *Team-Based Organization.* The department structure of old, consisting of boss and underlings, is being replaced by the work team. Groups work together to identify goals, manage themselves, and get things done. Some teams are so autonomous as to be self-managed, meaning they have the authority to hire, reward, and schedule their own work practices. You will learn more about empowerment and team-based organizations in Chapter 14 of this text.
- *Reengineering.* Companies are rethinking their organizations and the processes they use. **Reengineering** is defined by Hammer and Champy[12] as using the power of modern information technology to radically redesign business practices to achieve dramatic improvement in performance. It is about redesigning the organization around core processes rather than hierarchies. Several years ago the Westin

O'Hare in Chicago "reengineered" their bellstand, front desk, room service, and housekeeping departments to form a new department called "service express." When customers needed help, they called one number and could order a meal, ask for extra towels, or request directions.

As organizations change, so must leaders within these systems. The primary message for managers of the future is that you can't do it alone. To achieve success, you must work through others. You must act as a catalyst, energizing your work group to develop new and better ways of functioning.

The motto "Do it my way, or take the highway" has been replaced by "Your ideas are important. How do you think we can best serve our customers?" Yesterday's bosses make decisions and give orders; today's leaders coordinate groups of thinking adults who work together to solve problems and get things done.

THE IDEAL MANAGER

The ideal manager is one who is able to get the best from his or her work group at all times. Leaders have two primary objectives. The first is to contribute to the profitability of the organization, and the second is to maintain high morale among your employees.

To accomplish these dual objectives, you must become proficient in the following functions (Figure 1.4):

1. Planning. You must develop individual and department goals and create strategies for their achievement.
2. Communication. Not only must you keep people informed, you must also be able to listen and facilitate con-

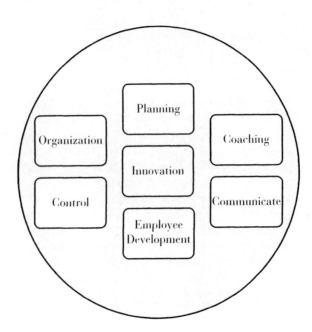

Figure 1.4 Management Proficiencies

versation with individuals and groups. You must be adept at presenting information to groups and communicating in written form.

3. Organization. You must be able to organize your own work and that of your department.

4. Employee Development. As a manager you must be able to select, orient, train, and motivate your employee group.

5. Coach. Today's work environment requires that managers empower employees to take on new responsibilities. This involves encouraging and teaching rather than just giving orders. The coach's purpose is to help each team member perform at his or her best and learn to improve.

6. Innovate. You will be required to continuously improve your department's function by identifying new and better ways to get work done. Innovation is most effective if it involves the employee group; thus the managers role not only is to develop creative solutions herself, but also to lead others to develop new ways to better meet guests' needs.

7. Control. This involves setting standards and objectives for yourself and your work group. You must evaluate performance, reward, and take corrective action when necessary.

Exercise 1 at the end of this chapter contains a brief assessment of managerial readiness. Complete it to identify your potential strengths and weaknesses.

THE KEYS TO LEADERSHIP

BEHAVIOR MODELING

As a manger, it is up to you to set the pace for your workgroup. One of the most powerful tools in teaching is **behavior modeling.** As children and as adults, we learn a great deal by modeling the behavior of people we respect. We observe important adults in our lives and mimic the behavior we see. You can make this powerful tool work to your advantage as a service manager by modeling the behaviors you expect of your employees. If you demonstrate enthusiasm for service, it is much more likely that your employees will feel the same way as you. When your employees see you using outstanding communication skills when dealing with difficult customers, they will "model" or copy your behavior when dealing with irate guests themselves. On the other hand, if you view guests as an inconvenience or an interruption of important work, your employees will quickly pick up on this and display the same lack of concern. Be very careful of the attitudes you demonstrate and display about customer service. A supervisor with a negative outlook toward his job or the company can spread this bad attitude like a virus.

SPECIFIC BEHAVIORS TO MODEL:

- **Good communication skills.** Demonstrate outstanding listening skills by paying attention to both employees and guests when they speak to you.
- **Respect for others.** Show respect for fellow employees, even those who perform less than adequately, by never criticizing in public or gossiping about their shortcomings.
- **Concern for guests.** Let employees see you going the extra mile for guests. Show them how you anticipate guests' needs and go out of your way to meet expectations.
- **Company loyalty.** Talk positively about your company to employees. If you have frustrations, don't let employees see them, or you will transfer your negative feelings.

To be an exemplary role model doesn't require perfection. Mistakes are important teachers too. We learn how to handle failure and frustration and how to recover from difficult situations from our mistakes, and behavior modeling *does* require knowledge. As a role model for employees, you must have a thorough understanding of leadership principles, human resources strategies, and management techniques. By carefully studying this text, you will be taking an important step toward becoming an accomplished leader and role model for others.

OPEN DOOR POLICY

Be available to your employees. Many managers have an **open door policy,** meaning that employees are always welcome to come and see them with ideas, problems, questions, or just to talk. But, more often than not, the open door is really a closed door in a literal or figurative sense. Employees may either be blocked from seeing their supervisor because he or she is too busy or always in meetings, or, if they do gain an audience, they may be met with annoyance for interrupting. Ideally a manager can still meet the job's administrative duties and have time for people by setting aside specific office hours, much like college faculty. During this time be prepared to give employees your full attention.

MBWA

MBWA stands for **managing by walking around.** It proposes that managers spend time with employees, not just to observe them at work, but to talk with them about how things are going. It can be a great way to make informal contact with employees and keep your finger on the pulse of your department. Managers in the hospitality industry typically spend a great deal of time with employees on the front lines, but as they reach higher levels within the organization, there is a tendency to become more office-bound.

BEST PRACTICES

Bill Marriott is famous for MBWA and makes a point of visiting each department in his hotels as often as possible. He is known for dropping by and introducing himself not just to managers, but to line employees when he visits hotels. It is truly awe inspiring for a server or room attendant to shake hands with the president of their company. MBWA can be a powerful tool for staying in touch with employees.

MAKE IT EASY TO SHARE IDEAS

Your more extroverted employees are likely to come to you freely with ideas and comments, but the more introverted group may find it difficult to speak out. There are many great ways to generate idea sharing from everyone. A great low-tech method that is experiencing a resurgence is the suggestion box. Here are a few suggestions that will keep your receptacle from collecting dust:

- Don't just place a brown wooden box on a table with a tacky, handwritten sign saying "Suggestion Box" and expect everyone to fill it with wonderful ideas. Instead, create a bit of a marketing blitz beforehand. Create posters and flyers that describe the new program. Distribute them ahead of time, so that when the attractive, large suggestion box is placed in a prominent location, employees will have had time to develop ideas to fill it.
- Create a committee to read and respond promptly to each suggestion. Using a point system. The committee will evaluate suggestions based on several criteria. High scoring suggestions will be reviewed at department meetings, with congratulations and small awards for those who developed the ideas.
- Publish great ideas in the company newsletter. This makes the employee look good and also makes you look good for fostering such a great program.
- Consider providing larger rewards for suggestions that are implemented and save the company considerable dollars.

Another way to get employees involved in customer service is to turn your employees into "idea scouts" by sending them out to see what other industries are doing with regard to service. Not only can hotel front desk clerks learn about service standards by visiting other hotels, but they can also be sent to Nordstrom's to find out what all the hoopla is about. Why does Nordstrom have such a great reputation for service? How can you get the same reputation?

Soliciting employee ideas and input does much more than just provide a steady flow of new information to your organization, it also makes your employees stakeholders in your organization. They no longer feel like employees, but like owners themselves. They are energized by their expanded role, and this renewal carries forth to the way they serve customers and do their jobs.

MAKE WORK FUN

What brings employees to our industry? More times than not, it is their preconception that working in hotels, restaurants, or travel will be fun. In turn a lack of fun often drives them away, according to the Industry of Choice study funded by the National Restaurant Association and Coca-Cola.[13] Taking this news to heart, managers are creating special events ranging from extensive staff dinners to department outings as a way to motivate their employees and build team spirit, creating a culture that is really fun and that increases the quality of the relationship between all employees. Togetherness also breaks down barriers between departments. Employees in the front of the house may spend little time with those in the back of the house. Fun activities help both groups get to know

BEST PRACTICES

Many companies are incorporating fun into their workplace. Below are just a few examples of successful programs that make work more enjoyable:

- A Chili's restaurant franchise holds daylong group competitions for all managers during quarterly meetings. Events such as scavenger hunts where groups head out into the city with instant cameras are sponsored. The employees must bring back articles or take pictures of themselves in areas around the city. Teams are awarded prizes and a party ends the event. Managers are inspired to go back and plan more fun events.

- A fine dining restaurant holds a "family meal" each evening before opening for back and front of the house employees. They taste new specials and wines and it helps both departments understand what the other is all about. The meal also includes some review of service and operational procedures. Employees who are too busy to participate in the meal can return to the restaurant on their day off for a free dinner.

- In the same restaurant, back of the house employees visit local farms and pick produce that will be included in special menus.

- A McDonald's franchisee sponsors monthly outings for employees including picnics, canoe trips, bowling parties, and river rafting.

each other a little better, and this translates to a better working relationship.[14] Companies that are struggling to retain good employees may find that adding a little fun to the workday can overcome some of the negatives in our industry such as long hours and stress.

SUCCESSFUL HOSPITALITY LEADERS OF THE PAST AND PRESENT

There have been many extraordinary people who have achieved great success in the hospitality industry through diligence, creativity, and their ability to lead their workforce to new heights of service excellence. Bill Marriott expanded the "billion dollar root beer" stand that his father began and has created a diversified corporation unlike any other. Hal Rosenbluth of Rosenbluth International, a highly successful travel agency, has built his business around employee happiness and satisfaction. Ray Kroc, founder of McDonald's Corporation, built a fast-food dynasty based on quality, service, and cleanliness. Mary Mahoney, of Howard Johnson International, is the first woman to be appointed president and CEO of a major hotel chain. Finally Walt Disney had a vision that has transformed central Florida into one of the world's premiere tourist destinations.

There is rich information to be found in the histories of these outstanding leaders. Let's examine some of the practices that led to their great success.

RAY KROC, FOUNDER OF MCDONALD'S CORPORATION

Ray Kroc did not invent McDonald's, he bought it. He had the foresight to recognize a winner in the small, drive-in restaurant created by the McDonald brothers. Ray developed their idea and created a worldwide corporation comprised of more than 14,000 restaurants that spends more than $1 billion on advertising each year. The reason behind his grand-scale success and his brilliance as a leader is demonstrated by the way he selected and motivated his managers, franchisees, and suppliers. He had a knack for bringing out the best in people. Thus he had the ability to unleash the entrepreneurial spirit in the men and women who franchised his restaurants.[15]

Kroc created the world's largest foodservice organization by giving his managers enormous decision-making authority. He chose a diverse management team—people who were themselves corporate entrepreneurs, who were competitive, who wanted to be the best, and who could make sound business decisions. Kroc encouraged managers and franchisees to take risks, to admit failures, and to learn from their mistakes. He strove to "shoot off a lot of cannons" or to come up with lots of new ideas, understanding that not all would land on target. Ray Kroc created an organization whose members adhered to strict standards of Quality, Service, Cleanliness, and Value (their QSV&C motto), without losing their individuality and creativity. Ray was a great listener. He had a habit of listening to all who offered ideas and suggestions, regardless of what their place was in the hierarchy.

Ray Kroc's genius rested in his ability to harness the power of hundreds of entrepreneurs and generate a successful, organized system from this chaotic energy. He bridged the gap between entrepreneurship and corporate bureaucracy.

Hal F. Rosenbluth, Chairman and CEO, Rosenbluth International

HAL ROSENBLUTH, ROSENBLUTH INTERNATIONAL

The philosophy behind Hal Rosenbluth's highly successful travel agency is "put the customers second and the employee first."[16] In fact his belief in this precept is so strong that he even wrote a book about it titled, *The Customer Comes Second and Other Secrets of Exceptional Service*, published in 1993. Rosenbluth's plan to promote happiness among his employees evolved from his need to attract the best people and ensure high-level performance. Rosenbluth and his colleagues believe that companies must address employee happiness and satisfaction if they are to truly increase customer satisfaction. He believes that it is impossible for employees to focus on their customers if they are dissatisfied with their company and their boss.

Workplace happiness is a strategic objective at Rosenbluth International. The company has set policy and adopted practices that not only address major employee issues, but also the minor ones that can either promote or hinder happiness. The first step is to carefully select the right people. Rosenbluth looks for people with positive attitudes and flexibility. The main criterion for hiring, even more important than experience or credentials, is "niceness." Next the company seeks to harness the excitement and curiosity of each associate's first day on the job by sending them to world headquarters in Philadelphia, so that they can become inundated with the corporate vision and values. New hires enjoy group projects and begin exploring such key issues as innovation, openness, and leadership. The two-day introduction ends with an afternoon tea served by Hal Rosenbluth himself.

Rosenbluth travel operates with an open decision-making structure. Service employees have added responsibility and can freely express ideas and opinions to top management. The company encourages all employees to really share their thoughts and ideas. In fact the company holds an annual idea drive to solicit as many creative inspirations as possible. Managers receive special leadership training to help them adapt to this open environment.

Rosenbluth stays closely connected to his associates with the "Hal Hotline," a phone line that any employee may use to provide a suggestion or express a concern or opinion. He also meets with employee focus groups to discuss such important topics as morale, fulfillment, and happiness in the workplace.

Recognizing that an important precursor to employee satisfaction is the opportunity for advancement, all associates are encouraged to create personal development plans with their supervisor to outline career paths that they want to explore. By becoming "associate of the day," employees can learn about a particular area of the company that interests them. They can even choose to spend a day with Hal, as more than a hundred associates have done to date.

Employee happiness has delivered big rewards for Rosenbluth International. Tom Peters dubbed it "Service Company of the Year," and Intel named it "Preferred Quality Supplier." The company has grown to include more than 1,000 locations worldwide and $2.5 billion in sales. Most important Rosenbluth's practices have made it easy to attract and retain top employees. The company's turnover rate is considerably lower than its competitors, and they have received thousands of unsolicited resumes and telephone calls from prospective employees.

Mary Mahoney, President and CEO, Howard Johnson International

MARY MAHONEY, CEO, HOWARD JOHNSON INTERNATIONAL

Mary Mahoney, as president and CEO of Howard Johnson International, is the first woman to lead a major hotel chain.[17] Mahoney began working in the hotel industry before she was twenty years old. She learned franchising, marketing, and sales while working for Days Inn Hotels. Later Days Inn and Howard Johnson were bought by what is now Cendant Corporation. Mahoney became the director of market development for Florida and later vice president of marketing for Howard Johnson. She demonstrated great marketing vision and is given credit for several successful campaigns that have increased the chain's occupancy to the highest rate in its history. Although she has made many sacrifices along the way, Mahoney finds her work very absorbing and interesting. She depends on daily exercise to help deal with the stress and exhaustion of long days and heavy travel.

Mary Mahoney has been blessed with many great mentors during her lifetime, beginning with her parents. She calls former Howard Johnson CEO Stephen Phillips the mentor of a lifetime, and credits him with preparing her for her current job. He was always willing to teach her and allowed her the opportunity to learn from her mistakes.

I had the good fortune to speak with Mary Mahoney about her leadership style and some of the new developments she is implementing at Howard Johnson. Her practice is to provide employees and staff with clear direction on Howard Johnson's corporate vision and mission, provide the skills they need to accomplish the goals, and then move out of the way, empowering her people to make good decisions.

Mahoney is also a visionary leader who is constantly developing new ways to solve organizational problems. She has implemented the national Mentor Partnership Program which pairs underperforming properties with top performers so they might form mentoring relationships that generate improvement. Owners, managers, and even line employees from both hotels meet, and the hotel that is having difficulties learns the secrets of success from its mentoring property. This practice has had a tremendous positive outcome, turning around problem properties quickly and effectively. It has had the added benefit of breaking down cultural barriers that sometimes hinder owners who are from other countries. They have a chance to make new friends in the organization and learn how to be successful in this cultural environment.

Under Mahoney's leadership, Howard Johnson also seeks to support their communities by joining Colin Powell's America's Promise—The Alliance for Youth. Through their participaton in this organization, the corporate staff, hotel general managers, owners, and staff have pledged to reach out to young people across the United States to provide them with encouragement and support as they seek to create a stable lifestyle and productive future.

When Mary Mahoney became the first woman president of a major hotel chain, a TV interviewer asked her what characteristics she had that a man does not. Mahoney's reply was "absolutely nothing." She went on to say that her job is not about gender, it is about leadership.[18] It is also about striving for a goal of peak-level performance and achieving it.

BILL MARRIOTT, CHAIRMAN AND CEO, MARRIOTT INTERNATIONAL, INC.

Although J. W. Marriott Sr. founded the Marriott empire, his son Bill is credited with much of the corporation's growth and continued success. He has carried on his father's hands-on, management-by-walking-around leadership style even though the organization has grown and expanded to mammoth size with more than 1,500 hotels. The Marriotts believe that the best way to make sure their business is running properly is to see it and hear it themselves. Today Bill travels more than 150,000 air miles each year visiting Marriott locations.[19]

Marriott's management style is built on the premise that employees come first, customers second. When employees are content, confident, and happy with themselves and their job, they are better equipped to serve guests. Marriott takes care of their employees by offering them excellent training, health benefits, and even assists them when they have problems with child care or immigration procedures. They have established a hotline where employees can call with any type of question, problem, or crisis, and they receive counseling. Marriott keeps their hourly staff motivated by looking to them first when managers are needed.

Another cornerstone of Marriott's success is his ability to instill a sense of teamwork in his associates. The company has successfully created an environment where rewards for working together outweigh those of the individual's interest. The company does this by hiring and promoting upbeat, involved, hands-on mangers who are excited to be part of the company. Marriott recognizes top performing workers with an Associate Appreciation Day that consists of parities, contest, special awards, and heartfelt thanks from the company.

Bill Marriott also has much to teach us on a personal level. In 1989 he suffered a heart attack. From this experience he learned important lessons. First he learned that the company that he had worked so hard to build had a constitution of iron and did not suffer any setbacks during his illness. Second although Bill is a self-described workaholic, he learned that he must improve the balance in his life between work and play. Finally throughout his life, Bill Marriott has decided to decide. To him this means making a strong commitment to certain behaviors and values and deciding to only make this decision once, never allowing temptation to sway him.

HORST SCHULZE, THE RITZ-CARLTON HOTEL COMPANY, L.L.C.

Mr. Schulze was promoted to president and chief operating officer of the Ritz-Carlton Hotel Company in 1988 after joining the property in 1983 as vice president, operations and general manager of the Ritz-Carlton, Buckhead. His leadership resulted in the company winning the 1992 Malcolm Baldridge National Quality Award, the first and only hospitality company to earn this prestigious award. Further the company won the coveted award a second time in 1999—the first and only service company to win the award two times. This honor is a great testimony to the tremendous leadership skills of Horst Schulze.

Mr. Schulze believes in empowering his employees. At the opening of every hotel, he conducts a leadership seminar for all employees. He begins by saying, "I am president of Ritz-Carlton . . . I am an important person." After a pause he then says, "You are as important because you make this hotel run. If I were absent for a day, no one would notice. But you, ladies and gentlemen, would be missed. You make this company the best in the world."

Mr. Schulze realizes the importance of giving frontline employees the power to make decisions. After all, he began his career as a dishwasher at age fourteen. He has worked in world-class hotels throughout Europe and the United States.

Horst Schulze was a member of the original management team who developed the service philosophy that guides Ritz-Carlton today. This philosophy includes the company's motto, "We are Ladies and Gentlemen serving Ladies and Gentleman," a guiding principle that permeates all levels of service throughout the organization.[20]

WALT DISNEY, FOUNDER, DISNEY ENTERPRISES

For as long as most of us can remember, Walt Disney has been a significant presence in our lives. This entertainer extraordinaire built perhaps the most far reaching empire in U.S. history. Behind Disney's amazing achievements lies a great visionary leader. He adopted quality management principles long before they became trendy. Everything that he and his organization produced—from animated movies to massive theme parks—was continuously improved until every last detail was perfect. Quality production, not volume or cost cutting, was in the forefront at all times. The notion of guests getting their money's worth became gospel at Disney.[21]

Walt Disney also sought to create a culture where employees were closely connected to each other. In his first major undertaking, Disney Studios, visitors noted that employees always smiled, were on a first-name basis with the leader of the company, and frequently had lunch with the boss. There was no time clock at Disney Studios because Walt believed that such devices hamper creativity. His innovative management style also encouraged employee participation and shared knowledge. He felt that it was important that every person who worked for him have access to information and that one man's knowledge is every man's knowledge. Walt also demonstrated some rather "quirky" management practices. He liked to make individuals with opposing views work closely together, causing them to fight harder for what they believed in. He enjoyed conflict and thought rivalry was good.

Long before customer service training became the norm, Disney was doing it and doing it well. Prior to the opening of Disneyland back in 1955, Disney University was established to provide training for park employees. New employees were indoctrinated into Disney lore and carefully taught that every guest receives VIP treatment.

Walt believed that he and his staff were one big team. He used informal talks to communicate his desires to workers and strove to make everyone feel that he or she was an important part of the Disney team. Today Disney employees still believe they are part of something very special.

CONCLUSION

Outstanding leadership skills are the foundation of career success in the hospitality industry. Great managers realize that their employees are their most important assets and hold the key to their own success. People bring added value to hospitality operations. Our industry can overcome the threat of poor service by concentrating on the motivation and training of its front-line employees. As organizations reinvent themselves, management's role has changed to that of coach, facilitator, and trainer. Managers must adopt new ways of leading others, including behavior modeling, open door policy, and MBWA. Leaders must actively solicit employee ideas and seek out new ways to make work enjoyable for their staff. There is much that today's managers can learn from past leaders in our industry. Vision, planning, innovation, and truly valuing front-line workers are the ingredients of successful leadership today, just as they were in earlier times.

K E Y   T E R M S

Experiential Learning	Reengineering
Internal Customers	Behavior Modeling
Flattened Organization	Open Door Policy
Empowerment	Managing by Walking Around (MBWA)
Team-Based Organization	

N O T E S

1. J. Cone, "Creating a Good Manager Is All in the Training," *Nation's Restaurant News*, 30, no. 16, (April 22, 1996): 34.

2. Roger Schank, *Virtual Learning*, (New York: McGraw-Hill, 1998), 17–18.

3. D. Ulrich, J. Zenger, and N. Smallwood, *Results-Based Leadership*, (Boston, Mass.: Harvard Business School Press, 1999), 136.

4. M. McCaffrey, "Proposal: Turn Your Signs to 'Internal Customers' for more Sales Success," *Nation's Restaurant News* 31, no. 40, (October 6, 1997): 70–71.

5. R. C. Whitely, *The Customer Driven Company: Moving from Talk to Action*, (Reading, Mass.: Addison-Wesley, 1991), 9–10.

6. C. R Bell and R. Zemke, *Managing Knock Your Socks Off Service* (New York: American Management Association, 1992).

7. V. Zithaml, L. Berry, and A. Parasuraman, "The Behavioral Consequences of Service Quality," *Journal of Marketing* 60, no. 2, 31–47.

8. R. Zemke, "The Service Revolution: Who Won?" *Management Review*, (March 1997): 10–16.

9. Ibid.

10. Roger S. Cline, "The Value of Human Capital," *Lodging Hospitality* 53, 20–24.

11. Julie Miller, "New Ramada Program Addresses Labor Issues," *Hotel and Motel Management* 211, no. 20 (Nov. 18, 1996): 4–6.

12. Michael Hammer and James Champy, *Reengineering the Corporation: A Manifesto for Business Revolution* (New York: Harper Business, 1993).

13. A. Zuber, "People—The Single Point of Difference—Motivating them," *Nation's Restaurant News* 31 no. 40 (October 6, 1997): 114–115.

14. Ibid.

15. J. F. Love, *McDonald's: Behind the Arches* (New York: Bantam Books, 1995).

16. David Bollier, *Aiming Higher: 25 Stories of How Companies Prosper by Combining Sound Management and Social Vision* (New York, AMACOM, 1997), 151–153.

17. P. Edwards, "Mary Mahoney: Taking HoJo's into the 21st Century," Thursday, October 29, 1998, 1–5, <*http://www. womenCONNECT.com/ businessprofiles.html*>.

18. Ibid.

19. J. W. Marriott Jr. and K. A. Brown, *The Spirit to Serve: Marriott's Way* (New York: Harper Collins, 1997).

20. Information supplied by the Public Relations Office, Ritz-Carlton Hotel Company, L.L.C.

21. S. Watts, *The Magic Kingdom: Walt Disney and the American Way of Life* (Boston, MA: Houghton Mifflin, 1996).

CASE 1.1: BACKGROUND ON RUNNING CASE

One or more case studies are included at the end of each chapter in your text. These are running cases, which means that each study builds on the previous one, and the main characters and setting remain the same. The cases deal with the issues and challenges faced by two new hospitality managers. Melissa Brooks is a newly hired front office supervisor at downtown property located in a major city; James Moore is a manager at a large, independent restaurant located in a busy district near a large city. You will serve as mentor or advisor to James and Melissa, offering them advice about how they might best handle the problems they face. Both the issues and their solutions are based on the material presented in the corresponding chapter.

Before you begin your mentoring role, you will need some background on your advisees. Melissa recently graduated with a B.S. in hotel management from a large state school. Her work experience includes internships and summer jobs as desk clerk and reservationist at resort properties. She was hired by her current company upon graduation and has just completed a three-month management training program. She has now been placed at a large convention hotel in her first job with her new employer as front office supervisor. She is responsible for hiring, scheduling, and supervising the fifteen desk clerks that work the evening shift. Melissa reports directly to the Front Office Manager, Grace Hernandez.

James Moore has a B.S. in foodservice management from a large urban hotel school. While studying, he worked as a host, waiter, and dining room supervisor, gaining lots of hands-on experience in the industry. Upon graduation, he was hired by a large, very successful, independent restaurant located near a major city. He received only two weeks of on the job training before taking on his new position. As day restaurant manager, James is responsible for hiring, scheduling, and supervising twelve servers, six buspersons, two hostesses, and one clerical worker who make up the front of the house day staff. James reports directly to Barry Rogers, the general manager of the restaurant. James also works closely with the chef, Gary Melone.

Both Melissa and James are highly motivated to be successful in their new positions. James hopes to learn everything he can in his new position so he can open his own restaurant one day. Melissa hopes to move up to front office manager, then crossover to sales, and eventually have an executive position in a major hotel. Although they have good technical knowledge, both realize that the most important aspect of their new positions is managing and motivating their staff. As they finish their training programs, both Melissa and James come to you, their mentor, for some advice about leadership. They ask you the following questions. What advice do you have for them?

1. How can I make a really great first impression on my new employees?

2. What specific leadership skills are most important for managers of service employees?

3. I want to create a fun, exciting work environment right from the start. How might I go about doing this?

R E V I E W   Q U E S T I O N S

1. The majority of customers choose not to do business with a company because of:
   a. High prices.
   b. Poor quality.
   c. Poor or disinterested service.
2. Your chapter described four benefits of outstanding customer service. Can you think of two more not mentioned in your text?
3. What does the concept, "internal customer" mean? How are the needs of the internal customer similar to those of the external customer? How are they different?
4. What are three specific actions a company might take if they want to "put people first" in their organization?
5. Match the following new organizational practices with their descriptions:
   ___ Flattened Organization   ___ Team-based Organization
   ___ Empowerment   ___ Reengineering
   a. Radically redesign business practices to achieve performance improvement.
   b. Reducing layers of management to eliminate bureaucracy.
   c. Involve employees in decision making and problem solving.
   d. Groups of employees manage themselves.
6. Describe in detail how you might go about performing the following key behaviors of effective leaders:
   - Behavior modeling.
   - Open door policy.
   - MBWA.
   - Sharing ideas.
   - Make work fun.
7. What are the significant practices that contributed to the great success of the following leaders in the hospitality industry?
   - Bill Marriott.
   - Ray Kroc.
   - Mary Mahoney.
   - Horst Schulze.
   - Hal Rosenbluth.
   - Walt Disney.

C R I T I C A L   T H I N K I N G   E X E R C I S E S

A. Imagine that you are about to meet the individual who has been voted the best manager in the world. Describe the qualities and characteristics that you expect this person to have.
B. Assess Your Leadership Knowledge.

Below are key competencies that middle managers must possess. Rate your degree of experience and knowledge of each area by entering a number from 0 to 10 in the space next to each. Keep in mind that this is not a valid test of your ability as a leader, but simply an inventory of your current knowledge level.

0	1	2	3	4	5	6	7	8	9	10

No knowledge or experience	Moderate understanding	Highly skilled and proficient

Self-rating

1. Coaching and facilitating work groups. _____
2. Getting employees involved in decision making. _____
3. Listening carefully to others. _____
4. Writing clear, accurate memos and letters. _____
5. Giving oral presentations to groups. _____
6. Solving guest problems by myself. _____
7. Working with others to solve guest problems. _____
8. Continuously improving my workplace. _____
9. Clear vision of where I want to be in the future. _____
10. Managing my own career. _____
11. Managing my time. _____
12. Creating a professional image for myself. _____
13. Conducting job interviews with employees. _____
14. Selecting service oriented employees. _____
15. Conducting new employee orientation. _____
16. Assessing training needs of my employees. _____
17. Delivering employee training. _____
18. Motivating service employees. _____
19. Evaluating employee performance. _____
20. Giving employees feedback. _____
21. Disciplining employees for poor performance. _____
22. Personal philosophy of management. _____
23. Organizational change process. _____
24. Equal employment opportunity. _____
25. Laws concerning sexual harassment. _____
26. Managing disable employees. _____
27. Supervising a diverse workforce. _____
28. Principles of total quality management. _____
29. Empowerment of employees. _____
30. Characteristics of quality organizations. _____

Total Score _____

0 to 100	**Novice leader**
101 to 200	**Moderate leadership expertise**
201 to 300	**Skilled leader**

C. List the five most important skill areas where you need to expand your level of expertise. Write action plans to describe how you will go about gaining additional knowledge and experience in each.

Skill   Action Plan

_____   _____
_____   _____
_____   _____
_____   _____
_____   _____

O N - L I N E   L I N K

An Internet-based exercise will be included at the end of each chapter in the text. If you do not have a computer at home that is connected, visit the student labs located at your college, university, or local library.

This first exercise is a very simple one, particularly if you are an experienced web master. Go to a search engine such as Yahoo and do a key word search using the words "hospitality industry" or "hotel industry" or "restaurant industry," depending on your career interests, and locate several web sites that provide important information about management and leadership. List the addresses of two of your favorite sites below and share them with your classmates. For each site, provide the following information:

- Site URL (site address).
- Site Name.
- What type of information did this site provide?
- What did you like about it?

P O R T F O L I O   E X E R C I S E

A portfolio is a collection of documents that demonstrate the skills and knowledge that an individual possesses. It typically contains letters of recommendation, a resume, college transcripts, sample projects, and other documentation of past achievement. At the end of each chapter in your text is a portfolio exercise that describes a brief project or activity that might enhance your professional portfolio. Several web sites also contain information about developing portfolios. You may want to visit *www.career.mag.com/portfolio.pdf* and *www.talent-net.com*.

In this, your first portfolio exercise, you will create a draft of a letter requesting a recommendation from either a past employer or a past teacher. Letters of recommendation are very valuable assets that you can use when you are seeking either new employment or a promotion at your current company. They provide proof of your abilities and reinforce your own description of your skills and abilities. This letter can later be used to solicit recommendations that will be placed in your professional portfolio. Your letter should be typed on quality paper in proper business format. It should include the following components:

- **Opening statement of your purpose:** To obtain a letter
  of recommendation that you might use as you seek a su-

pervisory position in the hospitality industry. Also includes a brief description of your career goals and how you are working toward their achievement.

- **Description of your past accomplishments:** Include some of your past achievements either on the job or in school. This gives the writer some background that he or she might use to write a more comprehensive letter. If writing to a past employer, include special recognition, promotions, or extra projects you were involved in. If writing to a past teacher, include your GPA, clubs and student organizations, or special activities you were involved during school.

- **Thank you:** Be sure to thank the teacher or employer for their assistance. Give a phone number and address where you can be reached if he or she has questions.

Positive Communication

2

ADVANCED ORGANIZER

Bill Marriott firmly believes that a manager who lacks people skills will never be successful in his organization. When visiting one of his hotels, he noticed that a new general manager looked great on paper—sales were up and costs were down. However, he also noticed that the workers at the property seemed subdued and uneasy. When Mr. Marriott talked with and observed the employees on his own, he learned that the new GM was bullying, punitive, and unsympathetic to the employees. The staff felt that they must walk on eggshells around him. Despite the financial and operating success of the property, Marriott decided to let the GM go because of his lack of ability to deal with his staff.[1]

One rarely thinks of a manager being fired because he cannot communicate effectively. As today's work environment changes and employees are more involved at all levels of the organization, communication becomes more important than ever before. Managers who lack strong communication skills will be left behind in today's workplace.

BEHAVIORAL OBJECTIVES

- Recognize poor communication practices in yourself and others.
- Differentiate between the three components of interpersonal effectiveness.
- Describe the aspects of skillful communication.
- Simulate the practice of giving challenging feedback.
- Distinguish between the different employee outcomes resulting from feedback.
- Describe the five steps in conflict resolution.

Network Operations Center, World Headquarters, Rosenbluth International, Philadelphia, PA, USA

SENDING QUALITY MESSAGES

All behavior is a form of **communication.** Everything that we say and do intentionally and unintentionally sends a message to others. Even when we choose not to respond, we send a message through our silence. Our tone of voice, choice of words, facial expressions, actions, listening ability, and writing skills shape the impression we make on others. We can choose to send quality messages that enrich the lives of others or negative ones that diminish the receiver. The quality of our lives is directly linked to the quality of our communication.

All of us began learning to communicate when we were very small. Some of us learned better than others. No matter what level of communication you are at now, as an adult you can choose to improve your relationships with others, both at work and in your personal life, by adopting a more effective communication style.

Good communicators have an enriched flow of information coming into their lives. They in turn send quality messages that benefit others. Good communicators find pleasure and satisfaction in life. They are successful, able to form close relationships, and feel a sense of accomplishment. Competent communicators are aware of the messages they send and their effect on the receiver. It's up to you. You can choose to improve your life and your career by becoming a better communicator.

LEADERSHIP AND COMMUNICATION

A supervisor or manager's ability to communicate dictates the level of success he can achieve as a supervisor. The following quote by Peter Block, author of *The Empowered Manager*, emphasizes the essential role of communication in management:

> There is no point at which people take more responsibility for their lives and their actions than when they put into words their own wants and their own feelings. Those two issues are at the center of motivation, at the center of responsibility, focus and action.

You are what you say and do. To be an effective supervisor, you must make a conscious decision to be an effective communicator. When dealing with employees, you must have the insight and ability to ask the right questions and the patience to listen and truly hear their answers.

TYPES OF RELATIONSHIPS

Your relationship with others, both at work and in your personal life, can be classified as **overt, covert,** and **task.** The type of relationship you have with someone dictates both the level of openness with which you communicate with him or her. Let's examine the three types of relationships:

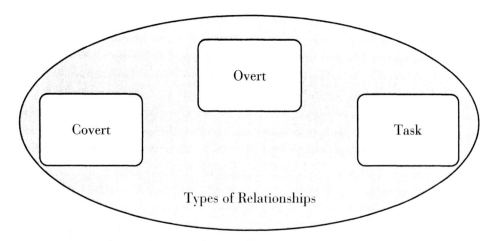

Figure 2.1 Types of Relationships

1. **Overt:** This is an open relationship where we readily express our thoughts and feelings to other people. If we like someone, we smile, tell them we like them, and we are helpful and friendly. If we do not like someone, we communicate this to them by frowning, closing ourselves off, ignoring them, or telling them that we dislike them. Overt behavior is very honest. It is when we readily communicate our feelings to others.

2. **Covert:** This is a more guarded relationship where we keep certain thoughts and feelings hidden from others. If a service employee is dealing with an irate guest, the service employee may be angry with the guest but the individual's job requires that this anger not be shown. The employee must keep his or her feelings covert or hidden. Our relationships with others, especially at work, often require that we keep many of our feelings hidden. We must practice tact and self-control to be effective in our careers.

3. **Task:** This is a relationship you might have with coworkers. Communication is very task oriented and less emotional that in covert and overt relationships. Interaction is limited to the sharing of information and communicating needs.

Few personal or work-related relationships are entirely covert, overt, or task but combine characteristics of each principle. When relationships are primarily covert, a great deal of distrust exists between both parties. People keep most of what they are really thinking or feeling hidden from each other. It is impossible for the people involved to solve problems because they never really talk about them. Unfortunately many employees have a covert relationship with higher management. Fearful for their jobs, they are reluctant to openly express concerns and feelings. It is impossible to empower employees when they have a covert relationship with management. Empowerment requires an employee-

management relationship that is a combination of task and overt. Workers must feel that they can share ideas, thoughts, and feelings openly with management without threat of reprisal.

A workplace that fosters overt relationships is a far more pleasurable place to work. Workers and managers share thoughts, ideas, and feelings without fear. Good communication skills facilitate openness. A supervisor who is adept at sending and receiving messages can do much to create an open, participative environment. Below are a few ways that managers can foster open relationships with employees:

- Encourage and accept employees' expression of ideas and feelings about the operation.
- Get to know your employees. Ask about their outside interests, family, education, etc.
- Ask for employee opinions when making decisions.
- When employees express ideas, don't shoot them down. Be careful not to be too critical.
- Reward and praise honesty. Thank employees for their feedback.

POOR HABITS

Communication is at the heart of all business relationships. Managers must give instructions, feedback, encouragement, discipline, and solve problems using interpersonal communication. When a manager is an ineffective communicator, his or her department will not operate successfully. Poor communication skills can have a very negative impact on career success. Employees may be denied promotions, demoted, or even terminated because they have poor communication skills. We spend virtually 100 percent of our working hours communicating in one way or another, yet most managers are "undertrained" in this skill. We develop many bad habits as we learn to communicate as children and receive little formal training to correct these flaws. As adults we can improve our interaction with others. Awareness of our deficiencies is the first step. Begin by examining the characteristics that work against good communication:

- **Resistance to Change:** Many people find it overwhelming to think of changing the way they communicate. Changing our communication style requires a large investment of time and effort. Change also leads to anxiety and insecurity. It takes courage, determination, and hard work to change our communication style. The first step in change is awareness. Without conscious knowledge of how others react to us, change is nearly impossible.

- **Send vague or unclear messages:** As our workplace becomes more diverse, the importance of sending clear messages increases. Language barriers, insensitivity of cultural groups, and just plain speaking before you think can lead to misunderstanding and miscommunication.

- **Failure to Listen:** Perhaps the most common barrier to good communication is failure to listen. Effective interaction requires a certain amount of selflessness on the part of each person. Otherwise we may be more concerned with what we want to say than with what the other person is communicating. Research has shown that people actually communicate better when others listen. Teachers whose students were attentive were more effective lecturers than those whose students were not.[2] Failure to pay attention is a "Catch 22." The less alert we are when others speak, the less interesting we find their conversation. If you find others boring, try paying attention. Perhaps they will respond to the positive reinforcement your attention provides by becoming more interesting, and a rich conversation will result.

- **Dear Abby Syndrome:** Many people are able to listen effectively, but fall into the bad habit of trying to solve everyone's problems. They constantly give unsolicited advice rather than responding appropriately. Instead of letting the speaker know they are heard and understood, they bombard the other person with suggestions and recommendations. Their conversation is peppered with lots of "you should" and "my friend Mary had the same problem" or "why don't you." This is a difficult habit to break. People share their thoughts and feelings to be understood and supported, not because they want others to provide unsolicited advice. A good rule of thumb is not to provide advice unless others ask for it directly. Or, if advice seems warranted, ask the other person if they would like to hear your suggestions before providing them.

- **Stereotyping and Generalization:** People are judged by their appearance and characteristics. We may assume that because someone is dressed poorly, they are also unintelligent. Often less affluent customers are ignored or provided poorer service than those who appear to be important. When I was a bartender at a prestigious banquet function, a man who was dressed poorly asked for a special wine I did not have on hand. Because he looked unimportant I was tempted to tell him we didn't have what he wanted and suggest something else. However, I was well trained. I located the manager and asked him to find the particular wine the man wanted. It turned out that the poorly dressed man owned part of a major sports team and gave me a $100 tip for my efforts. Not all avoidance of stereotyping pays off as well as it did in that instance, but good communicators avoid categorizing people.

- **Long-windedness:** It usually takes more words to say nothing than to say something. Avoid giving lengthy monologues when interacting with others. People who do this often speak without thinking. They start talking, realize that what they are saying is not on target, and keep speaking until they identify what they really wanted to say. Instead effective communicators develop a shared dialogue where each person responds thoughtfully to the other. Communication is not always spontaneous. It is not necessary to speak every thought that comes to mind. Focus on the core of what the other person is saying and respond to it. Make responses that are lean, concrete, and accurate.

These are just a few common communication errors. It is impossible to be an effective communicator 100 percent of the time. Improvement can be made if we become aware of bad habits and strive to eliminate them.

INTERPERSONAL EFFECTIVENESS

There are three components of successful interpersonal interaction.[3] Each component is necessary for successful communication. You must develop skill in all three areas, including social intelligence, technical competence, and assertiveness.

SOCIAL INTELLIGENCE

By understanding yourself, your environment, and other people you will be able to make appropriate responses in different social situations. Another name for this component might be common sense or social sense. When someone

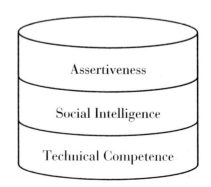

Figure 2.2 The Three Components of Interpersonal Effectiveness

says, "My father is very ill. I won't be able to work overtime this week," a supervisor with social intelligence will express sympathy and concern as well as offer support. A supervisor lacking this factor might say, "I don't know who is going to fill in for you. Can't the rest of your family take care of him?" Obviously this person lacks the ability to see beyond his concerns and express caring for others. Social intelligence does not just mean expressing sympathy, but it can also apply to giving appropriate feedback. When employees perform poorly, it is up to the supervisor to confront them. The supervisor who fails to give employees accurate feedback is also lacking in social intelligence.

> **Tip:** When employees come to you with a problem, express empathy. Let them know that you understand and that you are happy or sad for them, depending on the situation. This may sound simplistic, but if you let others know that you really understand what they are experiencing, they will sense that you are listening and that you care about their welfare.

TECHNICAL COMPETENCE

Social intelligence allows us to select the correct response in a given situation. Next we must have the appropriate skills to deliver the message. If the sender's language, delivery, or manner alienates people, even the most appropriate message will not have the desired effect. If a supervisor sees that an employee was discourteous to a guest and confronts him with this by saying, "You handled that situation badly. I can't believe you said that to the guest. How stupid can you be?" The employee will immediately feel defensive due to the accusing, blaming message the supervisor sends. The intention of improving employee performance will be defeated. If the supervisor had said, "I didn't like the way you dealt with the last guest. I thought you sounded frustrated and did not make the guest feel that you cared about his problem." This message gives the employee a more accurate picture of his behavior and is more likely to result in change. Notice that in the second message the supervisor used "I" statements in reporting his observations and feelings. The "you" statements in the first message are more blaming.

> **Tip:** Get in the habit of saying, "I think, I feel," or "I noticed that" when giving feedback to employees. It is less blaming than saying, "You did this" or "You didn't do that."

ASSERTIVENESS

Social intelligence and technical skill are useless if you lack the courage to use them when necessary. Supervisors, in particular, must have the courage to confront employees effectively when their performance is not acceptable. This must be done in a caring, nonjudgmental manner. Assertiveness without social awareness or communication skill is dangerous. Individuals who have the reputation of being uncaring, forceful, difficult bosses often have raw assertiveness but lack the finesse and skill to deliver feedback effectively.

Tip: Remember, employees cannot improve their performance and eliminate problem behavior if they are not aware of their limitations. One of your responsibilities as a supervisor is to act as a nonjudgmental mirror. You must let employees see how they are perceived by giving them specific, nonthreatening feedback about their behavior.

Being a skillful communicator involves the orchestration of all three components. Through awareness and steady, systematic practice, expertise in all three areas can be developed.

SKILLFUL COMMUNICATION

An excellent communicator focuses on what others say, asks for clarification, and responds appropriately. This sounds very simple, but most people fail in one or more of these areas. When we fail to communicate effectively, relationships crumble, trust is lost, and we feel disconnected from others. By developing interpersonal skills, we can build satisfying relationships with coworkers, family, friends, and even guests.

LISTENING

Have you ever met a good communicator who doesn't listen? Probably not. It is virtually impossible to communicate effectively without listening. Let's say you are telling a friend about a problem with your boss. She interrupts to make comments about her weekend, fails to maintain eye contact, and does not bother to ask for clarification of your input. Now you feel frustrated and perhaps even be-

INSIGHT 2.1

After more than forty years in business, Bill Marriott, president and CEO of Marriott International, concludes that listening is the single most important on-the-job skills that a manger can cultivate.* He believes that few of us are natural-born listeners, but that everyone can learn to listen more effectively. A listening strategy that he finds valuable is knowing to keep quiet. He also believes that body language is important and suggests mimicking the body language of people you know who are good listeners. This includes maintaining alert posture and good eye contact. Finally, he sees listening as an opportunity to learn. He suggests that we try not to make up our minds before having a chance to hear someone out. He cites an example of such an interaction that occurred in a Marriott executive meeting. Bill Marriott was very enthusiastic about a new idea. Responding to his enthusiasm, all executives present but one told him it was a great idea, even before they carefully thought about all the ramifications. One lone person had the courage to speak up and describe why he thought the project would be a disaster. Bill Marriott thought about what the employer had said and then told him that he was absolutely right. Going ahead with the idea would have been a disaster.

*J.W. Marriott, Jr. and K.A. Brown, "The Spirit to Serve: Marriot's Way." New York: Harper-Collins, 1997, pp. 50–60.

trayed by your friend. You may feel that she just doesn't care enough to listen. If you say, "I feel like you aren't listening." Your friend might say, "Of course I'm listening. I can repeat back everything you said." You don't want her to simply parrot your words; you want her to be there for you, to attend to what you are saying. As human beings we are very sensitive to any lack of attention from others. We notice immediately when someone fails to pay attention to us. At the same time, we often fail to give others our undivided attention. To become good listeners, we must learn to shut off our own thoughts, including the ongoing dialogue in our heads, to truly hear what others are saying. If we carefully attend to others and listen actively rather than passively, we are more likely to have an effect upon them. We are also more likely to be influenced by people who listen to us. Attending is a powerful communication tool that can transform casual, superficial interaction into rich, meaningful discourse.

PHYSICAL ATTENDING

Often overlooked when considering communication is the important physical component, listening. When we think of listening, we think of hearing with our ears, when in reality, our entire body is involved in this communication process. The physical elements of listening include the following:

- **Face the person squarely.** This lets the speaker know that you are interested in what he or she is saying and are willing to focus on that person. Busy service employees often fail to face customers squarely as they interact. It is important to take the time to make yourself available to the speaker by facing him or her completely.
- **Relax by maintaining an open posture.** Physically let the speaker know you are comfortable in his or her presence. Avoid folding your arms tightly, nervous gestures, or tapping hands or feet.
- **Eye contact is critical to good listening.** Look at the other person when you speak and maintain eye contact as the other person responds. This is not staring or glaring, but maintaining "soft eye contact." You are looking at the other person with acceptance, interest, concern, and caring. There is no criticism or judgment in soft eye contact.
- **Be aware of nonverbal cues.** Expressions on your face portray your feelings to others more effectively than any other physical component. Be aware of how others might interpret your facial expressions. You may frown when you are listening intently, but others may interpret this as dissatisfaction. You may smile when showing concern, but others may interpret this as a frivolous attitude toward their problems. As you listen to others, be aware of your facial expressions and make sure they match your feelings and intent.

We should not try to rigidly control our bodies when we communicate, but we must become more aware of the messages we are sending. A person might focus on everything another says, but if that person scowls, fails to maintain eye contact, or attempts to hold a conversation while engaged in another activity, the speaker will not truly feel heard.

NONVERBAL COMMUNICATION

We often think of communication as spoken or written language, but nonverbal communication, the physical component of the process is just as important. We have all heard the cliché, actions speak louder than words. Our physical behavior can be more accurate and honest than our words. We may try to conceal our anger, distrust, or skepticism by not expressing them verbally, only to find that these feelings are revealed physically. This nonverbal leakage occurs when our true feelings are expressed physically while we say something else verbally. A guest comes to the front desk to report his second missing key of the day, and the desk clerk says, "I'll be happy to make you a new key Mr. Gowen." At the same time he frowns, looks disgusted, and shakes his head. His frustration is not expressed verbally, but leaks out nonverbally. If the guest is at all perceptive, he is sure to spot these negative feelings.

Also be aware that different actions can be interpreted in a variety of ways. During a meeting with his supervisor, an employee folds his arms tightly across his chest. This could mean that he feels defensive, is not accepting what the supervisor says, or it could simply mean that he is cold. Different physical gestures can be interpreted in a variety of ways. Just think of all the different messages a smile can send. We smile to communicate happiness, irony, derision, joy, laughter, and condescension.

Not only must we be aware of what we say verbally, we must also be cognizant of what we say physically. As you communicate notice the feelings and emotions that you express nonverbally. Try to match your physical behavior to your verbal communication. If you are trying to portray a caring, helpful attitude to guests, or trying to let your boss know that you are willing to cooperate, just saying the right thing is not enough.

RESPONDING TO OTHERS

Hearing what the other person is saying is only one component of listening. If this is all you ever do, then you are a passive listener. Active listening lets the other person know they are heard and understood. The primary component of active listening is reflecting or summarizing what the sender has said. This not only lets the speaker know you are paying attention, but also lets the person know that you are interested enough to try to really understand what the speaker is saying. Responding to others can involve **paraphrasing,** reflecting meaning, or reflecting feeling.

Paraphrasing is when the receiver summarizes the message in his or her own words and repeats it back to the sender. If the sender says, "I am having major problems with my boss," the receiver might paraphrase by responding, "It sounds like you are having some problems at work." Paraphrasing provides clarification and assures that both parties have the same understanding of the message.

Reflecting meaning is a step beyond paraphrasing. It involves some interpretation on the part of the receiver. The receiver restates or summarizes

Responding to others

Paraphrasing
Reflecting Meanings
Reflecting Feelings

Figure 2.3 Responding to Others

what the sender is trying to express. This is more than just paraphrasing and may involve identifying information the sender may not have directly expressed. If an employee says, "I've been here for five years and haven't been promoted. People who joined the company after me are managers now," the supervisor might interpret the meaning of this statement and reflect, "You're wondering what our criterion is for promoting employees." This invites the speaker to agree and expand on his or her feelings or disagree and correct the supervisor's interpretation.

Reflecting feelings is when the receiver attempts to express understanding of the message by reflecting the sender's feelings. If the sender says, "I've had a terrible day at work," the receiver might reflect his interpretation of the feelings expressed by saying, "It sounds like you are very frustrated about something that happened at work today." This opens the door for the sender to either correct the interpretation or elaborate.

Reflecting is a powerful tool that allows both the sender and receiver to determine if the message is being expressed as intended. In reflecting the receiver does not give advice, or state an opinion; the receiver simply checks to make sure the message that is sent is understood. Just saying, "I don't understand" or "Tell me more" will illicit response from the sender, but it still does not let the sender, know that you are hearing the message correctly. A server might say, "I'm really tired of working with Mary" to another coworker. The coworker might say, "I can understand that" to indicate agreement and understanding, but the two might be talking about totally different concerns. The sender might mean that he is tired of working with Mary because she is popular with customers and they request her station instead of his. The receiver might have interpreted it as a personality conflict. He might think that the sender felt Mary was difficult or bossy and did not like her. He might even tell others that the two are not getting along, and an innocent statement is completely blown out of proportion. Had the receiver reflected back "You don't like working with Mary because she's too bossy," the sender might have then continued on to say, "No, that's not it. She is really a great person. It's just that the customers like her so well they all request her station."

Reflecting is crucial in bridging the communication gap that can separate people. It increases the accuracy of the message and consequently leads to better understanding. It also lets the sender know that you are interested and concerned.

QUESTIONING

The appropriate use of questioning is also critical to good communication. Have you ever been involved in a conversation with someone who asks so many questions you feel like an ace detective is interrogating you? "Where do you work? Where do you live? Why do you feel that way? What do you think about this?" Such questions can certainly express interest on the part of the speaker, but the receiver might feel defensive.

Questioning should follow these guidelines:

- Use **open-ended questions** that require more than just a yes or no answer. "How do you think we can solve this problem? " is more effective than "Do you think we can solve this problem?"
- Ask questions infrequently. Instead, use minimal encouraging such as nodding, or saying, "Yes, I see," "Oh," and other brief expressions to let the person know that you want to hear more. Another alternative is to use reflecting to clarify and encourage the speaker to continue.
- Stay on the topic. Avoid changing the subject by asking questions that have little to do with what the speaker says.
- Ask only one question at a time.
- Use silence instead of a question to give the speaker time to think about what is being said and to clarify the message. Do not fill silence with questions.

FEEDBACK

Giving feedback is "strong medicine" in communication. It can have a dramatically positive or negative effect upon both personal and work-related relationships. Feedback can either stimulate another person to self-examine in a new way, or if given incorrectly, can alienate the recipient. Positive feedback confirms and reinforces desirable behavior. Telling an employee that you like his or her haircut lets that person know that a more conservative cut is appropriate for a business environment. When a server handles a difficult guest with finesse, you might say, "That guest was very demanding. I like the way you explained exactly what you could do for her. You stayed very calm and professional during the entire conversation. Keep up the good work." This positive feedback is very specific: It lets the employee know exactly what was done right. It also reinforces the behavior you want to see in the future.

CHALLENGING FEEDBACK

Feedback that has the greatest effect on others is not always positive. **Challenging feedback** gives the recipient new insight into his or her behavior. It can build relationships and help others grow. We cannot change unless we are aware of how others see us. Trying to evoke change without feedback is like trying to create a new recipe without tasting it. If an employee has great skills but is continually passed over for promotion because the employee's appearance is untidy, the supervisor who fails to give this person accurate feedback is doing a disservice. By relating accurate feedback about appearance, the supervisor can have a tremendous impact on this person's career. Challenging feedback requires skill or it can damage relationships rather than solidify them.

The following are conditions that lead to effective feedback:

- **Trust:** It is important that both parties trust each other. It is particularly important that the receiver respects the sender's judgment.

- **Purposeful:** Feedback should have a purpose, particularly in a work-related setting. It is important to know exactly why you are giving feedback and what you hope to accomplish by doing so. Purposeful feedback can build relationships.

- **Invitational:** When possible, feedback should be given by invitation only. Before expressing your thoughts, ask the receiver if he or she would like to hear your feedback. Supervisors must give employees feedback whether they want to hear it or not, but simply saying, "I have some feedback I need to discuss with you. Is this a good time?" is certainly much better than just barging in.

- **Positive Attitude:** Avoid being confrontational or expressing anger when giving feedback. This can be difficult, but anger only serves to cloud the issues and leads to feelings of resentment and reduces cooperation.

- **Use "I" Messages:** Instead of saying "You just aren't checking your work closely enough," Use **"I" messages** such as, "I have noticed several errors in your work." Rather than accusing the employee of some shortcoming, an "I" message simply makes the employee aware of your observations or feelings and opens the door for further discussion. **"You" messages** lead to negative feelings whereas "I" messages lead to a clearer understanding of the situation. "I" messages communicate feedback honestly and accurately, and "you" messages are threatening and provoke resistance.

- **Feedback should be specific:** Most errors in feedback occur when the sender makes broad, general comments. Instead of saying, "You need to improve your performance," be more specific and give feedback in behavioral terms. More appropriate feedback regarding a performance problem might be, "We have had several customer complaints regarding the speed and accuracy of your performance."

- **Check for Accuracy:** This is very important and can help rebuild a relationship that might have been stressed by challenging feedback. Ask the recipient "Does this seem accurate to you?" or "What do you think about this?" to give the recipient an opportunity to respond and react to the feedback.

CHALLENGE AND SUPPORT

Feedback is particularly important in the workplace. Employees cannot grow and develop if they do not receive feedback. They need input from others, particularly supervisors, to improve performance. Optimal employee growth occurs when supervisors provide both challenging feedback and support. Challenging feedback identifies areas where employees need to improve performance. Supervisors can challenge employees by helping them set goals, encouraging self-direction, asking and answering questions, and giving accurate performance feedback. Accurate feedback is the mirror that gives employees an honest picture of how they are doing so they can change their behavior. When a supportive environment accompanies feedback, employees feel that they can grow and learn without being severely punished for mistakes. Supervisors provide support by developing trust, by not penalizing attempts at growth, by truly caring about their employees, and by being available to employees. Supervisors who provide both challenging feedback and encouragement help employees grow and learn from their mistakes.

Four conditions can occur, depending on the various levels of feedback and support:

- **Apathy:** When supervisors fail to give challenging feedback and fail to support employees, they feel completely ignored and will withdraw from the situation. Employees have no idea how they are doing and feel that the company does not really care if they perform well or not. They become apathetic, caring little about the quality of their work.
- **Withdrawal:** Some managers give employees plenty of challenging feedback but offer little support to go with it. This is like sending a fighter pilot out to do battle with no ground control. They may regularly point out employee weaknesses, but not offer help or guidance in correcting them. Employees feel threatened by the challenging feedback. Not knowing how to correct their behavior, they withdraw. The feedback becomes more of a source of punishment than an opportunity for growth.
- **Stagnation:** Employees who are given only support, but no challenging feedback, do not improve their performance. Their skill levels do not improve, and they may find themselves in the same job twenty years later.
- **Development:** When supervisors provide both challenging feedback and support, employees will grow and develop. They are aware of skills they need to develop and feel that they can successfully improve their performance because their supervisor is backing them all the way.

CONFLICT MANAGEMENT

Unfortunately we cannot choose our coworkers. A feminist female may have to work with a chauvinist male. A twenty-one-year old graduate of a culinary program may have to supervise cooks who have had the same job for the past ten years. Immigrants from two warring countries may share the same work space. People with different backgrounds, views, values, skills, and experience must come together to produce a product or service. In light of the tremendously varied history that people bring to the job, it is not surprising that conflict occurs. Perhaps the healthiest attitude to have toward conflict is to view it as a necessary part of a relationship. Just as few personal relationships can exist without conflict, few work relationships can exist without occasional differences of opinion.

CONFLICT MANAGEMENT STYLE

Conflict is a form of communication that is defined as the interaction of interdependent people who perceive opposite goals, aims, and values and who see the other party as possibly interfering with the realization of these goals.[4] Some conflict is healthy and can foster high levels of achievement and effective communication.[5] In fact a complete lack of conflict often signals group stagnation. Because conflict is part of organizational life, it is important to consider how people manage it in the workplace. Researchers suggest that people react to conflict by emphasizing concern for self or concern for others and also by degrees of assertiveness and cooperation (Figure 2.4).[6] Those with the most effective conflict management style emphasize high assertiveness along with competition and collaboration. Compromise is considered less effective in resolving conflict because neither party really gets what they need. Collaboration leads to more creative solutions that meet the needs of both parties. Accommodation is effective but can cause stress for the accommodating team member who must concede to the needs of others. Successful conflict management occurs when differences are recognized and accepted and both parties are committed to working together to consider each side's perspective and to arrive at creative solutions that meet everyone's needs.

The key to conflict management is awareness. Managers must be sensitive enough to their employees and the environment to identify conflicting or potentially conflicting situations before they become all out battles. Just as customers who fail to complain harbor negative feelings about a business, so do employees. If employee concerns, gripes, and problems are kept hidden, they

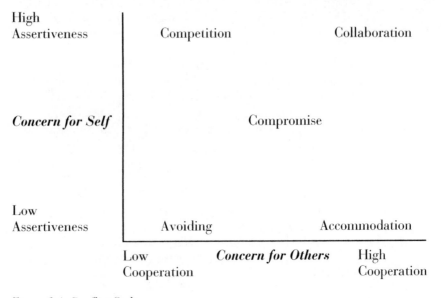

Figure 2.4 Conflict Styles

cannot be resolved. It is difficult to develop an open, trusting work environment when employees foster negative feelings about a supervisor or the company. There are several ways that supervisors can bring conflict out into the open:

- **Seek feedback from others.** The simplest way to find out if employees are having problems is to ask them. Let them know they will not be penalized for their comments.
- **Learn to read others.** When instituting new policy, try to be aware of the facial expressions and body language of the work group. It is very easy to see when people are responding negatively to something. If you see non-verbal leakage, comment on it. Let your employees know that you sense their dissatisfaction.
- **Use informal surveys.** If employees are uncomfortable or afraid to air their gripes verbally, use a confidential survey from time to time to find out what they really think. Issues from the survey can then be brought up in a group meeting and dealt with.

When conflict is brought out in the open, small problems can be resolved before they become major issues. For example, if you do not deal with your employees' dissatisfaction with scheduling, this could lead to such major problems as absenteeism, tardiness, and termination.

RESOLVING CONFLICT

Once conflict is identified, it takes effort on the part of both parties to resolve it. This is where effective communication skills become extremely valuable. There are three primary ways to deal with conflict: assertively, aggressively, or submissively. The quality of the resolution will depend on which method is chosen.

- **Aggressive Resolution:** When one or both parties react aggressively, anger often results. The issues become concealed by emotions, and it is difficult to deal effectively with the problems at hand. Aggression often occurs when one party feels threatened by the other. Like a cornered animal, this person comes out fighting. The only way conflict can be resolved in this situation is when one party dominates the other. There is always a winner and a loser.
- **Submissive Resolution:** This occurs when one or both parties are uncomfortable with conflict resolution. A submissive response limits the honest discussion and resolution of the problem. The person or persons reacting submissively are not participating in conflict resolution. When a domineering, aggressive supervisor presents a problem, most employees tend to react submissively, because there is little hope of satisfying their concerns. They realize the potential damage from confronting the problem outweighs the benefits.
- **Assertive Resolution:** When both parties assert their concerns and work together, conflict is resolved effec-

tively. Neither party is the aggressor, but both feel comfortable expressing their thoughts and feelings about the issue. When conflict is resolved assertively, it is likely to remain resolved. When aggressive or submissive responses lead to conflict resolution, it is short-lived. The same problems will reoccur, and the cycle will begin again.

When conflict arises in the work group, it is the supervisor's responsibility to see that it is resolved quickly and effectively. By taking an assertive role in the process, the supervisor lets the employees know it is acceptable to air problems and that difficulties can be resolved without losers.

There are five steps in effectively resolving conflict:

Step 1: Identify the Conflict

This is a critical step in conflict resolution. Supervisors must communicate the conflict to the employee and get the employer to buy-in to solving it. Imagine that an eager young cook in a busy restaurant decides to change the ingredients in a recipe. The executive chef disagrees with the cook's decision, but doesn't want to squelch his creativity. To bring the conflict out in the open, the cook begins by describing her concerns, "I do agree that we could improve on this recipe, but it's one of our signature items and customers expect us to make it the way we always have. Let's make the way we usually do this time, but I'd really like to hear your ideas about new recipes. How about if we meet later today after the lunch rush is over?" Notice that the chef has described the problem, expressed her feelings about it, and let the employee know that she needs his help to solve it.

Step 2: Generating Solutions

Later in the day when the two meet, the executive chef can open the door for the employee's participation by saying, "I realize that some of our menu items need updating. How can we make them more interesting, but still please our regular customers?" First, she might encourage the employee to offer solutions, and at the same time, offer several of her own. This is a brainstorming session, and, as such, ideas are noted but not judged.

Step 3: Analyzing Solutions

The chef might start by asking the employee, "Which solutions looks best to you?" They will eliminate solutions that are unacceptable to both parties and narrow the list until they arrive at a mutually beneficial resolution. In the example, the chef and cook might decide to try out several new dishes and offer them as seasonal specials, rather than commit to a menu overhaul at this time.

Step 4: Implementation

After choosing a solution, the next step is implementation. Decide when the solution will be implemented, by whom, and to what degree. A written contract should be formulated so each party knows what is expected of him.

In our example the cook will develop recipes for several new items, test them, and if successful, plan to offer one new item each week. The executive chef will provide feedback and assistance as needed.

Step 5: Evaluation

Follow up to find out if the solution is effective. Encourage the employee to discuss difficulties and identify ways to rectify them. In our example follow up might include the collection of feedback from staff and customers about the new menu items. Changes or improvements can be made until the final product is successful. Next plans can be made to test additional recipes and perhaps incorporate some into the regular menu.

In our example the busy chef has taken the time to listen and work with her employees to resolve conflict in a positive manner. She might have missed this opportunity to get the cook involved and excited about improvements if she had simply told him what to do and left it at that. Instead she recognized his interest in menu improvement, brought the conflict out into the open, and dealt with it effectively. For more about principles of effective communication during conflict resolution, see Figure 2.5.

At times the source of conflict may not be as obvious as that in our example. Employees may generally seem dissatisfied without a clear reason. If this is the case, prior to Step 1, ask the employee or a group of employees what problems they are having with you as their supervisor or with their job. If they trust you, they will be honest. If they fear recrimination, little valuable information will be generated.

The key to successful conflict resolution is to first get the problem out in the open and then focus on solving it. Unfortunately problems are often solved by a supervisor simply telling an employee what was wrong, then telling the employee what should have been done, and finally punishing the employee. This

---

1. Maintain a nonjudgmental demeanor and avoid judgmental comments or criticism.
2. Deal only with the present behavior.
3. Pay attention to nonverbal behavior.
4. Use "I" messages.
5. Avoid words that make the other person angry and defensive, such as "you" messages.
6. Reflect incoming messages.
7. Avoid inappropriate questions. Avoid asking "why" which may lead to defensiveness. Instead ask "what" and "how."
8. Use strategic silence and delayed reactions.
9. Do not give advice.
10. Stay calm. If you feel yourself becoming angry, remind yourself that you are negotiating a conflict and must stay calm.

Source: M. Roberts, *Managing Conflict from the Inside Out*, Learning Concepts, San Diego, CA. 1982.

Figure 2.5 Strategies for Effective Communication during Conflict Negotiation

system fit well with the old authoritarian management style, but if companies expect their employees to take initiative, they must assume they are responsible adults who can be trusted to solve problems. Supervisors must give employees the freedom and support they need to identify and solve problems.

CONCLUSION

Once we say something, it cannot be erased. We can offer damage control by saying "I'm sorry" but what has transpired will be remembered. By using effective communication practices, we can avoid errors that we will later regret. When we correct such bad habits as failing to listen, constantly offering advice, dominating conversation, and stereotyping, we are on the way to improving our interactions.

When we practice social intelligence, we let others know we understand and care. When we listen, attend physically, reflect, question, and provide appropriate feedback, we are able to send and receive clear messages. These are critical skills for successful supervision. It is virtually impossible to be an excellent supervisor without also being an excellent communicator.

K E Y   T E R M S

Communication	Reflecting
Overt Relationship	Open-ended questions
Covert Relationship	Challenging feedback
Open Relationship	"I" messages
Paraphrasing	"You" messages
Conflict	

N O T E S

1. J. W. Marriott and K. A. Brown, "The Spirit to Serve: Marriott's Way" (New York: HarperCollins, 1997): 45–46.

2. Ivey, A. and Hinkle, J., "The Transactional Classroom" (unpublished paper, University of Massachusetts, Amherst, 1970).

3. G. Egan, *Interpersonal Living: A Skills Contract Approach to Human Relations Training in Groups* (Monterey, Calif.: Brook/Cole Publishing, 1976)

4. L. Putnam and M. Poole, "Conflict and Negotiation," in F. Jablin et al., eds., *Handbook of Organizational Communication* (Newbury Park, Calif.: Sage Publications, 1987), 549–599.

5. C. Franz and K. Jin, "The Structure of Group Conflict in a Collaborative Work Group during Information Systems Development," *Journal of Applied Communication Research* 23, 108–122.

6. R. Kilmann and K. Thomas, "Interpersonal Conflict Handling Behavior and a Reflection of Jungian Personality Dimensions," *Psychological Reports*, (1975 #3, Pt 1) 37, 971-980.

CASE 2.1: A DIFFICULT CHOICE

Melissa has a very difficult decision to make. The director of Front Office Operations has asked that she recommend candidates for the management position that has become available in her department. Two of the best Front Office associates have applied for the position. Both have degrees in hospitality management and have demonstrated high levels of success in their positions. Of the two, Mary is the more technically proficient. She knows standard procedures backward and forward. John is also technically proficient, but not to the same degree as Mary. He can certainly perform his job well, but when big problems arise, Mary's expertise is invaluable.

Melissa held formal interviews with each of the candidates to help her assess their qualifications. She asked several key questions to find out how each would handle difficult employee situations.

Melissa asked, "If you had a new employee who did not perform up to your expectations, what would you do?"

Mary responded, "Assuming we were still within the probationary period, I'd have to let this person go."

John responded, "I guess I'd start by telling the person about the problems I am seeing, then I'd ask what's going on. Depending on what the answer would be I'd either beef up my training efforts or help the person find a more appropriate job in the hotel."

In response to similar questions, Mary always referred back to the company policy and recommended written warning notices and termination. It was obvious that she would be fair to employees, but felt that by penalizing them, she would change their behavior. On the other hand, John favored talking with the employees and finding out why they were having problems. He tended to want to work with the employees to improve their behavior.

Melissa isn't sure which of the two individuals to recommend. She likes John's management style, but he is lacking in technical knowledge. Melissa is also concerned about losing the employee she does not promote, and this would be a serious blow to the operation. She visits her mentor for some advice. Who do you think she should recommend for promotion? Why?

CASE 2.2: CAN THIS EMPLOYEE BE RETAINED?

James is trying to collect his thoughts after meeting with one of his waiters. Bill, the best waiter he has ever worked with, has given two weeks' notice. James called a meeting with Bill, hoping to find out why he is leaving and convince him to stay. Losing Bill during their busiest season is really going to hurt his operation. Looking back on their conversation, James wonders what went wrong.

James: So why are you leaving us?
Bill: I want to pursue other activities.
James: You can't leave us now. It's our busiest season. I can't believe you're doing this to me.
Bill: I'm sorry, but it's important to me to do these things.
James: What are these "things" you're going to do?
Bill: It's personal.
James: You've been here for ten years now. You can't leave now. Just stay through the summer. Okay?
Bill: I'm sorry, but I can't do that. My last day will be two weeks from today.

James came away from the meeting feeling very frustrated and discouraged. Not only did he fail to convince Bill to stay, he didn't even find out why he was leaving. James visits his mentor to try find out where things went wrong. He asks you the following questions:

1. What communication mistakes did I make in the conversation above?

2. What could I have said or done to encourage Bill to talk more openly about his reason for leaving?

3. Do you think there is any way I can salvage this situation and still get Bill to stay?

R E V I E W   Q U E S T I O N S

1. List four common communication errors identified in the chapter. Place a check mark by those that you need to improve on.

2. A person who responds incorrectly or inappropriately to others lacks:
   a. Social intelligence
   b. Technical competence
   c. Assertiveness

3. A supervisor who does not use "I" messages lacks:
   a. Social intelligence
   b. Technical competence
   c. Assertiveness

4. Give an example of nonverbal leakage.

5. The primary component of active listening is:_____.

6. After a very busy night, Karen tells Margaret, the supervisor, "I can't believe how disorganized this place is. I was so busy, I couldn't even take care of all my customers. I'm completely exhausted and didn't make as much in tips as I usually do. A few more nights like this, and I start looking for another job." Margaret can reflect Karen's feelings in one of the following three ways. Indicate which of the following possible statements is:
   a. Paraphrasing
   b. Reflecting meaning
   c. Reflecting feelings
   ____ You've had a very bad night. Things were disorganized, and you didn't provide the service you usually do.
   ____ It sounds like you are very frustrated. You are working hard, but not making the income you would like to. You are becoming pretty unhappy with your job.
   ____ You think we need to improve our service system. If we don't, we are going to start losing customers and employees.

7. The following questions are close-ended, requiring only a yes or no answer. Convert each one to an open-ended question.
   a. Did you enjoy your meal?
   b. Did your customers like our new menu?
   c. Did you learn a lot about the company during orientation?

8. What is strong medicine in communication? Why?

9. What is the key to conflict management?

10. You have just told the hostess in the restaurant that you manage that it seems that she is having trouble keeping up with her workload. What can you say next to check the accuracy of your feedback?

11. Convert the following "you" messages into "I" messages:

"You are 15 minutes late again today!"
"I" message:

"You didn't tell me you were going on break."
"I" message:

"You need to clean up your work area."
"I" message:

CRITICAL   THINKING   EXERCISES

Part I: Review the situations described below. Give an example of specific feedback a supervisor might provide in each instance.

1. George, a line cook in the main kitchen, has been arriving late to work at least two times per week during the past month. He always has a reasonable excuse, but his tardiness is slowing production.

2. Jack, a desk clerk at a large hotel, has just handled a guest problem using active listening, reflecting, and effective questioning techniques. The guest, who happened to be the president of a major corporation, was so pleased that he has promised to send all his business to the hotel chain.

3. At the Hill Street Diner, quality standards state that guests' orders are to be taken within five minutes of their being seated. Alice, a new server, has not been meeting this standard consistently.

Part II: The Melrose Inn

The Melrose Inn has four separate dining rooms. Each dining room has a different supervisor, each with their own particular way of providing feedback and support to employees. Review the situations below and indicate which condition you believe each situation will lead to. Indicate the rationale behind your choice.

a. Apathy.   c. Stagnation.

b. Withdrawal.   d. Development.

1. Louis is well liked by his employees. He always gives them plenty of positive feedback and encouragement and he rarely finds fault with their performance, overlooking their shortcomings.
   Condition:_____
   Rationale:_____

2. Joe is not very popular with his employees. He constantly points out their deficiencies, but never follows up to help them improve their performance. He gives more written warning notices than any other supervisor. Employees who do not shape up are terminated.
   Condition:_____
   Rationale:_____

3. Mary seems to always get the best from her employees. She gives them accurate, honest feedback about their performance and helps them find ways to improve. Servers in her area are frequently promoted to positions of more responsibility.

Condition:_____

Rationale:_____

4. Jerry operates his dining room by keeping a low profile. He rarely gives employees feedback of any sort, preferring to focus on budgeting and cost control. He spends most of his shift in the office doing paperwork and only gets involved in service when there is a serious problem.

Condition:_____

Rationale:_____

O N - L I N E   L I N K

In today's high-tech workplace, communication practices are changing. Many managers communicate directly with coworkers or customers via e-mail. Compose a brief (2 paragraph) e-mail message and send it to your professor or to a business contact you would normally call or fax. How does communicating by e-mail differ from face-to-face or telephone interaction? Is it easier for you, or more difficult? (Note: If you do not have an e-mail address. get one! Most search engines, like Yahoo, will supply one free of charge. It will only take a few minutes to set it up.)

P O R T F O L I O   E X E R C I S E

As you interview for supervisory positions in the hospitality industry, potential employers will focus carefully on your communication skills. Some may even ask behavioral interview questions (see Chapter 5 for more on this) where you are required to describe particular situations you have experienced and how you handled them. Add to your portfolio and become better prepared for tough interview questions by describing three challenging interactions you have been involved in and how you dealt effectively with them. These situations might include a difficult situation with a guest, dealing with a difficult or unreasonable coworker, giving your supervisor suggestions for improving operations, or helping a coworker or friend solve a difficult personal problem. Refer to the skills you have learned in this chapter to describe how you handled each situation. For example, did you use active listening, reflecting, or paraphrasing?

Creative Problem Solving
and Decision Making

3

ADVANCED ORGANIZER

You are the restaurant manager in a busy airport hotel property. You arrive at work one morning and find the following in your mailbox: a letter of resignation from your best server, a grievance from a busperson saying she is not receiving adequate tips from servers, a telephone message saying call the general manager immediately regarding a drop in revenue this month, and a complaint from a customer saying he developed food poisoning after eating in your restaurant last night.

No, this isn't a particularly bad day. You will face challenges like these every day, and learning to solve problems quickly and effectively will allow you to zip through a stack of messages like these in no time. This chapter will help you develop the problems-solving and decision-making skills you w need to deal with the challenges ahead.

BEHAVIORAL OBJECTIVES

- Differentiate between various methods us to identify workplace problems.

- Apply creative problem-solving techniques management issues.

- Describe and apply the four elements of t decision-making process.

- Identify the benefits of win-win conflict re lution.

- Describe the processes involved in skillful gotiation.

The Opryland Hotel

AN EXPENSIVE LEARNING EXPERIENCE

Managers today must deal with problems that are more varied and complex than ever before. They must be able to quickly and skillfully solve problems arising from union disputes, legal issues, labor shortages, and customer complaints, just to name a few topics. Problem solving and decision making definitely improve with experience, but lessons can be costly. Company lore at IBM describes an experience that a young manager had with its founder, Thomas Watson.[1] The young manager entered into a risky venture that cost the company $10 million. When he went in to talk to Watson, he began by saying, "I guess you want my resignation." Surprisingly, Watson replied, "You can't be serious. We just spent $10 million educating you." Although companies are becoming increasingly supportive of the idea of learning from mistakes, getting things right the first time can certainly make your life easier and your career progression more rapid.

PROBLEM IDENTIFICATION

There are few things as useless—if not dangerous—as the right answer to the wrong question.
—Peter Drucker, *The Practice of Management*

The most difficult aspect of problem solving is first identifying those issues that are important enough to warrant consideration. By definition a **problem** is a question offered for consideration, discussion, or solution. The identification of problems either in our personal lives or in the workplace is a very powerful act in itself. Knowledge is power. We cannot change that which we are unaware of, so by acknowledging a concern, we open an entire new realm of possibilities. For example, if an individual has the very bad habit of constantly interrupting others, that person has no chance of changing this annoying behavior unless he or she first identifies the problem either through personal introspection or through feedback from another person.

How do we go about identifying problems that are important enough to warrant our attention? Some might be so critical that they are hard to miss. College students who are failing classes, restaurants that have escalating food costs, or hotels that are facing a severe labor shortage are just a few of the "fires" or more obvious problems that require immediate attention. Other problems, perhaps just as important, are much more subtle and covert. When guests are very dissatisfied with an aspect of their service or stay, but fail to bring this to the attention of the hotel staff, the problem escalates without the benefit of a solution. We cannot solve guest problems unless we are aware of them, and we cannot always be aware of them unless guests report them. The same holds true with employee problems. Your staff may be disgruntled about the new scheduling policy to such a degree that many of them are seeking positions at other companies. If they do not bring their dissatisfaction to your attention, you may have no idea of the severity of the problem until it is too late and your best employees have gone elsewhere. Figure 3.1 contains some quantitative or measurable indicators of problems or opportunities for change.

H.R. Measures	Guest Service	Financial	Miscellaneous
Increased employee turnover	Increased customer complaints	Decreased average check	Fewer guests served per employee
Increased accident frequency	Slower service	Decline in sales volume	Higher labor costs
Frequent absenteeism	Fewer positive guest comments	Increase in accounts receivable	Increased spillage and waste
Increase in frequency and seriousness of grievances	Decline in repeat guests	Increase in operating expenses	
Rise in overtime	Fewer new customers	Change in inventory value	

Figure 3.1 Quantitative Indicators of Potential Problems

GOING TO THE SOURCE

So how do you learn about problems before they escalate and become "fires"? Begin by going to the source, or directly contacting guests and employees to uncover their concerns and opinions. Here are a few simple measures that will help you stay abreast of difficulties:

- **Written surveys.** These can be used with both guests and employees to solicit feedback in an anonymous manner. The most important aspect of written surveys is the correct handling of the information once it is received. Every comment deserves a reply. This may involve a letter or phone call to a guest or a meeting with all employees to share the results of the survey and discuss actions that should be taken in response. As described in Insight 3.1, Marriott used a survey method to uncover difficulties employees were having with managing their jobs and family life.
- **Focus groups.** These consist of group sessions held with either guests or employees led by an impartial third party. A series of questions are asked to guide the discussion, but **focus group** members are encouraged to digress a bit and discuss issues with each other. Focus groups that have a specific purpose yield the most valuable information. You might hold a customer focus group to assess a new menu or advertising campaign. An employee focus group might be held to examine morale problems or a high turnover rate. A detailed summary of the results of the focus group is written and distributed to the departments.

INSIGHT 3.1

DIAGNOSING WORK-FAMILY CONFLICT AT MARRIOTT

Organizational surveys are an excellent way to gather objective information from your employees. Marriott Corporation learned that employees were having difficulty meeting conflicting job and home demands. This difficulty resulted in increased turnover and lowered productivity. To assess the nature of the problem, Marriott surveyed 1,600 employees, including both line workers and managers, about their family responsibilities.* They found that 35 percent had children younger than twelve with 15 percent of workers having very young children under the age of five. The results of the study showed that those with children below the age of twelve were absent four days per year and late five times because of their child care needs. Within a year's time, 33 percent of working parents had to take at least two days off because they lacked child care. Twenty percent of those surveys left a previous job because of work-family conflict.

From these results Marriott concluded that the personal lives of their workers is affecting job efficiency and that work-family conflict is experienced equally by men and women. Child care arrangements produce a great deal of stress and limit work schedules and overtime. An unexpected finding was that care of elders is a growing concern.

As a result of survey findings, Marriott developed innovative family and child care programs. They developed a referral program to help employees located affordable child care, tax deferred accounts for child and elder care expenses, work and family seminars, a newsletter addressing dependent care, and a child care center at their corporate headquarters.

*C. Soloman, "Marriott Family Matters," *Personnel Journal* (October 1991): 42–44.

- **Guided interviewing.** Much information can be gleaned from just sitting down with employees or customers and asking them a few key questions. If approached in a non-threatening manner, both customers and employees will usually open up when asked such questions as, "What do you think about our operation?" "How might we make working here more satisfying?" or "What could we do to improve your stay?" Simple questions that address important issues often bring concerns to the forefront.
- **MBWA.** Chapter 1 introduced the principle of "managing by walking around" (MBWA), which emphasizes the importance of getting out of the office and finding out first-hand what is going on in your operation. This practice can yield a wealth of useful information about both customer and employee satisfaction. Walk around, introduce yourself, and ask customers how they like the food or if the service is fast and courteous. Spend time talking informally with employees, asking about their career aspirations, hobbies, or families. Once you have established a rapport with them, ask employees how they like their jobs and the company. Also ask for their ideas about how the operation could be improved. Valuable information can be gathered from such unscientific methods of inquiry.

BEST PRACTICES

There is much that managers can learn about problem solving from common practices used by airline pilots. Problem solving in the air can truly be a life or death situation. Managers can apply the following flight rules to problem solving on the job:*

- **Flight Rule 1:** Anticipate the next crisis. Even if you are currently embellished in a crisis, think ahead and try to predict the next challenge you will face. If you are a restaurant manager who is faced with the task of increasing customer traffic dramatically or closing, focus not only on the task at hand, but also look ahead to the challenge you will face if droves of new customers show up. How will you produce and serve food to a larger client base?

- **Flight Rule 2:** The best way to learn from a mistake is to identify the first error in the sequence. You cannot say that you were late in delivering a long-term project because you had the flu. Perhaps you were slowed down when you became ill, but proper planning would have allowed for built-in delays in your productivity and resulted in an on-time delivery despite a setback.

- **Flight Rule 3:** Pilots are held responsible for all errors on their flight. Managers are also held responsible for errors committed not only by themselves, but also by employees. Rather than looking for someone else to blame when difficulties arise, accept responsibility and focus on solutions.

*Peak, M. "The Right Stuff," *Management Review*, 86, no. 2 (February 1997): 1.

ENVIRONMENTAL SCANNING

Another important aspect of problem identification is **environmental scanning.** This involves the gathering of useful information from the environment that can help you identify and anticipate problems. Many external factors affect our industry, such as politics, competition, legal issues, the labor market, and area demographics to name just a few. External changes can have long-reaching effects on our business environment. For example the Gulf War all but shut down the travel and convention businesses for many months, and the passing of the Americans with Disabilities Act required that hotel and restaurants spend large sums of money to upgrade facilities to bring them up to standard. Anticipating these changes before they become major concerns allows for more effective management.

When we fail to recognize external threats and potential problems, we are lulled into a false sense of security similar to the frog in the following story.[2] According to the parable, if you place a frog in a pot of boiling water, it will try to climb out. However, if you place it in water that is room temperature, the frog will relax. If the temperature is gradually increased to 70 to 80 degrees, something interesting happens. The warm water lulls the frog and he become groggier and groggier, until he is unable to climb out of the pot. Why doesn't the frog realize the threat and try to jump out? Because he gauges external threats only when there are sudden changes in his environment; when the changes are subtle, he is unable to recognize them as threats.

To avoid the fate of the boiled frog, both people and organizations must slow their pace and pay attention to both dramatic and gradual changes in their environment. Failure to anticipate problems can be deadly in our fast-paced, competitive hospitality industry. You may be the owner of a successful coffee shop, satisfied with your customer base and profits. Your success may lull you into a false state of security. One day a major chain opens a similar shop just down the street from you, overrunning your territory and gobbling up your customer base. Suddenly you may have an insurmountable problem on your hands. In contrast McDonald's did an excellent job in anticipating a potential problem. In 1983, when it discovered that one of the toys it planned to promote had a choking hazard, the company undertook the largest toy recall ever, yet this potential scandal went largely unnoticed by the general public. A disaster was avoided because the company was aware of subtle difficulties.

Keeping a close eye on the environment is an effective method of anticipating problems before they strike. Just like earthquake forecasters scan fault lines for signs of abnormal activity, so must you scan your environment for unexpected threats. When scanning, consider how social, technical, economic, environmental, and political developments might affect your operation. Pay constant attention to developments in your external world. Use the following practices to uncover emerging issues and trends that may affect your operation:

- **Stay tuned to current events.** Read newspapers, watch the news on television, and stay abreast of all issues or opportunities that you run across. Create an "issues" file that contains clippings about changes that might affect your operation. Keep these in mind as you plan and forecast your operation's future.
- **Read trade journals.** There are a number of excellent trade journals such as *Restaurants and Institutions, Lodging,* and the *Cornell Hotel and Restaurant Quarterly* that address issues of concern to managers. If possible, subscribe to several trade journals and read them carefully each month.
- **Become a secret shopper.** Visit your competitors frequently to identify changes in traffic patterns, menus, décor, or service. See what is working and what isn't. Also visit operations outside your immediate market to identify regional trends. Many successful restaurateurs visit trendy California or New York to learn about the latest developments in the food industry.

BEST PRACTICES

Several years ago, Sara Lee employees complained about repetitive stress disorders. The company could have ignored the complaint, attributing it to typical employee grumbling, but instead they chose to take a proactive response.* Sara Lee hired a physician and an ergonomics engineer to observe the workers as they did their jobs. These professionals recommended changes in work habits that reduced complaints of repetitive stress injury by 80 percent.

*P. Senge. *The Fifth Discipline.* (New York: Doubleday, 1990).

CREATIVE PROBLEM SOLVING

As your radar develops and you acquire the habit of constantly examining both your internal and external environments for important changes and concerns, problem identification will become second nature. After problems are identified, of course the next step is to solve them. In this portion of your text, you will learn about practices that facilitate creative problem resolution.

MANAGEMENT THINKING

To thoroughly understand how we go about solving problems, we must first examine the cognitive processes that contribute to creative assumptions. There are three modes of thinking that managers use:[3]

1. **Rational thinking.** This mode involves using reason and logic to solve problems and reach conclusions. Decisions are based on observable facts and information.
2. **Intuitive thinking.** Ideas simply arise from the unconscious mind and are based on fragments of stored information and impressions that have accumulated over time.
3. **Creative thinking.** Creative thinking reaches beyond what is now known to what could be. New ideas and visions are formed from past knowledge by drawing on observation, experience, and our ability to form new patterns with old information.

Certainly there is a time and a place for rational decision making. Facts, figures, and observable information can support courses of action. Yet, too often, managers rely only on rational thought to solve problems. Many great ideas are lost because managers do not think intuitively or creatively. According to Disney CEO Michael Eisner, the main reason many companies do not progress is because the do not know how to manage people who have a creative orientation and who work with their imagination.[4] To release the creative energy of your workforce, you must first invite them to buy into your vision, and then foster a work environment that encourages and rewards creative problem solving.

Creative problem solving differs greatly from rational problem solving. By unleashing your creativity, you focus on the best way to handle a difficult situation. Think about how you feel when you sit down and try to solve a problem rationally. Immediately you focus on your anxiety and fear. You worry and become stressed. The problem grows in stature until solving it seems insurmountable. However, when your orientation is creative, problem solving can actually become fun. When you work with others to brainstorm and discuss new ideas, the creative juices flow and you become more relaxed, less focused on the problem, and more focused on solutions.

Break through the rigidity of traditional problem solving and get your creative juices flowing by considering these techniques:

JANUSIAN THINKING

One way to stimulate your creative ability is to engage in **Janusian think-ing.** This idea is based on the Roman deity, Janus, who has two faces looking in op-posite directions. Janusian thinking refers to one's ability to cope with conflicting ideas, paradoxes, ambiguity, and doubt by looking at both sides of an issue.[5] When we consider opposite sides of an issue, we often bring to the surface hidden as-sumptions and concerns that can then be dealt with. To practice Janusian think-ing, apply these two simple questions to your current work situation: "Wouldn't it be nice if . . . ?" and "Wouldn't it be awful if . . . ?" Jot down your answers on a sheet of paper. Next identify factors that influence each scenario. Ask yourself, "How can I minimize the negative factors and maximize the positive factors?"

DIVERGENT THINKING

Often we jump to the most obvious conclusion when problem solving without looking for alternatives. **Divergent thinking,** or thinking that is differ-ent from the norm, will allow you to explore less obvious, but often more effec-tive, options.[6] Imagine that hotel guests are complaining that the wait for elevators is too long. The obvious solution, to install more elevators, is also the most costly. A divergent thinking manager might come up with the creative al-ternative of reducing guests' perceptions of the length of the wait by giving them something to do. The manager may suggest posting information about the hotel by adding a rack that holds a company newsletter, information about area at-tractions, and dining. This low-cost option might just solve the problem more effectively, and certainly less expensively, than the initial alternative.

ROLE SWITCHING

When you are in conflict with another person, or faced with a difficult problem, try putting yourself in the other person's shoes. **Role switching** involves taking on another person's view within the organization.[7] For example, if servers are having a conflict with cooks regarding the accuracy of orders, ask each group to participate in a role reversal, with cooks looking at the problem from the per-spective of the servers and servers seeing the problem from the perspective of the cooks. Ask each group to answer such questions as, "What is important to our de-partment?" "How can we solve this problem?" "How can we best meet customer needs?" Role reversal not only allows each group to better understand the other, but also will result in more creative solutions to the problem at hand.

CHALLENGE ASSUMPTIONS

> *The problems we face today cannot be overcome at the same level of thinking we were at when we created them.*
> —Albert Einstein

Do not accept your current reality at face value, but look for ways to challenge your thinking. As the quote by Albert Einstein suggests, old ways of thinking cannot always solve the new and unique problems we face today. At one time many believed that the Internet was just a fad, that no one would pay $3 for a cup of designer coffee, and that the hospitality industry would always have an abundance of cheap labor. Each of these beliefs was proven wrong. Truly creative ideas and great solutions to problems are often where we least expect them. Read about innovative solutions to common problems in Insight 3.2.

WRITE SCENARIOS

If you or your organization is considering a particular course of action, scenarios can help you determine the possible outcomes that might occur. For example, if a restaurant considers changing its menu, the following scenarios might occur:

1. The new menu is a major improvement, customers are happy, and the kitchen finds it operates with greater efficiency when preparing the newer menu items. Overall, costs decrease by 10 percent and sales increase by 12 percent.
2. Customers and employees dislike the new menu. Customer complaints about menu choices are up by 20 percent, with many refusing to return if they cannot have their old favorites. The kitchen staff finds it difficult to prepare many of the items quickly enough, and as a result, labor costs increase by 15 percent.

INSIGHT 3.2

INNOVATIVE SOLUTIONS

Here are some examples of problems that were solved through creative thinking. In each instance, innovative solutions were discovered that involved changing the environment to resolve the issue.

*   Visitors at Disneyland pay a high admission price and wait hours for rides that last no more than five minutes. Why do they respond so well to a situation that might otherwise cause great dissatisfaction? One reason is that the theme park provides extra service wherever they can. They lend cameras at no charge to their guests at designated photo sites. People remember the fun picture with Mickey Mouse and forget the long lines. Superclean facilities and extra-friendly staff also go far to erase the negative experiences.

*   Hotels with less than adequate elevator service conquer complaints about slowness by changing guests' perceptions of the wait. They install mirrors on the walls to give people something to do—fix their hair, adjust their tie, and so on.

*   Ever notice that there is only one line at Wendy's Restaurants? The company adopted this system when they found that a single, serpentine line reduces guests' perceptions of unfairness when waiting for their turn.* In other restaurants, if you pick the slow line, you may wait longer than someone who just arrived.

*   Travelers in Houston complained about long delays to retrieve their luggage.† It took them only a minute to get to the claim area, but they had to wait as long as seven minutes for their luggage to arrive. The airline restructured the situation by moving baggage pick up to the farthest carousel. It then took passengers six minutes to walk there, and they only had to wait for a minute or two for their luggage. Complaints were eliminated, and guests perceived their luggage as arriving quickly even though there was no difference in the overall time involved.

*"The Line on Waiting," Washington Post. (November 10, 1988): E02.
†Ibid.

3. The new menu results in little change. Old customers complain a bit, but seem willing to try new items. A few new customers are lured by the lighter fare. The kitchen staff finds that the new menu items are similar in preparation to the old items, so they experience little change.

Scenarios are one way to play "devils advocate," allowing you to identify all the factors that can go wrong depending on your course of action. They also let you consider the potential positive outcomes of decisions so that you may weigh the options and make the best choice.

MAKE TIME FOR INNOVATION

If you spend most of your time solving problems and resolving crises, you will have little time for innovation. We have a tendency to race headlong into the future while depending on our rearview mirror to see what was done in the past and our side windows to assess competition instead of carefully mapping our journey. How can you find time in your busy schedule to think of new ideas, find solutions to complex problems, and just daydream about the future? Here are a few ideas that have worked for me:

- Get up earlier than usual. An extra hour in the morning can make all the difference by providing quiet, uninterrupted time just to think.
- Explore new ideas during repetitive exercise. Turn off the "Walkman" while you run, bike, or walk and just let your mind wander. You will be surprised at the number of creative ideas that just come to you as you exercise.
- Take a thinking break. Occasionally take lunch by yourself and sit on a park bench or in a quiet café and jot down new ideas and thoughts. Protein stimulates our cognitive ability, so take advantage of this phenomenon by engaging a little mental activity while you eat.

There are many other ways to slip a little quiet time into your day. Some people think creatively while driving, showering, or folding laundry. Just find something that works for you so you won't miss out on all those great ideas just waiting to be recognized.

THE VALUE OF CREATIVITY

Imagination is greater than knowledge.
—Albert Einstein

When a company achieves profit through a new product, service, or market, it becomes vulnerable. Competition often moves in and survival depends on the company's ability to continue to outpace its rivals. One way that hotels, restaurants, travel agencies, and other hospitality-related organizations can maintain their profitability and uniqueness is by staying at the leading edge of the market by creating innovative products and services that imitators cannot quickly copy. Restaurant and quick serve concepts such as Starbucks and Rain-forest Café have unique properties that are difficult to re-create. Companies depend on employees and managers at all levels of the organization to produce new products, solve customer problems, and make sound business decisions.

DECISION MAKING

Managers enter the workforce with little formal training in decision making. By the authority of their titles, managers are just expected to make good decisions all the time. Often this is not the case. Even the best managers may fall victim to decision traps such as the following:[8]

- Plunging in. Gathering information and reaching conclusions before you have taken time to think about important aspects of the decision you are about to make.
- Overconfidence. Failing to collect essential information because you believe your assumptions and opinions are facts.
- Taking shortcuts. Relying on "rules of thumb" or the ways things are always done without exploring other options.
- Group failure. Assuming that when many smart people are involved, good decisions will always follow.

These traps can result in serious and far-reaching mistakes. It is important that you learn to be a good decision maker. This doesn't mean that you will always make perfect choices, but your success will be more consistent.

THE PROCESS

The decision-making process consists of four elements.[9] All good decision makers must consider each element during this process.

- **Framing.** This involves structuring the question that you must answer with your decision. Think about the issue from several viewpoints and decide what are the most important aspects of the decision that must be made. For example, if you are asked to select an employee from your department to promote, initially, you might frame the decision as "choosing the person who is most likely to motivate the work group." This view fails to consider how the individual will interact within the organization. A more effective frame not only would include "choose a person who is likely to motivate the work group," but also has the "ability to work with other departments, possesses skill in handling customers, and is committed to organizational success."
- **Gathering Intelligence.** Before making your decision, you must collect facts to make the "unknowable" become "knowable." If you are considering accepting a new job with a different company, you must do lots of research to make the right decision. Consider the company's past success, benefits, opportunity for advancement, culture, policy on relocation, and, of course, salary offered.

- **Coming to Conclusions.** This involves following systematic decision-making rules. For example, if you are fortunate enough to have a large group of applicants for a position available in your department, and must weed out those you do not want interview, the development of a systematic judgment method will save you time and increase accuracy. You might decide only to interview those with at least one year of experience in a similar job and who have completed two years of college.
- **Learning from Feedback.** There is much to learn from both good and bad decisions. When things work out, assess the process you followed in making the decision. Consider aspects of it that you can apply in the future. When you make a bad decision, identify what went wrong. Did you take shortcuts or fail to consider the issue from several viewpoints?

CONFLICT RESOLUTION

We spend a great deal of time managing conflict in the hospitality industry. In fact great managers are often great mediators. They can negotiate peaceful solutions to the problems that arise in their departments. Conflict occurs at all levels of our organizations and the players involved can include guests, employees, and managers.

Conflict is typically resolved in one of three manners:[10]

1. **Imposed solution (win-lose).** When conflict is resolved in this manner, one side gets much more than the other. There is a definite winner and a definite loser. For example, if an

BEST PRACTICES

Benjamin Franklin developed an approach to decision making that has stood up well to the test of time.* He recommended making a list of pros and cons relating to the choice to be made. Next he crossed off the pros and cons of equal weight or importance. He would then choose the alternative with the most reasons left after canceling out those on the other side of the sheet. Here is how Ben Franklin's list might look:

Choice: *Should I accept the post as ambassador to Great Britain?*

Pros	Cons
* ~~Higher salary.~~	* ~~Increased cost of living.~~
* ~~Opportunity to see Europe.~~	* ~~Will miss friends and family.~~
* Can negotiate peace.	* ~~Must take time away from inventions.~~
* Will meet royalty.	* Ocean travel is dangerous.

As you can see, it was more advantageous for Ben to accept the ambassadorship to Great Britain. Even today Franklin's method is an excellent decision-making system when only two alternatives are available.

*J. Russo and P. Schoemaker, *Decision Traps: The Ten Barriers to Brilliant Decision-Making and How to Overcome Them*, (New York: Fireside, 1990).

employee comes to a manager and asks for a weekend off due to family obligations and the manager states a resounding no because that's policy, the manager is exerting his or her authority and wins, whereas the employee loses.

2. **Compromise.** When two sides have roughly equivalent power and must resolve a conflict, they often use compromise. Each side gives something up so that neither party really has their needs met. For example the front office manager might ask the housekeeping manager to turn rooms around or have them cleaned two hours ahead of schedule for the early check-in of a very important group. Housekeeping may compromise by offering to have the rooms available one hour ahead of time. The guest needs are not really met, and housekeeping is still inconvenienced by the need to speed up their schedule.

3. **Mutual agreement (win-win).** This third method of conflict resolution involves coming to mutual agreement in a manner that allows both parties to have their needs met and be satisfied with the outcome. Such resolutions are far less common than compromise or win-lose. In our earlier example, the front office manager and housekeeping manager would have to work much harder to develop a solution that meets the needs of both parties. As they discuss their dilemma, the housekeeping manager might explain that he simply cannot ask his employees to come in two hours earlier than scheduled without offering them a higher pay rate for the inconvenience. The front desk manager might decide to pay for the overtime rather than risk losing the business, realizing that the potential profits the group will produce will more than offset the increase in labor costs. In this situation both parties would win. Housekeeping would contribute to the profitability of the hotel without inconveniencing its employees, and the front office would satisfy important guests by allowing them an earlier check-in.

WIN-WIN EVERY TIME

It is obvious that win-win conflict resolution is best for the individuals involved and for the company as a whole. Nevertheless, how do we go about resolving conflict in such a manner that the needs of both parties are met? The following steps will lead you through the process of win-win resolution:

Step 1: **Talk about the issues.** Each party must have the opportunity to clearly and concisely state their position and describe their needs. Using our earlier example, both the housekeeping and front office managers describe their needs and their concerns.

Step 2: **Write an issue statement.** Both parties, to the best of their understanding, should describe the issues in writing

Front Office Manager	Housekeeping Manager
1. Just require the room attendants to arrive early on this one day	1. Just let the guests know it can't be done.
2. Hire an outside cleaning crew to service the additional rooms.	2. Pay employee double time for the early hours with the front office assuming the extra labor cost.
3. Pay the room attendants extra money for early arrival.	3. Require employee to come in early.

Figure 3.2 Possible Actions Resulting from Brainstorming

and share the results with the other party. This will clarify any misunderstanding and reduce the emotional component of the conflict. For example the front office manager might write the following **issue statement:** "Meet the needs of an important group by allowing them to check in two hours ahead of schedule. If we fail to meet this need and our competition succeeds, it is likely that we will lose the account." The housekeeping manager might write, "We cannot accommodate this request without greatly inconveniencing our staff. Morale in the department is currently low and this might result in loss of good employees. We could offer a pay incentive for the earlier start time, but we are currently way over budget and cannot afford the extra labor charges."

Step 3: Identify the objective. Both groups must work to arrive at a common objective. In our example this common goal would be to satisfy the guest needs and allow early arrival without sacrificing the needs of the room attendants.

Step 4: Brainstorm possible actions. Both parties list several actions that might support the desired objective. Figure 3.2 contains lists from both the front office manager and housekeeping manager. This is called **brainstorming.**

Step 5: Breakthrough solutions. Both parties review the lists and cross off solutions that they just cannot live with. The remaining actions are carefully discussed and implementation procedures agreed upon. For example the front office manager realized that having the current staff clean the rooms was certainly the best solution for her. Because money was available for extra wages for the staff, and would satisfy the housekeeping manager's needs, this would be the best solution available.

SKILLFUL NEGOTIATION

All managers are negotiators. You must negotiate with guests as you help solve their problems, with your employees as you ask them for their assistance, and with top management when you go to them for support. In **negotia-**

tion, each person takes a position, states their side of the story, and eventually makes concessions to reach agreement. Great managers and great negotiators do not focus only on their needs, but help their staff, coworkers, customers, and top management get what they want personally and professionally while at the same time, meeting their own needs. If this sounds like a tall order, you're right, it is. There is an art and skill to negotiation that once perfected allows you to meet both your needs and those of the other party. Fisher and Ury, in their book, *Getting to Yes,*[11] describe a negotiation method designed to produce wise outcomes without hard feelings. It consists of four basic points:

1. **Separate the people from the problem.** Do not allow your emotions or feelings about the person with whom you are negotiating to become confused with the problem itself. You and your counterpart must put your feelings aside and work together to solve the problem without attacking each other.

2. **Focus on interests, not positions.** The positions people take in negotiation don't necessarily reflect their interests or needs. In fact your negotiating position can actually hide your real needs. For example if you hold the position that you will not allow your company to transfer you to a new geographic location, your position may mask your real reasons for not wanting move. These might include concern over relocation costs, desire to be with your family, and fear of change. If the negotiation focuses on these interests rather than your stated position, there is a good chance that your company might be able to overcome your objections and make an offer that is acceptable to you.

3. **Invent options for mutual gain.** Prior to an important negotiation, brainstorm a list of possible solutions to the impasse that promote mutual gain and will creatively reconcile differences. For example, if your director plans to reduce your workforce by 10 percent, eliminating two key positions, prior to meeting with the director, come up with a list of your own ideas regarding other ways the issue might be resolved. Your list might include a reduction in hours across the board, reorganization of job duties so costs are shared with another department, or a reduction in costs in other operating areas. All solutions focus on mutual gain, allowing you to maintain your workforce while allowing your director to cut costs.

4. **Insist on using objective criteria.** Avoid focusing on position or power when negotiating, but instead focus on a standard of behavior or principle. Managers should not win negotiations because they have more power, but should remain open to reason, by focusing on principles, not pressure. If your company requires that all employees be available to work weekends, but one of your staff members tells you he or she is no longer available to work at that time, you could exercise your power and just tell

the person that he or she must work weekends if that person wants to continue with the company. Instead, if you were to negotiate based on reason, you might first listen to the employee's needs, then negotiate on principle by forcing that person to see that his or her unwillingness to work weekends inconveniences both the department and the coworkers.

These simple principles will allow you to skillfully negotiate solutions that result in "win-win" resolutions, where both parties' needs are met. Win-win negotiation not only has an immediate positive effect, but also offers long-term benefit. Both parties feel greater confidence about their ability to come to agreement when future differences arise and their relationship is stronger and less adversarial. The parties now have a history of working together and will be more likely to use the same practices in the future.

CONCLUSION

Your ability to make sound decisions and creatively solve problems is extremely important. In this chapter you learned about ways to initially identify problems by going directly to the source and also by scanning the environment for threats and opportunities. When it's time to solve existing or potential problems, creative thinking techniques such as the Janusian method, divergent thinking, role switching, challenging assumptions, and writing scenarios can help you to see less obvious but more effective solutions.

Managers make literally hundreds of decisions each month. Bad decisions can cost companies thousands or even millions of dollars and can certainly put a damper on your career. Avoid decision traps and instead practice effective methods, including framing, gathering intelligence, coming to conclusions, and learning from feedback as you solve complex issues.

As a manager you must also facilitate the resolution of differences between employees, guests, and other managers by learning to deal with conflict. You must strive to achieve solutions that are mutually beneficial, or win-win, rather than resorting to imposed solutions or compromise. Finally managers must also be skillful negotiators to effectively run their departments and to solve guest problems. Great managers negotiate solutions that not only meet their needs, but also the needs of employees, guests, and the company as a whole.

K E Y   T E R M S

Problem	Janusian Thinking
Focus Group	Divergent Thinking
Environmental Scanning	Role Switching
Rational Thinking	Issue Statement
Intuitive Thinking	Brainstorming
Creative Thinking	Negotiation

N   O   T   E   S

1. D. Garvin, "Building a Learning Organization," in *Harvard Business Review on Knowledge Management*, (Boston, Mass.: Harvard Business School Publishing, 47-80. 1998).

2. P. Senge, *The Fifth Discipline*, (New York: Doubleday, 1990).

3. C. Kepner, "Calling All Thinkers," *HR Focus*, 73, no. 10 (October 1996): 3.

4. S. Covey, "Where's Our Imagination?", *Incentive*, 172, no. 11 (November 1998): 27.

5. T. Verbene, "Creative Fitness," Training & Development, August, 1997, Vol. 51, No. 8, pp. 68-71.

6. Ibid.

7. Ibid.

8. J. Russo and P. Schoemaker, *Decision Traps: The Ten Barriers to Brilliant Decision-Making and How to Overcome Them* (New York: Fireside, 1990).

9. Ibid.

10. Dettmer, H. "The Conflict Resolution Diagram: Creating win-Win Solutions." *Quality Progress*, 32, no. 3 (March 1999): 41–47.

11. R. Fisher and W. Ury, *Getting to Yes: Negotiating Agreement without Giving In* (New York: Penguin Books, 1991).

CASE **3.1**: IN BOX EXERCISE

Melissa arrives at work on a Monday morning after a long weekend away from the hotel. As she sits at her desk, she notices a stack of telephone messages that need her attention.

A. The night auditor arrived for work thirty minutes late on Friday. He said that he had car trouble.

B. The hotel general manager called this morning at 7 A.M. and wants to talk to you about your ideas for improving performance in your department.

C. The sales manager called and the number of guests expected for check in this morning has increased from 100 to 150 people.

D. The human resource manager called about several job candidates he has for the reservationist position that is open.

E. There is a letter of resignation from Lucy, one of your best desk clerks, saying she is leaving to accept a supervisory position with one of your competitors.

F. A guest just called to complain about noise from the room next door. He would like to be moved to a different floor.

She has just ten minutes to respond to the most important messages before she must attend the morning's staff meeting. In what order should Melissa attend to the issues? List them in order of importance, with the most important issue listed first and the least important issue listed last.

R E V I E W   Q U E S T I O N S

1. A _____ is a question offered for consideration, discussion, or solution.

2. The process of gathering useful information about politics, the labor market, or your competition is called _____.

3. In _____ each person takes a position, states their side of the story, and eventually makes concessions to reach agreement.

4. _____ negotiation has an immediate positive effect on an organization and offers long-term benefits.

5. List the four elements of the decision-making process and give an example of each.

6. Put yourself in the place of an employee in the hospitality industry. How might you react if your managers were to consistently resolve conflict using:

   a. Imposed solutions.

   b. Compromise.

   c. Mutual agreement.

Which problem identification method would you choose to use in the following situations?

   a. Written survey.   c. Guided interview.
   b. Focus group.   d. MBWA.

____ 7. You want to learn more about your current customers and their satisfaction with your restaurant.

____ 8. You are in the process of choosing a new uniform for your restaurant servers and you want to find out what they think as a group about the possible choices.

____ 9. You want to find out how satisfied all the employees in the hotel are with their jobs.

____ 10. You want to ask employees about their career goals and find out how you might help them reach them.

What type of conflict resolution occurred in the following situations?

   a. Imposed solution.   c. Compromise.
   b. Mutual agreement.

____ 11. Morale has been low in housekeeping and the room attendants would like to have a longer lunch break. The housekeeping manager allows them to take an extra fifteen minutes at lunch if they shorten their morning and afternoon breaks by five minutes, causing their overall workday to be reduced by five minutes. The room attendants are very pleased with this decision and appreciate the extra time at lunch, while management feels that the loss of five minutes of work productivity is well worth the improvement in attitude.

____ 12. Door attendants carry luggage into the hotel, but the bell attendants make more than twice what the door attendants earn in tips. The door attendants feel this is unfair because they handle the luggage as often as the bell staff. Bell attendants agree to pool their tips with door attendants and split the total equally at the end of each shift.

____ 13. The front desk staff wants overtime for working weekends, even when their total hours are under forty for the week. The front desk manager refuses the request and states that no overtime will be paid for weekend work.

CRITICAL THINKING EXERCISES

1. Gary manages a full-service restaurant in a suburb of a large city. He has had the same chef and cooks in his kitchen for the past fifteen years. Little has changed with his menu, products, or cooking methods. Business was always good in the past, and even though newer restaurants were opening up around him, he always seemed to maintain his customer base. But last year things began going down hill. First there was a 10 percent drop in revenue; next he lost his best cook to a competing restaurant because they offered more money; and finally his dining room manager said the servers are unhappy because they just aren't making the tips they did in the past. How is this situation similar to the fate of the boiled frog? What could Gary have done to avoid the problems he now faces?

2. Review the following issues and use creative problem-solving techniques to examine possible solutions:

Issue 1: Dealing with a labor shortage

There is a tremendous labor shortage in your area. It is becoming increasingly difficult to find full-time servers who have the skill levels you are seeking. You have decided to abandon your original plan to employ only full-time employees and instead will seek to hire a number of part-time servers who are students, housewives, or working in other fields.

Examine this idea by using Janusian Thinking. List both the positive and negative aspects of your decision to seek out and hire part timers. How will your restaurant benefit from this decision and, on the other hand, what problems might arise?

Issue 2: Dissatisfaction with cafeteria food

Your employees constantly complain about the quality of the food in the employee cafeteria, even though they are allowed to dine there free of charge. When you have brought this issue to the attention of the executive chef, he says the food quality is the best that he can supply with the budget that he has to work with.

Use the principles of divergent thinking to develop alternative ways to solve this problem.

Issue 3: Improve quality with cleaning pairs

Currently, each room attendant is responsible for cleaning a total of fourteen guest rooms each day. You have had many complaints about poor cleanliness from guests and to improve cleaning quality you are considering having room attendants work in pairs rather than individually and reducing the number of rooms they clean together. Each room attendant pair would then be responsible for cleaning twenty-five guest rooms rather than the twenty-eight rooms the two would clean individually.

Try to predict what the consequences of this action will be by writing three scenarios describing the different possible outcomes that might occur.

3. Read the following situation and then describe how you would use the four elements of the decision-making process to help you choose whether you should accept a job offer.

You have been working as a room service supervisor for the past year in a large convention hotel. The money is good and you are well liked by your staff. You heard about a position available at a competing hotel in banquet management, which is the job you'd really like to have. You apply for the job, come through the interviews successfully, and sense that the hotel is about to offer you the position. You're really happy in your current position, and like the company you work for, but this is a great opportunity.

Use the four elements of the decision-making process in making this decision.

Step 1: Framing:
    What is the question that you must answer in making your decision about whether or not to accept the offer?

Step 2: Gathering Intelligence
    What information must you collect to help you in making your decision?

Step 3: Coming to Conclusions
    How would you systematically make this decision?

Step 4: Learning from Feedback
    After you make the decision and either stay with your current employer or accept the new job, how will you know whether you have made the right choice?

O   N   -   L   I   N   E   L   I   N   K

One of the decisions that you must make as you begin your career in hospitality management is where you want to ultimately live. You may be very happy with your current location and plan to stay indefinitely because you like the area or you want to be close to family or friends. But for the purpose of the exercise, let's assume that you'd like to live and work in a different part of the country or the world. First you would begin the problem-solving process by framing your question. Let's say, the question you want to answer is, "What city or town would provide the best possible career and recreational activities for me?" Next we will proceed to step 2, gathering information. There is lots of information about various cities and communities available on the web. Visit Convention and Visitor's Bureau sites for two different locations and review information available on topics such as recreational activities, climate, and hospitality organizations. You might contrast San Diego and Miami or Phoenix and New York.

What methods would you use to systematically decide which city would appeal to you the most? What is your decision—where would you rather live?

P O R T F O L I O   E X E R C I S E

Employers want to know why you have chosen to seek a career in the hospitality industry. They want to make sure that you are seeking a future in the field for the right reasons—not just because you think it is glamorous or because you enjoy travel. Be prepared for inquiries about this topic by adding a segment to your portfolio titled "The Hospitality Industry: My Career Choice." In this segment include several paragraphs that provide insight into your career decision-making process. Describe why you have decided to seek a career in the hospitality industry. Include the reasons why you are particularly suited for a career in this field and why you believe that you will be successful. This will be a great addition to your portfolio. Employers look very favorably on candidates who have given thought to their career aspirations.

Personal Mastery

4

ADVANCED ORGANIZER

Four years have passed since you completed your college degree. You have been working for a large hotel chain since leaving school, but your career just hasn't progressed as you thought it would. You are still holding the same supervisory position in the front office that you had when you graduated. Although you like your work, your ultimate career goal is to become a director of sales and marketing at a large convention hotel one day. At this rate you might achieve it by the time you are eligible for social security!

The person in the above narrative has suffered from "stalled career syndrome." Although she managed to get her foot in the door after graduation, she just hasn't gone anywhere since. Stalled careers are costly both in lost wages and lost opportunities. To avoid this fate, read this chapter carefully and plan ahead for a successful, fast-track career. You will develop expertise in job hunting, portfolio development, career progression, and other important skills to help you master your future.

BEHAVIORAL OBJECTIVES

- Describe the characteristics of those who have achieved personal mastery.

- Create a personal vision of your future.

The Hotel Allegro Chicago

- Identify and create a plan to eliminate your time-wasting behaviors.

- Develop a plan to use mentoring and networking to advance your career.

- Identify the components of a successful job search.

- Define the characteristics of highly successful workers.

- Assess the skills needed to achieve your career goals.

MANAGING YOURSELF

Perhaps the most important skill you will bring to your career is your ability to manage both the personal and professional aspects of your life. You must manage yourself before you can manage others. In this chapter you will develop skills in **personal mastery,** the discipline of personal growth and learning. Those who seek personal mastery engage in a quest for learning and continually expand their abilities to create the results in life that they desire.[1]

CHARACTERISTICS OF PERSONAL MASTERY

Those with high levels of personal mastery share several basic characteristics. First they have a sense of purpose in their lives. Their career is not simply a job they go to each day, but a calling. Your purpose as a manager may involve leading and accomplishing success through others. As a skilled manager, you have the important calling of providing gainful employment to others and giving them the opportunity to develop as individuals with your guidance and support as their leader.

Second, those who have achieved high levels of personal mastery are constantly learning. They find value in the learning process and see their careers as an enjoyable journey. Specifically these individuals become lifelong learners and enhance their knowledge by reading, taking courses, and conversing with knowledgeable people.

The final characteristic of those who have achieved personal mastery is their ability to delay gratification. When we set important long-term goals for ourselves, it may take many years of "paying our dues" to finally achieve the end result we desire. We must be able to make sacrifices and commit to staying the course over the long term to achieve important goals. This may involve several years of college, lower level jobs, and long hours before we reach a career level that provides the authority and responsibility desired.

In this chapter you will learn a simple formula that will help you ensure a long and satisfying professional and personal life. The first step in achieving mastery is to identify your personal vision. Having a life goal or mission will help you focus on what you hope to accomplish. You must have a clear idea of where you want to be both in the near and distant future if you are to have a satisfying career. If you don't know where you are going, others will make decisions for you, and you might find yourself in an unsatisfying career.

Next you must motivate yourself to achieve your vision. Often the motivation to work toward career goals comes from the practice of identifying them.

By identifying your mission in life, you will unleash great energy and enthusiasm that will provide the impetus for achievement. If you have a clear idea of what you want to accomplish in the next decade or two, your motivation level will naturally increase.

Third you must be able to market yourself by letting others know what you hope to accomplish. You may achieve this by taking on visible responsibilities that pertain to your career goals, by building relationships with mentors, and by participating in networking activities.

Finally it is impossible to achieve personal mastery if you fail to manage your time. You must include activities in your daily "to do" list that will ultimately help you achieve your major career goals. Try to do something each week that moves you a little closer to your long-term goal.

In the remainder of this chapter, you will learn the specific steps you need to take to achieve personal mastery. You will begin by developing a personal vision of your future. Next you will learn to activate the energy you will need to make your vision a reality. You will also gain expertise in additional important practices necessary for success such as time management, locating and working with a mentor, and networking. Finally, you will develop skill in managing your career progression, from job hunting to ascending the corporate ladder. Initially the chapter will provide background information regarding each of these important practices, and then you will have the opportunity to complete a series of exercises at the end of the chapter that will allow you to apply these principles to your own life.

PERSONAL VISION

Goals and objectives are fine for managing your day-to-day activities, but a **personal vision** offers much more than just a way to organize your activities. It is a specific destination that you want to reach—a picture of the future you desire. When creating your personal vision, you must consider several factors that will affect your long-term satisfaction by answering such questions as:

- What kind of future do you desire?
- Where do you want to live?
- How important is money and income to you?
- How much freedom do you desire?
- What type of family life do you want?
- How important is your physical health and well-being?
- What type of work will make you feel satisfied and productive while supporting your other desires?

As you answer these questions, you may realize that certain aspects of your personal vision may be in conflict. You may desire to remain close to your extended family, but at the same time, wish to live in a different part of the country or the world. Such conflicts require compromise. At one point in my life, I was working toward achieving my vision of becoming a corporate training executive with a major hotel chain. I was making great progress through career advancement and had completed an appropriate master's degree program when another desire took hold. I wanted to have children. As I learned more about the life of a corporate trainer, I realized that this would severely conflict with my desire to be a parent. Corporate trainers work long hours and spend most of their time traveling. This conflict led me to a new personal vision when I realized that many of the skills I had been cultivating could be very useful in higher education. I then changed gears and began to pursue a career as a college teacher.

Your personal vision is certainly not set in stone and may be revised as your life situation and desires change; it is not a rigid set of rules you must follow, but simply a target that you are working toward. Remember the adage, "Be careful what you wish for, you just might get it." Similarly we often achieve goals or a vision that we set for ourselves, so be careful of what you strive to achieve. When setting goals ask yourself the following questions:

- Is this something I really want to do?
- Am I likely to enjoy it in the future?
- What personal or professional price might I have to pay?
- Is the price worth it?
- Will I be able to live with myself if I accomplish it?

If the answers to these questions are positive, your vision is likely to bring you great satisfaction. If you find lots of nos when you ask the questions, give careful consideration to your decision before you immerse yourself in working to achieve it.

CREATIVE TENSION

Once you have identified your personal vision, how do you go about achieving it? According to author Peter Senge,[2] this is accomplished with **creative tension** caused by the gap between where you are now and where you want to be in the future. To benefit from creative tension, first begin with a clear vision or idea of what you want to achieve. Then you must have a clear picture of your **current reality,** or where you stand now.

To assess your current reality, apply benchmarking techniques to your personal development. Begin by listing the skills, knowledge, and abilities that you possess in all areas of your life. Next talk with individuals who are the best and brightest in your field. Ask them, to what do they attribute the success they have achieved. Identify the skills, knowledge, and abilities that have been most useful to them in their careers and their personal lives. Next conduct a gap analysis. What skills, knowledge, and abilities do they possess that you lack? The gap between your skills and theirs can then be used to formulate developmental goals that will foster your career development.[3]

The gap between where you are now and where you want to be in the future creates tension resulting in the strong desire to somehow move your current reality closer to your vision. You can accomplish this movement in one of two ways. First work diligently to achieve goals related to your vision and move yourself closer to where you want to be. Or, less effectively, you might readjust and reevaluate your vision to make it less rigorous and easier to achieve. For example consider a desk clerk in a hotel whose vision it is to become general manager of a resort property in the Southwest. This goal creates a certain tension or desire. To move his current reality closer to his vision, this individual must complete a baccalaureate degree, gain years of experience in several departments, and develop the political savvy needed to move up in the corporate world. To achieve this vision may require years of commitment. The desk clerk may feel overwhelmed by the time and effort required to achieve this vision and set his or her standards lower, deciding to aim for the position of front office manager at a resort property. Thus the vision has moved closer to reality. Assess your own ability to deal with stress by completing the short quiz in Insight 4.1. Then review "Stressbusters" in the next Best Practices box.

Sometimes we do set our goals too high, and an adjustment is a realistic way of dealing with the frustration we might feel in trying to achieve more than we can. But all too often, life becomes a series of vision adjustments until we are totally unchallenged and simply seek to fill our time with such meaningless activities as television, surfing the net, gambling, and watching sports. Eventually all this escapism catches up with us, and we realize that we have achieved little in our lives and have literally wasted our time. To avoid such disillusionment, don't be afraid to identify a challenging vision. When tension mounts don't let

INSIGHT 4.1

ARE YOU STRESSED OUT?

Find out how stressed you are by taking this short quiz. Rate how closely you agree with each statement by filling in a number from 1 to 10.

Strongly Disagree				Agree Somewhat					Strongly Agree
1	2	3	4	5	6	7	8	9	10

1. I have little control over my life at school and work.
2. I have lots of responsibility, but little authority.
3. I rarely have time to do a good job at things.
4. I rarely receive the praise I deserve.
5. I just don't have enough time for my family and friends.
6. I can't be my real self at school or at work.
7. I feel that I cannot use my talents to their full potential.
8. Other people discriminate against me.
9. I am not satisfied with the quality of work I produce.
10. Friends and coworkers get on my nerves.

If you scored between:

10 and 30:   You have low stress levels. Your current situation seems to be working well for you.

31 and 59:   You are moderately stressed. Consider implementing some of the "stress busters" in "Best Practices."

60 and 100: You are overstressed and should consider making changes to reduce your stress levels. If you score at the high end of this range, you may want to speak with a professional about your situation.

your goals erode. Instead use this tension to generate energy that supplies the motivation to change. Perhaps you may never achieve your ultimate goal, but by setting your standards high, you will accomplish far more in your life than you ever dreamed possible.

For example, Bill Russell, a legendary center for the Boston Celtics, kept his own scorecard and graded himself after each game on an asending scale to 100. He never gave himself a rating higher than sixty-five. Based on this relatively low score, we might think of Russell as a failure, but in reality, he played in over 1,200 basketball games and is considered one of the best basketball players of all time.[4]

MANAGING YOUR TIME

The world is filled with people who have great ideas and wonderful visions yet accomplish little in their lives. To avoid this fate, you must use your time well. Each day contains twenty-four hours. Those who use those hours to achieve their vision will have a successful personal and professional life, while those who habitually waste time will accomplish little. Steven Covey, in his best-seller *The Seven Habits of Highly Effective People*, has identified practices that, if followed, can help you better manage your time so you can achieve success. See Insight 4.2 for a synopsis of the seven habits.

As a student you face a particularly difficult time management challenge because the primary responsibility for organizing your day is up to you. Later as a busy manager in the hospitality industry, your day will be more

BEST PRACTICES

"STRESSBUSTERS"

High levels of stress can lead to both physiological problems like heart disease and high blood pressure and emotional problems like depression and insomnia. It is important that you take good care of yourself during periods of high stress to avoid or minimize the negative consequences. Here are just a few ways that you can reduce the negative impact of stress:

- Spend time outside. Nature is a natural stress reducer. Go for a walk, hike, fish, canoe, swim, and so on.

- Reduce life to essentials when you have too much to do. Eliminate all unnecessary activities until you catch up.

- Eat healthy foods. It is important to provide good fuel for your body when you are asking it to work on overdrive.

- Exercise aerobically. Run, walk, bike, or do an exercise class to greatly relieve stress.

- Talk to a friend. If life just seems overwhelming, talk to a friend.

- Turn off the TV. Reduce the amount of noise and negative energy that you are experiencing by turning off the television for a week or so.

77

INSIGHT 4.2

THE SEVEN HABITS OF HIGHLY EFFECTIVE PEOPLE

In his best-selling book *The Seven Habits of Highly Effective People*, Steven Covey identified seven qualities that enhance your success in life and as a leader. According to Covey, time management, personal discipline, and ethics lead to effectiveness.* The seven habits are:

1. Be proactive. Have a personal vision.

2. Begin with the end in mind. Base your actions on the results you hope to achieve.

3. Put first things first. Base your actions on priorities you have set in both your professional and personal life.

4. Think win/win. Seek mutual benefit in your relationships.

5. Seek first to understand, then to be understood. Listen with empathy to others.

6. Synergize. The whole is greater than its parts or teamwork is more effective than going it alone.

7. Sharpen the saw. Become a lifelong learner of new habits. Renew yourself physically, mentally, emotionally, and spiritually.

Covey believes courage and consideration are the key building blocks of emotional maturity. We are emotionally mature when we can express our feelings and convictions with courage, balanced with consideration for the feelings and convictions of others.

*"Character First," *Executive Excellence* (May 1994): 3–5.

structured, but then you may become overwhelmed by multiple tasks. You may have a list of daily operational responsibilities, special projects from your boss, peppered with a variety of "fires" or unforeseen emergencies that must be handled quickly. No matter what situation you face, time management will always be a challenge. Here are some basic principles that will help you achieve more in less time:

- **Keep your vision front and center.** If possible, post your vision or goals where they can be readily seen throughout the day. Make sure that many of the activities that you pursue during the day correspond to the achievement of these goals or vision.
- **Use a daily "to do" list.** A simple but effective system involves listing all tasks on the left-hand side of a bound notebook. Use the right-hand page to jot down notes relating to your tasks. Each day pick five or ten of the most important tasks and start working on them. Cross them off as you get them done. Add to the list as new tasks arise.[5]
- **Just get started.** When faced with an unpleasant task, force yourself to work on it for just ten minutes. Often you will find that the task wasn't as terrible as you thought

and that working on it gives you a great sense of accomplishment.

- **Reward yourself.** When you complete a large or unpleasant task, reward yourself with a favorite activity.
- **Seek out a mentor.** If you have big problems getting things done, seek out a friend or coworker that can act as your mentor. Meet once each week to review goals and accomplishments. The act of being accountable to someone may be enough to motivate you to get things done.
- **Use the Jesuit Test of Conscience.** To help you stay on track and assure that what you are doing each day is truly important, use the Jesuit Test of Conscience. Review your actions one or more times each day, and ask yourself whether what you have been doing in the past few hours is consistent with your long-term goals. If it is, carry on; if it isn't, decide how you can get back on track.

PROCRASTINATION

Are you a **procrastinator**? Do you put off similar tasks every month, or do you postpone most tasks until they become emergencies? Even when you use effective time management tools, you may still find yourself failing to finish important projects. To slay the procrastination monster, it may be necessary to understand the principles behind your avoidance behavior. What makes us procrastinate?

- **Fear.** Perhaps you aren't certain that you can perform a particular task adequately. You lack confidence in your ability to be successful. The first important step in eliminating fear is to become aware of it. Then you can deal with it by reminding yourself that you have been successful in the past and that you can perform this task well if you give it your best shot.
- **Perfectionism.** Often responsible for the fear we have of performing difficult tasks is our belief that everything that we do must be absolutely perfect. Certainly perfection is a goal to strive for, but if we put too much pressure on ourselves, we freeze and become fearful of trying new things. Try to avoid mistakes, but when they do occur, accept them as learning opportunities.
- **Crisis Addiction.** Some of us are addicted to the thrill of a crisis. We can only meet deadlines when under the gun. We allow simple tasks to escalate to the crisis level simply because we put them off. Although last-minute performance can be adequate, it is not optimal. Students who study consistently during the semester usually outperform those who cram the night before a final exam. Try to build the habit of completing tasks as soon as you become aware of them. Plan ahead, prepare, and you will find

that you must deal with fewer crises, and as a result, become a more efficient and effective manager.

- **Overextended.** People who accept every task asked of them often find themselves overwhelmed by all they must accomplish and just can't get anything done. Setting goals, prioritizing tasks, and a daily "to do" list will help avoid overextension. Accept those tasks that help you meet your goals. Tasks that have little value to you can be delegated or even refused.

The ability to use time wisely is perhaps one of the most valuable skills we can foster. If you master this principle, you will be head and shoulders above your competition because you will accomplish important things quickly and efficiently. Continue to work on time management principles so that your vision can become a reality.

MENTORING

Behind many successful managers are great mentors. If you are a woman, a mentor may be the crucial factor that helps you break through the notorious "glass ceiling," with more than 91 percent of female executives reporting that they have had a mentor at some point in their careers.[6] **Mentors** can help you identify career goals, training opportunities, and support your pursuit of promotion. But how do you go about developing a mentoring relationship?

- **Explore formal mentoring programs.** First talk to your human resources department and find out if your company has a formal mentoring program that will match you with an upper-level manager and guide you through the process. If your company has no formal program, don't give up. You will simply have to locate your own mentor.
- **Locate potential mentors.** Identify an experienced, supportive person within your organization that you think would make a good mentor. Some choose mentors who are similar to them in race and gender, but many successful mentoring relationships consist of diverse combinations of individuals. Once you have identified a potential mentor, make an appointment with this person. During your initial appointment, ask about the individual's career progression—how that person's goals have been achieved. Share your career aspirations and ask for advice about how you might achieve them. If this person seems interested and supportive, you may have found a mentor. If not simply select another individual until you find that right person who is interested in you and your career.
- **Look outside the organization.** Mentors may also be found outside your place of employment. College professors, religious leaders, neighbors, and fellow students may

all prove to be excellent mentors. You certainly don't need to limit yourself to one mentor. You may identify several individuals who can positively impact your life and career.

Once you have identified your mentor or mentors, next it is time for relationship building. At all times, maintain a professional demeanor with your mentor and don't slip into the habit of becoming too casual in your relationship. After the initial contact, stay in touch by sending brief notes or scheduling short meetings to discuss your ideas and achievements. Keep the discussions upbeat and positive; never "dump" on your mentor by focusing only on complaints and problems. Finally the best mentoring relationships are two-sided. To facilitate this mutual relationship, think of ways that you can help your mentor. For example, if you notice a new book or article dealing with an area of interest to your mentor, send a copy with a brief note. Ask about your mentor's future aspirations and perhaps even become a sounding board for his or her ideas, just as your mentor is for yours. Finally look for ways that you might assist your mentor and offer your time and expertise.

NETWORKING

Networking involves planning, making contacts, and sharing information with others for personal and professional gain.[7] It is similar to mentoring, but the networking relationship involves more give and take. In a mentoring relationship, the focus is primarily on your needs; in networking, the focus is on shared benefits.

Networking, once used primarily by those working in sales, offers many advantages to individuals hoping to advance their careers. By developing relationships with individuals both within your area of expertise and in other professions, you can become aware of emerging career opportunities. You may receive inside information about new developments within your organization or field of study. Once a network friend told me that the general manager of our hotel was being transferred before this person was even aware of his impending career change. I was able to use this information to my advantage. I had planned to approach the general manager with some issues and ideas, but realized this might not be the best time. Instead I waited and spoke with the incoming general manager who was very open to my ideas.

Finally networking gives you the opportunity to socialize, make new friends, and develop a support system that can be invaluable if you find yourself out of work or faced with a difficult decision. If you have a solid professional network, you have a valuable resource that can greatly facilitate your job hunt by providing additional contacts and references.

Some of us are natural networkers. We enjoy meeting new people, talking with them, sharing information, and developing lasting relationships. Others may find these activities a bit intimidating or perhaps even unpleasant. Even if a wide social network is just not your preference, forming professional relationships can expedite your achievement of your career goals. If you're not a natural, how do you go about networking?

- **Begin by looking within your organization or school.** Be friendly, smile, and make small talk with coworkers and fellow students. Most people are happy to talk about themselves and their lives. Without getting too personal, ask questions and encourage others to open up to you. Share your ideas without dominating the conversation. Soon others will view you as friendly, outgoing, and approachable—just the type of person to network with.

- **Get involved.** Do not limit your network to those individuals who are readily accessible. Join organizations that pertain to your career area, and attend both the social and educational programs they offer. Talk to people, hand out business cards, and set the goal of making one valuable contact during each function.

- **Identify those you would like to network with.** As you build relationships, identify individuals who have similar career interests to yours and who are willing to share information and provide encouragement in a positive manner. These are the people you want in your network. Don't be afraid to network up or to form relationships with those in more powerful positions than yours. These individuals can have the greatest positive impact on your career.

- **Nourish your relationships.** Once you have identified those you want to include in your network, the next step is relationship building. If you had a particularly interesting conversation with someone regarding a specific topic, locate more information on this area and forward it to that person with a brief note. If appropriate meet for lunch or coffee with new friends. Look for opportunities to maintain contact with important network members. If the person receives an award or promotion, send a congratulatory note. Think of projects on which you might collaborate. Just as with mentors, maintain professional relationships at all times. Mixing networking with romance can often backfire.

- **Networking is a two-way relationship.** Always begin networking relationships by thinking of ways you can be of service to the other person. Never begin by asking for large favors, or your network member may feel used. First form the relationship. Then, ideally, provide a service to your network member. Finally, if you are in need, ask for assistance.

- **Maintain Contact.** If you are really working hard at networking, you may find yourself with numerous people to stay in touch with. Prioritize your network by choosing those individuals that you enjoy the most and who are closely aligned with your current career and life goals. Be sure to include powerful individuals who can positively impact your career. Make it a priority (include it on your to-do list) to stay in touch with these individuals. Make periodic phone calls, send e-mail messages, cards, and notes. Look for opportunities to get together. You have put a great deal of effort into forming your network, but if you allow the relationships to fade, you will find yourself without a support system when you might need it most.

MANAGING YOUR CAREER

Our workforce is in a constant state of flux. Workers no longer stay with the same company or in the same occupation for the balance of their careers. You must be prepared to "reinvent" your career several times over to stay current with technological advances and build marketable skills. Career management must be viewed as a lifelong process. You must dedicate yourself to learning and development. If you have worked to master skills that are in demand, you will never have to worry about your employment prospects. Those who have desirable skills and knowledge will be the first to be promoted, the best paid, and the last to be downsized.

What skills are in demand today? In a study completed by the National Association of Colleges and Employers, the most desirable skills include:[8]

- The ability to communicate well both verbally and in writing.
- Technical skills including both job knowledge and computer literacy.
- The ability to lead and motivate others.
- Interpersonal skills.

PREPARING TO ENTER THE JOB MARKET

Perhaps one of the greatest concerns held by college students is the fear that they will not be successful or happy in the career they are preparing to enter. Advanced preparation will allay these fears and make for a smooth transition from student to trainee or manager. There are several things you can do while still in school that will prepare you to enter the job market and provide you with confidence in your career choice.

THE PROFESSIONAL PORTFOLIO

One way to manage your professional development is to maintain an ongoing **professional portfolio** that details important projects, seminars, workshops, and educational experiences you have completed. The portfolio not only provides a record of your progress, it also demonstrates to employers that you have the skills they need. If you have completed the portfolio exercises included in this text, you have made significant progress toward creating a valuable record of your accomplishments. Employers prefer to interview candidates who either present their portfolios before or during initial screening.[9] See Figure 4.1 for more information about constructing a professional portfolio.

BEST PRACTICES

The Internet is an excellent resource for educating yourself about job searches, professional development, and potential employers. Of course, it is no substitute for face-to-face meetings, but it can certainly be an excellent resource when you are beginning your career search. Here are a few strategies to use:

- Learn more about career opportunities by visiting some of the on line job banks such as Career Mosaic at www.careermosaic.com, My Job Search at www.myjobsearch.com, the Monster Board at www.monster.com, or CareerNet at *www.careers.org*. To get an idea of just how big on line job sites are, visit Yahoo!'s listing of job lead sources which includes a collection of mega-sites at *dir.yahoo.com/Business_and_Economy/Employment/Jobs*.

- To explore trends in electronic recruiting and to learn about innovative sites, visit www.Interbiznet.com and explore their site map that has clusters of valuable sites organized by topic.

- Visit sites hosted by your states' hotel or restaurant association to learn about upcoming career fairs and career opportunities.

- Find out how to develop and use electronic resumes effectively by visiting eResumes and Resources at www.eresumes.com .

- Finally, visit web sites of companies you would like to work for to learn more about opportunities. Most larger companies will allow you to submit your application and resume online.

INFORMATIONAL INTERVIEWS

In addition to creating a portfolio, another great way to prepare for career success while you are still in school is to schedule several **informational interviews** with industry managers. Choose individuals who currently hold positions that are consistent with your career vision. Contact them and ask if they would be willing to talk with you about their current positions and how they achieved them. Ideally informational interviews should be conducted face to face. Come prepared with a list of questions that you will ask them regarding current job responsibilities, job qualifications, and both positive and negative

---

The contents of your professional portfolio depend on your career goal and your field of study. Below are some recommendations of information that you might include:

- Professional resume and cover letter.
- Transcripts from higher education.
- Letters of recommendation from past employers and faculty.
- Positive letters from guests and customers.
- Certificates from on the job training or seminars completed.
- Documentation of awards or special recognition.
- Samples of projects completed in relevant courses or internships.
- Other material that demonstrates valuable skills you possess.

Figure 4.1 Contents of Your Professional Portfolio

aspects of their current positions. You will come away with both valuable information about a career direction that you are considering and a possible future contact that might be helpful when you enter the job market.

RESUME

The resume is a marketing tool that advertises your outstanding skills, competencies, and achievements. Its primary purpose is to briefly introduce you to potential employers and generate a face-to-face meeting. Today resumes may be on hard copy or paper or electronic. See Insight 4.3 for hints on creating an "intelligent resume."

An important component of your resume is a standout cover letter that supports information supplied in your resume and provides details about your career aspirations and your strong desire to join a particular organization. In your cover letter, let the employer know what you can do for their company. Research companies ahead of time so you can match your particular abilities to those most needed by the organization. Cover letters should always be personalized or addressed to a specific person in a specific organization. Figures 4.2 and 4.3 contains a sample resume and cover letter that can guide you in preparing your own. Additional help is available from your college placement office or from the many books written about resume development.

INSIGHT 4.3

THE INTELLIGENT RESUME

Your skills and accomplishments are the key ingredient of your resume. Begin a draft of your resume by first listing all your skills, knowledge, and abilities, then formulating these characteristics into a coherent document. Format is just as important as content. (See Figure 4.2 for a sample resume format.) Once your resume is complete, assess it using the following checklist:

- Use achievement-oriented phrases rather than sentences.

- Resume length is not longer than one to two pages.

- If submitted electronically, use key words from the job description in the advertisement to avoid being "scanned out."

- Use a chronological format listing most recent experiences first.

- Include your address, phone number, fax number, and e-mail address.

- List your GPA if it is good (B average or better).

- Use high quality bond paper in white or eggshell only.

- Make sure print quality is high. Take your disk to a copy store to have it printed on a laser printer if possible.

John Smith
_____

2341 N. Wilmington Blvd.   **Telephone:** 312-555-1234
Chicago, Illinois 60605   **e-mail:**   *jsmith@aol.com*

Career Objective: Challenging position in the meetings and convention industry
where I can utilize my skill in technology, service, and marketing.

Educational Background
B.S. Hospitality Management, May 2000
Roosevelt University, Chicago, Illinois
Cumulative G.P.A. 4.8/5.0
Major area of study: Meeting and Convention Management

Relevant Coursework:
- Technology in Meeting Management.
- Exposition Management.
- Convention Management.

Experience in the Hospitality Industry
Prism Convention and Meetings Management   (September 1999 to May 2000)
Chicago, Illinois   312-555-2345
Position: Intern, Convention Planning
Supervisor   Mary Prism, President

Responsibilities
- Worked with clients in all phases of convention planning.
- On-site management of major events.
- Developed client-management database.

The Hotel Excelsior   (September 1996 to August 1999)
Chicago, Illinois   312-555-3456
Position: Lead Guest Service Representative
Supervisor   Adam Hunt

Responsibilities:
- Provide exceptional service to guests at check-in and checkout.
- Lead guest service representative responsible for training and supervision of staff.
- Inspect all VIP rooms for cleanliness and accuracy of amenities.

Professional Activities
President, Roosevelt Hospitality Club, 1999 .
Student Delegate, CHRIE Conference, 1998
Student Member, Meeting Planners International

Figure 4.2 Sample Resume

THE SUCCESSFUL JOB HUNT

The perfect time to begin your job search is during your final semester in college. By this time you will have a representative portfolio and a clear idea of the career direction that interests you. Your primary goal is to land interviews with those who have the authority to hire you and handle them so well that job offers result. Here are some tried and true steps that will lead to the desired outcome:[10]

John Smith

2341 N. Wilmington Blvd.   Telephone: 312-555-1234
Chicago, Illinois 60605   e-mail: *jsmith@aol.com*

June 10, 2000

Mr. James Bartholomew
President, Corporate Meetings International
400 N. Michigan Avenue
Chicago, Illinois 60601

Dear Mr. Bartholomew:

As a recent graduate of the Convention and Meetings Management degree program at
Roosevelt University, I am hoping to begin my career in this exciting field with an outstanding company such as yours. My commitment to the meetings industry was reinforced by the excellent internship I completed at Prism Management. In fact, my
experience was so successful there that my tenure was extended for a second semester.

As my resume indicates, I have completed all coursework for the B.S. degree in Convention and Meetings Management and graduated with honors in May. I particularly
enjoyed courses in technology and international meeting planning and am seeking an
entry-level position that would allow me to practice the skills I have developed.

I would welcome the opportunity to discuss current or future careers opportunities at
Corporate Meetings International. I will contact you next to explore the possibility of
visiting your organization.

Sincerely,

John Smith

Figure 4.3 Sample Cover Letter

1. **Begin with a plan.** Start with a list of potential employers. Research these companies and learn about their business environments, profitability, product lines, and
   leadership. Choose several companies that are profitable,
   and seem to be a good match for you. Send resumes directly to the department heads of those areas in which
   you want to work. Follow up a week later with a telephone call to find out if there is any interest and to ask
   for an interview.
2. **Network.** Contact people that you know well and not so
   well and let them know you are seeking a job. These
   might include professors, fellow students, neighbors,
   clergy, or relatives. Don't forget to contact the managers
   that were part of your informational interviews. Let your

contacts know that you are entering the job market, and ask that they inform you of any opportunities they might hear of.

3. **Visit your college's career placement center.** You can receive assistance with resume and cover letter development, find out about job opportunities, and even receive help developing your interviewing skills from your college placement office.

4. **Be organized.** Develop a database or file that lists all you have contacted in your search. Note dates of correspondence, phone calls, and interviews along with their outcomes.

5. **Follow up.** Send thank you letters to potential employers following interviews and to those in your network that provide job leads. Thank you notes should be professional letters that are typed, not handwritten, on standard paper.

6. **Don't become discouraged.** Look upon the job search as a project or challenge. Interviews that do not lead to offers can still be great learning experiences and will help you better prepare for future interviews. Remember that you may need to interview with as many as ten or twenty different companies before you are offered the right job.

INTERVIEWING

The job interview is the most important component of the job offer. A face-to-face interview is the best way to sell potential employers on your suitability as a job candidate. When interviewing, dress professionally, always arrive on time, bring an extra copy of your resume, smile, shake hands, use the interviewer's name, and thank the interviewer for his or her time.

There is much that you can do to prepare for the interview ahead of time by anticipating some of the questions you might be asked and rehearsing your answers. Figure 4.4 contains some commonly asked interview questions. Think about how you might answer them, and if possible, even rehearse your responses with a friend.

Interviewers not only assess you based on your answers to their questions, but they also form opinions based on the type of questions you ask them. Well-researched, intelligent questions about the company tell the interviewer that you have done your homework and already know what the organization is about. When interviewing, do ask:

- What are the job responsibilities? As the interviewer answers, use your past experience to support your expertise in the job requirements.
- What do you personally like about this company?
- Where do you see this company in the next five years?
- What opportunities for advancement are there?
- Questions tailored to your research regarding mergers, new products, or new opportunities.

- Where do you see yourself in five (or ten) years' time?
- What are your greatest strengths?
- What are your weaknesses?
- Are you willing to relocate?
- What type of relationship have you had with supervisors in the past?
- How do you get along with your coworkers?
- Why do you want to leave your current job?
- What are your salary expectations?
- What professional organizations are you involved with?
- What excites you about this industry?
- What qualities do great managers have?
- What type of leader are you?
- What technology skills do you possess?
- How do you plan to upgrade your current skills?

Figure 4.4 Commonly Asked Interview Questions

- What are the characteristics of an individual who would be highly successful in this position? Follow up by describing the match between your own skills and those needed in the job.

Not all questions will add to your viability as a candidate. Avoid asking the following questions such as:

- How much money will I make? Certainly at some point salary must be discussed, but avoid bringing up the money question too early in the process or the interviewer will think that is all you are interested in.
- How much freedom will I have? This may lead the interviewer to believe you are not a team player and might be difficult to control.
- How much vacation/sick leave will I receive? These questions are best left until after the job offer is made. If brought up too soon, they can make you appear to be too interested in fringe benefits.
- How long will it be before I am promoted? Questions about career progression are important, but if asked in the wrong manner they can make you appear to be more interested in future opportunities and less interested in the job currently available.

AFTER THE INTERVIEW

The initial interview is only the first step in the process of being hired. Once again you must take responsibility for your success by following up. Immediately after the first interview, send a thank you letter typed on professional stock. Never send a handwritten card or note. In addition to thanking the interviewer for his or her time, also reiterate your interest in the position and remind the interviewer of your qualifications. In your thank you letter, mention that you will contact the interviewer during the next week to follow up on the status of the job search.

Do call the interviewer a week to ten days after your meeting to ask about your candidacy and the status of the job search. Be very polite. Once again express your interest in the position, but do not attempt a "hard sell" approach during this conversation. If you receive bad news and learn that another applicant has been offered the position, end the conversation on a positive note, once again thanking the interviewer for the time spent with you. Express your continued interest in the company, and ask your contact to keep you in mind for future positions.

If you have several interviews, but job offers just aren't made, carefully evaluate your interview skills. Visit your career placement center and ask one of the counselors to conduct a mock interview. Reassess your personal appearance and grooming. The conservative look is always preferred in the business environment. For men, this includes a neat haircut, polished shoes, and a good suit in blue or gray; for women, add natural looking makeup, little or no jewelry, and either a short- to mid-length haircut or longer hair that is off the face.

Look upon each interview, successful or not, as a valuable learning experience. Try to improve your interviewing practices, so that with time you will perfect this important aspect of the job hunt.

MOVING UP THE CAREER LADDER

Getting the job is only the first step in career progression. Next, you must focus on managing your performance so you advance quickly to achieve your vision. Learn more about career advancement in the hospitality industry in Research Brief 4.1.

Below are some important rules that will help you get your career on the fast track:

- Keep a record of what you do. Eventually your supervisor will ask you what you have accomplished during the past month, quarter, or year. Keep an ongoing record of your activities so you can promptly alert the supervisor to your achievements.
- When you tell your boss about a problem, always suggest solutions. Today's managers and supervisors must be creative problem solvers, not whiners.
- Try to arrive at work before your boss. Although long hours do not necessarily mean promotions, the early bird is often seen as the harder worker.
- Only use your sick days when you are really ill.
- Avoid involvement in the rumor mill. Never say anything negative about your manager to a coworker. Avoid becoming part of gripe sessions. Negative feelings are often communicated to managers and supervisors, and your comments could backfire on you.

- Treat everyone in the organization well. Develop informal networks with other departments. You never know when you might need help from a room attendant, guest service attendant, or maintenance person.
- Never lose your temper with guests, coworkers, or managers. Instead develop a reputation for being cool and calm in the face of tension.
- Never say, "It's not my job." Those who say this rarely leave the ranks of line employee.

DON'T BE PIGEONHOLED

One of the most difficult transitions to make within a company is moving either from line employee to supervisor or from a lower level management position to department head. Your career advancement can be hampered if you have been pigeonholed in your current position. Perhaps you are viewed as stable and dependable, but not quite management or upper management material. You may be hiding your true abilities under a bushel basket, or you may have been unfairly pegged by your current employer. So what do you do if your desired image is much different from reality? Begin by observing those who are highly regarded in your company. These may be top managers, or employees or supervisors who are on the fast track, being promoted quickly. How do they dress? How do they behave? What are their qualifications? Meet with these individuals and ask how he or she learned to manage so effectively. If possible model some of their appearance standards and behaviors. This worked well for me early in my hotel career. At one point I wasn't moving ahead as quickly as I expected although my job knowledge and work habits were sound. I observed those who were getting the jobs I wanted and found that they dressed more professionally and often had graduate degrees. I dressed more formally and decided to pursue a graduate degree. The response to these changes was almost immedi-

RESEARCH BRIEF 4.1

GETTING AHEAD IN THE HOSPITALITY INDUSTRY

What factors will help you achieve rapid career advancement in the hospitality industry? In a study of career progression that included 205 hotel and restaurant employees, it was found that certain factors increased rate of promotion.* Those who worked for large, nationally recognized firms rather than smaller companies moved up 69 percent faster. Educational attainment in the form of college education and a bachelor's degree increased the rate of promotion over those with just a high school education by 76 percent to 78 percent. The study also found that women moved up just as quickly as men did, suggesting that gender equity is increasing in our industry. This study highlighted the importance of staying in school and completing your degree if you want rapid career progression.

*R. Sparrowe and P. Popielarz, (1995) "Getting Ahead in the Hospitality Industry: An Event History Analysis of Promotions among Hotel and Restaurant Employees," *Journal of Hospitality and Tourism Research* 19, no. 3, 99–119.

ate. I was assigned to more visible projects, my opinions were sought, and I moved up quickly.

Here are just a few of the characteristics that can hold us back from getting the recognition we deserve:

- A sloppy, casual appearance.
- A lack of confidence.
- Inability to get things done.
- Seen as a chronic complainer.
- Overly shy and quiet.

An effective way to find out what might be holding you back is to ask for feedback from a trusted manager or mentor. Their advice can be invaluable and help you to better understand yourself and how others perceive you.

Moving up may also involve taking risks. You will not be noticed for your positive contributions if you are shy and stay in the background. You must overcome your reservations and volunteer for committee work and visible projects. Write memos, supply opinions, and volunteer your ideas. Force yourself to speak up at meetings. It may be difficult at first, but it will become easier the more often you do it.

Always be prepared for changes in your organization or in the industry. Try to anticipate both crises and opportunities so you can take full advantage of options that come your way. For more on this, review the information in Insight 4.4.

INSIGHT 4.4

THE MENTAL FIRE DRILL

A little paranoia may be beneficial to your career. When we become too complacent with regard to our jobs, we are at risk for being hit blindside with unexpected occurrences such as a layoff, denied promotion, or even termination. One way to avoid surprises is to put yourself through a mental fire drill with regard to your career.* Act as if you were the CEO of a large company. Read newspapers, attend industry conferences, network with colleagues at other companies to collect information. When your sources indicate that a change might be in store, such as a downslide in our economy, the selling of your property or company, or expansion of your organization, ask yourself the following questions:

- How will changes in your industry affect your company?

- Will these changes affect you and your position?

- What will you do if you are affected by these changes?

- What can you do now to prepare for the future?

The last question may be the most important. Anticipating change is valuable, but being prepared is even more so. Focus on the new skills you may need to develop or the additional education or credentials you may need to acquire to stay ahead of the game. By doing this you not only will weather the sea of change, but also you can actually use it to your advantage to leverage a higher paying, more responsible position than you have had in the past.

*A. Grove, "Andy Grove on Navigating your Career," *Fortune*, March 29, 1999, 187–192.

DIFFICULT TIMES

What is the worst thing that can happen to you career wise? Probably being told that you're fired may initially seem like one of the greatest career reversal possible, but later, this may turnout to be more of a blessing than you initially thought. Losing your job can actually be a liberating experience that provides the impetus for you to find a position that you really like and are good at. The following steps will help you transform the negative experience of a firing into a positive one:[11]

- **Find out what went wrong.** Your initial reaction may be to only blame the company for your poor treatment, but you must be objective and understand what action on your part led to your termination.
- **Develop an exit statement.** Don't burn all your bridges behind you. Work with your company to develop a statement that will be a permanent part of your file and will be used when references are requested. The exit statement should begin with a paragraph stating what you have accomplished in your job followed by a reason for the termination that neither condemns you or the company.
- **Start looking for a new job immediately.** Avoid a long sabbatical. The longer you put off starting your search, the more difficult it will be.
- **Consider outplacement services.** Your company may provide outplacement services or you can contract them yourself. Counselors help you develop your resume, interview skills, and provide an office to work from during your search. As an alternative, contact your college placement office for assistance.
- **Use your agreed upon exit statement during subsequent interviews.** Assume that companies will contact your previous employers for references. Be honest and tell them what happened without becoming defensive. Practice answering the question, "Why did you leave your last position?" with a friend or counselor until you feel comfortable with your response.
- **Stay positive.** At times, termination can lead to new opportunities and a more rewarding career or life. Many successful or entrepreneurs weren't successful until they struck out on their own.

CONCLUSION

Personal mastery refers to your continued growth and develop as both an individual and as a leader. When you strive for personal mastery, you work to continuously improve yourself. The process begins with a clear personal vision identifying those long-term goals you hope to achieve. All challenging goals create tension which can drive your current reality closer to your vision.

A second important component of personal mastery is time management. To use your time effectively, keep your vision front and center, use a daily to-do list, get started on hard tasks, reward yourself for work well done, and frequently ask yourself if what you are doing is consistent with your vision. If you procrastinate, find out why so you will be able to overcome this debilitating habit.

A good mentoring relationship can offer a tremendous boost to a lagging career. Mentors can help you to identify career goals and training opportunities and to pursue promotions. The first step is to find one or more mentors who see your potential and have the time and energy to help you fulfill it. Although a mentoring relationship focuses primarily on your needs, networking forms two-way relationships of mutual benefit. Through networking you will make new friends, develop a support system, and gain access to contacts and resources you would otherwise miss.

When it is time to seek employment, advanced preparation can facilitate this process. Develop a professional portfolio that details your accomplishments, schedule several informational interviews with industry managers, and create a standout resume before you get started. Then develop a plan of attack; contact your mentors and network friends, and, most importantly, don't get discouraged. Remember your primary goal during the job hunt is to get interviews so you can sell employers on your value as a potential employee. When you are invited to interview, make the most of this opportunity by dressing professionally, bringing your resume, smiling, and, of course, arriving on time. Follow up by sending a thank you letter and making a phone call a week or two later.

Once hired, keep your career on track by carefully managing your performance at work. Stay on the promotion fast track by volunteering for extra assignments, keeping a record of your accomplishments, getting to work early, keeping your cool, and developing a network of friends and mentors within the organization. Every career will have peaks and valleys. Learn to weather the difficult times by looking at setbacks as opportunities to make necessary changes and adjustments.

K E Y   T E R M S

Personal Mastery	Procrastinator
Personal Vision	Mentors
Creative Tension	Networking
Current Reality	Professional Portfolio
Jesuit Test of Conscience	Informational Interviews

N O T E S

1. P. Senge, *The Fifth Discipline: The Art and Practice of the Learning Organization* (New York: Doubleday, 1990), 141.
2. Ibid, 150–153.

3. J. Epperheimer, "Benchmarking Career Management," *HR Focus* 74, no. 11 (November 1997): 9-10.

4. B. Russell and T. Branch, *Second Wind: The Memoirs of an Opinionated Man* (New York: Random House, 1979).

5. J. Wesman, "The Simplest System: All You Need to Plan Your Work Is an Ordinary Notebook," *Inc.* (September 1996): 109.

6. S. Van Collie, "Moving Up through Mentoring" *Workforce* (March 1998): 36–41.

7. R. N. Sanyal and J. S. Neves, "Networking: A Simulation of Job Search Behavior," *Simulation & Gaming* 29, no. 2 (June 1998): 260–265.

8. S. Powell and Jankovich, J., "Student Portfolios: A Tool to Enhance the Traditional Job Search," *Business Communication Quarterly* 61, no. 4 (December 1998): 72.

9. Ibid.

10. "Keys to a Successful Job Hunt," *Changing Times* (September 1985): 71–73.

11. "How to Recover from a Firing," *Fortune*, December 7, 1998, 239.

CASE **4.1**: DEVELOPING A CAREER PLAN

James is pleased to have his current position as restaurant manager, but he really feels that he is not learning as much as he hoped to. The general manager is very authoritative and controlling and doesn't seem willing to teach James new skills. James's primary responsibility is to oversee the operation of the dining room during dinner service, and although his supervisor is very pleased with his performance, he does not seem to be in any hurry to expand his responsibilities.

James's ultimate career goal is to own his own restaurant one day. He is well aware of the statistics on early restaurant failure and hopes to avoid such a fate by being as prepared as he possibly can be before starting his business. But James has done little planning for his future, other than setting the ultimate goal of owning his own full-service restaurant one day. James comes to you, his mentor, for some advice on developing a career plan and maximizing his learning potential.

1. How would you go about helping James to develop a detailed career plan?

2. How can James learn as much as possible from his current job?

3. If James comes to a point in his current job where he has learned all that he can but he still doesn't feel ready to start his own restaurant, what should he do?

R E V I E W   Q U E S T I O N S

1. List several characteristics of an individual who has achieved personal mastery.

2. What is the simple formula that will help you ensure a long and satisfying professional and personal life?

3. What is creative tension? What are effective and ineffective ways of dealing with it?

3. Describe how each of the following concerns can lead to procrastination:
   a. Fear.
   b. Perfectionism.
   c. Crisis addiction.
   d. Overextended.
4. How might you go about locating a mentor in an organization that does not offer a formal program in this area?
5. How does a networking relationship differ from a mentoring relationship?
6. Once you have developed a professional network, how can you nourish these relationships?
7. How does an informational interview differ from a job interview?
8. List three questions not included in your text that you should ask when applying for a job and three that you should avoid asking during the interview:
   a. Three questions to ask:
   b. Three questions to avoid:
9. What might your boss assume about your job performance if you engage in the following behaviors at work?
   a. Tell your boss about problems without including solutions.
   b. Always arrive exactly on time for work.
   c. Gossip frequently with coworkers about department problems.
   d. Do only those tasks that are expected of you—no more, no less.
10. List several characteristics of someone who is likely to be on the "fast track" or move up quickly within an organization.

CRITICAL THINKING EXERCISES

1. Instant Millionaire
   To help you identify your most important values, complete this brief exercise. You have just inherited $1 million from a long lost relative who has placed several requirements on your receiving the money:
   • You must spend all the money in one year.
   • You can spend it however you would like to, but you can't save the money or invest it in any way.
   Make a list of the items you would buy with the $1 million and roughly estimate what each item would cost. When you have finished this exercise, review the results. Examine those items that you listed first and also those items that are most costly. This will indicate what you currently value in your life. If the first item was buy a house for your parents, your family is very important to you. If it was buy a new sports car, having impressive possessions is important to you.
2. Write Your Eulogy
   This next exercise will help you identify what it is that you hope to accomplish in your life. Fast forward into the future and assume that you have passed away after living a long and active life. Write a eulogy or

statement describing the kind of person you were and what you accomplished in your life that you would want someone to read at your funeral. Be fairly specific and talk about all aspects of your life, including your career, family, social issues, and achievements.

3. Your Personal Vision

Exercise 1, the Instant Millionaire, and Exercise 2, Write Your Eulogy, both provide insight into your values and your aspirations for your life and career. Using this information, create a vision statement detailing what you hope to achieve in your life. Describe what you hope to accomplish in the following areas:

a. Career.

b. Family.

c. Financial.

d. Possessions.

e. Social.

f. Community.

4. Gap Analysis.

Select one aspect of your vision that is very important to you and perform a gap analysis similar to the example below. Then describe measures you will take to deal with the creative tension that your skill gap creates. In the example below, the student who hopes to own her own restaurant might gain knowledge of management, customer service, and food production by working for a highly successful restaurant company for five years prior to opening her own business.

Where you are now	Skills you need	Where you want to be
• Student	• Legal issues	• Restaurant owner
	• Management	
	• Financial knowledge	
	• Customer service	
	• Food production	

5. Write down ten time wasters that you engage in. Review the list and circle your biggest time waster. Identify ways that you might reduce or even eliminate several of your time wasters.

6. Imagine that you have been selected to be part of a company task force assigned responsibility for developing a mentoring program for your hotel. How might you go about developing this program? How would you pair mentors and employees?

ON-LINE LINK

There are many excellent career sites on the Internet. For information on resume writing, visit www.golden.net, www.jobsmart.org, www.eresumes.com, and www.tripod.com; for help with a cover letter, see www.careerlab.com/letters/. Once you have visited these sights, you are ready to try a "virtual interview." Go to http://www.aboutwork.com/ace/virtual.html to try the exercise "Ace the Interview." It supplies you with a series of interview questions and multiple choice answers, then tells you whether you chose the best answer. Write a paragraph describing your virtual interview experience and what you learned from it.

P O R T F O L I O   E X E R C I S E

Develop a statement of your goals to include in your portfolio. Focus on the professional achievements, skills, and knowledge you want to develop over the next few years. A goal statement shows employers that you have given thought to your career and highlights your interest in advancement. If you include this goal statement in your portfolio during a job search, make sure that your goals and those of the company are in harmony. For example, if you state that your goal is to own a restaurant and you are applying for a position with an independent restaurateur, the employer might see you as a potential competitor and refuse to hire you. Your goal statement should help you get job offers, not prevent them.

Hiring Top Performers

ADVANCED ORGANIZER

Recently a high-volume independent restaurateur reported that his kitchen manager, lead cook, beverage manager, and general manager were enticed away by a new restaurant. They were lured away while at work by members of the new chain who posed as customers. The beverage manager was offered a $5,000 bonus and the lead cook $2,000 for joining the new company. They were also given annual salary increases of approximately 23 percent.

This situation demonstrates just how competitive and cutthroat our labor market has become, even within our own ranks. Companies must do battle to find, hire, and keep top performing employees. In this chapter you will learn the latest techniques for recruiting, interviewing, and hiring star performers. These skills will give you a distinct advantage over others as you enter the staffing race.

BEHAVIORAL OBJECTIVES

- Recognize the characteristics of desirable job applicants.

- Differentiate between discriminatory and non-discriminatory practices in hiring and selection.

- Describe the components of the in-depth selection interview.

- Demonstrate the ability to plan the selection interview.

- Differentiate between internal and external recruitment efforts.

- Recognize and construct behavioral interview questions.

- Gain understanding of the process involved in evaluating job applicants.

Paris Las Vegas Employment Center

THE STAFFING PROCESS

Organizational **staffing** refers to a number of activities that relate to the screening, selection, and hiring of employees. Few tasks that you will undertake as a manager will be as important as selecting and hiring great people. When you place the right person in the right job the first time, you will avoid costly hiring errors leading to increased turnover, reduced customer satisfaction, lower employee morale, and decreased profitability. Optimal staffing procedures can cure these ills, leading to higher organizational performance and increased customer satisfaction.

As a manager or supervisor, your role in the staffing process depends on the size of your organization and the type of human resources support it provides. In smaller companies such as independent restaurants, managers typically hold sole responsibility for all staffing activities. In major corporations such as a hotel or restaurant chains, department managers work cooperatively with human resources in performing the staffing function. The human resource recruiter will screen applicants and forward the names of candidates to managers for in-depth interviewing and selection.

SURROUND YOURSELF WITH TALENT

Surprisingly your ability to successfully staff your operation is determined by your willingness to hire people who are smarter than you. As a successful leader, you must learn to value the talent of others. It makes great sense for a front office manager to hire the smartest, brightest, most adept service workers that he or she can possibly find. Unfortunately there are managers who feel threatened by top-notch applicants, who instead choose mediocre candidates that will not outshine them. Smart managers surround themselves with an outstanding work group, not employees that make them feel secure in their superiority. Remember, hire, reward, and promote convivial, customer-obsessed folks. Disney has had great success in hiring workers who are service oriented (see Insight 5.1). As you recruit, screen, interview, and evaluate job applicants, look for such behaviors as listening, caring, smiling, saying thank you, and being warm.[1] Individuals who display these behaviors during the job interview are also likely to use them with your guests. Review a study on selecting customer contact employees in Research Notes 5.1.

It also is important to seek out and hire diverse applicants. Diversity and creativity are synonymous. When you have a work group diverse in age, gender, race, religion, sexual orientation, and physical ability, you have created a collective source of brainpower that provides a variety of attitudes and ideas that create competitive advantage for your organization. Hire those who bring unique skills and talents to the job to complement others in the department.

This chapter will provide you with the knowledge you will need to recruit, interview, and hire top performers for your organization. When properly executed, selection takes time and careful consideration. But time invested up front will lead to better hiring decisions and fewer serious problems with poorly chosen employees later. Sound selection procedures can certainly man labor problems in our industry, leading to reduced turnover, increased customer satisfaction, and ultimately, greater profitability.

INSIGHT 5.1

Companies must seek out employees who are strongly motivated to serve customers, who are excellent communicators, and who will respond enthusiastically to the company's values and mission. Disney has built their success on just such a recruiting process.* Disney doesn't hire employees, they hire cast members. In fact the selection process does not take place in human resources or personnel, but in the "Casting Center" where innovative hiring techniques are used to locate new cast members.

Prospective employees enter a building called "Central Casting," turning a handle that resembles the doorknob character from *Alice in Wonderland*. They continue down a long hallway filled with Disney art and memorabilia. Next they see a ten-minute video that reveals the good and bad of working for Disney. They are informed of the tough schedule, strict appearance guidelines, and the need to provide their own transportation. After this, approximate 20 percent decide Disney is not for them. This procedure allows applicants to screen themselves out of the process if they learn early on that this isn't right for them. Disney magic doesn't stop here. The company offers employees continuous training with a curriculum of courses and seminars. They mentor and train both new hires and existing employees to help them keep their skills sharp.

*R. Hiebeler, T. Kelly, and C. Ketteman. *Best Practices: Building Your Business with Customer-Focused Solutions* (New York: Simon & Schuster, 1998).

IT'S THE LAW

Before studying the fundamentals of selection and interviewing, it is important to have some understanding of the legal issues surrounding staffing decisions. Much of employment law is governed by **Title VII of the Civil Rights Act of 1964**, as amended by the Equal Employment opportunity Act of 1972, which prohibits discrimination based on

RESEARCH BRIEF 5.1

SELECTING CUSTOMER CONTACT EMPLOYEES

As companies seek to find the right person for frontline jobs, they must differentiate between candidates who have a passion for providing excellent service from those who work best in positions with less customer contact. A research study examined the possibility of identifying differences between low-customer contact workers and front-line employees.* The researchers developed a survey that tested employees' need for affiliation and responsiveness so they could identify people who really aren't motivated to work in high-customer contact positions. People who scored lower on affiliation, or the need to interact with people, and low on responsiveness to others, or willingness to help, were less likely to choose customer-contact positions than those that scored higher on these factors. The researchers suggested that hospitality students' needs for affiliation and responsiveness could be measured, and those who score low on these factors could be steered toward positions that have less customer contact, such as accounting or food production, whereas those who score high on these factors could be directed toward customer-contact positions.

*E. Sirakaya, D. Kersetter, and D. Mount. "Modeling the Selection of High Customer-contact Personnel," *Journal of Hospitality and Tourism Research* 1999 23, no. 2, 139–159.

- Age.
- Race or color.
- Religion.
- National origin.
- Disability or physical handicap.
- Sex or marital status.

This applies to all phases of employment, including recruiting, interviewing, hiring, promotion, training, transfer, discipline, layoff, and discharge.[2] This law applies to companies employing more than fifteen persons and affects private employers, employment agencies, and labor organizations. Small companies with less than 15 employees may also fall within the jurisdiction of state law and are not necessarily exempt from legal guidelines.

Before we move on to explore employment law in greater detail, take a few moments to calculate a baseline reading of your current understanding of legal issues by completing "The Discrimination Quiz" outlined in Figure 5.1.

If you answered yes to all statements in "The Discrimination Quiz," you are correct. Each statement pertains to situations that have the potential for discriminatory action. In particular, if you are forty to seventy years old, of a minority race, a woman, pregnant, or disabled, you are a member of a **protected class**. This means that the EEOC under the federally enacted Civil Rights Act of 1964 will provide protection against unfair labor practices. When applicants or employees are treated unfairly, litigation can result in the awarding of significant damages. These include job reinstatement, back pay for time unemployed, recovery of legal fees, and punitive damages. The best way to avoid costly litigation and penalties is to hire fairly. In the following section, you will learn about basic principles of employment law as it relates to the staffing process. The information provided here is an attempt to supply some helpful guidelines to direct the interview process, but it does not represent a source of legal advice. Employment law can change with court rulings and also varies by state, so it is

---

Read each employment practice described below and check "yes" if you believe it could be discriminatory and "no" if you believe it is acceptable.

	Yes	No	
1.	___	___	Refusing to hire women with preschool-age children.
2.	___	___	Restricting certain jobs to men (i.e., bellman, room service waiter, fine dining waiter).
3.	___	___	Pay men more than women for the same type of job.
4.	___	___	Refusing to hire pregnant women.
5.	___	___	Refusing to hire older applicants because they are overqualified.
6.	___	___	Requiring a college degree for all employees.
7.	___	___	Refusing to hire the disabled.
8.	___	___	Requiring all employees to work on weekends.
9.	___	___	Refusing to hire someone with AIDS.
10.	___	___	Hiring only young college students.

Figure 5.1 The Discrimination Quiz

important for you to consult a legal professional regarding the applicability of principles set forth in this text to your situation.

BONA FIDE OCCUPATIONAL QUALIFICATIONS

The best way to avoid legal problems is to recruit, hire, and promote applicants based on **Bonafide Occupational Qualifications (BFOQs).** These are qualifications or attributes necessary for successful job performance. All aspects of the selection process, including the job description, recruitment efforts, application, interview questions, and the hiring decision, must be based on BFOQs. If you are searching for male bellstand attendants because you believe that women are not strong enough lift and carry luggage, you are not basing your recruiting efforts on BFOQs. Gender is not a requirement in this job. Instead a job requirement that all applicants be able to lift and carry a twenty five-pound suitcase may be an acceptable BFOQ for bellstand attendants.

AVOIDING LEGAL PITFALLS

Discrimination can occur before the applicant even arrives at your door. Advertising in newspapers that reach only nonprotected class members can be discriminatory. By running ads that specify applicants that are young, recent college grads, male, female, or able bodied, you may risk adversely affecting protected groups on the basis of age, gender, or physical ability. It is certainly acceptable to require experience, service orientation, a good work ethic, a flexible schedule, and reliability because these qualities may be required for successful job performance and do not adversely impact minority group members. Occupational qualifications that do adversely impact some individuals may be acceptable if the employer can prove that they are required for successful job performance, example, the height and weight requirements of airlines were acceptable because flight attendants needed to be of a certain height to reach overhead compartments and a certain weight so they could maneuver in tight spaces. Read more about legal issues in human resources management in Chapter 11 of your text.

QUESTIONS YOU CAN'T ASK

In earlier years employers could ask applicants about marital status, arrests, their credit history, their age, number of children, and even their child-bearing plans, but this era ended more than twenty years ago. Today's interviewers must be particularly sensitive to protected classes. As a result, you must be very careful to only ask questions that directly bear on job performance. Figure 5.2 contains a series of common areas that merit exploration during the interview along with discriminatory and nondiscriminatory questions relating to these areas.[3] This chart should be used only as a guide. Special situations and job requirements may vary the questions you ask. For example, if your intent is to avoid hiring gays by only selecting married men, asking marital status could be potentially discriminatory. The problem lies not only in the ques-

Topic	Discriminatory	Nondiscriminatory
Name	Have you ever changed your name? Is that name Arabic (Italian, Chinese, etc.)?	Have you ever worked under a different name?
Age	How old are you? What is your date of birth?	Are you between the ages of eighteen and sixty five? If not, state your age.
Family	Do you have children? What does your spouse do?	What is your marital status?
Citizenship	What country are you from? Do you plan to become a U.S. citizen?	Are you a U.S. citizen? If not, can you demonstrate your legal right to work in this country?
Disability	Do you have heart disease, back trouble, AIDS, cancer, etc.?	Do you have any impairments that might interfere with your ability to perform this job?
Arrest	Have you ever been arrested?	Have you ever been convicted of a felony?
Language	What is your native tongue? What language do you speak at home?	Do you speak a foreign language?

Figure 5.2 Discriminatory and Nondiscriminatory Inquiries

tions you ask, but also with how you use the information. The potential for discrimination in hiring increases when:

- You ask applicants for photographs.
- You ask questions of your protected class candidates that you don't ask of others.
- You ask discriminatory questions on job applications or medical forms filled out before hiring.
- You ask discriminatory questions informally over lunch or during polite conversation.

Remember that employment law was created to promote fairness and justice in the workplace. Do not view it as a legal hindrance, but as a set of guidelines that help ensure that you do not violate the rights of applicants and employees. Remember, if you interview and hire based on BFOQs, in most instances, you will also be adhering to fair labor practices.

A SYSTEMS APPROACH TO SELECTION

Employee selection is not a series of isolated events. It is a complex system or series of interrelated practices that form a coherent whole and result in an excellent hiring decision. Figure 5.3 contains a diagram of the staffing system beginning with job standards and followed by recruitment, screening, interviewing, decision making, and finally ending with the job offer. Errors or inconsis-

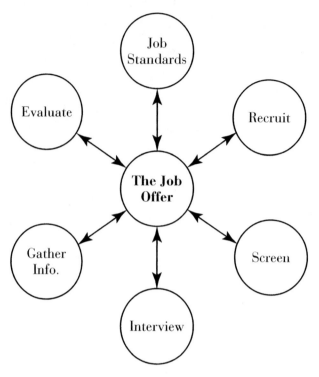

Figure 5.3 The Staffing System

tencies in any phase of the staffing system will result in less than desirable results. Recruiting great applicants will not result in successful hiring if you fail to screen them correctly and do not collect adequate information for decision making. Even if you recruit and screen carefully, eliminating all but the best people in your applicant pool, you might still hire the wrong ambitious, well-adjusted person for the job if you don't interview and check references thoroughly.

We will begin our examination of the staffing system with an overview of that important first step, the development of job standards.

DEVELOPING JOB STANDARDS

Before recruiting and interviewing job applicants, you must have a clear idea of the standards and requirements of the position that you want to fill. The type of candidate you will recruit, the questions you will ask, and interviewing procedures you will use are all based on the job's standards. Many organizations have detailed job descriptions on file that consist of a written statement detailing the duties and responsibilities that someone holding that position is expected to perform. If these are not available in your organization, you will want to begin the staffing process by developing a job description for the positions you directly supervise. This need not be a time-consuming or laborious procedure, but can be done relatively quickly if you follow a standard format and involve your current employees in the process.

JOB DESCRIPTION

Step 1: Develop a questionnaire that will be distributed to all employees currently performing the position you are evaluating (see Figure 5.4). This questionnaire asks current employees to describe their actual work activities, the standards at which they perform them, the materials they use to do their jobs, their personal characteristics, and their qualifications.

Step 2: Schedule a meeting and let employees know that you need their help in developing position descriptions. You are not "testing" them, but simply need their input. Have each employee complete the questionnaire and return it to you (see Figure 5.4).

Step 3: When the questionnaires are completed, review the information. Next, identify key skills, activities, work materials, employee characteristics, and qualifications that are mentioned frequently by your employees. Do this by first listing key skills and then noting how frequently they are mentioned. Those skills referred to most often are likely to be most important.

Step 4: Based on the information provided by employees, create a detailed job description (see Figure 5.5) for each position you supervise.

The job description becomes an invaluable tool that you use as you plan your selection process. The qualifications segment will help you target the type of workers you need to recruit and help you develop ads that will attract qualified applicants. The section labeled "Core Tasks Performed" serves as a resource as you develop specific questions to ask applicants. The job description is also a key component of your performance appraisal system and skills training program.

RECRUITMENT

Once an accurate position description is developed, the next step in the staffing process is recruitment. The effective selection of new employees is not possible without strong recruitment efforts. No organization can build a skilled, motivated, high-performance workforce unless great applicants are knocking on their doors. The applicant pool is the all-important basis of a great staff.

Recruitment is defined as those activities involved in locating the people needed to fill an origination's staffing requirements. Just as a discriminating chef must always have the highest quality ingredients to prepare a consistently outstanding meal, so must organizations have the highest quality applicants if they are to consistently employ outstanding individuals.

Directions: We are in the process of developing detailed position descriptions for each job in our department. Who better to help with this process that you, the person currently performing the job? Please answer each question below in detail and as accurately as possible. The information you provide will help us develop detailed position descriptions that will be used in the selection process.

Part I: Position Information

Position title:_____

How long have you held this position?_____

How many hours do you work each week?_____

Part II: Job Responsibilities and Standards

List all the duties you perform in a typical day and the standards at which you perform them. For example, if you are a host/hostess, you might describe one of your duties and standards as, "Greet guests as they enter the restaurant within 30 seconds of their arrival by saying 'Welcome to Harbor Inn. Will you be dining with us this evening?'"

1. _____
2. _____
3. _____
4. _____
5. _____
6. _____
7. _____
8. _____
9. _____

Part III: Materials and Resources

List all materials you use in performing your job: _____
_____

List people in your department and in other departments that you work with closely:
_____
_____
_____

Part IV: Qualifications and Background

What particular characteristics make you great at your job? (Example: patience, time management, ability to get along with others, etc.)
_____
_____
_____
_____

What education, training, and previous job experience have contributed to your success in your current job?
_____
_____
_____
_____
_____

Figure 5.4 Job Standards Questionnaire

Job Title: Dining Room Server
Job Function: Greets guests, takes food and beverage orders, answers questions
                     about products, and serve meals in the main dining room.
Supervisor: Dining Room supervisor and restaurant general manager.

Core Tasks Performed

- Set tables according to specifications.
- Perform daily sidework including filling salt and pepper shakers, folding napkins, filling condiments, and organizing workstation.
- Greet customers within three minutes of seating.
- Communicate daily specials.
- Answer questions about products accurately.
- Use upselling techniques by suggesting specified food and beverages.
- Recommending and serving beverages.
- Use accurate order-taking procedures by repeating each order to verify.
- Enter orders into the cash register.
- Monitor food production to ensure proper timing.
- Inspect food for quality and accuracy.
- Deliver food in the proper sequence.
- Process special requests.
- Clean and clear the table within two minutes of dining completion.
- Question customer satisfaction at least three times during service sequence.
- Use safe work practices.

Staff Contact

The dining room manager and the general manager provide direct supervision. Servers work cooperatively with the host/hostess, bussers, other servers, cooks, chef, and stewards.

Personal Competencies

- Excellent verbal communication.
- Ability to allocate time.
- Skill in problem solving and decision making.
- Ability to perform basic arithmetic.
- Listening skills.
- Ability to sell products to guests.
- Works cooperatively in a team setting.
- Physical ability to carry six meals on a single tray and serve from a tray stand.

Related Equipment

- Cash register
- Microwave, toaster, coffeemaker, beverage machine, ice machine.

Qualifications

- Physical ability to perform the job—lifting trays, handle hot plates, maneuver through the dining room.
- Ability to communicate in English.
- Basic math competency.
- Ability to serve customers in a friendly, caring manner.

Figure 5.5 Job Description

ATTRACTING GOOD PEOPLE

According to Gary Tharaldson, president of Tharaldson Lodging, the key to attracting quality employees is simple: You must pay more and train them better than your competitors. By doing so, your organization will create the image of being a great place to work, and you will attract top applicants both from your competitors and from other sources. John Leavitt of Prime Hospitality Corporation agrees. He believes that training is the key to attracting and retaining good employees. Organizations must have a training program that facilitates advancement in addition to offering benefits and competitive wages whether they are hiring housekeepers or general mangers.[4] Thus recruitment depends on the image and practices the organization has adopted. If your organization has a reputation for paying well and developing employees, great people will be attracted to it. Recruitment, in the broadest sense, begins with the implementation of many of the organizational practices described in this text.

Through trial and error, each organization must develop recruiting practices that are successful. Recruitment practices will differ with the labor market, the type of business, and the degree of skill that employees must possess. In recruiting applicants Motel 6 concentrates on job fairs, closing military bases, and a good relationship with the National Association for the Advancement of Colored People to attract potential employees. Other companies may focus on newspaper ads, college recruitment offices, or employee referrals. As you read in the Advanced Organizer for this chapter, others are virtually stealing employees away from competitors. Signing bonuses, once limited only to high-tech fields are being used by such lodging organizations as Red Roof Inn. New employees are offered a financial bonus award after successfully completing their initial ninety-day period.[5]

INTERNAL RECRUITMENT SOURCES

Promoting from Within   Often overlooked and underutilized, the current employees within an organization can be an excellent recruitment source. "Promoting from within" not only makes sense from the origination's perspective as it provides a ready source of trained labor, but it also can provide positive benefits to employees in the form of opportunity for advancement. Employees who perceive their company as one that first looks within when opportunities arise will be less likely to leave. Some companies go so far as to offer their current employees the first option to apply for openings. Job availability is posted either on a bulletin board or via computer, and internal employees have first opportunity to apply for these jobs.

Some organizations take this a step further and not only post job openings, but also offer employees the benefit of sophisticated career planning. Data about current employees in the form of education, work history, career interests, and performance history are entered into the computer. When a position opens up, a list of possible candidates are matched to the job. Human resources then contacts this matched group to see if they are interested in applying for the available positions.

Employee Referrals   An additional form of internal recruitment involves employee referral of friends and relatives for available positions. Often companies encourage this practice through the use of a bounty system where a reward is offered if the referred applicant accepts the job and successfully completes the probationary period. The cost of the bounty or reward is easily recouped by the organization in the form of reduced advertising and recruitment costs.

EXTERNAL RECRUITMENT

Even companies that are fully committed to promotion from within must look outside their organization to fill entry level and sometimes higher level positions. There are several effective methods of external recruitment that can yield a pool of qualified applicants.

Educational Institutions There are many fine community college and university level programs in hospitality management located throughout the country. Most have active placement offices recruiting both current students for part-time work and internships and graduating students for full-time positions. Recruiting from schools first guarantees that you will have applicants who are committed to working in our industry—not just those who are bartending until they get that job in graphic design that they really want. Current or past hospitality majors also bring a strong desire to learn and progress in the industry. Unfortunately most colleges find that the number of job openings far exceeds the number of students they have in their programs, but by starting here, you will greatly increase your chance of hiring the right person for the job the first time. You might attract more college students by offering organized internship programs, offering your services as a guest lecturer, or by serving on the college's advisor board.

Placement Services Government agencies operate a number of placement services designed to help those who are unemployed or have limited job skills become part of the workforce. These agencies screen applicants and will send you individuals that they feel are qualified for your open positions. Agencies provide an excellent source of unskilled labor for our industry and are certainly worth contacting. Check your area yellow pages under the heading "community employment agencies" to find listings.

Applicant Files You are required by the federal government to keep all applications on file for a total of thirteen months. Most good recruiters will maintain two systems of files—inactive and active. The inactive files contain applications supplied by candidates who are not qualified to work in your organization. These are arranged sequentially, so when the thirteen-month period expires, they can be tossed. The active files, consisting of applications from individuals who either applied for positions you currently do not have open or who were unqualified for the position for which they applied but may be qualified for other jobs in the organization, can be a rich source of future labor. Their value depends on your organization skill in filing these important applications. The best way to maintain active files is to create a separate folder for each position within your department. When an application is to be placed in the active file, simply place it in the appropriate folder that pertains to the position you think they might qualify for in the future. If an applicant might be qualified for more than one position, place a note in auxiliary files stating where the application form can be found. Later, when you need reservationists, pull the active file and begin your search by first contacting previous applicants.

Advertising   Placing ads in local newspapers can be one of the most cost-effective methods of recruiting applicants, but does require caution. One of my biggest mistakes as a new recruiter at a major downtown hotel was to place an ad for "dishwashers" and "buspersons" for one of our restaurants during a major recession when unemployment was very high. The ad came out in the Sunday paper, and when I came to work at 8:00 A.M. on Monday morning, I had literally hundreds of out-of-work, unskilled individuals waiting to see me. Our company required that we interview each person who applied for a job, so needless to say, I interviewed for ten straight hours, sending people away at the end of the day.

The moral of that story, and what I quickly learned, is that ads work great for fairly skilled positions like servers or bartenders, but for unskilled, lower level positions, your best bet is to rely on agency referrals and active files.

An important consideration when placing an ad is to make sure the wording is nondiscriminatory. You cannot ask for "waiters who are as charming as Cary Grant and as handsome as Robert Redford" as one restaurant advertised in a major newspaper, without risking possible discrimination. Obviously that particular fine dining restaurant was trying to use humor to attract some great applicants, but the actors mentioned in the ad were both male and both Caucasian, leaving the company vulnerable to a lawsuit based on both gender and racial discrimination. Instead companies can communicate their need for top-quality applicants in their want ads by saying they want to hire passionate, flexible, exciting people. In any case avoid reference to age, gender, race, or physical characteristics in your want ads.

Placement of ads is also important. The most common ad placement is in a major metropolitan newspaper. Other possibilities include local papers with limited circulation, college newspapers, magazines, and, of course, web-based ads linked to a home page or part of a recruitment web site.

On-line Recruiting   Web-based job searching has revolutionized the recruitment process. It is possible to both advertise your career openings on your own web page or on a general employment page on the World Wide Web. The Council for Hotel, Restaurant, and Institutional Educators (CHRIE) also allows hospitality organizations to both advertise positions and review applicant information on their career web site. Many colleges and universities have their own internal, Internet-based system that allows organizations to both display openings and review their students' resumes on-line.

One advantage of recruiting on the web is that you are more likely to access brighter, more technologically sophisticated applicants. The disadvantages are negligible, and there is little reason not to benefit from recruiting via Internet.

Career Days   If you are seeking management interns or large numbers of employees, you may choose to host a career day. When Marriott International had more than 400 job openings at Chicago properties, their recruiters held a career fair.[6] The event was free and open to the public. In addition to job opportunities, they offered applicants workshops on resume writing and job interviewing. Another type of career fair might be held on a college campus. This is particularly beneficial if you are seeking entry level managers or interns. College or university career fairs offer you the opportunity to interview students on-site for available positions.

THE SCREENING PROCESS

The **screening process** involves the careful review of the applicant's resume and application and, depending on your company policy, may also include a brief interview. The purpose of screening is to simply reduce a large applicant pool to more manageable numbers prior to in-depth interviewing. During this phase you will rule out those individuals that are not qualified for the positions available.

SCREENING APPLICATIONS AND RESUMES

Screening applicants involves a quick assessment of the individual's background. It is used to determine whether the applicant should be included in the interview process. Some individuals have clearly inappropriate work skills and can be quickly eliminated during this process. In screening the application and resume provide important insight into the individual's attention to detail, qualifications, and consistency in work history. As you initially review the application and resume, ask yourself the following questions:

- Are the resume and application neat and visually appealing?
- Are there any breaks in work history?
- Does the student report an acceptable grade point average?
- Is the college major and minor appropriate for the job?
- What skills were practiced in the past?
- Is the career objective consistent with the position available?

BEST PRACTICES

The Caspers Company, a franchised operator of forty-seven McDonald's outlets, uses an automated screening tool called HReasy.* Potential applicants call a toll-free number and are then asked to respond to a series of questions about their education, experience, skill, work availability, and work ethic. They respond by pressing telephone keys that correspond to yes or no answers. A questionnaire is then faxed to Casper Company managers within twenty-four hours. Candidates who are qualified are then interviewed. The service also appeals to job seekers because it allows them to call the service any time, even after normal business hours. Ed Shaw, Caspers's senior vice president, reports that twenty three of the twenty six people recently hired were recruited with HReasy. They are receiving more applicant inquiries, and Caspers says the system has allowed the company to attract the best people.

*Ed Rubenstein. "McD Franchisee Streamlines Employee Screening with Touch-tone Technology." *Nation's Restaurant News* 32, no. 16 (April 20, 1998): 78.

A number of applicants will be eliminated at this stage due to an inappropriate match of skills and experience, poor grades, or other critical reasons.

THE SCREENING INTERVIEW

The next phase of the screening process involves holding a fairly brief interview with the applicant. The human resources department in larger organizations typically does this, but in smaller companies, managers may need to take on this task. During the screening interview, review the applicant's past work experience, interest in the job, education, and availability for work. It is also a good time to ask about major red flags such as breaks in work history, felony convictions, or terminations. If all seems well, then this individual is referred on to speak with the manager who is making the hiring decision for an in-depth interview. In smaller companies screening interviews and in-depth interviews can be combined. In this case you begin with an initial screening interview, and if the candidate seems qualified, immediately follow-up with the in-depth interview, eliminating the need to invite the applicant back for a second visit.

THE IN-DEPTH SELECTION INTERVIEW

The in-depth selection interview allows applicants and managers to meet and exchange important information. To qualify for an in-depth interview, the candidate must have passed muster during screening. This means the applicant has the required level of experience, education, and skill as specified in the job descriptions. Although the interview can be time-consuming, it provides key information necessary to make the right decision.

Ideally at least three, but more than five, individuals will be chosen as final candidates following screening. These individuals will be asked to return for in-depth interviews. Just a few basic guidelines when scheduling interviews include:

- Allow adequate time for the interview. Be sure to schedule a minimum of fifteen minutes and ideally a good half-hour for each interview. Also hold all calls and interruptions during the interview. There is nothing more annoying than

BEST PRACTICES

Doubletree Hotels and Resorts has focused on selection strategy by implementing a **peer-based interviewing** process to decrease employee turnover. After receiving special training, employees interview job applicants and become involved in the hiring decision. They develop and ask interview questions, review the applicant's work history, and meet after the interview to evaluate the qualifications of different applicants. Not only are employees choosing who they work with, the "old-timers" are also more likely to take interest in the success of the new hires and provide greater support. Overall, turnover rates have dropped since the program was implemented.*

*Kathy Kennedy, "Doubletree Takes on Employee Turnover," *Hotels* 32, no. 3 (March, 1998): 28.

being interviewed by someone who spends more time talking on the phone than talking to you.

- Plan to spend at least ten to fifteen minutes getting ready for each interview. During this time you will review the application and prepare the questions you will ask.
- Make a great first impression. Be on time; greet the applicant with a warm handshake and friendly smile.
- If possible have more than one person interview the candidate before making the hiring decision so impressions can be compared. Interviewers might include the department supervisor or manager, department head, coworkers, the human resources manager, and the general manager.

STEP-BY-STEP GUIDE TO THE IN-DEPTH INTERVIEW

When orchestrated properly the in-depth selection interview will yield critical information about the applicant and the applicants candidacy for the job. Effort expended during this stage of the staffing process will lead to better hiring decisions and reduced turnover.

Step 1: Preparation
- Time spent in preparation will pay off big when it is time to make the hiring decision. Just walking into an interview cold leads to slipshod results and poor hiring decisions.
- Review the application and resume thoroughly.
- Develop a list of at least ten questions you will ask the applicant. Questions should include a mix of open-ended questions, or those requiring more than a yes or no answer, and probing questions, or those that require specific answers. The questions should be tailored to query each particular applicant's background. If the applicant has frequent breaks in work history, explore their outside activities and interests to get a feel for what they are doing during nonwork time. If an applicant has changed jobs often, you will definitely want to focus on relationships with supervisors and work habits. When planning choose those most appropriate to your applicant and the job available.
- Block out a halfhour of your time for the interview. Schedule the interview during a time when you will not be interrupted.

Step 2: Create a Great First Impression
Remember, it's a job seekers' market right now and just as applicants must sell their qualifications to you, so must you sell your organization to them. It is truly disappointing to identify the perfect person for the job and lose this individual to a competitor.
- Make sure your office is neat and tidy, you are professionally dressed, and that all staff is in top form.

- Greet the applicant.
- Give the applicant a few moments to relax before asking questions. During this time, make small talk, offer a beverage, and, remember, you are the host and applicant is your guest.

Step 3: Background Interview

- Open by setting the stage. For example you might say, "Bill, I appreciate your coming in today. What I'd like to do is explore your background, interests, and goals to see if we have a good match. I'm going to begin by asking you some questions, and then, when I'm done, you may ask me anything you'd like about the company, the job, or what I'm like as a manager." This lets the applicant know up front, in a nice way, that you will answer questions about the job after discussing his background. Never allow an applicant to pump you for information about the job early in the interview before you question him. If you do this, you will only give the applicant the opportunity to tell you what you want to hear or to adjust his or her answers to meet job requirements. This puts you at a disadvantage.
- Also, let the applicant know early on that you will be asking permission at the end of the interview to check references and verify the applicant's background. This is just a way of encouraging the applicant to be honest and forthright during the interview.
- Ask open-ended questions requiring more than just a yes or no answer to examine key areas such as education, work history, relationship with past supervisors and coworkers, goals for the future, and strengths and weaknesses.

Step 4: Answer Questions

Now it is your turn to be interviewed by the applicant. Today's savvy job candidates may ask you tough questions about what it is like to work in your organization.

- It is important for you to answer honestly and accurately. You want to paint an encouraging picture, particularly if you really like the applicant, but you don't want to make it too rosy. You want to give the applicant a realistic idea of what will be expected and what it is like to work for your company.
- Have information about company benefits on hand so you can answer all questions quickly and accurately.

Step 5: Ending the Interview

At this time you will have developed a "gut feeling" about the applicant's candidacy for the job. Whether it is very positive, or very negative, you must still leave some suspense about the outcome. Never offer a candidate a job immediately following an interview. Always take time for reference check and evaluation.

- If you are very interested in a candidate, warmly say, "I'm really glad that we had the chance to meet today. Your background is impressive. I just want to let you know that we have several applicants that we are interviewing and will not make a final decision until next week. But in the mean time, please feel free to call if you have any questions."

- If you are lukewarm, or feel negatively about the applicant, say, "Thank you very much for coming in today. We will be interviewing several candidates before making a hiring decision."

- Ideally you will write a letter to all candidates who did not get the job to let them know formally of your decision.

- Escort the applicant to the door and end with another firm handshake.

HOW TO GET MORE FROM YOUR JOB INTERVIEWS

- Use silence effectively. After asking a question and getting a very brief answer, just remain silent and odds are the applicant will tell you more. Don't jump in and rescue the applicant by asking another question.
- Use open-ended questions that require more than a yes or no answer.
- Use encouraging responses such as uh-huh, I see, that's interesting, and so on.
- Say "tell me more" when you get brief answers or when you think there are potential hot spots not being divulged.
- Make the applicant feel comfortable and accepted. People will open up to interviewers whom they trust.
- Act sympathetic. The applicant will often divulge important material if they sense a sympathetic ear.
- Don't monopolize the conversation. The applicant should do 80 percent of the talking during an interview—this means you do 80 percent of the listening. Your goal is to find out about the applicant, not tell the applicant about yourself, your background, or the company.

ADDITIONAL METHODS OF GATHERING APPLICANT INFORMATION

The majority of organizations rely on information gathered during screening and in-depth interviewing to make hiring decisions, but others want additional information about applicants before employment. Below some common methods for gaining insight into applicant's background and qualifications are described.

PREEMPLOYMENT TESTING

To gain further understanding of candidates' suitability for the job, organizations often collect additional information from paper and pencil or computer delivered tests or medical evaluations. Although these investigations can lend useful information, you must be careful that you do not violate the rights of employees or applicants. In the past paper and pencil tests that evaluate aptitude or personality have come under a great deal of legal scrutiny. Many tests do not measure job-related attributes or may adversely impact individuals of different races or national origin. Organizations that use testing often employ licensed psychologists to develop and validate tests that reliably measure only job-related factors. Many organizations have found that the risks of paper and pencil testing far outweigh their benefits and have adopted other methods of data gathering such as simulation or behavioral interviewing.

Medical tests must also be handled carefully. Some companies make the job offer contingent upon the applicant's ability to pass a physical test and, frequently today, a drug and alcohol screening. When in doubt about the appropriateness of testing, consult an attorney for legal advice.

BEHAVIORAL SIMULATION

The best way to evaluate people is to watch them work. This isn't practical in the selection process, so the next best method is to use simulation. A **behavioral simulation** is an exercise that demonstrates how well an applicant can perform key job responsibilities, such as those listed on the job description. These simulations are particularly useful in evaluating applicants with little previous experience in the area. For example, if you are seeking servers who can use suggestive selling techniques effectively, you might give then an assignment to role-play upselling products on your menu. You would provide the applicant with a role description, information about menu items to upsell, and a partner to role-play the situation. If you were interviewing bell staff attendants and you wanted to hire individuals who have knowledge of the city, you might ask applicants several questions about area restaurants and for directions to area attractions to test their ability to answer guest questions in a knowledgeable manner. Or, if you were interviewing a cook, you might ask the applicant to describe the process he or she would use in preparing some common dishes. Many job skills can be tested using simulation. In fact, the procedure of giving an office worker a typing test is a form of simulation because it tests a job-related skill.

Behavioral simulations are built around the specific requirements of the target positions, not the person's intelligence or personality, and thus their ability to measure objective job skills is generally viewed as highly valid. Even though they have strong ties to job success, care should be taken in assuring that simulation is nondiscriminatory in the sense that it is not used to rule out individuals based on their gender, race, religion, or age.

Types of Behavioral Simulations

- **Case Studies:** Applicants review guest or employee situations and either describe verbally how they would deal with each or give a written response to a series of questions.

- **Role-Play a Guest or Employee Situation:** The applicant takes the role of either the manager or guest service employee and acts out a problem situation.
- **In-basket Exercise:** These are typically used with applicants for management positions. The participant is asked to review a series of job-related tasks and prioritize them in the order of their importance and need for attention.
- **Job Replica Test:** These tests are common and might include a typing test for a secretary or a cooking test for a chef.
- **Problem Analysis:** Each participant is required to analyze data or information involving several possible solutions to a problem related to the job. Participants choose a course of action and defend their decision both verbally and in writing.
- **Task direction exercise:** The applicant takes on the role of a manager who has just been given a task to organize and complete. Participants must develop a project plan detailing their work activities as well as the activities of their subordinates.

BEHAVIORAL INTERVIEWING

Behavioral interviewing is hybrid, combining the ease of the in-depth interview with the thorough examination of job-related skills of behavioral simulation. In the **behavioral interview,** questions are asked that require applicants to give specific examples of previous job skill performance. Instead of asking applicants how they got along with past supervisors, the interviewer asks for specific instances or examples of when they had positive and negative experiences with their supervisor. When querying customer service ability, the behavioral interviewer would ask for an example of when, in the past, the applicant exceeded guest expectations with superior service.

Any job-related question can be transformed to a behavioral one simply by adding the preface, "Tell me about a time when...," or "Describe a situation when...," or "Give me a specific example of a time when..." Figure 5.6 lists some common behavioral interview questions.

Behavioral interview questions can also be asked about nonjob specific attitudes, such as ability to organize, lead others, work with others, and accept responsibility. If you want to explore leadership ability, ask for examples of when the individual has taken charge of a group and made things happen. This may have occurred in school, sports, or other nonwork related activities. Care must be taken in developing nondiscriminatory, valid behavioral questions. One company that hires creative designers asks applicants how they organize their CD collections at home. They believe that this provides them with insight into the individual's thinking and organizational habits, but it would be hard to prove legally that the organization of one's CD collection is a valid precursor of job success. Behavioral questions must be closely related to established skills and abilities that relate strongly to job performance.

If you choose to add behavioral questions to your interview, be sure to give applicants adequate time to formulate their answers. Also be aware that the

- Please describe a situation where you worked with very little supervision. How did you handle this?
- Describe a situation where you were required to perform tasks that were unfamiliar to you. How did you handle this situation?
- Give me an example of a time when you performed more than was required of you to get something done.
- Describe a time when you were faced with problems or stresses that tested your coping skills. What did you do?
- Give me an example of time when you were unable to finish a task because you didn't have enough information.
- Tell me about a time when you were able to build motivation in your work group.
- What goals have you set for yourself in the past and how have you gone about reaching them?
- How do you go about organizing your work space?

Figure 5.6 Behavioral Interview Questions

detail supplied by applicants with limited work experience will be not be as extensive as that supplied by someone with years of experience.

COLLECT INFORMATION

During this phase of staffing, the interviewer checks references and compiles information about all applicants interviewed prior to evaluation and decision making. If the applicant has passed both the screening process and the in-depth interview with flying colors, it is time to check references. It is becoming difficult to get useful information from past employers due to increased litigation in the area of employee references, but it is still worthwhile to pursue the verification of past employment. The reference check allows you to verify the facts that the applicant communicated for accuracy and honesty. In its simplest form, this includes dates of employment, position held, and salary. This information is typically supplied by the human resources department of the past employer and can either be communicated in writing or on the phone. Many organizations require a release form signed by the applicant before they will provide any information.

You can obtain valuable insight into the individual's qualifications by also contacting the applicant's past supervisor. If the supervisor is willing to talk, ask questions referring to the applicant's ability to handle pressure, relationship with coworkers and management, guest relations skills, and reliability. Personal references are supplied by the applicant, but are often poor sources of useful information. They are usually slanted to promote the applicant in a positive light and will not give an accurate picture of the individual's workplace behavior.

Companies that fail to explore the background of applicants can experience some very negative consequences. A beverage manager says, "We need to find a good bartender yesterday. Just send me a warm body." Sound familiar? In this case an employee recommended an applicant, and his background went unchecked. The result led to this headline "Bartender Shoots Customer." The bartender had a past criminal record for assault with a weapon. The company was sued for negligent hiring because they did not do a routine background check.[7] To protect themselves from such dire consequences, employers must establish a policy requiring a background check of all applicants.

ACCURATE BACKGROUND CHECKS

1. Carefully examine the work application. Make certain that it has been filled out completely. Also make sure that the applicant has signed it. On most application forms, the applicant's signature also verifies the truth and accuracy of what he or she has written on the application form.
2. Look for gaps in the work history. During the screening interview, find out what the applicant did during that time. Make sure the applicant's story is reinforced by tangible proof (college transcripts, etc.).
3. Look for an unstable work history that involves frequent job change, or more than an average of one or two job changes each year.
4. Obtain a signed release form from the applicant granting you permission to conduct a background check.
5. Contact former employers to verify dates of employment, job title, duties, performance, eligibility for rehire, and the reason the applicant is no longer employed.
6. Contact an attorney for advice in conducting a criminal-records check. This procedure allows you to gain knowledge of felony convictions of current employees and applicants. You cannot immediately rule out candidates with previous convictions, but a good attorney can help you make the right decision in such instances.
7. Use and retain a screening checklist that carefully documents each step taken in the screening process. Save all records and information in a hard copy filing system.

EVALUATING CANDIDATES

Finally we reach the last segment of the staffing system, candidate evaluation. In this phase you will review all the information collected during screening, the interview, testing, behavioral simulation, and background check. No one source of information should outweigh all others. For example, if your applicant receives glowing references from past employers, did a great job during the interview, and aced the behavioral simulations, a job offer should be the next step. But more often than not, concerns in one or more areas arise. If the applicant receives mediocre or poor references from one employer, but did well in all other assessments, this is not sufficient to eliminate an otherwise good candidate. Perhaps there was a personality conflict that was not the fault of the applicant, or the job was not a good match and yours might be better. In this case you may choose to gather additional information by bringing the individual in for another interview, or checking additional references if available.

Prior to making a formal job offer, you will want to meet with all key players in the selection process and combine and review the information collected. In larger organizations this will include the supervisor, manager, department head, and human resource recruiter. Compare impressions, information gathered during interviews, and test results if appropriate, to thoroughly analyze the individual's candidacy.

You may want to use an evaluation rating form like the one shown in Figure 5.7, where job dimensions are listed down the side and candidates across the top. Job dimensions should be taken directly from the job description if available, or developed after interviewing and observing current employees at work. The candidates are assessed in terms of these skills by listing a number from one to ten in the matrix with one indicating the candidate did not possess that skill to ten giving the candidate the highest possible rating on that skill. Total the columns and compare the numbers at the bottom of the page. The accuracy of the rating form depends on the interviewers' ability to objectively rate candidates on job skills that are closely connected to success in a particular position. It is unlikely that all raters will arrive at complete consensus, but a thorough discussion of the impressions of several raters, rather than just one individual, is likely to result in a more accurate decision.

THE JOB OFFER

Finally it is time to make the job offer. If you have completed the entire staffing process in a thorough manner, you can feel confident that the candidate you have chosen is the best available. Usually jobs are offered over the phone, but if time allows, a better vehicle for this important step is a face-to-face meeting. You will want to briefly "sell" the candidate on your company, focusing on benefits, opportunities for advancement, and any key features you think that candidate will find important. Next tell the candidate why you have chosen him or her from all others interviewed. Discuss the salary or wage the applicant will receive at this time. Hopefully all will go well, and the candidate will accept on the spot. More often than not, some negotiation involving money, scheduling, or

BEST PRACTICES

The dining services at University of Pennsylvania uses a point matrix system to evaluate applications.* Different characteristics within the matrix carry different values. For example, with regard to education, if an applicant has a bachelor's degree in hospitality management, he or she gets 25 points or 22 points for a degree in another field, 15 points for an associate's degree, 10 points for completion of a nondegree program, and 5 points for completing high school. Applicants also receive 5 extra points for ServSafe certification.

*Susie Stephenson, "Which Suit Suits? When a Manager's Position Opens Up, How Do You Choose the Best Individual for the Job?" *Restaurants & Institutions* 106, no. 5. (February 15, 1996): 92–95.

Position: Front Desk Clerk

Rate each candidate on the job skills listed below from 1 to 10 with 1 at the low end and 10 at the high end.

Job Skills	Candidate 1	Candidate 2	Candidate 3
Verbal Communication			
Job Experience			
Service Skill			
Education			
Computer Applications			
Reliability			
Professionalism			
Friendliness			
Team Experience			
Career Goals			
Total Score			

Figure 5.7 Applicant Evaluation Matrix

the start date might occur. If you have room for negotiation, try to meet the candidates needs—remember, this is your top choice.

Occasionally negotiation fails, and the candidate does not accept the offer. This can be very discouraging, but is certainly unavoidable at times. Always end on a positive note. Your top candidate may have good reasons for not accepting the job at this time, but could change his or her mind and reapply at a later date. Next you must decide whether to offer the job to your first runner up or next choice. If it was a close call between the two, this is an easy decision. If the person was clearly much less qualified, and if time allows, you may decide to continue recruiting and interviewing in hopes of finding another great applicant.

CONCLUSION

Management often undervalues the benefits of good selection procedures. If more time is spent up front recruiting, interviewing, and hiring the best people for the job, many expensive problems can be avoided. When organizations make the effort to recruit and hire better employees, a number of beneficial results occur:

- Turnover is decreased because the right people are placed in the right job.
- Training expenses are decreased because you do not need to constantly train new hires and because better selected employees will need less training.
- The organization will have a larger pool of high-producing employees to develop and promote from within.
- The organization will experience fewer lawsuits due to better compliance with
- EEOC guidelines.

K E Y   T E R M S

Staffing

Title VII of the Civil Rights Act

Protected Class

Bonafide Occupational Qualifications (BFOQs)

Screening Process

Peer-based Interviewing

Behavioral Simulation

Behavioral Interview

N O T E S

1. Tom Peters, *The Circle of Innovation* (New York: Alfred A Knopf, 1997), 465.
2. Steven M. Sack, *The Employee Rights Handbook* (New York: Facts on File, Inc, 1990), 6–9.
3. Ibid.
4. "Attracting Quality Employees Remains Top Pirority," Special Report, *Hotel and Motel Management* 212, no. 15 (Sept 1, 1997): pp. 19–21.
5. Kathy Woodard, "Hotels Bonus Workers Who Find New Job Candidates," *Business First-Columbus* 14, no. 33 (April 10, 1998): 39.
6. Mike Malley, "Help Wanted: Hotel Operators Search for New Solutions to Solve Labor Shortage," *Hotel & Motel Management* 212, no. 21 (November 17, 1997): 29–30.
7. Ben R. Furman, "Solid Screening Procedures Minimize Workplace Crime," *Hotel and Motel Management* 210, no. 10, (June 5, 1995): 29.

CASE 5.1: SEARCHING FOR TALENT

Two star desk clerks have given notice and will be leaving in just two weeks. Human resources has run ads in local papers, but so far only two individuals have applied, neither with any customer service experience. Grace, the front office manager, has asked that Melissa take over the replacement of the employees. She wants her to develop both creative recruiting methods to bring in great applicants and incentives to make sure that they accept their offer.

Melissa thinks this assignment may be a bit more than she can handle. If ads didn't bring in job applicants, what will? Melissa visits her mentor for some creative advice.

As Melissa's mentor, how would you suggest that she:

1. Recruit great applicants for the front desk positions.

2. Identify incentives that will make top candidates join the company.

R E V I E W   Q U E S T I O N S

1. Title VII of the Civil Rights Act of 1964 prohibits discrimination based on which characteristics?

2. Who would not be a member of a protected class?

    a. A thirty-nine year old Caucasian male.

    b. A Hispanic/Latino woman.

    c. A Caucasian woman.

3. List five BFOQs for a server position:

4. Which section of the job description is particularly useful when you are developing interview questions?

5. Indicate which of the following practices are:

    a. Internal recruitment methods.   b. External recruitment methods.

    _____ Employee referrals.

    _____ Job opening posted on the Internet.

    _____ Government placement services.

    _____ Applicant files.

6. Check the factors below that might be "red flags" during applicant screening.

    _____ Changing jobs every two years.

    _____ Breaks in work history with no explanation.

    _____ Time off to raise children.

    _____ Employment with one of your competitors.

    _____ Failure to complete all information on the application.

7. How might you prepare for the in-depth selection interview?

8. List the five steps in the in-depth selection interview and at least three important tasks to be completed during each step:

9. Place a check mark next to those questions that are behavioral:

_____ Tell me about your last supervisor.

_____ Give me an example of a problem guest.

_____ What did you like about your last job?

_____ Tell me about a time when you and your supervisor disagreed.

10. What benefits might a company experience from good selection procedures?

CRITICAL THINKING EXERCISES

1. Develop a series of behavioral interview questions that you can ask an applicant to find out more about each performance area:

   a. Can the applicant handle demanding customers?

   b. Is this person dependable?

   c. Is the person creative?

   d. Will the person be happy working here?

2. List some BFOQs for each position listed below:

   a. Banquet server.

   b. Front desk clerk.

   c. Busperson.

   d. Secretary.

3. Below are several scenarios. Which actions might be potentially discriminating in each? Why?

   Scenario 1

   To upgrade the quality of service at the front desk, a major downtown hotel has decided to only hire desk clerks who have bachelor's degrees.

   Scenario 2

   A restaurant has experienced an increase in on the job accidents due to back strain from bending and lifting. As a result, the owner has decided to have each applicant lift a thirty-pound box, do fifteen sit-ups, and touch their toes. If they can do these activities, he believes it will be unlikely that they have a bad back.

   Scenario 3

   A hotel located on the border of a major city has decided not to place job ads in newspapers that circulate to minority readers, but instead to focus ads in papers with a predominantly white audience.

   Scenario 4

   A restaurant that requires its female servers to wear revealing uniforms has decided not to hire larger women. They justify this by saying that they do not have to hire anyone who will not fit into their uniform, the largest of which is a woman's size fourteen.

4. What's wrong with this ad copy?

We are one of the finest restaurants in town and we are looking for top dining room servers. If you are as handsome as Robert Redford, as charming as Cary Grant, and as glib as Robin Williams, you have just the qualities we are looking for. Please contact us at 555=1234.

How could you rewrite this ad to still bring in top-quality applicants?

5. Meg has applied for a job as a reservationist in your hotel. She seems to be a great candidate with four years of experience at another local property. She was rather vague about why she left her last position, so you have decided to call her past supervisor to check her references. You want to find out as much as possible about her past performance on the job, although of course you aren't sure just how much information the supervisor will share. List three questions you will ask the supervisor to find out about Meg's past job performance as a reservationist.

O N - L I N E   L I N K

1. Give the complete address of at least three Internet sites that you would visit if you were searching for hotel, restaurant, or travel employees.

2. Visit the sites of a few major hotel or restaurant companies and see how they are marketing themselves to applicants. Print a copy of the materials they are displaying on the Internet, and briefly describe which methods you think have the most potential for bringing in quality applicants.

P O R T F O L I O   E X E R C I S E

All managers and supervisors in the hospitality industry will be involved in the selection process during most of their careers. Add to your portfolio by creating a detailed checklist that you can use when you prepare to interview job applicants. Include the following sections: recruitment of applicants, screening, planning the in-depth interview, steps in the in-depth interview, and evaluation of applicants. The checklist should be typed with check boxes or lines to the left and specific actions you must take to the right. Action statements should be brief and clear. When you are preparing to interview applicants on the job, you can simply pull this checklist out and use it as a job aid to help you apply the information you have learned in this chapter.

Training for Optimal Performance

6

ADVANCED ORGANIZER

When an applicant interviewed with a major hotel chain for an entry-level position, one of the first questions she asked about the company was, "What type of training will I receive?" Unfortunately all this company provided line employees was a one-day orientation and a few days of skills training. When offered the job, this ambitious applicant declined, stating that she had an offer from a competitor that promised to provide her with more than forty hours of training each year plus tuition reimbursement.

Training is one way that outstanding hospitality-related companies can distinguish themselves from competitors. Not only will training lead to higher levels of service performance, it will also help companies attract and retain the best employees. Applicants who are planning careers in the hospitality industry will often take the long view when comparing job offers. Immediate salary is important, but savvy applicants will seek out companies that will support lifetime learning to facilitate their career progression.

BEHAVIORAL OBJECTIVES

- Understand the important role that training plays in the hospitality industry.
- Recognize the unique training needs of the adult learner.

Opryland Hotel. The Delta

- Know the importance of both the physical and emotional training environments.

- Be familiar with common types of training programs offered in the hospitality industry.

- Know the important components of new employee orientation.

- Understand the training cycle, including needs assessment, program development, delivery, and evaluation.

NARROWING THE KNOWLEDGE GAP

An old proverb states: *If a man comes to you hungry, you may give him a fish and feed him today; or, you may teach him to fish, and feed him for a lifetime.* A significant portion of your job as a manager is to teach your employees to do their jobs well so they may have a lifetime of success. Today's managers must wear many hats; they must serve as coach, leader, and trainer. Helping employees grow and develop on the job by expanding their skill set is an enormously important function that managers perform today. In this chapter you will learn about the types of training activities you must undertake with your employees if you are to teach them to "fish" so they may go on and become productive members of your organization.

To maintain competitive advantage, today's organizations must narrow the gap between the skills employees have and the skills they need to provide high-level guest service. Training is the most effective way to increase performance skill and narrow the knowledge gap. For more about this, see Research Brief 6.1.

Historically the hospitality industry has faced a dilemma with regard to the training of employees. On the one hand, everyone agrees that training is valuable and is the vehicle by which we keep businesses competitive. Top management "talks the talk" with regard to training, vowing to its importance, but still fails to implement employee training in a consistent, thorough manner. All agree that training increases employee skill levels and, in turn, elevates guest service and satisfaction. But why the lack of follow through? Perhaps the biggest drawback to training is its expense. Currently, American employers are investing $210 billion in formal and informal training.[1] Hospitality-related businesses have difficulty justifying massive expenditure in employee development due to their high rate of turnover. Spending thousands to train new servers, dishwashers, and desk clerks only to lose them to a different chain or even a different industry only underlines the negative aspects of an investment in training. According to Horst Schultze, chief operating officer of Ritz-Carlton Hotels, the stone-age attitude toward training in our industry was "don't teach employees anything. Someone in another hotel is just going to steal them, so we might as well keep them stupid."[2] Schultze and other astute leaders realize that this attitude toward training is self-defeating.

As evidence builds that today's rank and file workers lack the basic job skills that customers require, hospitality companies are putting their fears about return on investment from training aside and are reacting to an even greater threat—lost business. As guest requirements escalate, companies realize that they must teach employees to handle complaints quickly, to clean a room thor-

RESEARCH BRIEF 6.1

TRAINING AND EMPLOYEE COMMITMENT

Does training increase your employees' commitment to your organization? In a research study designed to answer this question, it was found that training was positively associated with several important organizational factors, including morale, awareness of workplace rules, and perceptions of supervisor quality in addition to commitment to the organization.* The study showed that training has both short- and long-term positive effects on lodging organizations by increasing commitment behaviors such as acceptance of organizational goals and values, willingness to work, and intent to stay.

Further the research suggested that to receive the greatest benefit from training, managers should:

- Revise existing training programs to make sure they are consistent with the mission of the organization.

- Be aware of employees' attitudes toward managers, and maintain open lines of formal and informal communication through scheduled meetings, surveys, and taking time to speak to employees personally.

- Make employees aware of rules and expectations.

- Maintain a productive, interesting, meaningful work environment.

- Control the quality of service delivered to guests through training and organizational commitment.

*W. Roehl and S. Swerdlow, "Training and Its Impact on Organizational Commitment among Lodging Employees," *Journal of Hospitality and Tourism Research* 23, no. 2, (1999): 176–194.

---

oughly, and to be sensitive to the needs of disabled guests. According to hotelier extraordinaire Horst Schultze, "the role of training is to create consensus between the employee and the customer," thus giving the employee the skill set needed to provide each guest with a positive experience. Without the correct tools, employees will not be able to "wow" customers and provide the level of service that clinches repeat business. Even smaller chains, such as Fargo, North Dakota–based Tharaldson Lodging, have tripled their training expenditures in the past five years.[3] Other hotels and restaurants are offering, even requiring, that managers and employees participate in training programs dealing with guest service, diversity, empowerment, communication, technology, and sanitation and safety.

How committed is your organization to training? Consider the following questions to assess your company's support for training:

- Is your training and education budget untouchable in bad times, or is it the first to be cut?
- Is the training budget increased when profits are high?
- Is your training conducted by both internal and external trainers?
- Does your human resources staff have expertise in training?
- Have you provided adequate space and equipment for training?

BEST PRACTICES

Compass Group USA, a large foodservice organization with more than 48,000 employees, has launched CHAT, Communication, Help, and Training, to supplement its orientation and service training program.* CHAT involves unit managers holding monthly twenty-minute "power training" sessions with their employees that focus on a variety of topics which change monthly. Managers receive packets containing both visual aids and step-by-step discussion manuals to help them carry out the monthly training. These monthly CHATs keep both managers and employees focused on the importance of training.

*A. Zuber, "Human Resources: Reaping the Rewards," *Nation's Restaurant News*, 32, no. 9, (March 2, 1998): 106–107.

- Is training continuous? Do employees at all levels of the company participate in training regularly?
- Does top management support training?
- Does your company evaluate the training effort to identify needed improvements?
- Are employees excited about being involved in training, or do they dread it?
- Does management encourage employees to pursue training?
- Is there a continuing education or training reimbursement policy for employees?
- Is participation in training activities required? Is it included in the performance assessment process?

If you can answer yes to most of these questions, your organization is highly committed to training their workers. If not, it is time for your company to

INSIGHT 6.1

Training is the building block upon which Ritz-Carlton Hotels have created their empire.* Its success begins with top management's commitment to training employees. This commitment is so evident that Horst Schultze, chief operating officer, is frequently introduced as "our president, our chief trainer, and our friend."

After a careful selection process, training at Ritz-Carlton includes:

- An orientation that introduces employees to the "heart and soul of the company."

- New hires are trained in eighteen key processes. Upon mastery, they are certified to deliver excellent service. The certification test is administered during the sixty-day orientation period. If mastery is not achieved, further training and testing are provided.

Training is an ongoing part of the job. Managers strive to create good work habits by constantly reinforcing the importance of being on time, being tidy, and being friendly. This commitment to training is how Ritz-Carlton has distinguished itself from its competition. Even during the lodging recession in the late 1980s, this chain remained committed to training. Ritz-Carlton is committed to developing people who can become significant contributors to the organization.

*P. A. Galagan, "Putting on the Ritz," *Training and Development*, 46, no. 12 (December 1993,) 41–47.

reassess their commitment to ongoing employee training. As guests become more sophisticated and more demanding, companies must respond by continuously upgrading the skill level of their managers and employees. Those that do not seek to elevate their employees' knowledge and abilities will be left behind. Customers will choose to do business with those companies staffed by highly competent, well-trained individuals.

THE NEEDS OF THE ADULT LEARNER

Training involves teaching adults new skills that they will use in their work. The traditional education system in our country is based on **pedagogy,** where the teacher determines the content, sequence, and presentation of instruction. However, during the middle of the twentieth century, educators realized that the pedagogical assumptions that were successful with children were not appropriate for adult learning. These were adapted through the addition of **andragogy,** or learner-directed approaches to teaching adults. Andragogical learning differs from pedagogical methods in that it is problem centered and based on the specific behaviors adults must master to increase their workplace performance. Mutually agreed-on objectives are set, and learners are actively involved in the training process.

Adult learners have unique needs and requirements. You will be more successful as you develop and deliver training to your employees if you remember that adult learners:

- Set personal goals for learning.
- Link new knowledge and skills with what they already know.
- Want time for sharing and dialogue.
- Prefer team and peer learning activities.
- Have comfort needs that must be attended to.
- Are highly motivated to learn. They view training as a way to increase their career opportunities and move ahead.
- Need to feel that the training is relevant. Adults want to learn new skills that they can take back to their jobs, not spend time in philosophical discussion.
- Want to be treated as equals.
- Prefer to ask questions in a "risk-free" environment where their ideas and concerns are accepted and not judged.
- Want to understand the how and why behind principles that are presented.
- Need to be involved in their learning. They need to be consulted about training content, scheduling, and delivery.
- Must have practice that is meaningful. Adults need to practice with actual work skills in the learning environment to help them learn.

PRECONCEIVED NOTIONS

When we were children, first entering the learning environment, we came with fresh minds and few biased notions about our abilities. Later, as adults, we carry around a huge knapsack filled with myths and preconceived notions about our limitations and our ability to learn. Consider the following example of a common preconceived notion. Jennifer is convinced that she is not artistic. She was told by her second-grade teacher that she had little talent in art because her drawings were not neat and orderly like those of the other children. She didn't color between the lines, her trees did not have green leaves, and her houses were asymmetrical. Over the years Jennifer has avoided situations that test her artistic abilities.

Adult learners bring with them many preconceived notions that may limit their ability to learn successfully on the job. If you have a server who is "math phobic" and was always told how badly he or she performs in this area, teaching this person to total checks, calculate service charges, and perform other basic math functions may be particularly challenging. As a trainer you can help adult participants overcome emotional blocks to learning by:

- Including introductions and icebreakers in your training programs. Icebreakers might include having participants interview, and then introduce a partner or working in small groups, ask participants to identify three things they have in common
- Spend time talking about expectations. You might ask participants to write down three concerns they have about the training program, and then the instructor reads the concerns out loud and describes how to address them.
- Help trainees set learning goals. Ask participants to create a "learning contract" at the beginning of the program which describes their commitment to the learning process and their responsibilities such as arriving on time, participating in discussions, and doing external assignments.
- Incorporate fun and comfort-producing activities in your programs. If you are teaching participants factual information, use trivia games or "Jeopardy" to review the information. Some training environments even include stress reducing "toys" for participants to use such as Koosh or Nerf balls, Tinkertoys, Legos, and so on.

THE LEARNING ENVIRONMENT

If training is to be effective, you must carefully consider the learning environment that you create. This includes both the physical and emotional environment in which training will take place.

THE PHYSICAL ENVIRONMENT IS IMPORTANT

Ideally companies will have a separate area devoted to training. Not only does this facilitate training frequency and ease, but it also sends a message to everyone in the company that training is very important in this company. Characteristics of physical environments that promote learning include:

- On-site facilities that are easily reached by all trainees.
- Temperature and noise are controlled.

- Seating is flexible and comfortable.
- Large meeting room and smaller break out rooms for group work.
- Technological equipment such as video and computer support.
- Neutral décor that is pleasing to the eye.

A SUPPORTIVE EMOTIONAL ENVIRONMENT

Supervisors, managers, and even employees within a company can do much to either make or break the success of the training effort. What you say and do provides cues about the value and effectiveness of learning. If the pretraining environment is supportive and encouraging, trainees will feel more positive about its usefulness, and, in turn, be more motivated to learn. Trainees whose supervisors are skeptical and negative about training have little incentive to learn new skills. They have few opportunities to practice these new skills back on the job.

What happens after training, or the posttraining environment, is also extremely important. The effectiveness of a training program can be influenced by events that occur after a trainee returns to the job. If you continue to give trainees feedback during skill practice and encourage them to use the principles learned, **training transfer,** defined as the extent to which trainees apply the knowledge, skills, and abilities gained in training on the job, is greatly increased.

THE TRAINING MENU

A number of training programs are delivered in the hospitality industry to enhance performance on the job. Some are developed in-house, by department supervisors or training managers employed by the company, and others are developed externally by consultants. Training may be generic in form or appropriate for use in all hotels or restaurants within a chain, or very specific, designed for use only within a single operation. The Educational Foundations of the National Restaurant Association and the American Hotel and Motel Association both offer generic skills training and management development programs, videos, and CD-ROMS that can be used "as is" or customized by the hotels and restaurant that use them.

NEW EMPLOYEE ORIENTATION: A GREAT BEGINNING

Orientation is designed to teach new employees about the history and philosophy of the company, inform them of rules and regulations, and develop their knowledge of general areas of operation such as guest service, safety, communication, and empowerment. Orientation can last anywhere from a few hours to a full week, with the typical length being one or two days. Several individuals, including the supervisor, the training manager, and the human resource manager, usually carry it out. In a larger organization, orientation typically includes a workshop conducted by the human resources department describing such topics as employee benefits, company policies, and an introduction to work safety and guest service.

BEST PRACTICES

When new hires start their careers with The Four Seasons Hotels, they receive an immediate message about their importance to this company. All new employees are asked to spend a night or two in the hotel where they will work prior to joining the company. The employee experiences firsthand what it is like to be a guest in a luxury hotel property. He sees his new workplace from the guest's eyes before being asked to see it from an employee's perspective. The company also lets new hires know right away that their ideas and input are important. The company asks that each new employee complete detailed reports about their stay, and from this information they glean valuable data to help them identify areas in the hotel that may need additional attention. Both the new employee and the hotel benefit from the experience.

Next, in large or small organizations, the new employee is typically paired with an employee or supervisor who has been designated as the department trainer. This person acts as a combination mentor and trainer, providing job instruction training as described in the section titled Teaching Job Skills.

The goals of new employee orientation are to:

- Introduce the new employee to the job, workplace, supervisors, and coworkers in a manner that shows respect and concern for the individual.
- Help the new employee to feel comfortable and productive in the new environment as quickly as possible.
- Provide positive on the job experiences that will help the employee feel confident of his or her ability to be successful in their new position.

Orientation includes the following components:

1. *Description of the organization, its history, mission, and function:* Provide new employees with organizational charts, company mission statements, and recent publications about goals and strategies so that the new employees clearly understand what the new organization is all about. Ideally, orientation is a great time to employees

INSIGHT 6.2

Whether top management, or clean-up crew, all new Disney World hires participate in a two-day initiation process known as "Disney Traditions."* As part of their training, new hires are taken to the Magic Kingdom to observe veteran workers. Experienced cast members ask new hires how they would respond to guest interactions as they occur. This helps Disney pass on their culture of service to new members.

After two days of orientation, new hires move to their specific work locations. They are met by their supervisors and also by their qualified trainer. Training programs are designed with the needs of the specific position in mind and are closely monitored by human resources managers.

*R. Hiebeler, T. B. Kelly, and C. Ketteman, *Best Practices: Building Your Business with Customer-Focused Solutions.* (New York: Simon & Schuster, 1998).

communicate the company mission and goals so employees might become aligned with them and work to help their organization achieve its mission.

2. *Company policies, rules, and regulations including dress code*: Employees need to know what they can and cannot do. The important rules and regulations should be thoroughly discussed—don't just leave it up to the employee to read the rule book. Review the most common reasons for firing (tardiness, no show, poor guest relations), and describe specifically what employees can do to avoid disciplinary action in these areas.

3. *Compensation and benefits*: Make sure employees know their salary, when they will be paid, and how they receive their paychecks. Misunderstanding of compensation is a primary source of new employee dissatisfaction and can damage the new relationship with the company. Also describe in detail the benefits package, provide insurance booklets, and let the new employees know exactly what they need to do to request sick pay, vacation time, or to use health benefits.

4. *Work schedules and department rules:* Each department has additional rules that you must cover that are not part of overall organizational policy. Prepare an additional checklist describing department rules, and provide all employees with a copy. In addition you should also discuss the work-scheduling process in detail, letting the new employee know policy with regard to schedule changes.

5. *Safety procedures:* New employees must know how to perform their jobs in a safe manner, preventing injury to themselves or others. Procedures to prevent back injury, slips and falls, fire, and other workplace mishaps should be covered in detail. In addition make new employees aware of emergency exits, emergency procedures, and the location of safety equipment. Also another very important topic is your company's accident report process. New employees need to know how to report on the job accidents correctly.

6. *Tour of the operation and introduction to key employees:* Tours are particularly important in hotels characterized by many interlinking departments. It is important for employees to become oriented to their new surroundings and to meet key people in other departments that interact closely with theirs. The tour is also an opportunity to "wow" the new employees', making them proud to work for your company. The tour usually includes back and front of the house employee areas and also a quick peek at guest rooms and suites.

7. *Introduction to the work group:* This is the most important socializing event for new employees. As you introduce your new employee to coworkers, be sure to

mention the individual's strengths or qualifications so the person can start out with equal footing and respect. Assign new employees to a trained, caring mentor who will provide some on the job training and also give attention to the social integration process.

TEACHING JOB SKILLS

Following orientation, employees are taught the basic skills they will need to perform successfully on their job. **Job Instruction Training,** or JIT, consists of the step-by-step teaching of job skills. To begin this type of training, first list all steps or procedures necessary in performing the job. Next indicate key points or specific behaviors that employees must carry out to perform the job correctly. Figure 6.1 is an example of a JIT segment that would be used to train hosts/hostesses to seat the guest.

Ideally job skills training is based on the job description. You may utilize workbooks, videos, and computer-assisted training to teach employees job skills. Job skills trainers may be department managers, supervisors, or a specially designated line employee. Depending on the experience level of the new employee and the complexity of the job, training may last from several days to several months. A four-step method is used to deliver job instruction training:

Step 1: *Prepare the trainee.* Review objectives, address any concerns, and talk about past experiences. The goals of this step is to put the trainee at ease, answer questions about the process, and motivate learning.

Step 2: *Demonstrate the task or skill.* This is most typically done live, but may also be demonstrated via videotape or CD-ROM. Regardless of the media, demonstration involves first telling the employee about the skill and then demonstrating its performance.

Steps involved in seating guests	Specific behaviors
1. Greet guests promptly.	*Stay in the front area of the restaurant. Watch carefully for guests.*
2. Make guests feel welcome.	*Say, "Welcome to XYZ Restaurant."*
3. Ask about seating preferences.	*Say, "Would you prefer our smoking or non-smoking sections? Would you prefer a booth or a table?"*
4. Take guests to their table.	*Walk slowly so guests can keep up. Help disabled guests to table.*
5. Seat the guest.	*Ask if table is acceptable. Pull out chairs for ladies. Hand each guest a menu. Tell guests their server will be with them shortly.*

Figure 6.1 Job Instruction Training Segment

Café Avanti, Opryland Hotel

Step 3: *Trainee practices task.* The employee is asked to demonstrate the task while the trainer looks on.

Step 4: Feedback is provided, and this step is repeated until mastery is achieved.

Step 5: *Implementation.* The trainee is now ready to perform the task independently on the job. The trainee must continuously evaluate performance by observing and asking about problems. Gradually the trainer provides less and less assistance until finally the trainee is performing proficiently.

DEVELOPING YOUR MANAGEMENT STAFF

Larger companies often put new managers through a thorough development program where they work in several departments throughout the operation and gain expertise in overall operations. Both new and experienced managers also participate in ongoing training to help them develop skill in leading and supervising employees. This might include training in communication, leadership, motivation, legal issues, diversity, and a number of other important areas. Internal or corporate training managers, human resources managers, or external consultants may carry out training.

TRAINING FOR TEAM EFFECTIVENESS

The movement toward increased employee involvement and empowerment has created the need for additional training for both employees and managers. Employees must learn to work in groups, communicate effectively, and fine-tune their decision making skills. Managers must learn to act as coaches and facilitate problem solving rather than leading it. Corporate trainers or consultants experienced in group process typically deliver this type of training. To be effective, training of this nature must be fairly detailed, offering lots of opportunity for skills practice both in the workshops and on the job.

TIMELY TOPICS

In response to legal, demographic, and environmental changes, training also focuses on such timely topics as sexual harassment prevention, diversity management, serving disabled customers, sanitation, responsible alcohol service, and other subject areas that have emerged as important learning needs of both managers and employees in the hospitality industry. These seminars and workshops are often delivered corporatewide by either internal trainers or external consultants. The workshops are usually brief, lasting no more than a day or two.

THE TRAINING SYSTEM

As companies are convinced that training will enhance their organizations, they want to get off to a quick start and immediately begin offering workshops and seminars to employee groups. They attempt to make up for years of inertia with regard to training by offering employees a variety of learning experiences. Although their intentions are good, training is not something that should be rushed into, but requires careful planning and assessment prior to implementation. Skipping the planning and assessment phase of training is comparable to a doctor prescribing surgery for a sore throat following a brief, initial exam. The treatment is obviously premature, may be unnecessary, and the condition would certainly require considerable testing prior to diagnosis. In the same manner, you must complete careful analysis of the organization, the employees, and the tasks they perform before offering training programs. The training system begins with need assessment and ending with evaluation. We will examine each component of the training system carefully to make certain you have a comprehensive understanding of this function.

ASSESS TRAINING NEEDS

Before committing to a training solution, it is important to carefully assess your company's training needs. In the needs assessment phase, you will examine three essential areas that are altered by the training effort: the organization, the task, and the person. Once needs are assessed and goals identified, the most effective and efficient training methods can be chosen and an implementation strategy developed.

Needs assessment is defined as the process of identifying what employees need to learn in order to do their jobs, to grow in their careers, and to allow the organization to achieve its performance goals. Needs assessment should answer the following questions:

1. Who needs to learn what and at what depth?
2. Why do they need to learn it?
3. What are the priorities?

There are three key areas that you must address during needs assessment. These include the organization, the task, and the person. When conducting the **organization analysis,** you must carefully assess the culture, or the "way things are done" in the company, to decide if training outcomes will fit the culture and climate. For example, if you want to teach employees empowerment skills and your organization has a very traditional, bureaucratic structure, conflict will arise. Your training dollars will be wasted. Teaching employees to take responsibility while the organizational structure hampers their decision-making power will result in confusion. You will learn more about both organization culture and empowerment in Chapter 14.

Task analysis consists of the dissection of job-related tasks into the knowledge, skills, and attitudes needed to perform them. The first step in task analysis is to identify all tasks or actions performed on the job. Next group the tasks together in a logical manner. Finally identify the knowledge skills and abilities (KSAs) employees need to perform each task. Prien, Goldstein and Macey[4] define KSAs as:

- *Knowledge:* an organized body of knowledge, which if used, makes job performance possible. Knowledge is necessary for job performance, but does not ensure it.
- *Skill:* The capability to perform job operations with ease and precision.
- *Ability:* The thinking skills necessary to perform a job task. Ability involves the application of knowledge.

Figure 6.2 contains an example of KSAs and tasks for a customer service worker. When task analysis is complete, you will have detailed information concerning the knowledge, skills, and abilities your employees need to perform each job task. This provides a detailed map for the design of training programs and ensures that the training you undertake is closely related to job performance.

Person analysis brings the focus to the individual employees to be trained. From the organization analysis, you have a clear idea of the challenges and goals faced by the organization and how training can facilitate increased success. In task analysis you determined what specific actions need to be performed and the KSAs needed to implement them. Now, in person analysis, you

---

KSA: Ability to communication technical information to customers in a way that they understand it.

Task Links:
- Clearly understand technical information.
- Ability to communicate with people from diverse backgrounds.
- Speaks clearly and concisely, using proper diction.
- Asks guests if they understand.
- Repeats information patiently if necessary.

Figure 6.2: Knowledge, Skills, and Abilities of Customer Service Employees

must determine how well current employees are performing the KSAs and target areas where improvement is needed. In person analysis, you will address two important questions: (1) Which employee groups need training? (2) What type of instruction do they require? Information regarding current abilities can be gathered from performance appraisals, supervisor assessment of employees, peer assessment, self-assessment, and customer evaluation. Figure 6.3 contains a series of questions that can be used to guide the needs assessment process.

Training goals are a final, but important step in needs assessment. In this phase you set specific goals and describe desired outcomes in terms of the organization, task performance, and personal ability. In setting goals you want to answer three questions:

1. In what ways will training improve organizational effectiveness?

Part I: Organizational Assessment

1. What are the current organizational goals?
2. What external forces or factors are affecting the organization?
3. What internal changes have affected the organization?
4. How satisfied are you with human resources outcomes such as turnover, customer satisfaction, productivity, and employee motivation?
5. What organizationwide efforts are in place at this time and how successful are these initiatives? For example:
   - Total quality management.
   - Team building.
   - Empowerment.
   - Diversity management.

Part II: Performance Analysis

1. What gaps in employee performance are you observing?
2. What are the performance standards that you hope to achieve?
3. What methods are you using to measure performance?
4. What have you done to solve performance problems in the past?
5. What effect does the performance gap have on your organization?
6. What benefits do you expect your organization to experience when performance is improved?

Part III: Person Analysis

1. Who within the organization needs training?
2. To what degree do current employees posses the desired skills needed to perform their jobs?
3. Specifically what new skill sets must employees learn?
4. What types of training experiences have employees had in the past?
5. How motivated are employees to participate in training?
6. Which instructional methods are most effective with this employee group?
   - Classroom instruction.
   - Case study/simulation.
   - Media based.

Figure 6.3 Conducting Training Needs Assessment

2. What performance improvement will employees demonstrate following training?
3. How will employees will bring added value to the company following training?

Organizational goals are rather broad statements about the desired outcome of the overall training effort. These goals will be refined during the development of learning objectives that takes place initially during the design phase.

TRAINING DESIGN

Training design is the process of planning and developing the programs to be delivered to employees. This is a time-consuming process often undertaken by corporate training managers or external consultants. If materials are to be job specific, managers and supervisors known as **subject matter experts** must be involved throughout the design process.

IDENTIFY THE LEARNING OBJECTIVES

A thorough, detailed needs assessment builds a sound foundation for well-designed training programs. It provides a clear picture of important job skills and employees' current performance levels. The needs assessment provides the necessary information for the first step in the design process, the development of learning objectives. A piece of simple, but sage advice, "If we don't know where we are going, we can't tell if we got there," supplies philosophical support for the development of clear learning objectives. They provide the basis for all the remaining steps in the development of a training program and serve as the criteria against which a program can be evaluated. Training objectives consist of three elements:

1. A statement of the desired performance.
2. An indication of important conditions under which the desired performance is to occur.
3. A criterion of acceptable performance that is measurable.

Figure 6.4 contains examples of learning objectives for a training program for new hotels sales managers. As you will notice, each objective states specifically the skill to be taught, how it will be demonstrated, the person who will perform it, and the degree of success expected. Such detail makes it simple to assess performance outcomes following training. The objectives are based on outcomes relating to:

- Knowledge.
- Attitude.
- Skill.
- Job behavior.
- Organizational results.

Knowledge:	All sales management trainees will demonstrate understanding of principles of selling by achieving a grade of 80 percent or better on a test designed to measure the principles of making the sales call, selling benefits, and closing the sale.
Attitude:	All sales management trainees will believe that their sales performance is important to the successful operation of the hotel. This will be judged by their statements in class and their behavior on the job.
Skills:	All sales management trainees will be able to accurately demonstrate skills in three role-play situations. All trainees will provide high-quality sales skills to their "customers" during the role-play.
Job Behavior:	All sales management trainees will utilize the demonstrated skills on the job and will increase customer satisfaction with the sales function by 15 percent as measured by a survey distributed prior to training and again six months after training.
Organizational Results:	All sales managers will improve their sales quota by 3 percent during the first year following training.

Figure 6.4 Examples of Instructional Objectives

BUILDING TRAINING MODULES

Once you have a clear idea of what trainees must learn, it is time to develop materials for programs and workshops to teach the desired knowledge, skills, and abilities. Programs can be broken down into training modules. Each module or component is based on a learning objective or series of learning objectives to be taught. Figure 6.5 contains a sample of a one-day new employee orientation program. Notice how it is based on six different modules containing individual and group activities, role-plays, a video, presentations by top management, and a review game. This variety in delivery keeps participants inter-

BEST PRACTICES

Marriott Management Services provides training materials in important areas such as food safety and hazard control in both Spanish and English.* It is of the utmost importance that staff members grasp the intricacies of safe food handling, and if teaching it in their native tongues facilitates their learning, then this is the best way to communicate vital information. The company has also developed a research library containing materials to teach English-speaking managers basic Spanish so that they can better communicate with their employees. The company receives more than 400 requests per month for titles from its audiotape library.

*M. Hanstra. "People, the Single Point of Difference, Training Them." *Nation's Restaurant News* 31, no. 40 (October 6, 1997): 110–111.

8:00 to 8:30 A.M.	Continental Breakfast	
8:30 to 9:00 A.M.	Module 1:	Welcome General manager's welcome Ice breaker (individual exercise) Introductions
9:30 to 10:30 A.M.	Module 2:	Company vision Defining your personal vision (group exercise) Aligning company and personal vision
10:30 to 10:45 A.M.	Coffee break	
10:45 to 11:45 A.M.	Module 3:	Company history New employee video Corporate growth and development Presentation by director of marketing
11:45 to 1:00 P.M.	Lunch	
1:00 to 2:00 P.M.	Module 4:	Customer service is our business Anticipating customer needs (role-play) Exceeding customer expectations (group exercise)
2:00 to 3:00 P.M.	Module 5:	Company facts and figures Trivial Pursuit company game
3:00 to 3:30 P.M.	Module 6:	Company expectations of employees Rules, standards of conduct Achieving success in our company
3:30 to 3:45 P.M.	Break	
3:45 to 4:30 P.M.	Tour of property	
4:30 to 5:00 P.M.	Summary of days activities Good-bye.	

Figure 6.5 New Employee Orientation Schedule

ested and enthused, sending them off to their first day on the job with positive feelings about the company and the training they received. If you eliminate the variety and simply lecture to new employees for several hours, they will be bored and tune you out from the very start.

You may also need to consider the language needs of your employee groups. Employees who speak English as a second language may need written training materials in their native tongue if they are to thoroughly understand them. More often operators around the United States are developing Spanish-language training materials for their Hispanic employees. Training is more efficient when materials are provided in the language best known by the employee.

ACTIVE INSTRUCTIONAL METHODS

The best training programs are those that involve participants in the learning process. Interactive design elements build participant interest and involvement. They can increase **retention,** or the amount of information participants actually remember and use after training, and they allow participants to practice the new skills and ideas as they learn. Interactive design makes training an active process rather than a passive one. When participants are engaged mentally, physically, and emotionally, rather than just intellectually, learning is elevated to a higher level. In this section we will explore some interactive design elements that you may want to incorporate into your training programs to increase participation and retention.

IMMEDIATE LEARNING INVOLVEMENT

Training programs that incorporate principles of immediate learning involvement ask participants to respond to questions about course content, try out learning activities related to the content, or view presentations or demonstrations early in the session. These activities help introduce the course in a dramatic, active manner that draws the participants into the training program right from the beginning.

Below are some methods that will help you create immediate learning involvement in your training programs:

- Display an interesting proverb or slogan and ask each participant to discuss how it applies to his or her life.
- Give small groups a series of pertinent questions that will stimulate group discussion of the topic to be covered. As each new question is addressed, have two members rotate to a new group so that class members eventually work with everyone in the group.
- Open with a game or fun-filled activity that will dramatically introduce the main points of the lecture.
- Begin with a work-related anecdote, fictional story, cartoon, or graphic that focuses the group's attention on your topic.
- Open with a short case around which the presentation will be structured.
- Open with a short quiz that tests the participants current knowledge of the topic you will cover. This is particularly effective when teaching legal issues such as sexual harassment avoidance or employment law.

THE CASE STUDY

The **case study** has been used in both education and training settings to provide participants with a simulated problem to solve. It is designed to foster critical thinking and facilitate discussion. The case study is one of the oldest interactive training techniques. A minicase can be used to introduce a topic or as an alternative to a lecture. An extended case study can be presented at the end of a training session to allow participants to practice the skills they have learned.

Here are the steps in creating realistic case studies that promote learning:

1. Decide on the principles you want the case to emphasize. What do you want the class to learn or practice?

2. Identify case goals that lead to problem resolution, persuasion, or the gathering of necessary facts regarding an issue.

3. If possible base your case on a real event or situation, using fictitious names and locations of course. Establish a realistic situation. Make sure the negative consequences are important to the participants.

4. Develop your characters. Make them interesting, yet believable.

5. Write the case. Open with your setting or background to let readers know how the problem came about. Make sure it fully describes important details, events, problems, and personalities that are relevant to the case.

6. Write actively and use a storylike format full of excitement and "gossipy" information and background on your characters. Add dialogue when possible and make sure the case flows logically.

7. Provide several open-ended questions that guide participants' thinking about the problem presented. Don't solve the case for your readers. Include some mystery, and let them come to resolution as they address your discussion questions.

ROLE-PLAY

A **role-play** is similar to a case study in that it is based on a realistic, job-related experience that trainees might encounter in the workplace. Where a case study is usually read and discussed or analyzed, a role-play is acted out. Participants are given limited information on the part they are to play, then asked to "act out" the situation. Trainees in a program designed to teach interviewing skills might ask one participant to act as the interviewer and another to act as the applicant and have them demonstrate the process from beginning to end. If you were teaching alcohol server responsibility, you might ask one participant to take the part of bartender and the other a guest who has had too much to drink. The two then act out the conversation that might take place if the bartender refuses to serve the guest more drinks. Although outgoing, gregarious adults enjoy participating in role-plays, individuals who are more introverted may not. When planning role-plays, it is important to keep the participants in mind, choosing the less risky case study if your group prefers not to role-play.

Although participants may role-play a situation in front of the entire class, most find it more comfortable to do so in small group settings. Here you would have one or two individuals act as observers. Typically, the observers' task in a role-play is a passive one. Here are some methods that will increase their involvement in this process.

- Give observers lists of key points they should watch for during the role-play.
- When participants are observing a role-play or group exercise, provide observation forms so they can answer questions and complete checklists.

- Provide key questions to help observers focus their attention.
- Provide an opportunity for feedback. At the end of the role-play, the observer shares the information they have noted with the participants in their group.

ADDITIONAL METHODS THAT INCREASE PARTICIPATION

In addition to the case study, role-play, and interactive lecture, there are a number of other practices that enhance learner involvement in training. After developing learning objectives and modules, you can incorporate some of these techniques into to your programs to add zest.

- **Open sharing:** Ask participants to share their experiences with the class. Begin by saying, "I'd like to ask 4 or 5 individuals to tell us about . . ." and follow by calling on individuals one at a time to describe their experiences.
- **Anonymous cards:** If your group is particularly reticent, you might be able to increase their involvement by making it anonymous. Pass around index cards and ask participants to write their answers to questions, but not include their names. Read the responses aloud or pass them around to groups for discussion.
- **Questionnaires:** Design a short questionnaire that can be completed and tallied on the spot. Questionnaires might deal with opinions about new organizational practices such as teams or empowerment, or might query participants' initial knowledge of the principles' your program will cover.
- **Whips: Whips** is a questioning technique where you quickly go around the room and ask each person to respond to short questions. You might use this method for review by asking the first question as you toss a softball to a participant. After answering that person must quickly come up with another question, asking it as the ball is tossed to another classmate, and so on.
- **Panels/talk show format:** Invite a small group to present their views to the class by forming a panel. One person acts as the "talk show host" and leads others to discuss relevant topics of concern that relate to the training program.
- **Fishbowl:** Half the class forms a discussion circle and the other half forms a listening circle around them. At the end, the listening circle or **fishbowl** provides their observations and feedback.
- **Games:** Formats like Jeopardy, Trivial Pursuit, or new game show such as Greed or Who Wants to be a Millionaire can be fun and educational. They are particularly useful in reviewing fact-based knowledge in programs dealing with legal issues, principles of sanitation, or company rules and regulations.

TRAINING DELIVERY

The next step in the training cycle is to plan for the delivery of the programs you have developed. Training may be delivered via **live instruction,** where a person teaches students in a face to face setting, or **mediated instruction,** where the teacher and learner communicate at a distance. Live instruction is still a common delivery method and has been with us since ancient times. Many learners find that they prefer live instruction to distance learning. They enjoy interacting with their peers and prefer the personal attention they receive from their instructor. Others are seeking out alternative delivery methods such as telecourses, computer-assisted learning, and satellite courses to allow them to fit education and training to their schedules. When selecting a delivery method, you must consider the needs of the participants, the cost, time available, and, of course, the method that best facilitates learning. We will carefully examine several frequently used methods of delivery that are used today.

LIVE INSTRUCTION

When you train you will typically deliver instruction to large or small groups of participants. This is the method that we are most comfortable with due to our years of experience in traditional educational settings. Live instruction presents many advantages. Participants can interact readily with each other, and they can form relationships among themselves and with you without interference from time, space, or technological barriers. On the other hand, live instruction is expensive, rather inflexible, and requires the talents of experienced trainers if it is to be delivered effectively.

HIGH-INVOLVEMENT LECTURES

Lecture, or the individual presentation of material by a subject matter expert or teacher, is a commonly used method of sharing information and knowledge. Lecture is the least interactive of the training methods, and, unless the speaker is particularly skilled, the most likely to result in boredom and monotony. It's hard to fall asleep during a small group discussion, while acting out a role-play, or performing a demonstration, but all too many participants doze off during a lengthy lecture. Below are some methods you can use to ensure that your participants stay alert and involved during your lectures.

- Let participants know that they will be asked to clarify, summarize, or complete a quiz on the topic.
- Ask participants to listen carefully so that at the end of the lecture they can summarize the important principles for another person in class.
- Distribute a list of questions for participants to answer as you lecture. Participants must then search for information in the lecture, and their attention will be captured.
- Give participants a skeleton worksheet listing the main topics of the lecture. Ask them to complete it by summarizing the ideas presented and also writing any questions they still have.

THE SOCRATIC METHOD

Socrates, a well-known philosopher and teacher in ancient Greece, did not present information to his students as is commonly done in lectures. Instead he questioned them. The **Socratic method** of delivery involves leading students to a desired answer or conclusion by asking them a series of questions that requires them to reason and think for themselves. Only experienced trainers can utilize this method efficiently as it is easy to get off the topic at hand. If you were leading a workshop on sexual harassment, you might begin by asking "What are your rights as individuals?" leading participants to conclude that we all have the right to be physically respected by those we work for and highlighting the importance of avoiding behaviors that might result in sexual harassment. This type of delivery can be more meaningful to participants, as opposed to just having them memorize principles of sexual harassment avoidance.

SMALL GROUP INVOLVEMENT

An important component of live training is involving participants in small group activities and discussion. Optimal group size is from three to eight people. This is the best method for obtaining everyone's participation. People who never say a word in a classroom setting usually become very involved in small group work. Supply your groups with topics for discussion or tasks to complete. Tasks for small groups may include the analysis of case study materials, acting out role-plays, or brainstorming problems and issues. When they are finished, ask each small group to briefly report their results to the class. This can be done creatively in a skit, videotape, or demonstration, or more typically through a verbal report. Provide small groups with materials that will facilitate creativity such as markers, flip pads, cameras, video and audio recorders, and building tools such as Legos or clay.

TRAINING AT A DISTANCE

In the past those who pursued training did so in person—either on the job or in a classroom setting. With the development of distance learning, it is possible for trainees to experience high-quality education in a nontraditional manner. **Distance learning** is defined as instruction to persons in planned education in a time or place that is different from that of the instructor.[5] The key ingredient to learning at a distance is that the instructor and learner are not in the same location during most of the program. Thus training can take place at home, over the weekend, or even while you commute. Types of distance education delivery that are commonly used in employee training include computer-based training, teleconferencing, correspondence, and so on.

Computer-Based Training In computer-based training, participants use a personal computer at home or at work to develop new skills and learn new information. Research indicates that computer-based learning increases individual activity and ownership, resulting in quick, efficient learning that is also retained for longer periods of time.[6] The most common form of computer-based training at this time is known as **computer-assisted instruction** (CAI) where programs are developed for delivery on CD-ROM disks and include text, graphics, games, simulation, problem solving, and full-motion video. Hospitality organizations can develop custom programs that specifically meet their needs or can purchase "canned" or generic programs that teach everything from sanitation practices to negotiation skills. Custom programs are very expensive and are only practical at this time for large organizations. The generic programs can be quite good, but may not specifically address an organization's training needs.

Teleconferencing In **teleconferencing** learners in remote sites communicate with an instructor via satellite communication. One-way conferencing systems allows the instructor to be seen and heard, while the more preferable two-way systems allow the instructor to also see and hear the participants. Video conferencing is much like traditional classroom training where participants can ask questions and receive immediate feedback from an instructor. This type of training could be very practical for multiunit operations such as hotels or restaurant chains. An instructor located in one city can simultaneously teach participants in as many three different locations, thus reducing travel time and training cost. Typically the video conferencing requires specially equipped rooms containing the necessary technology, lighting, and acoustics for transmission. Of course drawbacks to this type of training include start-up cost. Purchasing equipment for an up-link and down-link site that allows two-way communication is expensive, as is the cost of hiring professionals to operate these systems. More recently video conferencing has moved to the desktop due the development of compressed digital transmission technology. Individuals at their workstations can communicate with each other directly, making teleconferencing even more convenient than ever. Personal computers are equipped with fairly inexpensive cameras and microphones so that employees can be seen and heard through their computer system.

Other Methods of Delivery at a Distance An additional method of distance learning is **correspondence study** where participants are given a workbook to complete that the supervisor later reviews and evaluates. Although low-tech and comparatively inexpensive, this can be an effective training method if participants are very self-motivated. Other distance training methods include participants listening to audiotapes or watching videotapes that address specific principles or tasks. Success depends on the quality of the tapes, the inclusion of quizzes, tests, and learning activities, and, once again, the motivation of the trainees. A last but up and coming delivery mode is Intranet-based training. Companies with their own in-house Intranet system can provide training to employees via their desktop computers.

Regardless of whether training is delivered traditionally or via distance learning, success depends on quality of the program, the expertise of the trainer, and the appropriateness of the material. Bells and whistles and high technology are not substitutes for sound-training principles.

EVALUATION: IS TRAINING WORTH THE INVESTMENT?

As company training expenditures increase, the need to assess the effectiveness of the training effort is highlighted. **Training evaluation** is the systematic collection of descriptive and judgmental information needed to make effective training decisions. Its goal is not to categorize programs as good or bad, but to gather information that can be used to continuously improve the training effort. Typical questions addressed in evaluation include:

1. Is training worth the money it costs?
2. Does the training target the knowledge, skills, and abilities that are critical to job performance?
3. Does learning occur during training?
4. Does learning transfer to job performance?
5. Does the training result in positive return on investment?

Kirkpatrick[7] suggests that evaluation should address four levels of criteria: reaction, learning, behavior, and results.

- **Reaction:** To measure this criteria, you assess what the trainees thought of the program. This provides a minimum of evaluation data and is the most common method of training evaluation. Instructors distribute questionnaires or "smile sheets" to participants to find out how well they liked the training experience. It is important to note that a positive reaction does not necessary denote training success. What people like and what results in long-term learning and practice may not be the same. Most effective reaction evaluations go beyond "smile sheets" to assess how the information presented is applied to trainee goals. A few principles to remember when measuring reaction to training include:

Instructions: Carefully read each statement below and write in a number from 1 to 5 that best describes how much you agree or disagree with each.

Strongly Disagree	Disagree	Neutral	Agree	Strongly Agree
1	2	3	4	5

_____ 1. Overall, I found this program to be an excellent learning experience.
_____ 2. This program will benefit me in my future at this organization.
_____ 3. The program objectives were closely related to my job.
_____ 4. The material was presented in a lively, interesting manner.
_____ 5. The instructor was helpful.
_____ 6. The instructor encouraged me to learn.
_____ 7. I will perform more effectively after attending this workshop.
_____ 8. The time I devoted to this program was well spent.
_____ 9. I would like to take another course from this instructor.
_____ 10. Overall I found this program to be very valuable.

Short answer:
1. How could this program be improved?
2. If a coworker asked you how beneficial this program was, what would you say?
3. What was the most valuable information you learned in this program?

Figure 6.6 Measuring Trainee Reaction

- Reactions do not indicate learning or transfer.
- Positive reactions do ensure future organizational support.
- Favorable reactions can enhance trainee motivation.
- Trainers may want to compare the results of different work groups.
- Reactions should be collected immediately after training and follow-up reactions should be collected three months after it ends.
- **Learning:** In assessing learning, the goal is to find out if trainees learned the principles, techniques, facts, and attitudes that were specified as training objectives. This evaluation may consist of paper and pencil tests or responses to simulation exercise or case studies.
- **Behavior:** To assess behavior, you must measure actual job performance following training or transfer of learning. Behavior back on the job is typically assessed with an on-the-job measure or performance assessment related to training objectives. Appraisal information is collected by interviewing or administering questionnaires to the trainee, supervisor, peers, and customers immediately after training and again three months later. It is important to note that you may find superior training performance or learning, but this doesn't always result in a high level of transfer. Remember, transfer is the change in behavior that takes place on the job after training.
- **Results:** This type of evaluation relates the results of the training program to organizational objectives. Factors that may be evaluated include cost of training, changes in turnover, absenteeism, grievances, and increases in morale. Results measures can be quite involved and include a detailed measure of training's return on investment or cost-benefit analysis that lets the company know the value of the benefits that they reap from training.

CONCLUSION

As customers become more demanding, jobs become more complex, and employees and supervisors take on new roles in our changing workplace, training will become more important than ever before. Finding top-notch employees that have the skills needed to communicate with customers, solve problems, and support quality service is becoming harder than ever. Organizations will have to provide on-the-job training to teach employees the skills they need to meet customer demands. Not all companies will be able to afford the services of an in-house trainer and will seek the help of educational consultations and industry associations to help them develop and deliver training.

As technology becomes more affordable and user friendly, the delivery of training via computer, satellite, or television will become a prominent, cost-effective way to provide employee instruction.

Finally companies must focus on individual responsibility in learning. Employees must take increased responsibility for their own training and development. One approach that shows promise in this area is the promotion of self-directed learning. The self-directed learner is someone who takes advantage of learning opportunities outside formal training.[8] We cannot possible gain all the knowledge we need for job success in the workplace from formal training alone. Self-directed learning might include:

- Independent completion of computer-based learning.
- Reading books and articles that address work-related topics.
- Furthering education at community colleges or universities.
- Informal cross-training resulting from visiting other departments.

In essence, self-directed learning can be any type of educational activity that employees initiate and complete on their own that may be directly or indirectly related to their job performance. We as individuals must take responsibility for our learning and development by challenging ourselves through reading, discussion, and continuing education.

K E Y   T E R M S

Pedagogy	Role-Play
Andragogy	Whips
Training Transfer	Fishbowl
Job Instruction Training	Live Instruction
Needs Assessment	Mediated Instruction
Organization Analysis	Socratic Method
Task Analysis	Distance Learning
Person Analysis	Computer Assisted Instruction
Training Goals	Teleconferencing
Subject Matter Experts	Correspondence Study
Retention	Training Evaluation
Case Study	

N O T E S

1. A. P. Carnevale, L. J. Gainer, and J. Villet, *Training in America: The Organization and Strategic Role of Training* (San Francisco: Jossey-Bass, 1990), XI.

2. P. A. Galagan, "Putting on the Ritz," *Training & Development* 46, 12, (December 1993): 41–47.

3. "Attracting Quality Employees Remains Top Priority," Special Report, *Hotel & Motel Management* 212, no 15 (September 1, 1997): 12–20.

4. E. P. Prien, I. S. Goldstein, and W. H. Macey. "Needs Assessment: Program and Individual Development," Paper presented at the 89th Convention of the American Psychological Association, Los Angeles, 1985.

5. M. G. Moore, *Contemporary Issues in American Distance Education* (New York: Perganon Press, 1990).

6. J. C Kulik and P. Cohen. "Effectiveness of Computer-based College Teaching: A Meta-analysis of findings," *Review of Educational Research*, 50 (1980): 525–544.

7. D. L, Kirkpatrick, "Techniques for Evaluation of Training Programs," *Journal of the American Society of Training Directors*, 13 (1959): 21–26.

8. C. C. Manz and K. P. Manz, "Strategies for Facilitating Self-directed Learning: A Process for Enhancing Human Resource Development," *Human Resource Development Quarterly*, 2 (1991): 3–12.

CASE 6.1: WRITE YOUR OWN CASE STUDY

Review the guidelines for developing case studies in the chapter, and then create your own case. Begin writing your case study by first outlining the goals, setting, and characters. First decide on a setting. What aspect of the hospitality industry and department function will your case be based on? Before you start developing the content, decide specifically what you want your participants to learn from your case. Next describe the situation. What is the nature of the conflict in your case? Then decide who will be your characters. What are they like? Finally consider the solutions your readers might come to. Now you are prepared to write your case. Make sure that it is no more than four or five paragraphs in length. Be sure to include several discussion questions at the end. When you are finished, check your case against the following checklist.

____   Subject matter is realistic and believable.

____   Facts are presented sequentially, clearly, and briefly.

____   Characters are interesting and believable.

____   The case includes conflict or friction.

____   The case is open-ended with solutions neither given nor implied.

____   The case is short so it can be read quickly in class.

____   The case is likely to provoke discussion or debate.

R E V I E W   Q U E S T I O N S

1. Although everyone agrees that training is important, why don't hospitality companies provide more opportunities to their employees?

2. What is the difference between pedagogy and andragogy? When is pedagogy the preferred method of teaching? When would andragogical methods be more effective?

3. Describe a preconceived notion that you have about learning. What experience caused you to have this belief?

4. What is training transfer and why is it important?

5. What should a good orientation program teach new employees?

6. What are the three key areas that should be addressed during needs assessment and why is each important?

7. Read the following descriptions of various training delivery methods and indicate the method that is being described

   A. Applicants review guest or employee situations and either describe verbally how they would deal with each or give a written response to a series of questions.

   B. Employees take the role of either the manager or guest service employee and act out a problem situation.

   C. Participants are asked to share their experiences with the class.

   D. Half the class forms a discussion circle and half forms a listening circle.

   E. Quickly go around the room and ask each participant to respond to short questions.

8. Complete the following comparison chart by listing the benefits of both live instruction and mediated instruction. Consider such factors as cost, learning quality, individual attention, and so on.

Live Instruction	Mediated Instruction

9. Below are several ways that training programs might be evaluated. Indicate which of Kirkpatrick's four levels of evaluation each addresses.

   A. Smile sheets.

   B. One month after completing training, have supervisors assess how often employees use the skills they were taught.

   C. After training all employees in guest service techniques, see if changes have occurred in guest comment cards—are they more positive?

   D. At the end of a training program, give employees a test.

CRITICAL THINKING EXERCISES

1. Give examples of several activities that you might use to create immediate learning involvement in the following training situations:
   - Guest Service Training.
   - Employee Skills Training.
   - Training in Interpersonal Communication.

2. What changes in the workplace have made training more important today than ever before?

3. How might training help solve the following organizational problems?
   A. High levels of turnover.
   B. Poor employee morale.
   C. Increase in guest complaints.
4. Think back to work-based training that you have experienced. Describe the training methods that were used—on-the-job, CD-ROM, lecture, and so on. How effective was the training? What are some ways that the program could have been improved?
5. Review the list of unique needs of adult learners included in your chapter. Which of these needs are most important to you as a learner? Why?
6. Create a Job Instruction Segment for a position in the hospitality industry that you are very familiar with. Choose just one small segment of the job like how a front desk clerk would check a guest into a hotel or how a server would take a guest's order. List all the steps one would need to take in order to perform the task and then identify the specific behaviors that the employee would perform to carry out each task. You should develop a JIT segment like the one in Figure 6.1.

O N - L I N E   L I N K

The American Society of Training and Development (ASTD) has an excellent web site for people involved in the field of training. Visit it at http://www.astd.org and browse through the information provided. You will see reports on important topics, an on-line magazine, chat rooms, discussion groups, and other useful information. Choose at least two topics to explore—review the magazine, read reports, or browse through some of the questions and answers in chat rooms or discussion groups. Write a one-page summary of what you saw and learned while at the site.

P O R T F O L I O   E X E R C I S E

Knowledge you have gained from training programs is a valuable commodity as you seek out new opportunities with your current employer or with other organizations. Add to your portfolio a segment "Training Programs Completed" and provide a list and description of the various training programs you have completed to date , whether they are on the job training, special seminars offered through your school, or workshops you completed through an employer. Be sure to describe the specific skills you developed as a result of the training. Include certificates of completion in your portfolio if you have them.

As an alternative for students who have had few or no training experiences (less than one or two) to report on, instead create a list of skills you would like to develop and specific training programs that you might complete to develop those skills.

As you progress through your career, maximize the benefits of training by keeping a list of all programs you have completed and certificates you received from each. You will then be able to document the knowledge and skills you have developed over the years.

Leading through Motivation

7

ADVANCED ORGANIZER

Newspaper and magazine articles continue to report the poor state of affairs with regard to service in the United States. Front-line workers make mistakes, display nasty attitudes, and just don't seem to care about customers. Plagued by a lack of skilled workers and high turnover rates, the service industry must instill new life into those having direct contact with customers and guests.

Motivated employees are anxious to provide guests with the best service possible. The key to solving service problems lies within employees. Management must ignite their desire to do their best by creating a highly inspiring work environment. In this chapter, you will learn about both theories of motivation and practical solutions that will help you create a high-performance service team.

BEHAVIORAL OBJECTIVES

- Develop a personal definition of motivation.
- Differentiate between several important theories of motivation.
- Apply motivational theories to common workplace problems.
- Differentiate between intrinsic and extrinsic rewards.
- Create reward systems that increase employee motivation and commitment.

Lobby, The Drake Hotel Chicago

BUILDING A HIGHLY MOTIVATED WORK GROUP

Unmotivated employees cost companies big dollars in absenteeism, turnover, and, most importantly, poor guest service. Guests can quickly gauge the motivation level of your staff. If your employees are inspired by their jobs, they will do everything they can to make sure that guest needs are met. They will go so far as to anticipate guest needs and be prepared to do whatever it takes to respond. Small acts of kindness are constantly performed by motivated employees. For example, when a hotel guest phones the front desk to ask about checkout time, the unmotivated employee will simply answer the question, whereas the motivated agent not only will supply the correct time, but also offer to send a bell attendant to assist with luggage. Motivated employees constantly seek out ways they can "wow" guests with extra service and attention; unmotivated employees watch the clock and just try to make it through the day while expending as little effort as possible.

So how do companies build a highly motivated staff? According to Daryl Harley-Leonard, CEO of Hyatt Hotels, much of the responsibility for employee motivation lies with the supervisor:

> *If there is anything I have learned in my twenty-seven years in the service industry, it is this: Ninety-nine percent of all employees want to do a good job. How they perform is simply a reflection of the one for whom they work. When people are unhappy at work, absenteeism increases, productivity goes down, quality is poor, and employee turnover increases.*[1]

According to Hartley-Leonard, there is much that you as a manager or supervisor can do to create a high-performance work team. In this chapter we will explore the important and rather illusive concept of motivation by first studying the theories developed by experts in the field and then applying this knowledge to managing service employees.

WHAT IS MOTIVATION?

Motivation is the driving force behind our actions, the spark that makes us behave as we do. It consists of the psychological processes that cause the arousal, direction, and persistence of behavior.[2] Arousal refers to our desire to do something, persistence is the time we spend doing it, and direction concerns those specific behaviors in which we engage. Our motivation is reflected both in what we do and how much effort we expend in doing it.

When we are highly motivated, we work hard. When we are unmotivated, we expend as little effort as possible. It is management's job to ignite and fuel the internal fires that will drive employees to achieve high-level performance on the job. This chapter will provide you with the knowledge and tools you will need to motivate your workforce.

THEORIES OF MOTIVATION

Management theorists argue that employees could make a greater contribution to the overall success of the business if they were supervised effectively. Overall, they hold that people like to be challenged, they appreciate and respond strongly to the sense of achievement they get when they meet or exceed high goals, they want to feel that they have made a contribution, and that their efforts are appreciated. When this occurs employees often achieve levels of performance much higher than expected.

Several important theories of motivation can provide a knowledge-base as you seek to understand this important but often illusive concept. Although no one theory is universally correct, each offers key ideas that will help you formulate your own motivating leadership style.

MASLOW'S HIERARCHY OF NEEDS

At the heart of Abraham Maslow's theory of motivation are human needs.[3] Much of what we do is based on the desire to satisfy physical and psychological needs. According to Maslow we are driven by a strict **need hierarchy,** or sequence of needs, as shown in Figure 7.1. As we progress through this hierarchy, we are motivated by the lowest or physiological needs first. As these are met, we progress upward toward higher order psychological needs. We cannot progress toward higher level needs until our lower level needs are satisfied. Once a need is satisfied, it no longer drives our behavior, because we act only to satisfy those needs that are not fulfilled. Thus we would begin by striving to fulfill our physiological needs for food, water, and shelter. Once these are met, we

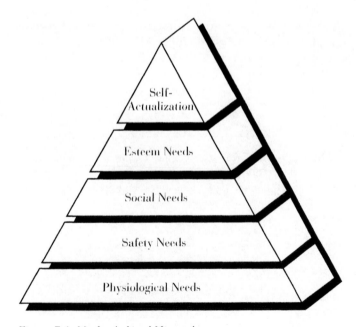

Figure 7.1 Maslow's Need Hierarchy

become aware of our need for safety, and our behavior is driven by our need for stability and protection. Once we meet our safety needs, we focus on our desire for social acceptance. When this need is met, we then focus on our need for esteem or recognition. Finally the most evolved or highly functioning people strive to satisfy the highest need level for self-actualization, which consists of our need to identify and utilize all our capabilities, to be the best that we can be.

Although there is no clear evidence that Maslow's theory is true for everyone, it does provide a much needed basis for understanding human behavior. Figure 7.2 shows how Maslow's theory might apply to needs employees have in the workplace. When a worker's basic needs are met, he or she is motivated by higher-order self-satisfaction needs. Thus, according to the Need Hierarchy theory, employees who are having a hard time supporting themselves are more likely to be motivated by a pay increase or a bonus than by opportunities to socialize with fellow workers. Those who have satisfied their lower order needs may appreciate a raise, but what they really want is increased recognition and responsibility.

Matching rewards to employee needs is one way to make certain that the incentives you provide get the results you want to achieve. Here is an example of an incentive program that initially failed to provide a desirable reward. A large hotel hoped to increase work performance and motivation among room attendants. First they designed a contest and then rewarded the winners with fruit baskets and dinners in the hotel restaurants. Unfortunately the rewards just were not something that the workers really wanted, and the program had little effect. But when the same contest was run using monetary rewards from $20 to $200 as an incentive, the employees worked very hard and dramatically increased their work performance. Finding the right reward made this incentive program a success.

IN PRACTICE

If rewards are to be motivating, they must match the particular employee's need level at that time. If you reward employees who seek self-actualization with money, their desire to be the best they can be will not be reinforced. Likewise, if you reward employees lacking physiological necessities with more responsibility and independence, but not more money, it is unlikely that they will be motivated to work

Physiological Needs	Regular breaks, employee cafeteria, attractive locker room facilities, reasonable amount of work to accomplish.
Safety Needs	Lighted parking facilities, nonslip flooring, up-to-date equipment, fire extinguishers.
Social Needs	Opportunity to interact with coworkers, holiday parties, after work activities.
Esteem Needs	Recognition programs, employee of the month, promotion from within, guest comment cards.
Self-Actualization	Employee training and development, career management, tuition reimbursement, opportunities to participate in community outreach.

Figure 7.2 Workplace Needs

harder. Take time to find out what need levels your employees are at by talking with them about their desires and aspirations. Find out what makes them do a good job and try to build such rewards into the work that they perform.

McCLELLAND'S ACQUIRED NEEDS THEORY

David McClelland's approach to motivation focuses on three needs that people might experience: the need for achievement, power, or affiliation.[4] Those driven by the **need for achievement** want to master complex tasks, work efficiently, and solve problems. Employees driven by the **need for power** want to control others, influence their behavior, and have an impact on other people and events. McClelland identifies two forms of the power need. The first is the need for personal power, or the desire to manipulate and control others. The second form is the need for social power, or the need to exert power more responsibly to achieve goals that are aimed at the common good or at organizational objectives. Those with a high **need for affiliation** want friendly, warm relationships with coworkers and customers.

This theory suggests that the best managers are those who have a high need for personal achievement, coupled with a high need for social power. Those individuals with high needs levels for affiliation may find leadership more difficult because their strong need for friendship and approval may cloud their decision-making ability. There are times when managers must take action that can make them unpopular. One manager I worked with was well loved by her employees. She became very close to several people in her department. Although her concern for the welfare of her employees was admirable, sometimes her judgment was clouded by her friendship with the people that worked for her. She would overlook tardiness, let employees take longer breaks than they should, and fail to enforce other company policies. She was unable to balance her need for affiliation with a need for achievement. Eventually she was replaced by a more task-oriented manager who was not as popular with the employees but did manage to greatly improve the work habits in the department by extending her focus to work quality.

According to McClelland we develop needs based on our life experiences. Our performance at work is driven by our desire to satisfy our needs. By understanding your employees' need orientation, you can create work environments that help them find satisfaction through fulfillment of their desires for power, achievement, or affiliation. The best way to achieve this is to match work assignments to employee need levels. Figure 7.3 suggests some ways to do this.

IN PRACTICE

As you select, hire, and promote employees, be sensitive to their needs for power, affiliation, and achievement. How do you find out what their individual needs are? By asking them about their goals, their desires, what's important to them, and what they want from their careers. Their answers will alert you to their individual needs. Those wanting rapid promotion are likely to have a high need for power. Those wanting challenging assignments are likely to be motivated by a high need for achievement. Employees who want a pleasant work environment and time to socialize are probably high in the need for affiliation.

Need for Power:	Individuals who have a high need for power often seek out leadership positions in organizations. In your department you might steer the power oriented-employee toward positions of authority such as chair of safety committee, leader of task force to improve customer service, train new employees, or act as shift leader.
Need for Affiliation:	Those with high needs for affiliation focus on social relationships with coworkers and customers. They need to feel accepted and to be an important member of the workgroup. Give them assignments that require cooperative interactions such as planning special events for employees and customer, the development of an employee relations committee, and conducting customer interviews and focus groups to identify service opportunities.
Need for Achievement:	These employees are highly motivated to learn and develop their skills so they can achieve their career goals. Provide them with a variety of learning opportunities and challenging tasks that might include development of training manuals for new employees, creation of new menu items, writing an employee or customer newsletter, and assessment of company technology needs.

Figure 7.3 Work Assignments Based on Need for Power, Achievement, and Affiliation

As you manage your employees' work, know that heavy supervision and boring work can squelch the efforts of even the highest achiever. If you fail to give those high in the need for power opportunity to lead, they may try to undermine your authority. Finally make sure that you place those with needs for affiliation in front-line positions where they have lots of opportunity to interact with your customers rather than disrupting their coworkers or talking with their family all day on the phone. As a manager your job is to recognize the differences among your employees. Rather than trying to make everyone the same, benefit from each individual's particular drives and needs by giving that person the right work to do.

EQUITY THEORY

According to the equity theory of motivation, we develop a set of beliefs about how much we should earn for the work that we perform.[5] We then compare our rewards with those received by others, and if we believe that an inequity exists, a tension is created that motivates us to reduce the inequity. If we feel that we are being paid more than comparable others, we are driven to work harder or longer to reduce the **positive inequity.** More frequently we experience **negative inequity** where we feel that we are not earning as much as comparable others. To reduce the negative inequity, people respond in one of the following ways:

- Become less productive.
- Ask for a raise.
- Work harder to earn more.

- Assume their situation is different from that of the person who earns more and accept the inequity.
- Compare themselves with others who earn the same or less as they do.
- Leave the company for a job that pays more.

Which option might your employees choose if they feel they are being underpaid? According to the equity theory, employees choose a method of equity reduction that is personally least costly. But predicting which action an individual will see as least costly is very difficult to do. Research has consistently shown that people who feel underpaid are more likely to reduce their work efforts to compensate for the missing rewards. Those who feel overpaid, more of a rarity, are more likely to increase the quantity or quality of their work to make up for the positive inequity.

IN PRACTICE

As a manager you can benefit from knowledge of the equity theory by realizing that rewards fairly given can lead to increased job satisfaction and higher performance; rewards that are viewed as inequitable can lead to decreased productivity and increased turnover. Seek to pay your employees the most generous wage your company allows. Be aware that employees feel they are underpaid and are often lured away by other companies. Also be careful when singling out one employee for higher rewards than others. Your work group will compare themselves with this person and feelings of inequity may arise if they sense that they are just as deserving, yet do not receive equal rewards.

GOAL SETTING

Developed by Edwin Locke, the theory of goal setting is based on the premise that effective goals are highly motivating.[6] A **goal** is defined as the level of performance an individual is trying to accomplish; it is the object or aim of behavior. Goals direct and energize our time while encouraging us to work hard and persist in our efforts.

To maximize the performance benefits of goal setting, several requirements must be met:

- *Goals must be challenging.* We work as hard as we must to achieve a particular goal. Research has consistently shown that if we accept difficult goals, our performance increases beyond the level achieved with easier goals. Thus, if we want to challenge ourselves to be our best, we must set our sights high.
- *Goals must be specific.* Vague goals such as "improve guest service" are not as effective as more specific ones like "decrease customer complaints by 10 percent by increasing our response time."
- *Goals must be accepted.* People work harder to achieve goals they set for themselves. Employees must be highly involved in setting goals to achieve performance improve-

ment. They must also be involved in planning the steps involved in goal achievement.

IN PRACTICE

Goal setting can be employed as much more than just an annual addendum to the performance appraisal. Set goals often with employees, meet with them frequently to gauge progress, and celebrate their achievement. Begin by setting goals with new employees for job development. When these are achieved, set new goals for further knowledge acquisition. Goals for seasoned employees should coincide with their career aspirations and help employees move ahead in your organization.

REINFORCEMENT THEORY

According to reinforcement theory, the behaviors that we engage in are determined by results that we experience. It is based on the **law of effect** which states that behavior that results in a pleasant outcome is likely to be repeated, whereas behavior that results in an unpleasant outcome is not likely to be repeated.[7] Although this sounds like common sense, what this theory assumes is that everything we do is determined by the external feedback that we receive as we engage in various activities. If we are rewarded for smiling at customers and giving good service with generous tips, we will continue that reinforced behavior.

B. F. Skinner developed the reinforcement theory of **behavior modification**.[8] This theory assumes that our behavior is controlled by manipulating its

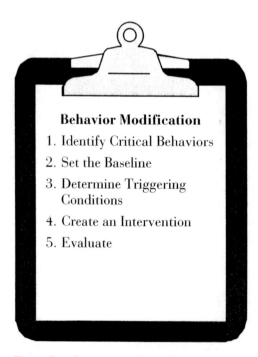

Figure 7.4 Organization-Based Behavior Modification

consequences. The frequency of a particular behavior will increase if the behavior is rewarded. Likewise undesirable behavior can be extinguished by either ignoring or punishing it. Reward or positive reinforcement is the strategy most highly advocated by Skinner. Although punishment can eliminate undesirable consequences, it is not as desirable as rewards for changing behavior.

Organizational-based behavior modification is the term that describes the application of Skinner's theory of reinforcement to employees in the workplace. Its purpose is to reinforce desirable behavior and discourage undesirable behavior among employees. Luthans and Kreitner[9] developed a behavior modification system that can be used to improve employee performance in the work place:

1. *Identify critical behavior.* Specify in writing those actions that employees must demonstrate to achieve performance.
2. *Set the baseline.* Measure the average rate at which employees perform these behaviors.
3. *Determine triggering conditions.* Identify factors that promote the desired behaviors and those that hinder them.
4. *Create an intervention.* Design a way to reinforce desired behavior and to discourage or punish undesired behavior.
5. *Evaluate.* Compare the baseline frequency of the critical behavior at the start of the program with its frequency at the end of the program to determine the level of improvement.

A particular hotel applied the principles of organization-based behavior modification to reduce its extremely high employee accident frequency rate. First the company identified its goals of a safer work environment by changing the critical behavior of accident frequency. The hotel's goal was to reduce overall accident frequency by 25 percent during the next quarter. Next the baseline was set by using the accident frequency rate for each department. Triggering conditions were identified in the form of safe work practices. These included proper bending and lifting techniques, having proper equipment, the avoidance of slippery surfaces, and so forth. If followed these key actions would decrease employee accidents. All employees received training in these practices with follow-up communication in the form of posters and newsletters focusing on safety issues. The intervention created consisted of a monthly contest designed to reward desired behavior. Each employee in each department that reduced their accident frequency by 25 percent received a valued prize. Managers of departments that failed to achieve this goal not only failed to receive the prize, but were also required to distribute prizes to employees who won. At the end of the quarter, the accident rate decreased by not just 25 percent, but by 50 percent!

IN PRACTICE

Positive reinforcement can be a powerful change agent. Use it often in the form of praise and rewards to encourage your employees to work hard and provide outstanding guest service. Use punishment in the form of disciplinary action only when absolutely necessary. Punishment alone as a management tool will reduce loyalty, commitment, and satisfaction, and can severely damage supervisor-employee relationships. Instead great managers find ways to identify desired behaviors and recognize and reward them frequently.

INTRINSIC AND EXTRINSIC MOTIVATION

Constructed by Frederick Herzberg,[10] the **motivation-hygiene theory** is based on two sets of factors that affect employee performance. Hygiene factors include compensation, supervisory style, working conditions, and company policies. If these hygiene factors are inadequate, dissatisfaction occurs and a lack of motivation results. If they are adequate, employees will be satisfied by their work environment, but not necessarily motivated to work harder. For improved performance motivators must be provided. **Motivators** are those opportunities supplied by the job itself for growth, achievement, recognition, responsibility, and advancement. Employees can be motivated by these factors only when the hygiene components such as fair pay and good supervision are in place. For example employees cannot be motivated by challenging work if they feel severely underpaid when compared with others. They must first feel that their hygiene factor, fair pay, is met before they can be motivated by the work itself.

Herzberg's theory consists of both extrinsic and intrinsic rewards. **Extrinsic rewards** are given by someone else, typically by a manager or by the organization. Extrinsic rewards are factors that are outside the control of the individual. When extrinsic rewards or hygiene factors are removed, dissatisfaction occurs. **Intrinsic rewards** are experienced internally and are based on pleasure taken from the work itself.

They result from the performance of work and consist of the feelings of competency, personal development, and control we experience in our jobs. We do not depend on others for these rewards, but find them within ourselves if we are given challenging work we enjoy. Herzberg believes that extrinsic rewards in and of themselves are not motivating, but will only result in satisfaction or dissatisfaction. Intrinsic rewards are the only true motivators, but can only affect us when we are satisfied by our work environment. Research has not proven this premise conclusively, but common sense tells us that when working conditions are poor and supervisory style is limiting, it is very difficult to feel a strong desire to do our best. Of course there are isolated instances of individuals who have such an inner drive to succeed that they do their best despite low pay, poor management, and little recognition, but these are the exceptions, not the rule.

IN PRACTICE

Managers can benefit from Herzberg's theory by recognizing that good pay and good working conditions are very important, but in and of themselves, may not motivate all employees to do their best. For high achievement many workers need interesting tasks that they can control. As often as possible, provide employees with additional responsibility and control over their work. Try to assign tasks that workers particularly enjoy so they will be intrinsically motivated to do their best.

BUILDING COMMITMENT

When you have found great employees, trained them, and incorporated them into your work team, you don't want to lose them. Investment in productive workers is lost if you don't hold on to them. The key to keeping great em-

1. Incompatible corporate culture.
2. Unsatisfactory relationships with coworkers.
3. Insufficient support to get tasks accomplished.
4. Inadequate opportunities for growth.
5. Dissatisfaction with compensation.

Source: R. Herman, "Hold on to the People You Need," *HR Focus,* 76 (June 1999 supp.): S11.

Figure 7.5 Five Reasons Why Employees Leave

ployees is recognizing why they might leave. Figure 7.5 contains the five principle reasons that people leave one organization for another. As the list indicates, employees leave because their values and norms are dissimilar from that of the corporate culture (see Chapter 13 for more on this topic), they can't get along with their coworkers, not enough support from management, few opportunities for growth, and, finally, employees leave because they are dissatisfied with their pay.

Intense competition coupled with high turnover and a shortage of qualified workers make employee commitment more important than ever. When you have a highly committed workforce, your employees see unity between their goals and the goals of the organization, and, as a result, do their jobs as if they owned the company. Committed workers do much more than just stick around; they are loyal employees who fully utilize their skills, knowledge, and abilities in the workplace.

According to the Workforce Commitment Index, an annual measurement of employee loyalty that includes 1,800 U.S. workers, commitment is growing with an overall score of 100.3 for 1999, up from 97.8 last year.[11] This year the number one concern of workers is recognition by employers of the importance of personal and family life. The study found that employees who have the opportunity to spend a moderate amount of time each week attending to personal matters have a higher than average level of commitment to their employers. See Figure 7.6 for the top workforce commitment factors identified in the study.

One way to increase employee commitment is to help workers self-actualize, or reach their potential, in both their careers and their personal lives. Employees are driven to realize their potential, and companies can facilitate this by providing opportunities for them to learn, take responsibility, and grow in their careers. Employers can also help their workers reach their goals in their personal lives by recognizing and valuing the importance of family. Companies that make it easy for their employees to care for their children, aging parents, or to meet other personal responsibilities and still maintain a successful career are rewarded by committed, loyal workers.[12]

1. Management recognizes the importance of personal and family life.
2. The organization provides opportunities for personal growth.
3. The company satisfies customer needs.
4. The company communicates employee benefits.
5. Coworkers' skills are keeping pace with the skill demands of the job.

Source: "Employee Loyalty Surprisingly Strong," *Management Review,* 88 (July/August 1999): 9.

Figure 7.6 Top Workforce Commitment Drivers

PUTTING IT ALL TOGETHER

Now that you have a better understanding of the foundations of motivation science, it is time to develop strategies that will enable you to tap the reservoir of talent in your work group. We will examine ways to apply the principles of motivation theory in hospitality organizations to generate high-level performance from all employees.

Our knowledge of human motivation and the factors that affect worker performance strongly support the potential value of reward systems, incentives, employee involvement, goal setting, and recognition. People enjoy a good challenge; they respond strongly to the sense of achievement they have when they reach hard goals; and they want to feel that they are an important and valued part of their organization. When this occurs, your employees will achieve levels of performance that far surpass not only your expectations, but also your guests'. Even workers in the least satisfying jobs can consistently demonstrate a strong commitment to quality service and hard work. When you treat your dishwashers with respect, let them know how important they are to the success of the overall operation, and reward them for their hard work, they will work harder and develop a stronger sense of commitment to the organization.

RECOGNITION FOR A JOB WELL DONE

> A well-placed "well done" is the most powerful motivator a manager has—and the least used.
>
> —Thomas Connellan,
> *How to Grow People into Self-Starters*

Acknowledging desired performance in a consistent, fair manner will reinforce desired behavior in your employees. We all want our hard efforts to be recognized, and when they aren't, we are more likely to leave our organization. Consistently compliments and praise have been found to be powerful rewards for service workers in the hospitality industry.[13] It is easy to notice when employees make mistakes or do not put forth their best effort, but it takes diligence to see employees doing things right. As a manager or supervisor, you must train yourself to constantly watch for good deeds in the form of extra service to guests, helping out coworkers, working overtime or on days off, always being on time, and so forth. Here are a few recognition systems that will help you catch your employees doing something right:

- *Look for quality performance*. Make a point of spending at least thirty minutes each day on the front line looking for positive efforts among employees.
- *Write it down*. Keep a running list of "random acts of kindness" that you observe and don't cross them off until you have thanked the employee for extra effort.
- *Chronicle your group's achievements*. Create a scrapbook complete with photos and work samples from your department highlighting each person's best achievements and overall group accomplishments.
- *Give special privileges*. Let top performers attend meetings or serve on committees when you aren't available.
- *Share the credit*. Always give employees credit for their work when you are discussing department accomplishments with top management.
- *Team logos create synergy*. Create team T-shirts, mugs, calendars, and so on that symbolize top-quality efforts.

- *Teach others to recognize.* Create a department climate of recognition by encouraging and thanking employees for praising each other's work.
- *Develop employee recognition programs.* Top employees are chosen by a committee of fellow workers and recognized monthly and annually for their extra effort. The best reward I've heard of was at the O'Hare Hilton in Chicago. The hotel is located on airport grounds so employees who drive must park in remote lots and be bussed to the property. Employees of the month are given a designated parking spot for thirty days right by the door, a truly valued reward on a cold, snowy day.
- *Get top management involved.* A thank you note from your hotel or restaurant's general manger to the deserving employee can be a big pat on the back.
- *Create publicity.* Take pictures of your team and publish a brief article in the company newsletter. If the accomplishment is newsworthy, contact local papers and see if they will pick up the story. People really like seeing their name in print, and positive publicity for your work group will make you look good too.
- *Celebrate success.* Schedule a special party or event for the department when they achieve their goals. By celebrating their successes, team members are encouraged to work hard to reach subsequent goals.
- *Increase participation.* Recognize employees as valued members of your team by asking for their input before making decisions that will affect them. If you are changing uniforms or revising the menu, ask employees for their

INSIGHT 7.1

REWARDS AND RECOGNITION

CA One, a company that manages foodservice operation in airports, has developed a number of successful methods of improving employee performance through rewards and recognition.* Joseph Taylor, general manager of CA One Services at the New Orleans International Airport, puts together a monthly newsletter where he recognizes hourly employees who have gone the extra mile for customers. In addition, he gives them rewards in the form of small gifts such as movie tickets to general prizes like stereos or luggage.

Dana Browne, general manager of CA One Services at the Denver Airport, an airport foodservice operation, had devised a way to reinforce positive behavior with rewards that are important to employees. Those who put forth extra effort by providing extra service to guests or working extra shifts receive "Dana Dollars" which resemble dollar bills. When these accumulate, employees can exchange them for a day off with pay. Since initiating the incentive program, many employees have received days off, and the restaurant's average check has increased by 8 percent.

*A. Zuber, "CA One Soars with Employee-incentives Program," *Nation's Restaurant News*, 31, no. 51 (December 22, 1997): 11.

ideas. Not only will you benefit from their added input, your workers will feel that their opinion is important.

REWARD SYSTEMS

Now that you have gotten in the habit of watching out for good performance, it is important to consistently and fairly reward employees for their efforts. Although the intangible rewards such as those mentioned earlier are very effective motivators, tangible rewards can also provide great incentives. Here are a few ideas for creating reward systems that will reinforce and encourage top performance:

- *Contests.* If you have employees who enjoy competition, contests can light a fire under even the most apathetic employees. Think of a behavior that you want to see more of, like suggestive selling of certain products. Calculate a baseline rate of your current sales. Reward employees who surpass the baseline by 20 percent or more during a period of time. Charts, diagrams, and posters can all reinforce the contest. Monetary rewards are often best, but tickets to sporting events, movies, or plays are often appreciated.
- *Training.* Most companies can't afford to send all employees to expensive training sessions, so continuing education can become a great reward for employees who want to get ahead.
- *Customer service awards.* A common method of encouraging quality service is a service award system. Employees who receive the most positive guest comments receive prizes in the form of money or gifts. This can be unfair to employees who do not have a lot of guest contact, so some companies have given tokens to managers to give to employees when they observe quality performance. The tokens are then exchanged for money or gifts.
- *Tie pay to performance.* Money is a tremendous motivator. If your company has a system for tying pay to perfor-

BEST PRACTICES

Another great way to provide employees with a reason to perform well is to allow them to become "partners" in the business. Starbucks is one of the few restaurant companies that offers stock options to its line employees. The "Bean Stock Plan" allows employees to buy shares of the company at some point in the future at today's prices.* If everyone shares in the fate of the company, they will have an interest in seeing that it is successful. Employees are winners if the company outperforms its competition and stock prices rise. Workers are committed to the success of Starbucks and willing to contribute through their own efforts on the job.

*R.L. Papiernik, "People—the Single Point of Difference—Paying Them," *Nation's Restaurant News*, 31, no. 40 (October 6, 1997): 124–127.

mance in the form of annual raises, bonuses, or spot-bonuses, use them effectively to encourage high-level performance from your employees.

As you design incentive programs, don't forget about back of the house employees. Contests work as well in the back of the house as they do in the front. Ross Racine, owner of the Grand Mere Inn, tailored a contest that increased performance of a hard to motivate group, the restaurant's dishwashers. On nights when the restaurant served 300 meals or more, the dishwashers received a monetary bonus that increased as the number of covers went up.[14] Many hotel housekeeping departments have ongoing contests awarding cash or prizes to those with the cleanest rooms. Camberly Hotels even award housekeepers for saving energy.[15]

SET GOALS FOR IMPROVEMENT

Goal setting is a valuable tool that managers can use to improve employee performance. In a study of senior managers in hospitality-related organizations, fully three-quarters of the respondents believed that goal setting boosts their organizations' bottom lines by at least 15 percent.[16] Supervisors can use an approach to goal setting called **Management by Objectives** (MBO) where goals are set jointly and rewards are based on the achievement of these goals. Often used only with management, principles of MBO can certainly improve the performance of line employees in our industry. Here's how the process might be implemented:

Step 1:   Employees list the performance goals they would like to achieve during the next six months. These are submitted to the supervisor for review.

INSIGHT 7.2

JUST REWARDS

One of the most important aspects of a successful incentive program is developing objective, unbiased methods of measuring behavior. Employees must feel that they are rewarded fairly and equitably for their performance. Sofitel Hotels has created just such a program by linking rewards and incentives to their carefully planned guest Satisfaction Program.* Rather than relying on comment cards, which can be biased, Sofitel sends questionnaires to randomly selected guests asking about their expectations, the quality of their experience, and performance in eight key areas, including the quality of service provided by employees. Each department member that achieves a rating of 90 percent or better gets a lapel pin and a personal thank you note. Department managers get cash awards when their team boosts performance. In addition recognition is given to high-scoring departments within the chain's seven U.S. properties. Next the company plans to develop a system to measure how one department assists another so they can reward internal cooperation and service.

*R. Selwitz, "Sofitel Boosts Staff Performance," *Hotel & Motel Magazine* 211, no. 19 (November 4, 1996): 29–30.

Step 2: The supervisor and employee meet to review the goals, assuring that both individual and organizational goals are in agreement. Together, measurable objectives for achievement are identified.

Step 3: The supervisor and employee meet periodically to review progress, make revisions, and evaluate.

Step 4: At the end of six months, the employee lists his or her accomplishments. If objectives are met, a reward is given. If not reasons for discrepancies are discussed, and new goals are set with rewards to come upon their achievement.

Goal-setting theory also highlights the importance of aligning individual goals with those of the organization. Ideally, individual goals will coincide with organizational goals. As employees work to fulfill personal goals, they also work to fulfill company goals. When we say that employees are not motivated, more likely what we mean is that employee motives are not aligned with organizational motives. Employees must feel that they have a stake in the business and that improving customer service is a goal that will also benefit them. Thus an important part of motivating employees is assuring that they feel they will benefit from working hard to achieve organizational goals such as increasing customer retention and improving guest service.

UPWARD MOBILITY

As we have learned by studying Maslow, McClelland, and Herzberg, most of us are driven by a strong desire to be successful and to do work that we find rewarding. Companies that fail to recognize their employees' innate desire to achieve all that they can achieve in their careers will lose their best employees to organizations that facilitate career development. As Abraham Maslow said, our ultimate need is to achieve self-actualization or to "become more and more

BEST PRACTICES

At Cameron Mitchell Restaurants in Columbus, Ohio, hourly employees receive help preparing for the jobs they will hold when they leave one of the chain's six restaurants.* The company hosts one-day workshops for employees focusing on interviewing and resume-writing skills. Although this practice may sound like a conflict of interest for the restaurant chain, the owner, Cameron Mitchell, believes that "there comes a point when they (line employees) will leave anyway. You can't hold a gun to their heads. But if we show them that we care, they ultimately will care about the restaurant and guest service." He believes that satisfied employees will also recruit their friends and often become loyal customers when they move on to a new job.

Over and over again, the owner is asked, "Where do you get such great employees?" According to Mitchell, he doesn't hire anyone different from those employed at other restaurants, but he does try to "get them excited about their jobs."

*Sally Woolchuk, "For Managers Only: Motivation and Empowerment," *Hotels* (November 1993): 21.

what one is, to become anything that one is capable of becoming." An important key to having a high performance work team strongly committed to your organization is to help them "be all that they can be" in their careers. Read more about how a restaurant supports career development for their employees in the Best Practices on page 170.

COMPETENCY MODELING

One way to systematically manage your employees' careers in a way that makes them motivated to stay with your organization and work hard to achieve their goals is competency management. Entry-level employees will be more motivated to stay and pay their dues if their company maps a career plan that shows them exactly how they can achieve their goals in the organization. **Competency modeling** is a process that can be used to couch, counsel, assess, recruit, and select staff. It is a systematic approach to the identification of skills that employees must have to advance and grow within a company.[17] The end product of competency modeling is the development of a competency map that describes those skills needed to progress to higher level positions within the company. Managers guide employees as they develop desired skills that will help them achieve career progression.

To create competency models, companies must:

- Analyze jobs and identify key skills required for performance. These skills should reinforce company goals and objectives.
- List the specific behaviors that must be performed in the demonstration of each skill.
- Make competency models available to employees so they can see exactly what is expected of them in their current position and in future positions to which they might aspire.
- Create a career map for each employee, showing where they are starting out and how they can progress as they develop necessary skills and abilities.
- Create an annual development plan for each employee identifying skills needed for career progression and ways they might be acquired through training, coaching, continuing education, or self-paced learning.

To increase their focus on career planning and development, larger hotels might invest in a career development center. This resource center would house information about career goals, educational opportunities in the community, company-sponsored training, and perhaps even a lending library filled with tapes and books concerning topics of importance.

Attention to the career development of your employees can pay off big in increased loyalty, commitment, and reduced turnover. In addition helping someone else realize their career aspirations is a tremendously satisfying experience. Many hotel general managers and top executives started as dishwashers, front desk clerks, and bellstand attendants. Who is to say that some of your entry-level workers couldn't become the next CEO of your company? Career planning allows you to contribute to the continued success of your organization by creating a top-flight workforce for the future.

CONCLUSION

As a manager, you have many tools available for motivating your staff. First you must be aware that each person is driven by a unique set of needs and desires. These needs and desires are what drive us to achieve great things. Next don't overlook the benefits of recognition and reward systems. In particular when you match rewards and incentives to employee needs, you get the greatest increase in motivation and performance improvement possible. Finally tap into the power of intrinsic motivation by giving employees interesting tasks that they enjoy. Also focus on career planning to give employees a clear sense of where they can go in your company. Facilitate their development of challenging goals that will help them achieve success in their careers and in your organization.

K E Y   T E R M S

Motivation	Law of Effect
Need Hierarchy	Behavior Modification
Need for Achievement	Motivation-Hygiene Theory
Need for Power	Motivators
Need for Affiliation	Extrinsic Rewards
Positive Inequity	Intrinsic Rewards
Negative Inequity	Management by Objectives
Goal	Competency Modeling

N O T E S

1. Noel Cullen, "Motivating Your Kitchen Team," *National Culinary Review* (November 1996): 24–29.
2. T. R. Mitchell, "Motivation: New Directions for Theory, Research, and Practice," *Academy of Management Review*, 7 (1989): 80–88.
3. Abraham H. Maslow, *Motivation and Personality* (New York: Harper & Row, 1970).
4. David C. McClelland, *The Achieving Society* (New York: Van Nostrand, 1961); and David C. McClelland, *Human Motivation* (Glenview, Ill.: Scott Foresmen, 1985).
5. J. S. Adams, "Toward and Understanding of Inequity," *Journal of Abnormal and Social Psychology* 67 (1963): 422–436.
6. Edwin A. Locke, "Toward a Theory of Task Motivation and Incentives," *Organizational Behavior and Human Performance* 3 (1968): 157–189.

7. E. L. Thorndike, *Animal Intelligence* (New York: Macmillan, 1911): 244.

8. B. F. Skinner, *Science and Human Behavior* (New York: Macmillan, 1953).

9. Frederick Luthans and Robert Kreitner, *Organizational Behavior Modification* (Glenview, Ill.: Scott, Foresman, 1975).

10. Frederick Herzberg, *The Managerial Choice: To Be Efficient and to Be Human* (Salt Lake City, Utah: Olympus, 1982).

11. "Employee Loyalty Surprisingly Strong," *Management Review* 88 (July/August, 1999): 9.

12. Ibid.

13. Karen Seelhoff, "Bring Out the Best in Your Staff," *Hotels* (January, 1992): 23.

14. Steve Brooks, "Managing: Shape Up or Ship Out," *Restaurant Business*, January 20, 1993, pp. 40–42.

15. E. Merrit and F. Berger, "The Value of Setting Goals," *Cornell Hotel and Restaurant Administration Quarterly*, 39, no. 1 (1988): 40–49.

16. A. Zuber, "Operators Explore Employee Motivation Programs," *Nation's Restaurant News* 32, no. 23 (June 8, 1998): 10.

17. P. McLagan, "Great Ideas Revisited," *Training and Development*, 50, 5, (May, 1997): 60–66.

CASE 7.1: A DIFFICULT CHOICE

Melissa has noticed that the productivity level and quality of work produced by the reservation agents at her hotel has declined steadily over the past few months. Guests have complained that when they call they have been put on hold for long periods of time, agents seemed unable to answer their questions, and have been unpleasant when asked for more information. In fact one disgruntled guest talked to Melissa personally and said, "I had hoped to book a suite at your property but your reservation agents couldn't answer any of my questions. I got the feeling that she had more important things on her mind and didn't want to take the time to find answers for me, so I went to another hotel."

When she observed them at work, the agents seem to put little energy into their work. Their tone of voice was negative or, at best, uninterested; they were quick to put guests on hold on the telephone; and they just didn't seem to care about the success of the department. Melissa realizes that this is a critical problem that must be addressed quickly. Reservation agents are often the guests' first contact with hotel personnel. They are directly responsible for selling rooms, and the revenue earned by the property depends on their success. If they are doing a poor job or have a poor attitude toward their work, it must be addressed.

First Melissa describes her observations to her supervisor, the director of front office operations. The director thanks her for bringing this to her attention and agrees that there is a serious problem and that it must be addressed. She says, "Melissa, I just don't have time to deal with this right now, but I want you to come up with a plan to solve this problem. I think it's important and I think you'll handle it well. Let's meet next week and you tell me your strategy."

First Melissa analyzes the situation and realizes that part of problem might be that the reservationists have not received adequate skills training in customer service and selling. So the first step in her strategy is to develop and deliver a quality training program to the agents to teach them how to interact effectively with customers and also how to increase revenue by using appropriate sales techniques. But she feels that training is just not enough in this situation. The agents seem to lack the desire to do a good job. If this motivation problem is not addressed, Melissa realizes that all the training in the world won't create a high-performance work group. Melissa needs help from her mentor in developing a plan to increase worker motivation.

1. How should Melissa go about investigating the root causes of poor performance among the reservation agents?

2. Assume that one of the causes she has found is that the workers feel that they are underpaid and overworked. Specifically, what should be done to address this problem?

3. Melissa plans to train the agents in customer service and sales techniques. How can she motivate the workers to continue using the techniques she teaches them when they are back on the job?

R E V I E W   Q U E S T I O N S

1. What behaviors do you engage in when you are highly motivated? How do you feel when you have something to do you just don't want to do—you are totally unmotivated? Based on your answers to these two questions, develop your own definition of motivation.

2. Based on the information provided in your text about the various theories of motivation, try to predict which theorist might have said the following:

   a. The best way to motivate employees to work harder is to set challenging goals for them to achieve.

   b. Even the most exciting, challenging tasks won't motivate employees if they feel they are being treated unfairly by their supervisor or disagree with company policies.

   c. If companies don't provide employees with adequate food while they are working, it will be difficult for them to do their best work.

   d. If employees feel that they are underpaid, the best way to motivate them to work harder is to give them a raise.

   e. When all employee needs are met, they can truly excel in their jobs and be the best they can be.

3. According to Maslow's Need Hierarchy, which need are employees reacting to when they do the following:

   a. Ask for a raise.

   b. Apply for a promotion.

   c. Request a one-year employment contract.

   d. Leave their current job for one with better insurance benefits.

   e. Offer to sponsor charitable events on their own time.

4. According to McClelland's Acquired Needs Theory, which need are we reacting to when we:

   a. Ask a group of employees to get together for dinner after work.

   b. Volunteer to head the marketing committee.

   c. Complete a training program to improve written communication skills.

5. Which of the motivational theories addresses the way employees respond to feeling that they are being underpaid for the work they perform? What do people do specifically when they feel underpaid? How about when they feel overpaid?

6. Give several examples of intrinsic and extrinsic rewards. Which rewards are more likely to motivate you to do your best? Why?

7. In their order of importance, list the five main reasons why you might leave a job. Compare your reasons with those listed in Figure 7.5. How do they differ?

8. How could you tell if your employees were highly committed to their jobs and the organization?

CRITICAL THINKING EXERCISES

Review each situation described below. Indicate which theory or theories of motivation you would use to address the problem and describe how you would go about solving it.

1. Your hotel has linked with a youth services organization to provide work experience to disadvantaged young people. Each day several teens work in your restaurant as buspersons, dishwashers, and runners. You have noticed that the teens just aren't putting forth their best effort on the job. They have trouble concentrating on their work and have poor hygiene practices. You also know that many of the group don't have enough to eat at home and live in poor conditions. What motivation theory might explain their behavior and how might you go about improving their work performance?

2. One of the reservation agents comes to you and says that she has heard that another agent was hired at a higher pay rate than she is currently earning and feels this is unfair because she has been with the company for two years. She indicates that she will only perform those tasks specified in her union contract—no more, no less. What theory best applies to this issue and how would you deal with the situation?

3. You know that restaurant revenue could increase dramatically if you could sell more beverages and desserts with meals. You have asked servers to encourage customers to order drinks and dessert, but they just aren't following through. What motivational theory addresses this problem and how might you go about encouraging servers to sell beverages and desserts?

4. In this chapter you learned about various reward systems that can increase employee performance, including contests, training, awards, or pay. Review each situation below and indicate which reward system or systems you might use motivate employees.

   a. You would like for your reservation agents to do a better job of up selling rooms by encouraging guests to instead choose more expensive suites or larger rooms.

   b. A really important group is coming to the hotel and you want to encourage the front office staff, including desk clerks and bellstand attendants, to really wow them with extra attention and service.

   c. You want your cooks to speed up their work on the line. You'd like to prepare meals more quickly and get them plated and garnished in less time so overall speed of service to customers could be increased.

O N - L I N E   L I N K

Organizations often hire management consultants to assess and improve performance and motivational problems. Most of the larger consulting firms have established web sites and web pages to describe and market the services they provide. Assume that you are a restaurant owner and want to hire a consultant to help you improve the quality and quantity of work produced by your front of the house staff. Go to the web and enter a combination of key search terms such as "motivation, management consultant, performance improvement, and work place or employee" and locate several sites of consulting organizations. Based on the information supplied by their web sites, which consulting company might you choose to help you with your performance problem? What made you choose this particular company?

P O R T F O L I O   E X E R C I S E

Employers are always looking for managers who can motivate their employees to do their best at work. Add to your portfolio of qualifications by developing a series of ideas that you might draw upon to increase performance in the particular department you hope to supervise one day, whether it be front desk, kitchen, dining room, housekeeping, or another area. Briefly describe four or five ways that you might motivate poor performers in areas you might supervise to improve the quality and quantity of work they produce. Describe a contest you might implement, ways that you might increase workers' feelings of intrinsic motivation, how you might use pay as a reward, a goal-setting program you might create, and measures that you would take to build employee commitment. This will be an important addition to your portfolio and will first indicate to employers that you recognize the importance of developing a highly motivated work group and second that you are a person who can develop creative and unique ways to deal with common performance problems.

Performance Management

8

ADVANCED ORGANIZER

You have been given the opportunity to "turn around" a troubled housekeeping department in a midsized hotel. If you can improve overall productivity and quality, you will be given the promotion you have been waiting for. You know that the previous manager was transferred because he just couldn't manage the people in the department. You have heard that several employees have problems with tardiness, another just has a bad attitude but her work quality is good, while others receive lots of complaints about the cleanliness of their rooms. There are several outstanding employees, but even they seem to be developing some bad habits. You're not sure that you can be any more successful than the last manager, but you are willing to give it a try.

In this chapter you will learn about an important aspect of leadership, performance management. You will begin to acquire the knowledge you will need to improve the performance of your work group. By developing skill in appraisal, coaching, discipline, and career management, you will have the ability to manage a challenging group of employees.

BEHAVIORAL OBJECTIVES

- Summarize key components of performance management.

- Define important components of coaching.

- Explain steps in planning, preparing, and conducting an effective performance appraisal.

The Broadmoor

- Contrast progressive and positive discipline.
- Design a BARS-based rating scale.

INTEGRATING HUMAN RESOURCES
WITH COMPANY OBJECTIVES

Performance management is a relatively new strategy that links key employee concerns such as goal setting, evaluation, development, and coaching with organizational effectiveness. Its purpose is to increase productivity, decrease turnover, and improve both service and employee satisfaction by integrating the human resources function with company objectives. Reducing turnover is an important outcome of performance management. Through good management practices, performance management reduces costly turnover and shapes the overall success of the organization.

A key criterion of a successful performance management system is the linking of pay to performance. Employees who improve their job skills and perform at high levels can reap monetary rewards within their particular positions. For exam-

Figure 8.1 Outcome of Performance Management Strategy

ple a hotel might assess the front desk clerk's key competencies such as communication, teamwork, and service orientation against specific business-related results that include guest satisfaction and repeat business. Desk clerks who display these competencies receive significant pay increases within their current position. An added benefit of performance management is that it provides an incentive for those not interested in promotion but who prefer to remain in their line position.

CUSTOMER-BASED SYSTEM

In many companies, the basis of the performance management system is customer opinion. The results of customer satisfaction measures are used to develop the performance review and resulting rewards. By doing this organizations directly link customer satisfaction and employee behavior. Employee performance is increased in a manner directly related to customer needs. Its primary goal is to focus employee performance on organizational goals based on improving customer satisfaction. Two powerful management tools are combined—customer satisfaction and performance assessment—to dramatically improve organizational effectiveness. Companies implement this process by:[1]

1. **Collecting Customer Satisfaction Data.** The company collects survey data to identify important service concerns of customers. Next the company asks customers to rate how well they are doing in each area. This provides a baseline measure of company performance before implementing the new program.

2. **Employee Goal Setting.** Based on the results of the customer service data, the company sets goals for employee performance. These goals should be measurable. For example, if customers rated a hotel poorly on speed of service at the front desk, a resulting goal might be to reduce check-in time by an average of two minutes during the next quarter.

3. **Link Goals to Pay.** Ideally goals are linked to incentive pay for employees. At the end of the quarter, customers are surveyed to identify performance improvement needs. If goals are met, managers and employees may receive a quarterly bonus. The bonus can either be all or nothing, or can be based on the level of success achieved. If check-in time is reduced by 1.5 minutes rather than 2 minutes, employees might receive a portion of the promised monetary reward for making progress.

To be successful performance management programs must be more "carrot" and less "stick," meaning that employees are rewarded for improved performance rather than simply punished for poor performance. Ideally employees will be involved in the development of the program from start to finish to ensure "buy-in" or commitment. In addition it is important to set fair and reasonable goals for service improvement. Make sure the factors you are basing employee evaluations on are within the control of employees. For example, if a

BEST PRACTICES

When The Parkway Hotel in Gwent, Wales, was refused the coveted AA four-star rating due to poor service in their restaurant, they developed programs to improve employee performance.* Parkway introduced formal training programs and incentive programs to bolster service in their hotel. Not only did they achieve the four-star status, they also went on to win a National Training Award for their efforts. How did they achieve this service transformation? Here are some of the programs they initiated:

- A "Hall of Fame" where all staff training certificates are displayed.

- An evaluation of all jobs describing the skills needed at each level.

- Training programs that include National Vocational Qualifications or standards that teach employees to perform up to four-star standards.

As a result staff turnover has fallen while room occupancy rates have risen. Customer complaints dropped by 61 percent the first year and are now virtually nonexistent. Net profit was up 276 percent following losses in the early 1990s.

*L. Curry, "Catering for Success," *People Management*, March 20. 1997. 40–43.

---

major area of customer dissatisfaction is the new fee for parking in the hotel garage, you can't blame employees for this gripe by saying they must do a better job of explaining the policy to customers. The fee is the problem, not the way employees tell guests about it.

Several hospitality-related organizations are implementing performance management programs to increase employee performance and guest satisfaction. See examples of such programs in both hotels and restaurants in the "Best Practices" boxes in this chapter.

MAKING PERFORMANCE MANAGEMENT WORK

In this chapter you will examine the key components of a performance management system. When using the system, managers and supervisors must coach their team members to get the best from them. They must have a system

BEST PRACTICES

Ramada Franchise Systems. headed by President Steve Belmonte. developed the "Personal Best" program to create a culture that focuses on both guests and line employees. Historically the lodging industry has not been successful at motivating line-level employees and presenting career paths to them. says Belmonte. Personal Best was designed to correct this shortcoming. "Typically, we hire an employee, put her in a uniform two sizes too big. tell her she has to clean eighteen rooms a day, and send her off." Belmonte states. Instead he says that we must tell new employees about customer service and also focus on career opportunities within our industry. Belmonte believes that "the key to motivating any employee is hope, whether you're management or line-level."

for assessing the performance of their employees on a regular basis. Both poor performers and top performers alike must be coached and counseled to do their best. At times it becomes necessary to take disciplinary action against problem employees in a fair and impartial manner. Finally a good performance manager also must help employees plan and develop their careers. Performance management requires commitment from management, but the increase in organizational success that it brings about is well worth the time and attention.

COACHING

The department supervisor is the key player in the development of a performance management system. The success or failure of such an undertaking lies in the hand of front-line leaders. Supervisors with a dictatorial, command-and-control leadership style cannot successfully take on the role of performance manager. How does one transform petty tyrants into coaches who possess the insight and sensitivity of Phil Jackson, the enthusiasm of Vince Lombardi, and the charisma of Yogi Berra? Begin by developing a strong foundation consisting of many of the basic principles of leadership addressed in this text, including skill in:

- **Communication:** The ability to listen and give clear directions both in writing and verbally.
- **Negotiation:** The ability to manage conflict.
- **Task management:** Skill in delegation, team development, and performance management.
- **Problem solving and decision making:** The ability to identify and resolve problems and make decisions both individually and with others.
- **Self-management:** Skill in managing your time, dealing with stress, planning your own career, and taking care of your personal life.

BEST PRACTICES

More than a year after Monical's Pizza, a Midwestern chain, reorganized its operations department to create a management structure that focused on employees and customers as well as bottom line performance, the results showed a reduction in turnover and higher guest satisfaction levels.* According to Harry D. Bond, president of the chain, "Operations is the key to our success. Our most important people are on the front line, dealing with the guest, but I think to some extent our industry has confused who that is. Store managers are tremendously important, yet sometimes we overlook servers and cooks and even dishwashers. But they have a huge impact on our success as well." Monical's new organization is divided into four teams: employee satisfaction, guest satisfaction, revenue growth, and profitability. One of the cornerstones of the overhaul is a new incentive program for both unit-level managers and hourly employees. The company has changed its focus from measuring labor costs to controlling guest satisfaction.

*A. Zuber, "Monical's Reorganization Cuts Turnover, Helps Performance," *Nation's Restaurant News*, May 3, 1999, 4.

Coaches typically work very closely with their team members, constantly monitoring their performance, providing encouragement, and helping them improve their skills. Figure 8.2 contains the basic principles of this leadership method presented in a five-step approach using the acronym COACH.

COACHING ACROSS THE BOARD

There are two important components of coaching employee performance. The first is to reward and encourage excellent performance, and the second is to correct poor performance. We often think of **coaching** in terms of improving the performance of difficult or lagging employees. Most leaders are well aware of the need to improve poor performance, but often fail to recognize the importance of encouraging outstanding contributions. Employees who have perfect attendance, receive the most positive guest comment cards, or are always well groomed deserve to be recognized.

COACHING PEAK PERFORMERS

Once again, as we explore a sports metaphor, we can see that those who coach professional athletes do not spend all their time encouraging poor performers, but do, in fact, focus the majority of their attention on developing and encouraging team stars. Unfortunately in the workplace we often take good per-

---

Contract. Just as top athletes sign contracts with their teams so must management coaches with their employees. The coaching contract identifies those key behaviors that both employee and supervisor agree must occur and specifies the rewards or outcomes that the employee will receive when the desired behavior is achieved. Putting everything in writing lets employees know exactly where they stand and specifically what is expected of them.

Observation. Coaches must carefully observe employees' progress noting both their achievements and their shortcomings.

Assess. Coaches must carefully assess employee performance on a regular basis. Ideally employees will receive a progress note each month indicating how far they have come in their effort to achieve their performance goals.

Challenge. Just as sports players must be constantly challenged if they are to improve, so must employees. Good coaches can tell when their employees are becoming bored with their jobs and need additional responsibilities or more stimulating work to stay engaged.

Handle failure. Not every employee can be a "Michael Jordan." Some will be unable to achieve the performance goals set forth in their contracts. Good coaches will continue to work with these poor performers to help them develop the skills they need to achieve success in their jobs. Unfortunately not every employee will improve, so coaches must be prepared to "cut" players who cannot meet company standards. Allowing poor performers to stay on your team will only reduce customer satisfaction and frustrate other employees.

Figure 8.2 Five-Step Method of Coaching.

formance for granted. For example, how much time do managers spend coaching and encouraging employees who are always on time, always do a good job, and always have a good attitude? Not much. Supervisors just assume that these employees don't need their attention and poor performers do. If the coach of a professional sports team made these assumptions, that coach wouldn't last long in the business. Professional coaches realize that team stars need attention and encouragement if they are to maintain their high level of performance. Even Mark McGwire and Sammy Sosa occasionally need guidance from their coaches. Outstanding performance is not an accident. It evolves from a carefully managed process of training, coaching, leading, and encouraging employees to constantly improve the quality of their work.[2] It is the result of a combination of both positive and negative feedback. Good employees need to hear about what they have done that's right along with areas of performance where they need to improve.

You might encourage a top performer by recognizing both verbally and in writing such accomplishments as perfect attendance, good grooming, a friendly attitude, or meeting deadlines. By specifically reinforcing the expected behavior, you show the employee that his or her efforts are noticed and appreciated. The best way to assure repeated behavior is to reinforce it. This is one of the best-kept secrets of successful people management.[3] When employees perform at the desired level, give them a reward and they will continue this behavior. Take the time to find out what your top performers want and what is important to them. An employee whose burning desire is to move up in the company would prefer career advancement to a monetary increase. Those who prefer to stay in their line positions may find higher wages or incentive bonuses motivating. Remember, not all outstanding employees are motivated by the same factors.

COACHING FOR PERFORMANCE IMPROVEMENT

Your job as a supervisor would certainly be easier if all your employees were top performers. Many attribute the great success of Phil Jackson, former coach of the Chicago Bulls, to the great basketball players on his team, particularly Michael Jordan. But remember, he also had Dennis Rodman to contend with, a talented player, but also very difficult to coach. As a supervisor you might find yourself leading an outstanding work team, but, unfortunately, as Chicago discovered, great employees and great basketball players do retire or move on to other places of employment. With high turnover and a lack of skilled applicants in the hospitality industry, more likely than not, you will be facing the challenge of managing employees whose performance is not up to standard.

How do you coach employees for performance improvement? Begin by setting high standards for new employees. Make certain they understand what you expect of them and receive proper training. Let employees know that you will not accept inferior performance. Investigate poor performance and meet with the employee to develop a plan of improvement. Make a point of rewarding creativity and innovation. Get employees involved in decision making and listen carefully to their ideas. Finally be a good role model. Demonstrate top-quality performance in all that you do. Avoid shortcuts and shoddy work habits yourself.

Below are a few common mistakes supervisors make when dealing with poor performers.

- Making vague statements about poor performance. Telling the receptionist that he or she just doesn't get to the phone fast enough is vague. Instead, remind the receptionist that the company standard is to answer the phone by the third ring.
- Focusing on the negative by saying, "You look very unfriendly when you serve guests." Instead say, "Watch your body language by smiling and nodding in a friendly manner as you serve guests."
- Failure to provide deadlines. Giving employees assignments without letting them know when you need the project completed can result in delays due to miscommunication.
- Being too soft. Bending over backward to accommodate poor performers. Allowing employees to play on your emotions and get away with shoddy work. Read more about dealing with "high maintenance" employees in Insight 8.1.

What is the right way to coach poor performers? The following coaching principles will help you avoid the pitfalls described above:

- **Set Clear Performance Objectives.** An important first step in coaching the struggling worker is setting clear performance objectives. As you learned in earlier chapters, job analysis is conducted to identify those specific behaviors that are required to successfully complete each job task. Very specific expectations are identified and job standards developed from this process. Let employees know exactly what you expect of them and how you expect them to achieve it. Instead of telling a host to be

INSIGHT 8.1

HIGH-MAINTENANCE EMPLOYEES

Every manager has an employee or two that takes up most of their time. These "high-maintenance" employees always seem to have a personal problem or a problem with another employee or a guest that you must help them solve. They might be great employees technically, but have a poor attitude, or, in contrast, have a great attitude, but poor performance. Most managers try to ignore the problems these employees create, but by doing so may be setting a precedent of poor performance that will affect all employees in their department. Instead, they should confront the employees about their performance or attitude problems.* Begin by making a list of behaviors that need to be changed. Tell the employee in a calm, objective manner about your perceptions of their performance. Once the employee recognizes the difficulties, ask what you can do to help the employee change. Identify a deadline for change and let the employee know what consequences he or she will experience if the deadline is not met. If confronting employees about poor attitude or performance is difficult, ask yourself, "Why should I work so hard only to see these employees scare off my guests or good employees?"

*T. Gunderson, "How to Deal with Bad Apples," *Restaurant Hospitality* (July 1998): 30–32.

friendly, you must communicate a specific behavioral object such as, "When guests enter the door, greet them with a smile and say, 'Welcome to the Hightop Café,' then promptly seat them and provide menus."

- **Emphasize the Positive.** Rather than giving employees a laundry list of things not to do, instead give them specific guidelines stating what they should do to be successful in their jobs. Instead of saying, "Don't forget to use the guest's name during check-in," be positive and say, "Guests appreciate it when we remember their names. Use the guest's name at least two times during check-in." The second statement is much more encouraging and more specific than the first.

- **Be Serious.** New supervisors, especially younger ones, may find that employees do not take their instructions seriously. Let employees know that you mean business and firmly tell them what you expect and what will happen if they do not perform the expected tasks. This isn't saying that you must turn into a tyrant to gain respect. To the contrary, younger supervisors who come on too strong automatically earn the disrespect of their employees. Instead clearly state what you expect; let them know this is not a request but a requirement, and explain the consequences. Of course, you must be prepared to enforce any consequences you set if the desired outcome does not occur. Check with your human resource manager or legal advisor before telling employees that they will be fired, disciplined, or demoted if they do not comply with job requirements. Firing an employee for failing to answer the phone by the fourth ring twice during a week's time is certainly unfair and could be potentially discriminating. Make sure the actions you take in response to poor performance are both fair and legally sound.

- **Give Frequent Feedback.** Ideally, poor performers will improve and meet the objectives set forth. If this is the case, praise them and let them know specifically what they have done right. Unfortunately, when dealing with poor performers, improvement does not always occur. You must then enforce the consequences you outlined quickly and fairly. Let employees know what you expected and how their performance fell short. When giving negative feedback, don't attack the person, only focus on desired and undesired behavior.

COACHABLE MOMENTS

Managers in the hospitality industry are often bombarded by numerous important tasks and may find the burden of setting aside time to coach employees nearly impossible. Instead of scheduling large blocks of time to meet with employees, consider utilizing **coachable moments** or opportunities that occur in the context of ongoing work and open the door for valuable, brief, career counseling.[4] To make this process successful, managers must recognize opportunities for coachable moments by picking up on cues from employees. Five common cues include:

1. **An employee demonstrates a new skill or interest.** Greg, a server in the dining room, shows you a very attractive flyer he has made using a computer graphics program to promote your restaurant's new menu. The insensitive manager might just say, "That's nice," and leave it at that. The manager who is receptive to coachable moments realizes that Greg is not only willing to share a valuable skill with your operation, but that he may be interested in taking on additional responsibilities.

2. **Request for feedback.** Lindsey, a banquet server, asks if the guests were happy with the way the function went last Saturday. This question can prompt you to provide Lindsey with some valuable feedback about her performance that night, whether positive or negative.

3. **Questions about the organization.** Employees who demonstrate interest in new policies or practices within the organization are often showing their commitment to the company. Answer such questions in detail. They provide an excellent opportunity to increase your employees' feelings of belonging and loyalty.

4. **Dissatisfaction with the job.** Just as a customer complaint provides a second chance to satisfy the guest, an employee complaint gives you the opportunity to respond to concerns before they result in turnover. Even minor complaints or concerns should receive your undivided attention. Let the employee know what you can do about the problem and when you will take action. Always follow up with employees to find out if the issue has been rectified.

5. **Opportunities for advancement.** Employees who ask about future opportunities with the company are telling you that they would like to have a long-term relationship with the organization. If you answer by saying, "Talk to human resources," or "We'll let you know when you're ready to move up," you risk losing this individual to a competitor with a better offer. Instead, ask the person about his or her career goals and help that person to identify career paths within your organization.

By taking advantage of coachable moments during the workday, you will greatly improve the work environment in your department and reduce employee frustration and dissatisfaction. Brief talks with employees will increase your accessibility as a manager and could go far toward reducing turnover in your department.

COACHING WITH RESPECT

Nearly 25 percent of respondents to a 1996 Gallup nationwide telephone survey of 1,000 adults age eighteen or older who were employed full or part time indicated they were generally at least somewhat angry at work. Eleven percent of those surveyed blame their anger on the actions of supervisors or managers.[5] An undercurrent of anger and resentment aimed at the workplace could potentially lead to explosions of rage. Read more about dealing with anger in the workplace in Insight 8.2.

What is the prescription that will dissipate employee anger and resentment? It is **coaching with respect.** If you lead your employees with an attitude of respect, you communicate your belief in their value as a human being and their ability to succeed. Specifically, how do you coach with respect? By incorporating the four principles of respectful coaching to make all employees feel like VIPs (Very Important Persons).[6]

- **Validation.** When you respect someone, you are willing to take the time to listen and explain things. For example, you might need to elaborate on the reasons behind a new company policy or department practice. Just telling employees what they must do does not portray respect for them as thinking people.
- **Inquiry.** Respect also involves taking the time to ask employees the right questions such as, "What do you want from your career? What do you need to achieve your goals?" and, "How can I make this a better place to

INSIGHT 8.2

WORKPLACE VIOLENCE

Recent high school violence across the country draws our attention to the important issue of workplace safety. Awareness is the key to risk prevention. Employers need to establish clear guidelines and policies regarding violent behavior in the workplace. This must be communicated to all employees. One company uses an anonymous toll-free telephone line as a tool for employees to report any threats or unusual behavior, thereby decreasing violent workplace episodes.*

When disturbing, potentially violent behavior occurs, managers should:

- Stay calm. Do not react with anger to the behavior.

- Focus on the behavior in question, not feelings and emotions.

- Always have a third party present when talking with a potentially violent employee.

- Never meet with this person alone, behind closed doors.

- Use "I" statements rather than make accusatory remarks.

- Watch for escalations in anger, and if they seem imminent, move farther away from the employee.

*R. Ruggless, " Preventing Workplace Violence," *Nation's Restaurant News*, June 14, 1999, 92, 116.

work?" When you inquire about employees' needs, you are demonstrating your respect for them.

- **Possibility.** Help your employees to see the possibilities in change. Avoid labeling difficult employees as "problems" and instead view them as works in progress. See the possibilities in both the people you lead and the company you work for.
- **Significance.** Sometimes difficult employees need to feel that they have a significant purpose in the organization. Rather than limiting their responsibility as punishment, expand it. Some employees view being taken for granted or underestimated as the ultimate form of disrespect.

A disrespectful atmosphere creates resentment, anger, and perhaps even violence in our country's workplace and schools. When employees or students feel that they are being "put down" by others, tension results that can erupt into instances of extreme violence. Instead keep the peace by creating an atmosphere of mutual respect in your department.

PERFORMANCE APPRAISAL

Ask seasoned managers what is their most dreaded task, and many will say annual reviews. Managers find it extremely difficult to sum up an entire year's performance on a single sheet of paper. One restaurant chain decided to make performance reviews optional. Outback Steakhouse has no corporate policy regarding employee reviews.[7] Managing partners decide whether their restaurant will use them. A form is available, but the annual review might be a waste of time for a supervisor who sits down with employees after every shift to provide feedback.

Most companies do not have such a flexible outlook with regard to performance evaluations, so managers continue to muddle through the process. The worst reviews are those where the manager has saved up all the bad news all year and dumps it on the employee during their annual meeting. This leaves the employee feeling overwhelmed and misunderstood. The best way to approach the review process is to view it as an opportunity to summarize the feedback you have been providing employees all year and to put their past performance into perspective. Good reviews also involve setting new goals, giving employees targets to reach in the future. Effective performance reviews have the following characteristics:

- **No surprises.** Employees should have a good idea of how they are doing before the annual review based on feedback they have received on a regular basis during the year.
- **Employee involvement.** Ask employees to provide information about their accomplishments either verbally or in writing. If there are deficiencies in performance, ask the employee how he or she might overcome them.

- **Separate reviews from pay decisions.** In some companies where pay raises are linked to the results of the performance review, managers must limit salary increases by also limiting how highly they rate employees. If excellent employees must be given a 6 percent raise, but your budget only has room for a 4 percent increase, you can't rate employees as excellent, even if they deserve it.
- **Base it on objective data.** Try to find measurable factors to include in the review rather than just opinion. Base your evaluation on such objective measures as days absent, positive customer comments, department revenue, individual sales data, to name just a few.

PREPARING FOR THE PERFORMANCE REVIEW

The first step in the performance appraisal process is to collect the necessary forms and review them. Figures 8.3 and 8.4 contain examples of appraisal forms. The first form is generic and can be used for all employees in the company. It contains several criteria, and the supervisor is asked to rate the employee on each one. Unfortunately generic forms like this are still used today and provide only the minimal amount of information about performance. An employee might be rated only average on quality of work, but still have no idea what he or she is doing wrong. The second form in Figure 8.4 is an improvement over the first. It is based on actual performance behavior and developed by using principles of the behaviorally anchored rating scales (BARS) method. The sample in Figure 8.4 is an abbreviated example of a BARS rating form that also provides space for another important component of performance management, goal setting. Appraisal forms such as this one take more time to develop, but provide a more accurate, informative assessment of performance. BARS scales are based on critical incidents of job performance as generated by supervisors or outstanding employees. These critical incidents are then grouped into common themes to develop the instrument. Each classification in the organization would have its own separate review form, allowing you to assess the employee on the actual job dimensions. In a restaurant you would have a review form applicable to your waitstaff, bus attendants, cooks, dishwashers, greeters, and another job categories you employ.

Once you have the proper forms, collect objective data about the employee's past performance. Summarize days absent, sales summaries, guest comment cards, and any other objective information that shows what the person has been doing during the past year. Make sure the employee has some advance notice of the meeting and has time to prepare also. Prior to the meeting, ask the employee to make a list of accomplishments and to briefly describe how the employer thinks he or she is doing in his current position. Also ask that he list some goals that he would like to achieve during the next year. Have the employee give you this information prior to the meeting so you have an idea of his perspective of his performance.

Next using your objective data and your general sense of how the employee is doing, complete a rough draft of the appraisal form. Be as honest as possible, realizing that you need to be fair, unprejudiced, and objective. Re-

Employee Name: _____   **Date:** _____

Position: _____   **Length of Service:** _____

Supervisor: _____   **Dept.:** _____

5 = Exceptional Performance   **2 = Improvement Needed**

4 = Very Good Performance   **1 = Unsatisfactory Performance**

3 = Average Performance

Job Dimension	Rating
Quality of Work: Accuracy, free of errors.	_____
Productivity: Ability to complete assignments on time.	_____
Attendance: Comes to work on time as scheduled.	_____
Work Habits: Neat, clean, orderly work area.	_____
Attitude: Interacts effectively with coworkers and managers.	_____
Service: Interacts effectively with guests.	_____
Empowerment: Able to solve problems independently.	_____
Grooming: Adheres to standards.	_____
Overall Rating:	_____

Comments: _____

_____

_____

_____

Employee's Signature: _____

Manager's Signature: _____

Figure 8.3 Generic Appraisal Form

member, employees really do want to know how they are doing. If there are areas of performance that need improvement, you are doing the employee a disservice if you do not make that person aware of them. As you write the review, base it on the following assumptions:

- People really do want to know how they are doing. They can't improve their performance unless they are aware of their shortcomings.
- It is better to have high expectations for employees than to set them too low.
- People tend to perceive feedback as more positive than it really is so don't be overly harsh, but don't sugarcoat your message either.
- Even the best employees have areas in which they could improve. Top performers are often the most open to hearing accurate feedback about how they can do even better.

Waitstaff Appraisal Form

Employee Name: _____   Date: _____

Dept.: _____   Length of Service: _____

Supervisor: _____

5 = Exceptional Performance   2 = Improvement Needed

4 = Very Good Performance   1 = Unsatisfactory Performance

3 = Average Performance

Performance	Rating

1. Provides **quick service** by taking guest orders within three
   minutes after they are seated.   _____
2. Provides **accurate service** by writing orders down and repeating
   them back to the customer.   _____
3. Provides **courteous service** by smiling, using the guests' names,
   and thanking them for their patronage.   _____
4. Practices **empowerment** by solving guest problems quickly and
   to their satisfaction.   _____
5. Demonstrates **reliability** by arriving at work on time as scheduled. _____
6. Is **flexible** and is available to work as needed.   _____
7. Practices **good work habits** by completing all side work.   _____
8. Keeps **work area neat** by practicing "clean as you go" principles. _____
9. Is **courteous and respectful** to other employees.   _____
10. Practices **teamwork** by helping others to more effectively serve
    guests.   _____
    Average Rating: Total Score divided by 10:   _____

Goal Setting

List goals that the server would like to achieve in the next six months:

1. _____

2. _____

3. _____

Employee's Signature: _____

Manager's Signature: _____

Figure 8.4 Behavioral Performance Appraisal

THE REVIEW SESSION

The actual appraisal interview will proceed much more smoothly if you
are well prepared. Schedule the meeting during a time when you will not be
busy with other duties. Create a relaxed atmosphere to reduce tension. Begin by
telling the employee the purpose of the annual review, and then briefly describe
the process you will follow. Next review the form with the employee. Give details
about the reasons for your assessment of each area of performance. Ask the em-

BEST PRACTICES

USING "CHECKRIDES" TO IMPROVE PERFORMANCE

Airforce pilots are given "checkrides" or tests twice each year to help them maintain important skills and recall little used but critical procedures. They keep pilots from falling into life-threatening bad habits. If pilots fail their checkrides, they can be grounded or forced to go through remedial training until they pass. A small, but growing number of companies are using "checkrides" to make sure their employees' skills are up to date.* The Ritz-Carlton Hotel Company uses a system like this to make sure that all their employees have been trained properly and have the same standards. New employees are certified within forty-five days of hire, and then tested annually so they keep their skills honed. Testing might include a written questionnaire or the demonstration of key skills. For example a telephone operator might have to call a customer while being monitored to make sure he or she is adhering to the standards of answering the phone by three rings and using one of twenty company-sanctioned greetings. A housekeeper might be asked what he or she would do if that individual noticed something spilled on the floor. Employees who have difficulty grasping required skills would be moved to another area.

Employees can also be certified as quality engineers after twenty-one days of employment. This means the worker understands the company's TQM philosophy and credo. To further reinforce standards, each hotel has a daily lineup where employees affirm their commitment to quality.

*J. McCune. "Testing, Testing 1-2-3." *Management Review* (January 1996): 50–53.

ployee for additional information about strengths and weaknesses. Make the review session a two-way conversation, not a lecture. Finally end the session with a discussion of goals for performance improvement and future development. This is also a great time to discuss the employee's career aspirations and to talk about opportunities within your company for advancement.

The appraisal interview may result in lots of new information, and you may need to make changes to your original form. If necessary rewrite the appraisal and ask that the employee stop back later to sign it. Give the employee a copy of the form and of course keep a copy in the personnel file. If several key areas of performance require improvement, schedule a coaching session with the employee in the near future—certainly don't wait until next year to follow up on these areas. The annual appraisal will never be an enjoyable event, but with proper planning it can become far less painful for both the supervisor and the employee.

An alternative, or an addition, to an employee appraisal system, is a certification program that requires employees to master a set of skills on which they are assessed and evaluated. Read more about this system in the "Best Practices" box.

360-DEGREE FEEDBACK

The latest trend in performance appraisal uses feedback from coworkers, customers, supervisors, and employees. It is an attempt to improve the process by providing more information than the traditional appraisal completed only by the individual's direct supervisor. It increases participation in the feedback process to include everyone who might have an opinion or information about the employee's work habits. When supervisors are reviewed, they not only receive feedback from their department managers, but also from their employees.

Here's how **360-degree feedback** works. Rating forms containing a series of questions about the job performance of the employee are distributed to the supervisor, coworkers, other department managers, regular customers, and even to the employee. Those being rated may have the opportunity to select those coworkers and customers who will participate. The information is then collected and summarized prior to the appraisal interview. Inappropriate comments may be filtered out at this time. A meeting is scheduled and proceeds much as the traditional appraisal interview.

Multiple reviews can make the supervisor's job easier and employee evaluations more useful. They can build a sense of teamwork and increase motivation when done properly.

DISCIPLINARY ACTION

Unfortunately not all poor performers respond to coaching efforts or appraisal. At times it becomes necessary to take disciplinary action when employees fail to improve their performance or do not follow company policy. Most managers find this to be one of the most unpleasant aspects of their job. Taking disciplinary action can be a particularly difficult step for the new supervisor who hopes to avoid being the "bad guy" at any cost. Yet it is a necessary part of the manager's job. Why is employee discipline so difficult? Here are some common reasons: are . . .

- Lack of knowledge or understanding of the process.
- Fear of causing a lawsuit.
- Don't want to hurt the employee's feelings.
- Not sure if it's really necessary—thinks maybe the problem will resolve itself.

No matter how difficult it may seem to write up or even fire an employee, not taking action when it is warranted can have a far-reaching negative effect on the entire department. The morale of other employees may plunge as they watch a coworker consistently abuse company policy or perform below standards with no response from management.[8] Ignoring poor performance can also have deleterious results for the employee in question. Employee performance may deteriorate so dramatically that termination is the only alternative. We also think of termination and turnover as negative, but there are some benefits to losing employees as described in Insight 8.3.

Employee discipline does not begin with the first infraction of company policy, but instead it begins before the new hire even starts working. Make sure that each new employee receives a copy of the job description and company policy manual before starting to work. Have the employee sign a statement that says that he or she has read the material, understands it, and agrees to abide by the rules set forth. Place this signed statement in the employee's personnel file. Also review the job description and company policy manual with the employee verbally. Make sure the new employee understands exactly what is expected. By doing this you have both communicated policy to the employee and gained written proof that the employee was aware of all rules and regulations.

INSIGHT 8.3

A POSITIVE SIDE TO TURNOVER

Most view turnover as a purely negative occurrence in the business world, but some are taking a new look at this phenomenon and seeing the silver lining.* Who wouldn't want to celebrate after a troublesome worker announces his resignation? Here are some of the benefits turnover can bring:

- Increased morale. When employees who are mean-spirited or negative leave, the remaining work group may experience a boost in morale.

- Eliminating Deadwood: When employees have their minds elsewhere and aren't really committed to your organization, they can be a drag on the department. Terminating the poor performer not only eliminates deadwood, it sends a message to all employees that performance is important.

- Creates Opportunities: When rungs on the career ladder are opened, this provides opportunities for employees to move up.

- Initiating Change: Even when great employees leave, there is always the advantage of bringing a new person with a fresh view of the operation. When employees stay in their job for too long, they stagnate. New people mean new ideas.

*R. McGarvey, "A Turn for the Better: Employee Turnover May Be Good for Your Business," *Entrepreneur* (March 1997): 81–83.

PROGRESSIVE DISCIPLINE

Before responding to an employee infraction, make sure that you know and understand your company's policies with regard to disciplinary action. Most companies follow a policy of **progressive discipline** that includes the following increasingly severe steps:

1. **Verbal Warning Notice:** This is written documentation of a conversation you have had with an employee regarding his performance. The **verbal warning** is not punitive and does not lead to termination. You might use this the first time an employee comes to work late or the first time the employee makes a fairly important error that results in a guest complaint.

2. **Written Warning Notice:** Written warnings are a more harsh action in response to an employee breaking an important company rule or making a severe error on the job. Most companies will terminate an employee if three written warning notices are issued within a year's time.

3. **Suspension:** Some companies suspend employees with or without pay for a period of one to three days following either a first or second written warning notice. The purpose of **suspension** is to require employees to think about their poor performance, and after such contemplation, come back to work more willing to follow policy or improve performance. Problems have arisen with both paid and unpaid

suspension. Many employees do not find a paid suspension punitive—some may even view a day or two off with pay as a reward. Companies who use the alternative of unpaid suspension may later find the disciplinary action was unwarranted and have to pay the employee for the time off.

4. **Termination:** If an employee breaks a very important company rule he or she might be fired immediately. Otherwise most companies require at least two to three written warnings before termination.

Before taking any disciplinary action against an employee, contact your human resources department or your manager to let them know your plans. Disciplinary action should be undertaken carefully to avoid such problems as claims of discrimination, grievance, arbitration, or even lawsuit.

IMPLEMENTING DISCIPLINARY ACTION

The primary goal of disciplinary action is not punish the employee, but to change the employee's behavior. Ideally it will be an ultimately positive experience for the employee that allows the employee to improve his or her performance in order to achieve career success. To make sure that both you and the employee find the experience as positive as possible, keep the following in mind when you take disciplinary action:

- **Immediate Response:** When employees fail to follow policy or perform poorly, respond quickly by taking corrective action. Waiting will only confuse the employee and reduce the effect of the disciplinary action.

- **Keep It Private:** All meetings and discussion of employee performance should be kept confidential. Do your best to keep other employees from finding out about the disciplinary action to avoid embarrassment for the employee. Never reprimand employees publicly for their shortcomings. You may lose the trust and respect not only of the employee who endures the public humiliation, but also of others who observe the incident.

- **Stay Calm:** Never discipline an employee when you are angry. First gain control of your emotions so you can be objective.

- **Listen:** Disciplinary meetings are discussions, not lectures. Unfortunately many managers dominate the meeting by doing all the talking. Instead get employees involved by not only asking for their side of the story, but also by getting their opinion about how to solve the problem.

- **Gain Commitment:** Before closing the session, ask the employee to summarize his or her understanding of what took place and agree to change the problematic behavior. You may want to get this commitment in writing by including it on the warning notice.

- **Follow-up:** Always meet with the employee in the near future (one to weeks later) to check progress. Schedule this meeting at the close of the disciplinary session so the employee knows you won't forget about the problem. In addition end your disciplinary session by letting the employee know what will happen in the future if the problem continues (either another written notice, suspension, or termination). This may include identifying possible actions to take if the problem is not resolved. The most effective disciplinary sessions end on a positive note. Let the employee know that you have confidence in his or her ability.

If you have done a good job in administering discipline and the employee in question is a reasonable person, he or she should leave the meeting believing that you are committed to helping the employee succeed.

POSITIVE DISCIPLINE

A new trend in management is **positive discipline** or discipline without punishment.[9] Instead of warning employees about the consequences of their actions, supervisors remind employees of the standards and ask for their agreement to solve the problem. For example an employee who is chronically tardy might be given a paid day off to reflect upon his or her employment and to decide if he or she is willing to commit to solving the problem permanently, often called a **decision leave.** Some employees take this action seriously and return with a new, better work attitude. But as you can imagine, some employees take advantage of their employers and enjoy the paid time off, but fail to make the desired behavioral changes. To circumvent this, many companies have changed to unpaid leave for disciplinary action.

So how does positive discipline differ from the old practice of suspension? It really doesn't in principle, but when using a more positive approach, most companies require employees to return with an assessment of their behavioral problem and a written commitment or contract describing how they will change. In one company the decisional leave is a timeout for the employee to reflect on specific questions relating to his or her job.[10] The employee must answer such questions as: How important is the job? What would happen if the job is lost? What is the employee willing to do in order to keep the job? The person is asked to come back with a written response, including specific commitments (buying an alarm clock, developing alternate car-pool arrangements, or switching shifts to accommodate child care needs). Often this is a last step in the disciplinary process. If the employee fails to live up to the written agreement, the employee will lose her job. Companies using this approach to positive discipline have had excellent results with the majority of employees solving their workplace problems.

CAREER DEVELOPMENT

Another component of managing employee performance is developing the careers of your employees. One of the best systems for reducing turnover and encouraging longterm employment is to provide workers with a game plan describing their future with your organization. In order to accomplish this, you must first begin by identifying the skills required by each position in your department or in your organization. Read more about developing job standards in Chapter 5. **Succession development,** a systematic method of identifying the required competencies for targeted positions, accomplishes this. Typically the human resources department initiates succession planning, but department involvement is necessary for its successful implementation. Below are the steps included in succession planning:[11]

1. **Job Profile.** Begin by identifying the competencies needed for successful performance in the job positions. Specify the knowledge, skills, and abilities employees must have to be successful servers, hosts, supervisors, and managers.

2. **Assessment.** Develop a system for assessing where employees currently stand. Create an assessment form that will identify readiness for promotion to manager or supervisor. It should be based on those competencies identified in the job profile.

3. **Analysis of Readiness.** After evaluating the readiness of department employees, managers and supervisors meet to identify those individuals who show strong potential for promotion in the future.

4. **Feedback.** Let the high-potential candidates for future management positions know that they are considered top-level employees. Create development plans for each person that identify the knowledge, skills, and abilities that they must develop prior to moving up.

5. **Evaluation.** Create a system to assess how well succession planning is working. Is the system encouraging employees to achieve their highest potential? Has the process reduced turnover and increased employee satisfaction?

MULTILAYERED JOB CATEGORIES

What about employees who cannot be promoted? Each department includes one or more employees who do not have the potential for promotion or who do not want to move up in the organization. How do you keep these employees happy and motivated in their current positions? One method of keeping good employees from leaving is to create **multilayered job categories.** If you have a great bell stand attendant who just doesn't have the potential for management, but still deserves extra recognition or responsibility, create both entry-level, midlevel, and top-level positions in the department. Top-level attendants may act as trainers or mentors to new employees, receive additional salary, and participate in special projects and committees. They are still line employees performing the basic job functions, but their elevated position may give them the recognition they need to be satisfied and motivated without career progression.

CONCLUSION

Performance management links goals setting, evaluation, employee development, and coaching with organizational effectiveness as defined by customer needs. Companies implement this system by collecting customer satisfaction data, setting employees' goals, and linking goals to pay. Coaching is a key component of a successful performance management system. Coaches possess skill in communication, negotiation, task management, problem solving, and self-management. It is important to focus on rewarding and encouraging excellent performance in addition to correcting poor performance. Coachable moments allow busy managers to provide encouragement in the context of ongoing work.

Many managers face performance review with dread, but by assuring that there are no surprises, getting employees involved, being objective, and separating reviews from pay decisions, the process is less daunting. Preparation for reviews involve completing the proper forms, collecting objective performance data, and identifying employee goals. Three-hundred-sixty-degree feedback is a multiple review process that provides additional information from supervisors, clients, and employees.

At times it becomes necessary to take disciplinary action when other measures fail. Employee discipline begins on the new hire's first day with the communication of expectations and company rules. Progressive discipline includes the increasingly severe steps of verbal warning, written warning, suspension, and termination. Suspension may be replaced with the positive disciplinary alternative of a decision leave or a nonpunitive opportunity for employees to consider their performance problems and commit to change.

Performance management also involves the fostering of employee career development. Succession planning identifies the competencies needed for target positions through job profile, assessment, analysis of readiness, feedback and evaluation. Multilayered job categories can help keep good employees who are ineligible or uninterested in promotion challenged

The successful management of employee performance can increase job satisfaction, reduce turnover, and improve guest service. Time and effort spent appraising, coaching, and disciplining employees can pay off in a more effective work force.

K E Y   T E R M S

Performance Management	Written Warning
Coaching	Suspension
Coachable Moments	Positive Discipline
Coaching with Respect	Decision Leave
360-Degree Feedback	Succession Development
Progressive Discipline	Multilayered Job Categories
Verbal Warning	

N   O   T   E   S

1. M. Yakovac, "Paying for Satisfaction," *HR Focus* (June 1996); 10–11.

2. M. Deblieux, "Encouraging Great Performance," *HR Focus* (January 1998): 13.

3. Ibid.

4. B. Kaye, "Career Development—Anytime, Anyplace," *Training & Development*, 47 no. 12 (December 1993): 46–50.

5. 1996 Gallup nationwide telephone survey of 1,000 adults age 18 or older who were employed full or part time; study by Marlin Co., a management consulting firm.

6. M. Darling, "Coaching People through Difficult Times," *HR Magazine* 39, no. 11 (November 1994): 70–73.

7. A. Liddle, "The Outback Way: More Training, Less Paperwork," *Nation's Restaurant News*, May 1, 1995, 11.

8. D. Day, "Help for Discipline Dodgers," *Training & Development* 47, no. 5 (May 1993): 19–23.

9. B. Paik Sunoo, "Positive Discipline—Sending the Right or Wrong Message?" *Personnel Journal* 75, no. 8 (August 1996): 109–111.

10. Ibid.

11. K. Nowack, "The Secrets of Succession," *Training & Development* 48, no. 11 (November 1994), 49–55.

CASE 8.1: RESPONDING TO POOR PERFORMANCE

Melissa has been experiencing some difficulties with Carol, one of the employees she supervises. Carol has been the lead desk clerk at the hotel for the past three years. Melissa has noticed that since she arrived on the job several months ago, Carol has been unfriendly and has refused to answer her questions about procedures. Carol admitted to Melissa that she had been hoping to be promoted into her job and was angry that someone from outside the company had been hired. Melissa has been concerned about how Carol would accept her as her supervisor. Melissa has noticed that several times Carol would be joking with other desk clerks, only to stalk off when she approached them. Melissa is convinced that Carol is trying to stir up resentment toward her in the other desk clerks.

Melissa noticed that although she is technically competent, Carol has some bad habits. She is often late for work and has had several guest complaints lodged against her for rudeness and lack of interest in solving their problems. Melissa went to Ms. Hernandez, the front office manager, to get advice on how she should proceed. Hernandez admitted that the previous supervisor had also had difficulties with Carol and suggested that she issue Carol a verbal warning notice next time she is tardy. Melissa pulled Carol's file and was amazed at what she found there. Not only was there a total absence of any past disciplinary action, but Carol's past performance reviews were all outstanding.

The next day, Carol was fifteen minutes late, so Melissa issued her a verbal warning notice. Although Carol became very angry when she heard about the disciplinary action, Melissa managed to keep her cool and calmly told her that if the problem continued, she would receive a written warning next.

Several weeks passed without incident. Although Carol was no longer tardy, she still displayed a very unpleasant attitude and was often impatient with guests. It was nearing the date for her next performance review, and Melissa would have to administer it. This was going to be a particularly difficult review because most of the documentation in Carol's file showed her to be an outstanding employee. Melissa felt that Carol was far from outstanding in her performance since she had arrived, but didn't know how to rate her. She felt that Carol deserved a poor rating, but on the other hand, it might be too extremely low in light of her previous evaluations. Melissa comes to you for some much-needed advice on this one.

1. What mistakes did previous management make in disciplining Carol?

2. How can Melissa now correct the situation?

3. What type of rating do you think that Melissa should give Carol?

4. Is there any way that Melissa can repair her relationship with Carol?

R E V I E W   Q U E S T I O N S

1. What are the key components of performance management?
2. How does performance management reduce turnover?
3. What two powerful management tools are combined in performance management?
4. What are the two important components of coaching employee performance?
5. What are several ways that you might encourage a top employee to keep up the good work?
6. Why aren't generic appraisal forms very effective? Why would a BARS form be a more accurate tool for appraising performance?
7. List the steps you would follow in preparing to review an employee.
8. Put the following steps in progressive discipline in the proper order from least to most severe: termination, written warning, suspension, verbal warning.
9. What is positive discipline and how does it differ from progressive discipline?

C R I T I C A L   T H I N K I N G   E X E R C I S E S

1. As a supervisor, how might you take advantage of the following coachable moments? Specifically what would you say and do to respond to the following cues from your employees?
   a. A room attendant tells you that she has decided to complete her associate degree at an area community college and major in hospitality management.
   b. A new cook asks if you are happy with his performance so far.

   c. You overhear employees complaining about the new scheduling system.

   d. A front desk clerk tells you that she is interested in becoming a concierge one day.

2. What do you think causes violence in the workplace? What might you do as a supervisor to prevent it?

3. If you were an employee, specifically, what would you want your supervisor to say and do during your performance appraisal? Why are these particular things important to you?

4. Identify a position in the hospitality industry (other than a restaurant server) that you are very familiar with. List ten actual performance behaviors like those in Figure 8.3 that might be included in a BARS rating scale.

5. If you were a department supervisor, would you like to be appraised using 360-degree feedback? Why or why not?

6. What difficulties do you have or anticipate having with regard to taking disciplinary action against an employee? How might you overcome your concerns?

Indicate which disciplinary action should be taken in the following situations:

   a. verbal warning   b. written warning   c. termination

7. A new employee is fifteen minutes late for work.

8. A long-term employee is caught stealing a box of steaks.

9. A manager is seen sexually harassing an employee.

10. An employee leaves his workplace for thirty minutes without permission.

11. An employee fails to come to work or call for one day.

O N - L I N E   L I N K

A rather new occupation that has grown in recent years is a professional career coach. These are individuals who meet with clients to help them with issues that affect their work. They provide individual attention, using many of the coaching skills described in your chapter. One of the first organizations to provide training and certification of coaches is Coach University. Visit their web site at www.coachuniversity.com to find out more about professional coaching skills. The site allows you to download articles on coaching, provides answers to questions, has a chat room, and will even let you sit in on a coaching telecourse. Explore the "free of charge" options on the site and write several paragraphs describing what you saw and learned while there.

P O R T F O L I O   E X E R C I S E

Act as your own career development coach and develop a succession plan for yourself. First identify a management position you would like to hold in the next few years. Next create a job profile by identifying the competencies needed for successful performance. Specifically describe the knowledge, skills, and abilities a person in that job would need. Then assess where you currently stand—how ready are you for the position? Finally describe those proficiencies you must develop in order to be considered "ready" for the job. What must you learn? What skills must you develop?

Later, when you're ready to apply for the job you just described, use this succession plan to create a summary statement of your qualifications. A summary statement is a brief (one page) document that tells the employer about your particular qualifications and specifically matches your abilities to the position requirements. You might include your education, specific past experiences, and the skills and competencies you have developed matching them to the published job requirements.

Protecting Employee Rights

9

ADVANCED ORGANIZER

It is easy to forget that not long ago life on the job was very different from today. In the early 1960s, pregnant women were expected to quit work when their condition became obvious and certainly couldn't return after the baby was born. Men earned much more than women because they were supporting families, African Americans were denied all but the most menial employment, and sexual harassment was just part of the job.

Our country has made great progress in the arena of employee rights. It is now illegal to discriminate against employees in hiring, promotion, termination, or treatment on the job. This isn't to say that all forms of unfair practice have been eliminated. In fact, litigation regarding employment practices is at an all time high. Most claims of discrimination are directed toward a particular manager or supervisor. To avoid costly legal battles, leaders must view fair labor practices in a positive manner by focusing on protecting the rights of their employees.

BEHAVIORAL OBJECTIVES

- Identify the various laws that protect the rights of employees.

- Describe ways to minimize legal risk by guarding against discriminatory practice.

- Demonstrate understanding of those behaviors that denote sexual harassment.

- Differentiate between acceptable and unacceptable preemployment inquiries.

- Describe the steps that must be taken to ensure termination for just cause.

- Apply the principles of employment law in decision making.

The Mansion on Turtle Creek, Exterior

AVOIDING LEGAL PITFALLS

Today's legal environment has a tremendous effect on how managers deal with employees. Years ago, the law always favored the company when employee disputes arose. Employers could hire and fire workers at whim, with little fear of legal reprisal. They could choose to hire only males for management positions. If they preferred, hotels could make sure that all their bell staff attendants were white, and all their door attendants were black. They could refuse to hire overweight cocktail servers or even fire a female employee if she refused sexual advances. Not so today. Unfair practices like these are forbidden by our legal system. Both the supervisors and the company as a whole must protect employee rights in the workplace. No company is immune to this necessity. Even small, family owned businesses that are exempt from federal guidelines with regard to legal practices might still be covered by state mandates. If state and federal laws differ, the law that takes precedence is that which is strictest. No one should assume that they are exempt from laws regarding fair practices in the workplace. Read about some of the legal difficulties hospitality companies have cause themselves through unfair labor practices in Figure 9.1. So how do you avoid legal pitfalls in your job as a supervisor? Make the protection of employee rights a priority in your department and in your organization.

Please keep in mind that the information presented in this chapter and in the remainder of the text does not represent legal advice of any kind, but is meant to simply provide details on various topics. If you have concerns about legal issues in the workplace, please contact an attorney, preferably one who specializes in labor law or employee rights.

Reverse Gender Discrimination
Hooters was sued by a man who accused the chain of sex discrimination for hiring only women to wait on tables. The claimant had previous experience as a waiter but was not hired by the company, resulting in a class-action lawsuit because males who have applied at Hooters throughout the country have been denied jobs.*

Inappropriate Use of the Number "8"
A hotel chain agreed to pay $1 million to hundreds of African-American job seekers after accusations that company managers used a racial coding system on job applications.[†] The suit claimed that the independently owned franchise marked instructed employees to mark the number 8 on applications filed by African-Americans for front desk and customer service jobs at the hotel. None of those 300 applicants were hired. The people who were unknowinly affected by the coding system will share the $1 million. The hotel will give hiring preference to those in the lawsuit, and managers will undergo recruitment training.

Whistle Blower Gets Fired
A white nightclub manager filed a discrimination suit saying he was fired from his job because club owners learned that he objected to their allegedly discriminatory policies.[‡] The manager said he was told to tear up employment applications from minorities and to make sure that minority attendance at the club did not get too large. According to his attorney, it is against the law to require an employee to engage in

---

Figure 9.1 Cases in the Hospitality Industry

racially discriminatory acts, and it is also unlawful to fire an employee in retaliation for objecting to a racially hostile work environment.

Religious Expression

The EEOC filed suit against an airport food court concession alleging that the company refused to hire an Islamic teenager because of a headscarf that she wore due to her religious beliefs.[§] The girl was hired, went to orientation, and was then told by another employee that the manager was having second thoughts about her working there. The supervisor told her the scarf does not go with the uniform.

In another case the Houston office of the EEOC filed a complaint on behalf of an employee who wanted to wear dresses or skirts to work rather than trousers as part of her uniform in order to comply with her religious beliefs. The commission claimed that the employee was not allowed to assume her job as cashier when the company learned that her membership in the United Pentecostal Church prevented her from wearing the trouser uniform. The EEOC attorney said the commission is pressing the civil complaint, "because companies have a legal obligation to adapt their employment practices to accommodate employees' religious observance, practice and belief."[||]

Antigay Discrimination

The Cook County Human Rights Commission ordered a restaurant chain to rehire a gay employee and pay him $45,000 in back pay and $50,000 in damages.[#] The waiter was harassed by his manager, who publicly announced that he planned to get rid of him. Later the waiter was fired for "creating a hostile work environment." This finding occurred in Cook County, located in Chicago, the only county in Illinois with an ordinance that outlaws antigay discrimination. In other counties employees can lose their jobs solely for being gay, without legal recourse.

[*]"Bias Alleged at Hooters Against Men" *Chicago Tribune*, Chicagoland, December 24, 1993, p. 3.

[†]"Oak Lawn Hotel Settles Bias Suit for $1 Million," *Chicago Tribune*, Metro Northwest, Sunday, May 31, 1998, 2.

[‡]J. Hanna, "Fired Manager Sues Club Over Bias," *Chicago Tribune*, Metro Du Page, Friday, April 3, 1998, 2.

[§]A. Pallasch, "Midway Food Company Sued by EEOC for Religious Bias," *Chicago Tribune*, Metro Chicago, August 5, 1998, 6.

[||]R. Ruggless, "EEOC Charges Whataburger Franchisee with Civil-Rights Violations." *Nation's Restaurant News*, October 12, 1998, 26.

[#]Editorial, "Anti-gay Bias Has No Place in Illinois," *Chicago Tribune*, Chicagoland North, September 12, 1998, 22.

Figure 9.1 Cases in the Hospitality Industry (*continued*)

EVOLUTION OF LABOR LAW

Laws that make discrimination illegal have been on the books for more than 100 years, but were not enforced until the early 1960s when the first of a series of legislation was passed to protect the rights of employees. These laws were designed to address the history of discriminatory practices aimed at women, minorities, older workers, the disabled, and Vietnam veterans. Let's examine each law in detail.

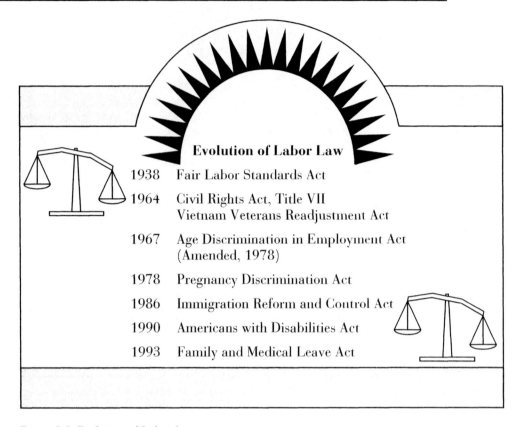

Evolution of Labor Law

1938	Fair Labor Standards Act
1964	Civil Rights Act, Title VII Vietnam Veterans Readjustment Act
1967	Age Discrimination in Employment Act (Amended, 1978)
1978	Pregnancy Discrimination Act
1986	Immigration Reform and Control Act
1990	Americans with Disabilities Act
1993	Family and Medical Leave Act

Figure 9.2 Evolution of Labor Law

TITLE VII OF THE CIVIL RIGHTS ACT

In 1964 Congress amended the **Civil Rights Act under Title VII** and outlawed discrimination based on race, color, religion, and national origin. This law applies to private employers, employment agencies, labor organizations, and training programs. In addition each state has its own discrimination laws, which further protect the rights of employees. This single act is credited with initiating the drive toward equality in the workplace that is still ongoing today.

EEOC

The **Equal Employment Opportunity Commission** (EEOC) was charged with the task of enforcing Title VII. The EEOC consists of five members appointed by the president of the United States. This commission investigates claims of unfair treatment by workers. If just cause is found, the EEOC first tries to bring about reconciliation between the employee and employer. If this is not possible, the commission will go directly to the court system to enforce Title VII.[1]

AGE DISCRIMINATION ACT

The **Age Discrimination in Employment Act** was passed in 1967 and amended in 1978. It is administered by the EEOC. This act makes it unlawful to discriminate against employees or applicants between forty and seventy years of age in hiring, recruiting, appraisal, and promotion. Employers cannot refuse to hire or promote someone because they think they are too old to do the work. They cannot force older employees to take early retirement if they do not want to do so. Due to the increasing age of our workforce, this act will become very important in the near future. Law with regard to older workers prohibits the following actions:

- Denying an older applicant a job because of age,
- Forcing retirement before age seventy.
- Denying promotions because of age.

VETERANS REEMPLOYMENT ACT

The **Veterans Reemployment Act** of 1942 requires employers to rehire veterans who leave a job for military service with no loss of seniority.

IMMIGRATION REFORM AND CONTROL ACT OF 1986

The **Immigration Reform and Control Act** of 1986 prohibits employers from discriminating against applicants on the basis of citizenship or nationality. The act also requires employers to verify the employment status of their

INSIGHT 9.1

THE PLIGHT OF THE HISPANIC WORKER

There has been a significant increase in the number of Hispanic workers in the hospitality industry during the last decade. By the end of 1998, 16 percent, nearly 1.1 million of the total workers holding restaurant jobs, were of Hispanic origin. Although they still dominate entry-level positions, Hispanics are increasingly more evident as business owners, corporate executives, general managers, and chefs in today's restaurants.

Yet not all Hispanics have positive experiences in our industry. Union officials believe that this cultural group is being abused because of their language limitations and unfamiliarity with labor law. A former Manhattan chef described immigrants as "nothing but a new generation of indentured servant—overworked, underpaid, fearful of the law, and just a snap away from being fired." In response Local 100 in New York has instigated lawsuits on behalf of Hispanic employees for company wage and hour violations.

While some unethical restaurant owners pay immigrant employees less than minimum wage and do not provide any benefits, others value their Hispanic workers. New York Restaurant operator Seven Hanson pays his Hispanic workers top dollar and promotes them to executive-level positions. Carol Greenwood, chef-owner of a successful Washington, D.C., restaurant pays her Hispanic employees better than the market average because she knows that if they want to stay with her, she must treat them properly.

workers. This means that employers must complete and retain an **Employment Eligibility Verification Form** or I-9 for each person employed or hired to demonstrate that this person is authorized to work in the United States. Applicants must provide employers with documents that demonstrate their identity such as a U.S. Passport, Certificate of Citizenship, or Temporary Resident Card, along with documentation of employment eligibility in the form of a U.S. social security card, birth certificate, or unexpired employment authorization from the INS. Employers then sign the I-9 form no later than three days after hiring a new employee and must keep it on file for three years following the date of hire or one year after the employee leaves, whichever is longer.[2] The Immigration and Naturalization Service is very strict about enforcing their laws regarding illegal aliens. In the hospitality industry, you will often hear stories about INS inspections that lead to the loss of entire departments staffed by illegal aliens along with costly fines. All department managers must make sure their organization hires only applicants who have the right to work in this country.

Some unethical companies take advantage of immigrants' fear of the law and fail to pay them a fair wage or provide appropriate benefits. Read more about the plight of the Hispanic worker in our industry in Insight 9.1.

PREGNANCY DISCRIMINATION ACT

The **Pregnancy Discrimination Act** was passed in 1978 as an amendment to the Civil Rights Act of 1964, Title VII. The act prohibits discrimination in hiring, promotion, suspension, discharge, or any other term or condition of employment based on pregnancy, childbirth, or related medical conditions. The act says that pregnancy and childbirth must be treated like any other disability.[3] If your company protects the jobs of those who have heart attacks, broken legs, or other illnesses, they must offer the same protection to those who are pregnant. Here are a few guidelines with regard to pregnant workers:

- Employers must provide pregnant workers with paid leave for the time they are disabled due to pregnancy and childbirth if paid leave is given to employees for illnesses or other disabilities.
- If unpaid leave is given to pregnant women, it must also be given to fathers and to those who adopt.
- You cannot refuse to hire or promote an applicant because she is pregnant.

FAMILY AND MEDICAL LEAVE ACT OF 1993

The **Family and Medical Leave Act** went into effect in 1993 and entitles employees to up to twelve weeks of leave per year for childbirth, adoption, foster placement, or to care for a child, spouse, or parent with a serious health condition.[4] It also allows employees time off if they have a serious health condition. The employee must also be reinstated to the position held before the leave or to an equivalent position. Employees who have worked for a company for twelve months and for at least 1,250 hours are eligible if their company has more than fifty employees.

AMERICANS WITH DISABILITIES ACT

In 1990 the **Americans with Disabilities Act** (ADA) was passed to prohibit employment discrimination against qualified individuals with disabilities. Employers must base their hiring and promotion decisions only on the applicant's ability to do the job, not on their disability. A disabled person protected under this law:[5]

1. Has a physical or mental impairment that substantially limits one or more major life activities. There is no specific list of impairments, but the ADA includes examples of people with AIDS, HIV, alcoholism, cancer, cerebral palsy, diabetes, emotional illness, epilepsy, hearing and speech disorders, heart disease, dyslexia, metal retardation, muscular dystrophy, and visual impairments.
2. Has a record of impairment. This refers to someone who was disabled or ill in the past, for example, someone who had cancer or back injuries.
3. Is regarded as having impairment. This includes people who are viewed by others as disabled although they may have no actual impairment. For example burn victims or those with severe scarring may create an impression of disability.

Under the governance of the ADA, employers must:[6]

- Eliminate questions designed to identify an applicant's disabilities.
- Make reasonable accommodations to known physical or mental limitations of an applicant or employee as long as doing so does not impose undue hardship on the employer.
- Not deny employment to the disabled because it requires reasonable accommodation.
- Avoid employment tests or physical screening that might rule out the disabled unless the criteria can be shown to be job related and supports business necessity.

FAIR LABOR STANDARDS ACT OF 1938

The **Fair Labor Standards Act** was passed in 1938 and requires that employers pay employees at least minimum wage and pay overtime to employees who work more than forty hours in one week at the rate of at least one and one-half times their regular pay. The regulation of wages in the hospitality industry is rather complex due to tipped income and exempt employees. An exemption to the minimum wage requirement applies to employees who routinely receive at least $30 per month in tips on the job. Employers can credit a percentage of tips against the hourly minimum wage requirement. As of September 1, 1997, up to 59 percent of wages can be replaced by tips, allowing restaurants and hotels to pay servers $2.13 per hour rather than $5.15 per hour, or minimum wage. In this case, the server must receive at least $3.92 per hour in tips. Laws regarding tipped income differ by state, so check with your local government.

A second area of concern with regard to wages is exemption of overtime. Employers may seek to avoid paying overtime to employees by making them salaried. To be **exempt from overtime,** the employee must be managing the business, must regularly direct the work of two or more employees, and be paid a salary of at least $250 per week or have the authority to hire, fire, or promote and be paid a salary of at least $155 per week.[7] Therefore you can't call a cook a food production manager and pay that person a salary to avoid overtime if a cook's job duties are performed.

MINIMIZE LEGAL RISKS

As a manager you represent your company to your employees. Most litigation results from interactions employees have with their supervisors. Two of today's hottest litigation topics are age discrimination, accounting for 20 percent of court actions filed by EEOC,[8] and **sexual harassment,** accounting for another 30 percent of court action.[9] In some cases employees not only sue their company, they also sue their individual managers, particularly in cases of sexual harassment. Litigation is not only time-consuming—you must spend countless hours in court and talking to lawyers—it can also be debilitating to your career. Having a lawsuit filed against you can certainly put your career on hold. Fortunately it is not difficult to avoid threats of legal action from disgruntled employees. You must be aware of employment law and let employees know that protecting their rights is a priority to you and that you will do everything you can to make sure they are treated fairly. Review the information below about specific types of discrimination you must guard against as a manager.

GENDER-BASED DISCRIMINATION

The law requires that men and women be treated equally with regard to employment policies, standards and practices in areas of hiring, placement, job promotion, working conditions, wages, benefits, layoff, and termination. Here are some illegal practices with regard to gender:

- Refusing to hire women who have young children.
- Restricting some jobs to men or other jobs to women.
- Denying a leave of absence to a pregnant woman.
- Harassing a pregnant woman so she will not return after her child is born.
- Paying men more for the same work.
- Failing to promote qualified women to top positions in the organization.

PERFORMANCE EVALUATION

The performance evaluation process can be a land mine of liability. Managers need to be cautious when assessing employee performance. When writing the evaluation, be careful not to include comments that might be discriminatory—those referring to a person's race, religion, age, gender, national origin, or physical appearance. Simply saying something as seemingly benign as "Mary needs to improve her appearance," could lead to charges if it is obvious that you are referring to Mary's weight problem. The same principles apply to face-to-face appraisal meetings. Never say anything that you wouldn't be comfortable putting in writing. Also make sure that employees see and sign all evaluations that are placed in their file. Never place information about employee performance in the file without the employee knowing about it. Unsigned evaluations or warning notices are of no use if legal action occurs.

DRUG TESTING

Although controversial, **drug testing** in the workplace is becoming increasingly prevalent. This practice does appear to be effective. A study showed a drastic drop in positive results during the past decade. In 1987, 18 percent of those tested showed positive drug use whereas in 1997 only 5 percent of 5 million employment-related tests were positive.[10] Drug testing is becoming more prevalent in organizations, and this trend is expected to continue. To reduce the risk of litigation with regard to drug testing:

1. Begin by having a specific policy prohibiting the use, possession, sale, or transfer of illegal drugs in your workplace.
2. If the hiring decision is based on a negative drug test, state this on the application.
3. Realize that drug testing of a single employee due to suspicion of drug use is risky. You might be challenged based on invasion of privacy.
4. Remember that action cannot be taken if legal drugs such as prescribed antidepressants or tranquilizers are found.
5. Review your state's laws. Some states require employers to provide unpaid time off for rehab if drugs are found.

RELIGIOUS DISCRIMINATION

Most businesses in the hospitality industry must operate seven days per week, often even twenty-four hours per day. This schedule has created the potential for claims of religious discrimination. Under Title VII of the Civil Rights Act, employers must make reasonable efforts to accommodate employees' religious needs unless it causes undue hardship. This means that if at all possible, you must give employees time off for religious observance on a weekly basis and also on special holidays. Make it clear to your employees that all reasonable effort will be made to accommodate employees' religious practices, but that helping the company achieve its objectives during business hours should be the employees' primary concern.[11]

APPEARANCE

Companies have the right to expect their employees to adhere to attire and grooming standards that are appropriate for business and that meet safety and health requirements. But some efforts to enforce appearance standards have resulted in claims of discrimination based on gender, race, religion, culture, or disability. Here are just a few recent situations that have occurred with regard to appearance standards:

- A manager who terminated a restaurant employee who was missing several teeth rather than reassign this person was sued for violations of the ADA.[12] The manager justified this action by saying that the company required that customer contact employees smile and that this person failed to portray a professional image with regard to this standard. The courts ruled against the manager in this case.

- The EEOC brought suit against a company for religious discrimination when they refused to allow Muslim employees to wear headdresses as part of their religious observance.[13] A decision has not yet been made in this case. In another case a Muslim employee was fired for wearing a knit cap and not keeping his shirt tucked in, both requirements of his religion. This employee was reinstated and given back pay.

A repeated topic of legal action in the hospitality industry has been the requirement that employees wear suggestive or provocative attire. Court rulings have consistently supported employee's rights to refuse to wear skimpy uniforms that can cause sexual harassment from customers and other employees. Most companies have done away with revealing costumes for cocktail servers and other staff, preferring to focus on quality of service instead.

SEXUAL HARASSMENT

Lawsuits based on sexual harassment are increasing in frequency. According to the EEOC, Americans filed 15,889 sexual harassment grievances in 1997, compared with 10,532 in 1992. Most people realize that inappropriate touching denotes sexual harassment as do **quid pro quo situations,** where requests for sexual favors are made in return for promotions, hiring, or pay increases. Less obvious forms of sexual harassment also include **hostile work environments** that are brought about by sexual jokes, suggestive comments, hugging, pinching, back rubs, sexually suggestive pictures or objects, and obscene gestures. Even if conduct isn't obviously sexual in nature, it can still be considered sexual harassment if it is offensive and aimed at someone because of his or her gender.[14] We had a manager who repeatedly asked his secretary to rub his feet. This was a case of covert or less obvious sexual harassment because the request was demeaning to the employee and dealt with unwanted physical contact.

How can you protect yourself and your company against sexual harassment claims? Begin by establishing a **sexual harassment policy** that includes:[15]

1. A clear statement that sexual harassment is unlawful, against company policy, and if violation of policy occurs, discipline and possibly discharge will result.
2. A statement that no one has the right to sexually harass any other employee and that everyone within the com-

BEST PRACTICES

Training for employees and managers in the prevention of sexual harassment has become more important than ever. The Supreme Court has outlined a path for employers to follow to avoid liability for sexual harassment, suggesting that they conduct training to ensure that supervisors and employees are aware of the harassment prevention program and know how to complain if they believe they are victims.* This makes sexual harassment awareness training vital for employees at every level of the organization.

*C. Kleinman, "Companies Dragging Feet on Training," *Chicago Tribune*, Jobs, September 20, 1998, 1.

pany must adhere to policy regarding this from the CEO on down.

3. Letting all employees and managers know what behaviors constitute sexual harassment. This should be communicated in writing, in employee handbooks, and also in training programs. See Best Practices for a Supreme Court ruling with regard to sexual harassment prevention training.

4. Assurance that all complaints will be investigated confidentially and without retaliation.

HANDLING SEXUAL HARASSMENT COMPLAINTS

Big problems occur for both managers and organizations when complaints of sexual harassment are either ignored or not taken seriously. A manager might simply chuckle if a secretary files a claim against a supervisor who requests a foot massage, but this is a valid claim and should be treated with the same seriousness as more overt cases. No matter how minor the complaint, investigate it thoroughly and promptly. Below are some steps to follow when a complaint is received.

1. Let the person know that the claim will be taken seriously and investigated thoroughly.

2. Notify human resources or your legal department immediately and follow any company guidelines with regard to handling sexual harassment complaints.

3. Offer to reschedule or reassign the complainant so he or she won't have continued contact with the allege harasser. Be sure not to force a change on the person claiming harassment. Instead, leave the decision to him or her.

4. Obtain a detailed report from the persons making the claim. Ask if other employees either witnessed the harassment or had similar experiences. Ask for any supporting evidence at this time such as notes or pictures.

5. Separately interview witnesses asking for details of the incidents.

6. Meet with the alleged harasser and explain the claim. Get this person's story regarding each incident. Once again ask for the names of witnesses that might support his or her position.

7. If it is obvious that the harassment claim was valid, take disciplinary action based on the severity of the situation, including written warning notice, suspension, or even immediate discharge. If you cannot decide with reasonable certainty that harassment occurred, avoid disciplinary action at this time and instead counsel the person accused and remind him or her that disciplinary action will be taken in the future if questionable conduct occurs.

8. Document in writing all the steps involved in the investigation and what action was taken as a result. This will provide some protection if a lawsuit occurs in the future.

Managers and supervisors get into big trouble with regard to sexual harassment claims when they ignore them and just hope that they will disappear. This is one employee problem that doesn't solve itself with time. Be prepared to show that you have taken all claims seriously and responded promptly and appropriately.

EMPLOYMENT APPLICATIONS

The hiring process is particularly vulnerable to legal action. The decision to hire someone is often based on subjective feelings, which may result in discriminatory action. Hiring a particular person because that person has a neat appearance, a good work record, and a pleasant personality seems safe, but if you only find these characteristics among your white applicants, you may be discriminating against people of color. Remember, your new hires should racially and ethnically represent your applicant pool.

Perhaps the most vulnerable part of the selection process is the application because all information is in writing and is easy to verify. If you have discriminatory questions on your application, they are obvious for all to see, and it will be easy to support in court. Here are some ways to protect yourself against discrimination claims stemming from your job application:[16]

- Include a statement on your application that says than any applicant who provides information not requested will be rejected. This is necessary because applicants may include potentially discriminatory information about themselves like height, weight, religion, or number of children and could later claim they were rejected because of it.
- Include instructions for disabled applicants stating how they can request accommodation if needed to complete the application.
- Include an equal employment opportunity statement in the instructions.
- Make sure all questions are recognized as lawful by the EEOC. Be prepared to show that all questions are related to the applicant's potential to perform the job. Avoid all questions relating to race, religion, gender, national origin, citizenship, arrest records, finances, military record, disability, or union affiliation.

PREEMPLOYMENT INQUIRIES

Financial Information   It is unlawful to ask if someone has filed for bankruptcy or if they have ever been arrested. You can't ask if they own a car unless it is required for the job (i.e., pizza delivery in their own car). You also can't ask if they own a house or make inquiry about their credit history.

Criminal History   You can ask about job-related criminal convictions and can reject an applicant due to criminal conviction if the offense is of a grave nature, the crime was recent, and it relates to the job under consideration.

Women   Because women are primarily responsible for child care, you must be careful in exploring this area during the interview process. Here are some unlawful preemployment questions that might discriminate against women:

- Are you pregnant?
- Do you have children?
- Are you planning to have children?
- Are you married?
- Do you have reliable child care?
- What will you do if your children are sick?

Disabled   The ADA prohibits both questions about disability and questions that might lead to information about an applicant's disability. Avoid questions about workers' compensation claims, days absent in the past due to illness, or health problems. Instead ask, "Can you meet the attendance requirements of this job?"

You must also avoid questions about height and weight because this could reveal obesity, which is a medical condition protected by the ADA.

Employees Taking Medication   Is an employee who controls a condition with medication protected under the ADA? The answer to this question is maybe. Some federal circuit courts are saying yes, and some are saying no.[17] Some are saying that they will determine that a condition is a disability by considering it in its unmedicated state. A diabetic would be disabled even if he could control his condition with medication. The same would hold true for someone with a mental illness like depression that is controlled with medication. Until the Supreme Court makes a final decision on this issue, employers should play it safe by considering employee's conditions in their unmedicated state when deciding if they require special accommodation under the ADA.

Age   Do not ask questions that directly or indirectly address age. Avoid questions that ask for the year of graduation from high school. Under federal guidelines, employers can only ask the applicant if he or she is over the age of eighteen. If the employee says "yes," that's all that can be asked. If the employee says "no," then it's legal to ask the person's age.

Other Sensitive Topics   Many companies want to avoid hiring smokers because they seem to take more breaks and may have more health problems than nonsmokers, but you can't even ask if the applicant is a smoker on a job application or during an interview. Also avoid questions about social clubs as this might relate to their race or religion. It is okay to ask if the applicant served in the military, but avoid questions about type of discharge.

Certification of Information End your application with a statement saying that the individual certifies that the information provided is correct. Make sure the applicant signs his or her name below this statement, confirming the accuracy of the information provided. Also warn applicants in writing that misstatements or omissions could result in disqualification from the interview process or termination if hired. Later, if you find the applicant has lied about information on the application, you have legal grounds to refuse to hire the person or even to discharge the person if the falsification is discovered after employment begins. This occurred several times in companies I worked for with regard to felony convictions. When it was later discovered that new employees had prior felony records but failed to note this on the application, they were then discharged, not for their felony conviction, but for falsification of company documents.

Also be very careful if unusually overqualified applicants apply for positions in your organization. Once I had a middle-aged male attorney apply for a receptionist position in a hotel where I worked. He was obviously overqualified for the position due to his professional status, and I strongly suspected that he was hoping I would tell him this so he might then file a lawsuit against us. I interviewed him and gave him the required typing test, and fortunately was able to disqualify him because he could only type thirty words per minute, not the required fifty words per minute. Typing ability was a bona fide occupational qualification and a legitimate reason to disqualify an applicant.

WHAT CAN YOU ASK?

It might seem like there is little that you can actually ask an applicant during the interview process. All the questions that used to be acceptable are now risky. So how do you find out if someone is qualified to work in your department or company? The answer is simple. Make sure that all questions are related to job performance or are based on bona fide occupational qualifications. Review the information in Chapter 5 relating to selection. Be sure to develop an accurate job description and base your pre-employment questions on this. It is okay to ask applicants about past job experiences, what type of supervisor they prefer, and how they got along with their coworkers. There is lots of valuable information to be gained both from the job application and the interview. Just remember that your goal is to hire the most qualified person for the job. Keep this in mind and ignore other factors such as gender, race, age, and disability, and you should be able to make a fair hiring decision.

TERMINATING EMPLOYEES FAIRLY

In the past decisions regarding termination were based on **employment at will** principles. Employers hire workers at will and are free to fire them at any time with or without cause and with or without notice. Until the 1960s employers could terminate employees for any reason whenever they wanted to. Since then many laws have been passed that protect employee rights in the workplace, as you know from your readings in the first part of this chapter. Yet many employers may still try to enforce an employment at will contract and feel that they have the right to fire employees without cause. This often leads to grievances or even legal action by employees who feel that their rights have been violated. Remember, you can't fire an employee because of:

- Age.
- Religion, gender, or nation origin.
- Disability.
- Reporting of illegal activity.
- A filed worker's compensation claim.

Be just as careful in your decisions regarding termination as you are in decisions regarding hiring.

The first question to ask yourself when you consider firing an employee is, "Do I have a legal basis for terminating this employee?" Remember, Title VII of the Civil Rights Act as amended by the Equal Employment Opportunity Act of 1972 states that employers cannot fire workers based on personal characteristics of sex, age, race, color, religion, national origin, nondisqualifying physical handicaps, or mental impairments unrelated to job qualifications. The law also protects reprisals against workers who exercise their First Amendment rights. If an employee loses his or her job because of speaking out against unsafe working conditions or because of a refusal to take a lie detector test, the employee may have grounds for a lawsuit.[18] Here are some other risky reasons to fire an employee:

- Because his wages have been garnished.
- So she can't receive her pension.
- Because he wants to organize a union.
- For missing work due to jury duty or performing other public duties.
- For refusing to commit an act that is illegal.

So what are valid reasons for terminating employees?

- Theft.
- Falsifying company records.
- Punching another employee's time card.
- Leaving the job without approval.
- Failure to follow company work rules.
- Fighting or unprovoked assault.
- Working under the influence of drugs or alcohol or using or possessing drugs or alcohol on the premises.
- Possession of weapons on company property.
- Excessive tardiness.
- Unreported absences.
- Sexual harassment of other employees.

To protect yourself and your company when termination occurs, always inform employees of company rules and regulations upon hiring. Be sure to identify serious offenses that lead to immediate termination such as fighting, theft, or drug and alcohol use. Have the employees sign a receipt stating that they understand the rules and will follow them. Be sure to place this receipt in each file. When infractions of company policy occur, take immediate disciplinary action as outline in Chapter 8. Lesser infractions such as tardiness, unreported absence, or leaving the workplace usually warrant a verbal or written warning notice. Most companies terminate employees for three violations of minor rules such as these within a year's time and terminate employees immediately for serious infractions of policy.

Make sure your terminations are air tight and legal by:

- Consulting human resources or an attorney before terminating an employee.
- Giving employees fair warning of infractions of policy so they have a chance to change their behavior.
- Showing employees all warning notices and performance reviews and asking for their signature. If the employee refuses to sign documents, have another manager witness them, stating that the employee saw the documents in his or her presence.
- Treating all employees the same with regard to discipline. If your best and worst employees are both tardy, you must give both of them warning notices. Make sure all employees, including minorities, women, and immigrants, are given the same opportunity to change their behavior.
- Sincerely trying to help poor performers improve. Document counseling, additional training, and other actions employed to help a poor performer come up to par. Firing an employee for poor performance without proper documentation of attempts to improve work habits can be risky.

TERMINATION FOR "BAD ATTITUDE"

We all know that employee attitude is a key component of quality service and can make or break an organization. Yet it can be very risky, legally speaking, to discharge employees for a poor attitude. Firing for attitude continues to be a trigger for many employment lawsuits.[19] "Poor attitude" is a vague characteristic that is difficult to make objective. You must objectify the behavior by carefully specifying what you mean by "bad attitude." Is it the employee's tone of voice, lack of respect, facial expressions, or is it poor work habits such as tardiness, absenteeism, or continuous errors? Next examine company rules to determine if the employee's behavior violates policy. If so standard disciplinary action can be taken. Then meet with the employee and give her specific examples of complaints or observations you have made about the behavior that is causing the problem. If a sudden variation in attitude occurred, utilize counseling skills to discover the underlying cause of the change. Explore ways to eliminate the problem and specify a reasonable period of time for behavior change. If it becomes necessary to terminate the employee, stay away from the word "attitude" and instead focus on the troublesome behaviors. If the employee is a member of a protected class, make sure there are no stereotypes

INSIGHT 9.2

FIRING FOR "ATTITUDE"

Can you fire an employee who is obnoxious, rude, sarcastic, hostile, and argumentative but who is technically very good at his job? According to attorney Thomas Schweich, you certainly can.* "Failing to get along with co-workers to the point where morale and productivity suffer is grounds for firing because dealing effectively with people is every bit as much a part of their job as the more technical aspects."

But there are a few exceptions that you need to be aware of. People who are protected from termination in this situation are those classified as "whistle blowers" or people who report unsafe or illegal activities at work along with those workers under employment contact. Of course civil rights laws prohibit termination due to race, gender, religion, and so on.. Also protected under the Americans with Disabilities Act are those who are clinically depressed. Over the past two years, EEOC complaints arising from mental illness have skyrocketed to 15 percent of total claims, making this the single largest category of complaints. For this reason companies try to get people with serious attitude problems into counseling. Even if you eventually let the person go, it shows that effort was made to help.

*A. Fisher, "Dumping Troublemakers, and Exiting Gracefully," *Fortune*, February 15, 1999, 174.

or bias affecting your decision to terminate this person. Read more about firing for attitude in Insight 9.2.

WHEN LAWSUITS OCCUR

Lawsuits today are not only directed toward the organization in question, but with increasing frequency, they are also brought against managers or supervisors in the company.[20] Most of these cases involve discrimination or situations where the employee claims that the manager or supervisor caused emotion distress.

What can you do to avoid being named in a lawsuit by a disgruntled employee? Begin by doing the best job you possibly can. Learn all you can about sexual harassment and workplace discrimination issues. Have another manager or human resources representative sit in to witness any conversations with employees about sensitive issues. Know how to identify and investigate employee complaints in a timely fashion. Learn how to identify small problems before they mushroom into big ones. Finally maintain a good rapport with employees so they don't see you as the cause of their workplace problems.

IS THE CLAIM VALID?

If an employee is fired, he or she can sue for lost wages and benefits, along with reinstatement. The employee can claim emotional distress and additional monetary damages when he or she sues for an illegal reason such as racial discrimination.[21]

? Questions Asked by EEOC

Was the employee fired justifiably due to excessive absence or
lateness?

Was the older employee fired because of his age and higher salary?

Were majority workers with the same number of absences merely
warned while minority workers were fired?

Was a female employee fired for complaining that she did not
receive the same wages as her male counterparts?

Was an older worker refused employment because she was
overqualified?

Figure 9.3 Questions Asked by EEOC When Considering a Claim

When a recently fired employee consults a lawyer or contacts the EEOC,
the first point considered is whether the person has a valid claim of unfair termination based on discrimination. The validity of a discrimination claim is determined by whether the company's decision was made because of age, race,
gender, national origin, disability, and so on or because of a reasonable, nondiscriminatory business decision. They might ask the questions listed in Figure 9.3
when considering a claim.

The answers to these questions help determine whether discrimination
has occurred.

FILING COMPLAINTS

In most instances employees who believe they have been treated unfairly
must file a complaint with the EEOC within 180 days of the alleged illegal act
to avoid expiration due to the Statue of Limitations.[22] If the EEOC determines
that the claim has merit, they will investigate at no charge to the claimant. The
following facts must be included on the complaint:

- The name of the person filing the complaint.
- The names, business addresses, and telephone numbers of all
  persons who committed or participated in the discrimination.

- Specific events, including dates and facts, to support the discriminatory nature of the act.

The employee will be asked to sign and notarize the complaint. The company is sent a copy of the document and requested to submit a detailed written response typically within thirty days. Where warranted instigators will look into the claim by interviewing company personnel and witnesses. A no fault conference may be convened with both the employee and the company to attempt resolution. The investigator may also visit the company and examine documents and records and talk to witnesses and other employees. If the case cannot be settled, the following options might be taken:

- The employee might hire a lawyer and sue the employer in a civil suit.
- The employee might represent himself or herself and sue the employer in federal court.
- The EEOC might file a lawsuit on behalf of the employee.
- The EEOC might file a class action lawsuit on behalf of a number of employees who have all received the same type of unfair treatment.

As a result of the enactment of the Civil Rights Act of 1991, employees who have been discriminated against are entitled to receive greater monetary awards for discrimination lawsuits about hiring, firing, promotion, and on the job behavior. The burden of proof required has been reduced, and minorities and women are no longer limited to only receiving retroactive back pay and lost benefits. They can receive punitive and compensatory damages up to $300,000 plus payment for legal fees.[23]

The best way to protect your company from lawsuits based on discrimination is to support all hiring, firing, and promotion decisions with proper documentation. This includes keeping records on file of all applicants, reference check information on applicants, written warning notices for employees, and a valid performance appraisal system. Read about how some companies are attempting to reduce costly litigation through arbitration in the Best Practices box.

BEST PRACTICES

To avoid expensive legal battles, companies are requiring applicants and employees to sign agreements stating that they will bring all employment disputes to arbitration rather take legal action. Such practices have met with mixed results in the court system. Despite this both Darden Restaurants and Hooters are adopting mandatory arbitration systems to resolve workplace disputes.* In Darden restaurants employees first take disputes to their managers. If they are not happy with the results, they can take their problem to human resources or upper management. Next peer review performed by a panel of employees and managers may work to resolve the complaint. If the problem is still not solved, next mediation and finally arbitration may result. To make sure the process is fair, arbitration should be conducted by a trained, impartial individual rather than by a company employee.

*Sack, The Employee Rights Handbook, 106–107.

THE ENLIGHTENED MANAGER

Management practices based on cooperation and the recognition that employees have rights to fair treatment create a better work environment. Adopt both ethical and legal principles in your treatment of employees by including:

1. A code of ethical conduct that guides your decisions.
2. A progressive disciplinary system.
3. A fair, consistent system of dismissal.
4. An impartial grievance and appeal system.

CONCLUSION

Federal and state government prohibits discriminatory labor practices. Laws protecting employee rights have been on the books for more than 100 years, but were not enforced until the 1960s. Employee rights are protected by Title VII of the Civil Rights Act of 1964, the Age Discrimination in Employment Act passed in 1967 and amended in 1978, the Veterans Reemployment Act of 1942 and Veterans Readjustment Act of 1964, the Pregnancy Discrimination Act of 1978, the Immigration Reform and Control Act of 1986, the Americans with Disabilities Act of 1990, and the Fair Labor Standards Act of 1938.

As a manager you can minimize the risk of legal action by being aware of employment law and by letting employees know that protecting their rights in the workplace is important to you. You must be particularly careful to guard against discrimination relating to gender, performance evaluation, drug testing, religion, physical appearance, inappropriate behavior of a sexual nature, hiring practices, employee illness, age, and other sensitive issues.

In the past employers had a great deal of freedom in their decisions to terminate employees. Today our laws protect employee rights and prohibit termination for reasons other than just cause. Managers must learn the difference between valid and invalid reasons for termination and carefully follow company rules regarding employee discipline. Before terminating someone contact human resources or your corporate attorney, give the person plenty of chances to change, document all disciplinary action, treat all employees the same, and sincerely try to help poor performers improve.

Employees who are refused employment, terminated, or denied promotion may file a discrimination suit with the EEOC or may initiate a civil lawsuit if they feel they have been treated unfairly. The validity of the discrimination claim depends on whether the company decision was based on age, race, gender, national origin, disability, or another sensitive area or a reasonable, nondiscriminatory reason. If the EEOC believes the claim has merit, they will initiate an investigation. The best way to protect yourself and your company from lawsuits based on discrimination is to make valid hiring, firing, and promotion decisions and support them with proper written documentation. Managers who protect employee rights by following ethical and legal principles can avoid legal pitfalls.

K E Y   T E R M S

Title VII of the Civil Rights Act

Equal Employment Opportunity Commission

Age Discrimination in Employment Act

Veterans Reemployment Act

Immigration Reform and Control Act

Employment Eligibility Verification Form

Pregnancy Discrimination Act

Family and Medical Leave Act

Americans with Disabilities Act

Fair Labor Standards Act

Exempt from Overtime

Sexual Harassment

Gender Discrimination

Drug Testing

Quid Pro Quo Stiuations

Hostile Work Environments

Sexual Harassment Policy

Employment at Will

N O T E S

1. G. Dessler, *Human Resource Management*, 6th ed. (Upper Saddle River, NJ: Prentice Hall, 1997), 35.

2. N. Cournoyer, A. Marshall, and K. Morris, *Hotel Restaurant, and Travel Law: A Preventative Approach*, 5th ed. (Albany, N.Y.: Delmar Publishers, 1999), 474.

3. Commerce Clearing House, "Pregnancy Leave," *Ideas and Trends* (January 23, 1987): 10.

4. Cournoyer, Marshall, and Morris, *Hotel Restaurant, and Travel Law*, 477.

5. J. Allen, *Complying with the ADA* (New York: John Wiley & Sons, 1993), 11–13.

6. S. Sack, *The Employee Rights Handbook* (New York: Facts on File, 1990), 97.

7. Cournoyer, Marshall, and Morris, *Hotel Restaurant, and Travel Law*, 441.

8. Bureau of National Affairs, *Fair Employment Practices*, October 8, 1992, 117.

9. Ibid.

10. G. Flynn, "How to prescribe Drug Testing," *Workforce* (January, 1999): 107–109.

11. "Religious Employees Challenge Companies," *Futurist*, March 1999, pp.21.

12. M. Zachary, "Regulating Appearance Poses Legal Risk," *Supervision* (February 1999): 21–23.

13. Ibid.

14. D. Garland, "Sexual harassment: The Risk One Can Control," *International Commercial Litigation* (April 1998): 35–38.

15. Ibid.

16. T. Bland, S. Stalcup, and S. Sue, "Build a Legal Employment Application," *HRMagazine* (March 1999): 129–133.

17. T. Bland, "ADA: The Law Meets Medicine," *HRMagazine* (January 1999): 99–104.

18. G. Flynn, "You Can Say Good Riddance to Bad Attitudes," *Workforce* (July 1998): 82–85.

19. G. Flynn, "When a Lawsuit Has Your Name on It," *Workforce* (June 1998): 119–120.

20. D. Greenberg, Common Myths of Employment Law," *Workforce* (November 1998): 2.

21. S. Sack, *The Employee Rights Handbook*, 100.

22. Ibid., 101.

23. A. Zuber, "Operators Eye Arbitration Policies," *Nation's Restaurant News* (January 1998): 1-3.

CASE 9.1: AIDS AT WORK

There was a very disturbing incident yesterday afternoon in the restaurant where James works. One of the newer cooks, Gary, who seemed to be working out very well, cut his hand quite badly while cleaning the meat grinder. Several coworkers rushed over to help him, but before they could give him aid, he yelled, "Stand back, I have AIDS." Needless to say everyone was stunned. The executive chef reacted calmly and called for emergency medical assistance. Gary was taken to the nearest hospitality where his cut was stitched and he was released. The emergency medical technicians also gave the chef the name of an organization that cleans up contaminated sites. They arrived quickly and thoroughly cleaned and sanitized the area.

Fortunately it was a slow night, and the accident occurred before the evening rush so there was ample time to deal with the situation. Somehow the back and front of the house crew pulled together and managed to get through the evening without further event.

The next day, the restaurant general manager, Tom Malone, called a meeting with all supervisors and managers to discuss the emergency. He thanked everyone for maintaining his or her cool and handing the difficult situation well. Malone said that Gary's cut was large, but that he would have full recovery and use of his hand. He also said that although Gary wanted to return to his position as cook when he recovered, he planned to ask him to resign instead. Malone just didn't feel that it was safe for someone with AIDS to be working around food. He was putting both customers and coworkers at risk. Also, if anyone in the media found out about the incident, the reputation of the restaurant would be severely damaged.

James felt very strongly that it was unfair to terminate someone because of an illness. He was concerned that the restaurant might get sued if they took action against Gary. James wanted to go to Malone and tell him his concerns, but he wasn't sure if he should.

James comes to you, his mentor, and asks the following questions. You may need to do a bit of additional research outside your text to respond to his questions accurately.

1. What does your particular state law mandate with regard to hiring and firing individuals with AIDS?

2. According to medical evidence, is Gary putting his coworkers and the restaurant's guests at risk of contracting HIV by handling food? What is the risk caused by his having an accident such as he did where there was a serious cut and heavy bleeding?

3. Based on the answers to the above questions, should James go to Tom Malone with his concerns? Why or why not?

R E V I E W   Q U E S T I O N S

1. Indicate which law would be broken in each of the following situations:
   a. Laying off older employees so they could be replaced by younger ones who will work for less pay.
   b. Failing to ask applicants for proof of availability to work.
   c. Telling a long-term employee that he cannot take a leave to care for his sick wife.
   d. Refusing to hire individuals who are not American born.
   e. Denying employment at the front desk to a qualified individual because she is in a wheelchair.

2. In some situations certain seemingly harmless behaviors might be viewed as sexually harassing. Under what circumstances might the following behaviors be considered sexual harassment:
   a. Telling dirty jokes.
   b. Putting your arm around a female employee.
   c. Telling another employee that she looks very attractive.
   d. Asking a fellow employee out for a date.

3. Why is the employment application perhaps the most vulnerable part of the hiring process with regard to the potential for lawsuit?

4. Which of the following statements are allowable on a job application form and which are not? Indicate "yes" if they are allowable and "no" if they are not.
   a. Have you ever been accused of a crime?
   b. What arrangements have you made for child care?
   c. Are you over eighteen years of age?
   d. Do you smoke?
   e. Have you served in the military?
   f. Do you own a house?

5. What is the reason for including a statement that says the individual certifies that all information is correct on the application followed by a signature?

6. What is employment at will?

7. What is the first question you should ask yourself when you think of terminating an employee?

8. What steps can you take to make sure that all terminations are air tight with regard to legality?

C R I T I C A L   T H I N K I N G   E X E R C I S E S

1. Think of a situation where an individual has been fired from his or her job. It might be something that happened to a friend, relative, or coworker. Describe the situation briefly and then answer the following questions:

    a. Was it a just termination? If so, what particular steps were taken to assure that the employees' rights were not violated. If not, what particular laws regarding employee rights were violated?

    b. If you were the manager in that situation, what would you have done—would you have terminated the employee, or taken some other action instead?

2. Imagine that you are conducting a preemployment interview with a woman applying for a position as a server. She is experienced, has a great attitude, and seems like she will fit in well. Your restaurant is very hectic and servers must really work hard. This applicant looks like she could handle the pace. Before you actually offer her the job, she says, "By the way, I just found out I'm pregnant. I'll be due in about seven months. I hope this won't cause any problems." You are very surprised. She certainly didn't look pregnant. What would you say in this situation to avoid violating the rights of the applicant and to make the best hiring decision for your restaurant?

3. You are interviewing a man who has applied for a position as a bus person in your restaurant. He is certainly older than the typical applicant, but he has had past experience and seems to have a good attitude. As you are talking with him, you hear a distinct ticking sound. Wondering what this is, you ask him, "Do you hear that ticking sound?" He chuckles and says, "Oh, that's just my pacemaker. It's an older model and a little noisier than I'd like." You are immediately on your guard. What should you say to him next? How should you handle the situation to avoid violating his rights and still make the best hiring decision possible?

4. One of the desk clerks comes to you and says that she is being sexually harassed by one of the guests. He repeatedly asks her out, makes suggestive comments, and has even tried to hold her hand. The man is also the president of a large corporation that books lots of business at the hotel. How would you handle this situation in a manner that would avoid violating the employees' rights and at the same time attempt to keep the client's business?

5. According the Civil Rights Act of 1991, employees who have been discriminated against can receive retroactive back pay, lost benefits, and punitive damages up to $300,000 in addition to payment of legal fees. What effect do you think this law might have on the way the hospitality industry handles hiring, firing, and claims of workplace discrimination?

O N - L I N E   L I N K

The Equal Employment Opportunity Commission has an excellent web site located at www.eeoc.gov. Visit the site and explore some the extensive information provided there. Included are the most recent court decisions, along with a detailed description of the many laws relating to employment practices. You can also learn more about the process that the EEOC follows when a discrimination claim is filed. Select one particular aspect of employment law that you want to learn more about—sexual harassment, medical or family leave, maternity leave, preemployment inquiries, and so on. Investigate this topic at the EEOC site and prepare a one- to two-page summary of what you learned. Include a description of several recent court rulings that pertain to your topic.

P O R T F O L I O   E X E R C I S E

The last segment of this chapter suggests that managers adopt both ethical and legal principles in the treatment of their employees. To do this it is recommended that your decisions with regard to employees be guided by a code of ethical conduct. Add a section to your portfolio and title it "Ethics." Next create a "Code of Ethical Conduct" that describes your own personal beliefs and values with regard to ethical behavior. Specifically describe what equality means to you, how you will go about protecting the rights of your employees, how you think others should be treated in the workplace, and how you will apply your ethical beliefs in your career as a manager. Companies seek out managers who have ethical standards, and this statement describing your values and beliefs will be a unique and valuable addition to your job portfolio.

Labor Relations

10

ADVANCED ORGANIZER

You have always worked for nonunion companies. In fact no one in your family has ever been a union member. As a result you know very little about labor organizations. You really don't know why employees want to join unions. All you have heard is that dues are high and that administration is ineffective. But all that is about to change. You have been offered a plum position with a large hotel chain and will be a department head at one of their union properties. Suddenly you realize how little you really know about unions and that you must expand your knowledge if you are to successfully manage your workforce.

In this chapter you will be introduced to the function of unions in the hospitality industry. You will learn about the history, organization, and function of labor organizations in the United States. In addition you will examine the manager's role in administering the union contract and working with union officials to resolve grievance disputes. You never know when you might manage a union shop.

BEHAVIORAL OBJECTIVES

- Recognize differences between the various types of union organizations and their structure.

- Understand why employees seek to organize unions.

The Breakers, Palm Beach

- Become familiar with the history of the labor movement in the United States.

- Know the various laws that govern union and management practices.

- Recognize the challenges that unions face.

- Know the process followed in an organizing campaign.

- Develop knowledge of contract negotiation.

- Understand the manager's role in contract application and grievance handling.

UNIONS AND MANAGEMENT

Unions can have a tremendous effect on the way you manage your operation and deal with your employees. Your relationship with your employees is not just defined by you and the organization you work with, but also by the union contract. The contract determines when you can give pay raises, what assignments you can give employees, and who must be considered first for promotions. Some equate managing in a union shop to marital life with interfering in-laws. Each time you and your spouse disagree, a family member is brought in to help you resolve the problem. This type of external control at work can make your job much more difficult if you are not well versed in union practices. Even if you are working in a nonunion company now, odds are that at some point in your career you will work for a union hotel, restaurant, or hospitality organization. In this chapter you will learn about the role of labor organizations, bargaining processes, grievance procedures, and the changing relationship between unions and management so you will be better prepared to lead in a union environment.

TYPES OF UNIONS

A **labor union** is defined as an organization of employees that use collective bargaining to represent its members' interests with regard to wages and working conditions. Unions provide employees with a voice in company decisions that affect their welfare. There are two main divisions of unions, craft and industrial. **Craft unions** represent workers who share similar skills and perform the same job duties such as electricians, plumbers, or carpenters. **Industrial unions** represent workers from a particular industry doing a variety of different jobs such as autoworkers, steel workers, or hotel and restaurant workers.

The most active union in the hospitality industry is the **Hotel Employees and Restaurant Employees Union (HERE)**. This is a national union with local chapters in different cities. In hotels, they organize service workers, cashiers, room attendants, and other line employees. In restaurants, their members typically include bus persons, servers, and cooks. Traditional "white collar" workers in hotels and restaurants such as clerical workers and desk clerks typically are not represented by HERE. In some properties a union targeting white-collar workers, such as the teamsters, may represent these employee groups. In larger, downtown hotels, engineering and building maintenance workers may be represented by individual craft unions. This makes the human resources manager's job very complicated since the manager must be well versed in the language of as many as fifteen or more different union contracts.

UNION STRUCTURE

The officers of the local union are involved in organizing the union, negotiating the contractual agreement, and assuring that the provisions it makes are enforced. They are watchdogs for employees, making sure that management treats them fairly. Typically the officers of the local union include the president, vice president, secretary treasurer, and business agent. The higher level officers administer union operations while the **business agent** works closely with employees and management to settle disputes. They may be called upon to counsel troubled employees and become involved in grievances that are not solved at lower levels.

The **union steward** or **shop steward** is both a company employee and a union representative. Although the company pays that person's salary, the steward spends much of his or her time reconciling disputes between union members and management. Employees often come to the union steward with questions and concerns before they file a formal grievance. The steward must serve the needs of employees while remaining on good terms with management. A good shop steward and business agent will try to settle problems quickly and avoid complicated grievances and arbitration.

WHY EMPLOYEES JOIN UNIONS

The majority of employees join unions because they believe it will bring them better working conditions, income, and benefits. A union's success in attempting to organize hotels or restaurants depends on the degree of dissatisfaction among employees. Employees who are happy with the way they are paid and treated are less likely to seek union representation. Unions can offer disgruntled employees better wages, benefits, and a way to challenge the unfair practices of supervisors. They may join a union because it makes them feel more secure in their position and less dependent on the whims of management. Employees who feel that they are paid fairly, have good benefits, and good relationships with management rarely feel compelled to organize. Only when they perceive that they are being treated unfairly do they seek the services of the union.

Some hospitality organizations work very hard to keep their employees happy so they will not seek the services of the union. Historically the majority of Marriott operations have been nonunion. In a strong union city, Marriott makes sure that their employee's wages are equal or better than union scale, they offer equal or better benefits, and they try to keep their employees happy by making sure they are treated fairly. These practices have allowed the company to operate nonunion hotels in very strong union markets such as Chicago, New York, and Los Angeles. Other organizations, like Hilton, prefer to work closely with unions to assure that employees receive standard wages, benefits, and have a formal system for airing their concerns. The majority of Hilton Hotels located in major cities are union properties. Hilton prides itself on forming cooperative relationships with labor with a minimum of disagreement.

THE HISTORY OF UNIONS

Unions have existed in the United States since the colonial era. The first union was organized in 1794 when shoemakers in Philadelphia picketed employers and conducted strikes for higher wages. Employers often resisted early efforts to organize. Unions were actually illegal until 1842, when the Massachusetts Supreme Court decided in *Commonwealth v Hunt* that it was not a criminal conspiracy for unions to organize. Even after this decision, employers still resisted organization by firing employees who joined unions. They made employees sign **yellow dog contracts** agreeing not to form or join a union when they were hired with the understanding that they would lose their jobs if they did.

Led by Samuel Gompers, the **American Federation of Labor (AFL)** was established in 1886 and was one of the first federations, or groups of unions, to achieve significant size and influence. The AFL consisted primarily of craft workers or skilled workers when it was developed. Shortly after the **Congress of Industry Organizations (CIO)** began to organize factory workers and mine workers in the United States. In 1955 these two organizations combined to form the AFL-CIO, a federation of about 100 labor unions.

LAWS GOVERNING UNIONS

There are three prominent laws that govern labor relations today: The Wagner Act, the Taft-Hartley Act, and the Landrum-Griffin Act.[1] The **Wagner Act** of 1935, also called the National Labor Relations Act, had the strongest impact on union and management relations. It was considered prolabor, and protects employees' rights to bargain with the union. In Section 7 of the Wagner Act, employee rights to form, join, or assist unions, to bargain collectively, and to engage in union activities are guaranteed. The Wagner Act also made the following unfair labor practices illegal. Employers cannot:

- Interfere with, restrain, or coerce employees in the exercise of their rights to form, join, or assist the union, to bargain collectively, or to engage in union activities.
- Interfere with the formation of any labor organization.
- Discriminate in the hiring or tenure of employees to encourage or discourage membership in a labor organization.
- Fire or discriminate against an employee because that employee has filed charges under this act.
- Refuse to bargain collectively with union representatives.

The power to implement the Wagner act was given to the National Labor Relations Board (NLRB). The NLRB conducts elections to determine whether a union will represent a group of employees and also investigates charges filed by both unions and employers regarding charges of unfair labor practices.

Just as the Wagner Act was prounion, the **Taft-Hartley Act** of 1946 was promanagement. It was passed to attempt to balance the power between labor and management and made it illegal for unions to:

- Restrict employees for exercising their rights according to the Wagner Act.
- Persuade employers to discriminate against their employees.
- Refuse to bargain collectively with an employer.
- Participate in secondary boycotts.
- Attempt to force recognition when another union is the certified representative.
- Charge excessive initiation fees.
- Require members to pay for services not performed.

The Taft-Hartley Act gave states the right to pass laws that further restricted union security. Before this act unions had the right to have a **closed shop** and could make union membership a condition of employment. Those who refused to join the union were also refused jobs. But the Taft-Hartley Act gave individual states the power to enact **right-to-work** laws banning closed shops. This meant that employees have a choice in deciding whether to join the union in their particular company. Nearly half the states in the United States now have enacted right-to-work laws.

In the 1950s a number of illegal practices on the part of unions were discovered. In response the **Landrum-Griffin Act** of 1959 was passed to protect the rights of individual union members. It provided a Bill of Rights of Union Members that stated that each member has the right to:

- Nominate candidates for union office.
- Vote in union elections.
- Attend union meetings.
- Participate in union meetings and vote on union business.

CONFLICT BETWEEN LABOR AND MANAGEMENT

Unions arose because of the power struggle between employees and management, and this conflict is still quite evident today. During the early days of union development, this clash often erupted into instances of violence. In 1870 Pinkerton detectives infiltrated a militant union organization called the Molly Maguires; ten union members were hanged, and fourteen sent to jail. In 1877 twenty-five railway strikers died when they took over company property, and federal troops were sent in to deal with the situation. Such instances of violence continued for many years, and relationships between union and management did not stabilize until the start of the Second World War.

CHALLENGES UNIONS FACE

The need for unions during the early part of the twentieth century was dramatic. Employees were treated very poorly by employers and often forced to work long hours with little pay in unhealthy working conditions. Until the formation of organized labor, workers had little recourse and had to just accept whatever employers offered. Unions granted employees a newfound power over the companies they worked for and gave them a voice in the decision-making process. Unions became so powerful that at one point, members of the United Steel Workers received thirteen weeks paid vacation every fifth year of employment, a generous benefit at the time.

Today we have fairly uniform working conditions and government laws that regulate wages, safety, and equal opportunity. Many question the continued need for union representation. As a result organized labor has had a hard time maintaining a satisfactory growth rate. The national rate of membership fell from an all time high of 40 percent of the civilian labor force in 1955 to 14.5 percent in 1996.[2] This same trend has also been evident in the hospitality industry. HERE membership has declined dramatically. In 1970 there were 507,000 members, and by 1989 that number had dwindled to 280,000.[3] Currently only about 8 percent of hotels in the United States are unionized, according to a survey of 535 hotels nationwide conducted by PKF Consulting.[4]

Although the hospitality industry is one of the largest in our country, it has proved to be difficult to organize. Many workers are part time and transient, making it difficult to gain any real commitment to representation. The hospitality industry also employs a large number of women and minorities. Historically women and minorities have not been actively recruited for traditional union jobs, particularly those in the trades, and this has weakened the support of these groups for union efforts. HERE has been most successful in organizing in major cities like Chicago, New York, San Francisco, Las Vegas, and Detroit.

Another challenge facing unions is the possible repeal of the closed shop. Initially unions had the right to a closed shop, meaning that all employees in a company where a union was recognized must join and pay dues or lose their jobs. States were granted the right to set their own laws with regard to closed shops and currently twenty-one states have right-to-work laws, giving individual employees within a company the right to decide whether they would join the union. There is a countermovement toward the passing of a national right to work law that would make closed shops illegal in all states.[5] Those supporting it argue that for more than sixty years, unions have been able to rely on dues from more than 8 million American workers who are forced to pay as a condition of employment. Unions collect more than $6 billion every year from private-sector workers, most of who would be automatically fired if they didn't pay up. The National Right to Work Act would make this practice illegal. Unions protest this act because the national right to work would greatly reduce union income by making forced dues illegal and further weakening their position.

THE IMAGE OF UNIONS

Over the years organized labor has developed a somewhat negative public image. Some argue that unions have become too powerful politically, charge too much for dues, and do not provide a good return on investment to its members. Publicized incidences of corruption and ties to organized crime have made many view unions as a whole in a negative light.

INCREASING THEIR APPEAL

Unions initially gained strength by representing blue-collar or factory workers. They expanded their efforts to other hourly employees such as service workers in the hospitality industry represented by HERE. Next certain professional groups such as teachers were organized. More recently the union has further directed its recruitment efforts toward white-collar employees and other professional groups. Unions have targeted many companies with large numbers of clerical workers. Typically secretaries and clerical workers of companies that already have union representation of other groups of workers are the focus of their efforts. Even physicians have been driven to seek union representation as a result of their dissatisfaction with managed health care.

ORGANIZING CAMPAIGNS

When unions seek recognition by employees of a nonunion organization, they instigate an organizing campaign. An **organizing campaign** is an all-out effort by the union to bring its services to employees of a particular hotel or restaurant. These all-out efforts can be very expensive, and are only undertaken when the union believes they have a good chance of convincing employees to bring them in. An all-out union campaign may consists of the following:

- Development of a committee who will contact targeted employees to inform them of union benefits.
- Flyers distributed to employees as they go to work.
- Holding of rallies to publicize the issues around which the campaign is centered such as wages, benefits, and job security.

SALTING

Unions may also attempt to organize from inside the company by **salting** or infiltrating the employee ranks with union sympathizers. In this technique a union organizer, the "salt," applies for a position with a nonunion employer. Once hired the salt begins placing pressure on the employer to form a union. In the past companies have often refused to hire or even terminated employees that they felt might be salts. But this practice is now illegal as a result of the Supreme Court's ruling that a nonunion company cannot impinge on the rights of an employee and union member to organize a union.[6] Union organizers or salts have full protection from termination under the National Labor Relations Act. Employers of a nonunion company do not have the right to refuse or terminate the employment of an individual on the basis of union membership because this would be counted as unfair labor practice. They must be considered viable job applicants, regardless of the possible consequences to the employer. Any attempt to exclude them from consideration, deny them employment, or terminate their employment based on their union membership or protected organizing activities would be considered an unfair labor practice.

UNION AVOIDANCE

Many companies seek to avert unionization because they believe that it is to their benefit to avoid the involvement of a second party in their relationship with their employees. Unions can limit the freedom of management in setting policies, rewarding employees, and identifying job responsibilities. In most cases management must negotiate with unions about wages, work schedules, benefits, job standards, job descriptions, and the hiring of nonunion workers to perform union tasks. Supervisors must discipline employees with care or risk being challenged by the union grievance procedure. Managers may feel that their authority is diluted by union regulations.

In response to the union's efforts to organize, the company cannot in any way threaten or coerce their prounion employees. They can inform employees of their right to revoke their authorization cards either verbally or through the distribution of pamphlets.[7] **Authorization cards** are signed by employees to indicate that they want union representation. Management can explain their views of the consequences of signing an authorization card. They can emphasize the advantages in wages, benefits, or working conditions that they provide in comparison to what the union offers, but they have little additional recourse in the event of a union campaign.

Once a union can show that at least 30 percent of the employees within their target group want it to represent them, demonstrated by their signing of authorization cards, the union can request a certification vote. More frequently employers are accepting the union without a formal vote if more than 50 percent of employees sign cards in favor of unionization. This recently occurred at the San Francisco Marriott where the majority of the hotel's 900 union-eligible workers had signed cards indicating they favored union representation, but without an election held by the National Labor Relations Board (see Insight 10.1). The union prefers acceptance after card checks because they can avoid lengthy appeals and court proceedings that can stall NLRB elections for many

---

Step 1:   Employees of a hotel or restaurant contact the local chapter of HERE.

Step 2:   HERE conducts a campaign, schedules rallies, and hands out flyers.

Step 3:   Employees sign authorization cards indicating they want union representation. If 30 percent or more sign, an election is held. If 50 percent or more sign, the union can ask to be certified without an election.

Step 4:   If necessary NLRB holds a certification election with secret ballots. If more than half or 50 percent of employees plus one vote yes, the union is in. If fewer than this vote yes, the union cannot hold another election for one year.

Figure 10.1 How Unions Organize

years.[8] In San Francisco the developers of a 400-room hotel agreed to the card-check process as have the Marriott on Fisherman's Wharf and the Sheraton Palace Hotel.

If the employer requests an election, or if more than one union is vying for recognition, the NLRB or a state labor agency conducts these formal elections. Elections are conducted by secret ballot with choices of "no union" or the name of the particular union or unions seeking representation. See Figure 10.1 for steps involved in union certification.

On rare occasions existing unions are voted out by employees through **decertification.** I experienced this firsthand when a nonunion company purchased a union hotel. After the new company took over, the employees were still represented by the union. A decertification election was held, but the majority of employees still chose union representation.

COLLECTIVE BARGAINING

In **collective bargaining,** union representatives and management meet to develop and reach a contractual agreement. There is a trend in the hospitality industry to negotiate longer contracts. In the 1970s and 1980s, contracts were usually two- to three-year pacts. Today, unions have been signing five- or six-year contracts to better allow companies to forecast labor costs into the future.

The union contract contains a detailed description of the rights of both employees and management. It typically contains the following information:

- Time limits of the agreement.
- Management rights.
- Employee rights.
- Job classifications and pay.
- Grievance procedures.
- Hours of work.
- Overtime and holiday pay.
- Vacation benefits.
- Seniority issues.
- Employee benefits.

Union and management progress through a series of phases during the collective bargaining process. In the **prenegotiation** phase, both parties collect information to help make decisions during the process. They must know the number of employees in each job classification, their current wages, overtime pay, demographic information, and the cost of benefits such as lunch, breaks, vacations, health insurance, and child care provisions.

Unions try to get the best contract they can for their employees. At the same time, management tries to reach an agreement that allows them continued profitability. Unions are recognizing the limitations faced by hotels and restaurants in a competitive marketplace. Companies argue that if they are required to pay union wages and benefits and adhere to strict job classifications, they will have difficulty competing with nonunion organizations. In response to this concern, Los Angeles has developed a joint committee to make contract changes and even allow a reduction in wages for restaurants that have had to close or cut operations.[9]

Next both parties must decide who will comprise their negotiation teams. The chief negotiator for management might be the human resources director or a corporate negotiator who is a specialist in collective bargaining. Other members might be line managers or nonunion supervisors from the organization, the benefits administrator, and the hotel or restaurant general manager. The union team might include the business agent, shop stewards, local union president, and representatives from the national union. Typically the union president will serve as chief negotiator for their side.

Each group meets individually to decide their agenda. First they identify their areas of concern and create a game plan of requirements and concessions that they will bring to the table. For example the primary issue for the union might be the need to increase wages while management's main concern might be to increase emloyee insurance deductions. Both groups also decide which concessions they are willing to make and where they are willing to compromise.

The bargaining process begins. Facing each other across a table, union and management present their cases. Rarely is an agreement reached in a first meeting. In some instances the collective bargaining process can last for months. Insight 10.1 describes the very lengthy contract negotiations between Marriott and HERE in San Francisco.

INSIGHT 10.1

SAN FRANCISCO MARRIOTT

A labor official has called the recent unionization of the San Francisco Marriott a model for the struggling American union movement.* Hotel management recently ended a seven-year dispute by agreeing to recognize Local 2 of the Hotel Employees and Restaurant Employees union as the collective-bargaining agent for its employees. This recognition took place after a majority of the hotel's 900 union-eligible employees signed cards indicating they favored union representation. The union was recognized without a National Labor Relations Board election. Back in 1980, when Marriott was negotiating for the land the hotel is built on, they agreed to a pledge of neutrality with the union. This meant that there would be no NLRB secret-ballot election, and that management could not speak to employees about the union during Local 2's organizing drive.

The next step in the unionization process is contract negotiation. In the case of the San Francisco Marriott, union and management are still at odds.† Marriott wanted employees to be able to serve outside of their job classifications on occasions. For example, management would like a banquet waitress to be able to add a chair to a table if requested by a customer rather than waiting for another employee. Job security, seniority, and benefits were concerns that were not dealt with adequately. The union wants Marriott to accept seniority as a primary determinant of promotions, reduced schedules, and shift choices. The union would like employees who work forty-eight hours in any month to be eligible for health and welfare benefits; the hotel would like to limit benefits to those who work sixty-four hours in any one month.

*"ADR Techniques," *Compensation and Benefits Review* 28, no. 4, (1996): 46.

†K. Seal, "Union, Hotel Negotiates Philosophical Differences in Customer Service," *Hotel & Motel Management* 212, no. 14 (August 11, 1997): 4(2).

When an agreement is finally reached, a formal contract is written. It is reviewed several times by both parties to make sure that all language and provisions are correct. The next step in the collective bargaining process is **ratification.** The contract is distributed to all union members, and a formal vote is held. A majority vote is needed for official acceptance of the contract.

FAILURE TO AGREE

In most instances labor and management negotiate smoothly during collective bargaining. On occasion an impasse is reached that is so severe neither side is willing to concede. When this happens one of four events can occur. The employees might call a **strike** where they refuse to work until management grants the concessions they want. Strikes in the hotel and restaurant industry, although typically very brief, can create tremendous hardship for the company. Organizations do have the right to hire replacement workers as of 1990, when the Caterpillar strike set this precedent, but it would be very difficult to find experienced workers who could step in and replace union workers in hotels or restaurants. Recently a hotel workers strike was called right before the Miss America beauty pageant in Atlantic City, but settlement was reached before the day of the event. Imagine planning a convention in a major city only to find that a strike has been called, and there are no workers cleaning guest rooms, preparing food, or setting up banquet facilities. Most managers know that few experiences are worse than a strike, and companies will go to great lengths to avoid them. See Insight 10.2 for more information on a new partnership between labor and management.

A less dramatic alternative to a strike during negotiation impasse is a **boycott.** Union members picket the entrances to the business advertising the dispute. They also ask members of other unions not to patronize the boycotted company. The union may contact suppliers and ask that they no longer do business with the organization. HERE is resorting to boycotts in their efforts to increase their success in organizing hotels and restaurants.[10] Boycotts often result when hotels meet organizing drives with counterattacks, stall in contract negotiations, or have complex grievance disputes. In response hoteliers question the legality of the boycott tactic. Two properties in the San Francisco Bay area plan to file civil racketeering lawsuits against local unions that have mounted boycotts against the hotels. They feel that the boycott efforts are creating severe business hardship and impeding their rights to free trade.

A third response to a contractual impasse is a **lockout.** Management shuts down the operation or runs it with only a skeleton crew of nonunion employees. Management may do this to force the union to agree to their demands or in response to work slowdowns by employees. Lockouts rarely occur in the hospitality industry because it is very difficult to close a hotel or restaurant or to operate with a limited number of workers.

Management and union negotiators might agree to resort to **third-party mediation** if they are unable to come to an agreement. A neutral third party is brought in to help the groups reach agreement. A professional mediator, trained to facilitate negotiations, listens to both sides and helps the disputing parties to reach agreement. In the case of **contractual arbitration,** the third party doesn't just help the two groups reach agreement; they impose a decision on them. The arbitrator reviews both sides' concerns and then makes a binding decision that management and labor must live with.

INSIGHT 10.2

A NEW PARTNERSHIP BETWEEN LABOR AND MANAGEMENT

Many hotels believe that a new partnership between management and labor is emerging where each side is becoming more sensitive to the needs of the other.* Hotel managers believe that the union is taking a more businesslike approach to the needs of the company by seeking mutually beneficial agreements. For example the union recently allowed Chicago hotels to combine job classifications allowing workers to perform various functions. Room service order takers were allowed to perform the duties of cashiers, and dining room servers were allowed to collect payments from customers. In San Francisco a living contract provides for labor-management problem-solving teams to meet regularly to modify contract language at once.‡ More flexible still, the MGM Grand in Las Vegas negotiated a contract that has only job classifications, not job descriptions, to allow the hotel to cross train and cross utilize workers. In San Francisco the city's twelve-member Hotel Group have formed a consortium to streamline handling of grievances, facilitate marketing, and jointly run training programs. In addition the general managers and human resources directors of these hotels meet monthly with union representatives to air problems that might otherwise become grievances. The teams also have the power to change the contract on a hotel-by-hotel basis to find solutions that meet the needs of both labor and employees. This allows hotels to better react to changing customer and market needs, rather than being forced to adhere to ineffective practices until the next contract negotiation.

*K. Seal, "Unions Flexing Different Kind of Clout," *Hotel & Motel Management* 213, no. 14 (August 1998): 42.

‡Ibid.

APPLYING THE CONTRACT

As a manager, you must become well versed in your employee's union contract. The major responsibility for administering this agreement is yours. You must make sure that your employees are treated fairly with regard to wages, overtime, promotion, and discipline as set forth in the union contract. When employees feel that their rights under the contract have been violated, they can file a grievance in response. A **grievance** is a formal complaint about an organizational policy, procedure, or managerial practice that creates dissatisfaction or discomfort for the employee.[11] See Insight 10.3 for a description of a rather complicated grievance involving alleged discrimination that was settled by labor and management.

Union companies usually follow a sequence of steps in the grievance procedure:

1. The employee meets with the shop steward to formally file his or her grievance.
2. The shop steward, supervisor and employee meet to discuss the problem. Most grievances are solved at this point. If they are not, the human resources manager may be asked to mediate.
3. If a solution is not reached, the individuals will meet with the department head and the union business agent.

INSIGHT 10.3

UNION INVOLVED IN SETTLING DISCRIMINATION CLAIM

The owners of Logan Airport's new Hilton Hotel have settled complaints by the hotel workers' union that the company planned to fire longtime workers who did not fit in with the hotel's new upscale image, including a trendy Irish theme pub.* The 600-room hotel replaces the smaller Ramada Airport Hotel. Three longtime Ramada waitresses filed gender- and age-bias complaints against Hilton with the Massachusetts Commission Against Discrimination, accusing management of trying to make them quit by making their work lives difficult. They claimed that Hilton only wanted a wait staff with Irish brogues for their new pub. Hotel officials denied the allegations. The conflict was settled when the union obtained written guarantees from hotel management covering a number of areas, including schedules, seniority, and allowing workers from the old hotel to transfer to the new hotel's pub.

*J. Hart, "New Hilton Hotel, Union Settles Workers' Bias Suit." *Boston Globe*, August 19, 1999, Thursday, City Edition. Metro/Region, B2.

4. In rare occasions an agreement is still not reached, and a grievance arbitrator must be called in to make a binding decision. This is an expensive last resort, and both the union and management share the cost.

A supervisor or manager who has lots of grievances filed against him or her might be viewed by the company as a poor leader. Managers who are promoted are those who can create a cooperative work environment. Grievances are counterproductive and can take a great deal of time and money to resolve. Your best bet is to stop grievances before they even happen. Practice good leadership technique and let employees know that you are willing to work with them to solve any problems they might have. Ask that they come to you first to air their gripes before resorting to a formal grievance. This way, problems can be solved between the two of you without resorting to formal procedures.

BEST PRACTICES

Legal action against companies has increased by 400 percent over the last 20 years.* To avoid costly litigation, companies are adopting **alternative dispute resolution** (ADR), a relatively new practice to settle grievances without costly arbitration or legal action.† A panel of employees and managers settles problems with compensation, benefits, promotion, or termination. External mediators and arbitrators become involved when necessary. They follow a process of internal review, fact finding, mediation, and, if required, arbitration. Company employees who agree to this process sign a statement saying they will abide by the decision of the panel and not resort to legal action. Both union and nonunion companies are using alternative dispute resolution to avoid costly legal battles.

*R. Kuenzel, "Alternative Dispute Resolution." *Compensation and Benefits Review* 28, no. 4,(1996): 43–51.

†"ADR Techniques." *Compensation and Benefits Review* 28, no. 4, (1996): 46.

Formal grievances cannot be avoided completely and are going be filed occasionally. The most important thing you can do is to respond quickly and carefully to the grievance. The union contract will describe the time limits that management must work within to respond to formal grievances. If you delay, it may mean that you lose the grievance simply because of negligence. A second important response to the grievance process is to make peace with the employee in question after a decision has been made. Talk with the individual after the process and let him or her know you have no hard feelings, regardless of the outcome of the grievance. You must continue to work with this employee, and hard feelings will only result in future grievances.

CONCLUSION

At some point in your career, it is likely that you will work for an organization where employees have union representation. Thus it is important that you understand the function of unions and their role in management. Labor unions are classified as either craft or industrial. The largest union representing hospitality workers is HERE, a national union with chapters in most major cities. Union administration includes the president, vice president, secretary treasurer, and business agent. The shop steward is an on-site representative who is both a company and union employee.

Employees join unions because they want to have a voice in the organization and hope to improve their working conditions, income, and benefits. Unions were initiated in the United States late in the eighteenth century and have had a volatile history. In 1955 two federations, the AFL and CIO, joined forces and represent most labor organizations in the United States. Union and management procedures are governed by the Wagner Act, the Taft-Hartley Act, and the Landrum-Griffin Act.

Unions arose because of the power struggle between employees and management, and this conflict continues today. Union membership has declined dramatically during the last twenty years, and organized labor faces many challenges today. It must overcome difficulties in organizing women and minority workers, the threat of the closed shop, image problems, and find ways to increase membership by approaching traditionally nonunion workers.

When unions mount organizing campaigns, companies cannot in any way threaten or coerce employees with regard to union membership. Unions can gain recognition through the signing of authorization cards or through a formal vote. Once the union is certified, collective bargaining begins. Labor and management must negotiate in good faith to develop a fair contract. Once a contract is written, a membership vote is taken to ratify it.

When labor and management fail to agree, one of four events can occur: the union may call a strike or boycott, management may lockout employees, or both groups might agree to third-party arbitration. With increasing frequency disputes are being settled out of court through binding arbitration.

Supervisors are responsible for applying the contract in their daily dealings with employees. When workers feel that their rights have been violated, they can file a grievance or a formal complaint with the union. The shop steward, business agent, the supervisor, and human resources manager can all become involved in the settlement of grievances.

Hospitality organizations are finding unions more receptive to their needs and more likely to take a businesslike approach in collective bargaining and negotiation. Labor and management are seeking to work together for mutually beneficial agreements that meet both employee and company needs.

K E Y   T E R M S

Labor Union
Craft Union
Industrial Union
HERE
Business Agent
Union Steward
Yellow Dog Contract
AFL-CIO
Wagner Act
Decertification
Collective Bargaining
Boycott
Third-Party Mediation
Alternative Dispute Resolution

Taft-Hartley Act
Landrum-Griffin Act
Closed Shop
Right-to-work
Organizing Campaign
Salting
Authorization Card
Prenegotiation
Ratification
Strike
Lockout
Contractual Arbitration
Grievance

N O T E S

1. W. Forbath , *Law and the Shaping of the American Labor Movement* (Cambridge, Mass.: Harvard University Press, 1991), 135–141.

2. *Bureau of Labor Statistics* (1997), Union Members Summary (*http://www.bls.gov/news.release/union2.nws.htm*).

3. S. Murrmann and K. Murrman, "Union Membership Trends and Organizing Activities in the Hotel and Restaurant Industries," *Hospitality Research Journal* 14, no. 2 (1990): 491–501.

4. K. Seal, "Worker Agreement Seen as Union Model," *Hotel & Motel Management*, 211, no. 21 (November 18, 1996): 3.

5. R. Larson and W. Clay, "Does America Need a National Right-to-Work Law?" *Insight on the News*, August 17, 1998, 24–28.

6. R. Fink, R. Robinson, and D. Nichols, "Paid Union Organizers as Protected Employees: *NLRB v. Town and Country Electric*," *Industrial Management* (January-February 1996): 24–27.

7. Commerce Clearing House, "More on Management's Pre-election Campaign Strategy," *Issues and Trends in Personnel*, August 20, 1982, 158–159.

8. Ibid.

9. Ibid.

10. K. Seal, "Unions Seek to Organize Via Increased Boycotts," *Hotel & Motel Management* 211, no. 16 (September 16, 1996): 3–5.

11. P. Salipante and R. Bouwen (1990), "Behavioral Analysis of Grievances: Conflict Sources, Complexities, and Transformation," *Employee Relations*, 12, no. 3, 17–22.

CASE **10.1**: UNION TARGETS HOTEL

The hotel where Melissa is working is currently nonunion. The company that owns it hopes to maintain its nonunion status, although there have been several attempts to organize in the past. Typically the front desk, where Melissa supervises, is nonunion even in a union hotel because desk clerks usually are not represented by HERE. There have been some rumors that a different union representing white-collar staff was trying to organize the office workers and desk clerks at the property. Flyers have been distributed, and union representatives have been seen meeting with employees off premises. Recently employees have been doing a lot more grumbling about their dissatisfaction with their pay, which is rather low, the poor quality of their health benefits, the fact that they only receive a week's vacation each year, and the current system of scheduling on a rotating basis, not by seniority.

Melissa suspects that Mark, a new hire, might even be a union salt. She has heard her family talk about the union practice of salting where they get one of their own people placed on staff so he or she can talk up the union to other employees. One of the long-term desk clerks told Melissa that Mark has been talking to all the employees about the benefits of joining a union and that he has even gone so far as to point out the many deficiencies in the current department that would be overcome if a union were brought in. He suggested that pay would be higher, benefits improved, and that long-term employees would be given more and better hours. Melissa has noticed that although Mark is great with guests, he often leaves his work area without permission and takes longer breaks than allowed.

Melissa tells her suspicions to the director of front office operations, Jack Hamilton, who thanks her for coming forward. Hamilton said that his first thought is to fire Mark, but realizes that this action could make the problem worse instead of better. He asks Melissa to do a bit of research and develop a plan of action for the department describing how they should proceed to handle the problem. The goals are to keep the union out without violating their rights. Time is of the essence, so Hamilton gives Melissa tomorrow off and asks that she work exclusively on the problem and then come back with her plan the following day.

Melissa immediately calls her mentor for some advice. She needs to know how her department can keep the union out without overstepping any legal boundaries. Answer the following questions to help her develop her plan of action:

1. Melissa wants to know what specific action, if any, can be taken against Mark. How would you recommend that he be handled?

2. Next she needs to know what action the department can take legally to counteract the union's campaign to encourage the front desk clerks to organize. What advice would you give her?

3. Melissa believes that some of the employees' gripes are warranted. Do you think Melissa should recommend that the hotel make changes in these areas to reduce dissatisfaction? What might happen if they continue to ignore the employees' complaints?

R E V I E W   Q U E S T I O N S

1. What is the name of the most active union in the hospitality industry and what type of service workers does it typically organize in hotels and restaurants? Is it a craft or an industrial union?
2. What is a yellow dog contract? Is this legal today?
3. Which act was considered prounion? Why?
4. Which act was considered promanagement? Why?
5. Why has it been difficult in recent years for organized labor to maintain a satisfactory growth rate? Why has it been particularly difficult to organize hospitality workers?
6. What is an organizing campaign? What activities might it include?
7. What actions can management take to avoid union organization?
8. When can a union gain recognition without a formal vote?
9. What are the various phases that union and management must pass through in collective bargaining?
10. When a severe impasse is reached in collective bargaining, what four events can occur?
11. What is alternative dispute resolution? What are its benefits?

C R I T I C A L   T H I N K I N G   E X E R C I S E S

1. As an employee in the hospitality industry, under what circumstances would you want to have union representation? When would you feel that union organization was not necessary?
2. Using the T diagram below, indicate the pros and cons for union membership for hourly employees:

Pros	Cons

Now list the pros and cons for having a union organization as they apply to management:

Pros	Cons

3. Do you support right to work laws? Why or why not?

4. When you think of unions, what image comes to mind? How might unions improve their image?

5. Imagine that you are a manager in a large union hotel and one of your employees files a grievance against you stating that you are showing favoritism in the scheduling of employees. Certain employees consistently get weekends and evenings off and others do not. Specifically how would you go about handling the grievance? What steps would be followed processing the grievance?

6. As a manager how might you stop grievances before they happen in your department?

O N - L I N E   L I N K

As described in this chapter, HERE, the Hotel Employees and Restaurant Employees Union, is the most active union in the hospitality industry. HERE has a website located at www.hereunion.org that contains information about its history, benefits, activities, and membership. Visit this site, explore the various sources of information, and answer the following questions:

1. What is the name of the local chapter in the city nearest you?
2. What are two pieces of news reported in the web site?
3. Are there any boycotts being held at this time? If so, what properties are involved?
4. Use the hotel guide to find union hotels in a city near you. How would you describe union membership in that particular city? Are there many hotels that are union, just a few, or none?

P O R T F O L I O   E X E R C I S E

It is very likely that at various points in your career in hospitality management that you will have the opportunity to manage at both a union property and a nonunion property. Although you may have strong feelings for or against unions, it is important that you are able to keep an open mind so that you will be successful in both types of organizations. This portfolio exercise will help you clarify your feelings about unions and help you develop a management plan of action that will prepare you for both a union and nonunion environment. Although you will not want to include the results of this exercise in the portfolio that you would show prospective employers, it is nonetheless a valuable activity. Write several paragraphs describing your feelings about unions and how you would be successful in both a union and nonunion environment. As you do so, organize your statement so that you answer the following questions:

• Would you prefer to manage in a union or nonunion environment? What is the basis for your preference?
• If you are a manager or supervisor in a union organization, specifically what practices will you follow to ensure

developing a positive relationship with the union and at the same time representing the best interests of your employer?

• If you manage or supervise in a nonunion property, how will you make certain that your employees rights are protected so they will not feel that it is necessary to organize a union?

Evolution of Management Theory

11

ADVANCED ORGANIZER

Publishing executives estimate that more than 1,600 management books hit the shelves each year. That's too much theory for overworked managers to absorb. Today's managers are confronted with a constant blur of new information and ideas. Survival depends on their ability to manage this information overload. The ability to pick and choose the good ideas from the bad is a necessary skill.

In this chapter you will learn about management gurus, or leading theorists of the past and present. You will study the evolution of management theory. Only by understanding the past can we understand the future. Next, you will review the ideas of some of today's "cutting edge" experts to bring you up to date in the discipline of management thought. Then it's up to you to continue your education by reading trade journals, books, and attending conferences and seminars so you can stay abreast of changes in the management studies.

BEHAVIORAL OBJECTIVES

- Understand the characteristics of a knowledge-based organization.

- Gain knowledge of the three evolutionary phases of management thought: the industrial revolution, the productivity revolution, and the management revolution.

- Understand the principles of Taylor's scientific management.

- Become familiar with the humanistic movement in management thought, including Theory X and Theory Y, participation, and quality of work life programs.

- Gain knowledge of contemporary management thought, including Japanese management, open-book management, federalism, Theory Z, and servant leadership.

- Apply your knowledge to the development of your own unique management philosophy.

The Ritz-Carlton Marina del Rey. © 1992 The Ritz-Carlton Hotel Company. All rights reserved. Reprinted with the permission of The Ritz-Carlton Hotel Company, L.L.C. The Ritz-Carlton © is a federally registered trademark of The Ritz-Carlton Hotel Company, L.L.C.

MANAGEMENT THEORY

There is much to learn from the ideas set forth by management experts from both the past and the present. In this chapter you will examine the ideas of recognized guides and leaders in the field of management. You will study the evolution of management thought and its impact on current practices. Management philosophy has an important purpose in the organization and is responsible for setting the type of climate that will prevail throughout the company. Leaders make assumptions about people: that they are lazy or hardworking, honest or dishonest, intelligent or slow. These assumptions guide the way we deal with employees and people at work. Assumptions serve as an unconscious guide to each manager's behavior. We think, therefore we are. The theories about people and about management that we adopt directly affect the way we lead. For this reason the study of management theory is an important part of leadership development.

Various management theories have evolved over time to help solve a particular problem faced during the era. For example, Scientific Management, explained in detail in this chapter, was developed to increase productivity and to create a more organized way of dealing with employees. Next, the humanistic theories were developed to address the emotional needs of employees in the workplace. Today companies face many challenges that emerging theories are attempting to address. Here are just a few of the challenges today's organizations face with regard to employees:

- **Lack of commitment.** Employees do not feel the same company loyalty as they did in the past.
- **Work-family conflict.** Today's two-income families are more likely to experience a conflict of interest with regard to workplace demands and family responsibilities.
- **Personal development.** Employees want to develop new skills and learn on the job, not just punch a time clock.
- **Cooperative relationships.** Employees today find it difficult to tolerate relationships with supervisors based only on their ability to follow orders and demonstrate obedience. They want to be partners, not underlings.
- **Decline in individuality.** Workers are no longer thought of as individuals, but as team members.

This is just a short list of challenges companies face. It is no wonder that the number of books providing advice for managers has grown to almost comic proportions. If you have been in a bookstore lately, you would have noticed that there are literally hundreds of books addressing management concerns. There has been an explosion in the development of modern leadership theory, making it difficult for managers to keep up with this expanding body of knowledge. Read more about how managers are staying abreast of new ideas in Best Practices, and see Figure 11.1 to find out which books are high on corporate America's reading list.

In this chapter you will be introduced to some of the more important ideas advanced today, along with an overview of their evolution from past theory. You won't agree with every perspective, but by examining both old and new ideas, you will progress toward developing your own leadership style that will allow you to meet the unique challenges faced by your particular organization.

A Simpler Way by Margaret J. Wheatley
Rewiring the Corporate Brain by Danah Zohar
Emotional Intelligence by Daniel P. Goldman
On Becoming a Leader by Warren G. Bennis
The Loyalty Effect by Frederick F. Reichheld
Healing the Wounds by David M. Noer
Synchronicity: The Inner Path of Leadership by Joseph Jaworski
Get Everyone in Your Boat Rowing in the Same Direction by Bob Boylan
Managers as Mentors by Chip R. Bell

Figure 11.1 Recommended Reading List

THE EVOLUTION OF KNOWLEDGE

According to Peter Drucker, a highly regarded management theorist, every few hundred years we cross a divide with regard to business practices and enter into a new era of thought. Over time organizations and our society as a whole transform themselves, adopting a new school of thought.[1] Drucker believes that we are experiencing just such a transformation at this time. Fifty years from now, the world that we live in and the organizations where we work will be so different from those we know that it will be as if we are living in a new world. Drucker believes that this new society will be built upon a foundation of knowledge. We are beginning to see the development of this evolution as technology controls more and more of the functions we perform at work and in our personal lives. Today we can shop for anything we need over the Internet from groceries to antiques. Hotels and restaurants are becoming highly automated, and the need for paper communication is all but obsolete. We are evolving into a knowledge-based society where planning and strategy become more important than physical labor. Knowledge work is replacing manual labor as evidenced by the fact that we have fewer employees responsible for making or moving materials. By 1990 only one in five employees were performing jobs requiring manual labor, down from three in five during the 1950s.

Today knowledge is king, and it is very difficult for people to reach a middle-class income level without a college degree. There are few viable career

BEST PRACTICES

To help managers get a handle on the new ideas that are emerging, a group of publishers formed the Consortium for Business Literacy to encourage companies to organize reading groups for their workers.* The Consortium suggests that the groups be limited to ten to twelve participants and that meetings be held no more than once a month. Members read the same books and then get together and hold spirited discussions centered on ways they can better serve clients and employees. The president of Berett-Koehler Communications, a San Francisco publisher, offers fifteeen free copies of current business books to any organization launching a new reading group. So far the club has given away 600 books.

*M. Groves, "New Management Theories Going Round in Company Reading Circles," *Los Angeles Times*, August 16, 1998, Part D, 5.

paths in the trades or manufacturing for those who do not choose higher education.

As our society becomes more strongly knowledge-based, organizations must change the way they operate.[2] They must find a way to put knowledge to work. Specialized knowledge or skills become increasingly important. Rather than valuing a chef who knows a great deal about cooking in general, the chef who is a specialist, perhaps an expert on Mediterranean or Oriental cuisine, will be in demand. Companies will focus only on what they do well and hire experts as contract workers to do the rest. We see this trend in the lodging industry today. Many hotels are hiring foodservice organizations to manage their restaurants, allowing them to focus solely on the rooms division.

In the knowledge-based organization, there will be no boss or subordinate. The desk clerk is not a superior of the room attendant; both are equally important. When you want a room cleaned particularly well, you don't call a desk clerk to do it, you call a room attendant. Both jobs are equally valuable in the overall success of the operation.

Finally knowledge-based organizations must be **decentralized.** This means that authority must be given to individual units within the operation. According to these principles, chains must allow individual hotels to run like independent properties, rather than trying to create cookie-cutter replicas.

It will certainly be a long time before technology takes over in our labor-intensive industry. We will always need people to prepare food, clean guest rooms, and set up meeting rooms, but there have been some dramatic technological changes in just the last twenty years. The drive-up window has transformed fast-food service, the computer has streamlined communication between departments in hotels, and technology allows us to create detailed databases on our regular customers so we can better anticipate their needs. Managers of the future will need to use their heads more than their hands to create new and better ways of serving customers.

How did management practices evolve? Let's examine a bit of history to better understand the creation of the knowledge-based society that is about to emerge. See Figure 11.2 for a summary of landmark events in management.

THE INDUSTRIAL REVOLUTION

The first phase of knowledge application in the workplace began around 1700 and lasted until approximately 1880.[3] During this time the first technical schools were founded. An initial attempt at large-scale production was made

1848	Passage of a law in Philadelphia that set minimum wage for workers.
1868	Passage of law requiring first eight-hour day for government employees.
1881	Frederick Taylor begins work in scientific management at the Midvale Steel Plant.
1886	Founding of American Federation of Labor.
1913	Establishment of the U.S. Department of Labor.
1927	Hawthorne Studies begun by Mayo, Roethlisberger, and Dickson.

Figure 11.2 Landmark Events in the History of Management

with the development of factories. Mechanical power made it possible to mass produce products that had been previously made in small shops and homes. This process also created tedious and repetitive jobs. Imagine working on an assembly line for forty years doing the same repetitive motion over and over every day. In early factories there was little concern for employee safety or job satisfaction. Workers became dependent on business owners for their livelihood and power became concentrated in the hands of the bosses.

THE PRODUCTIVITY REVOLUTION

The second knowledge revolution began in 1881 and lasted until after World War II.[4] During this period there was an attempt to use knowledge to improve work methods. Early in the twentieth century, the modern era of management theory began with the classical management perspective of **scientific management** pioneered by Frederick Taylor.[5] This revolutionary theory claimed that after careful study of individual situations, decisions about organizations and jobs should be based on precise, scientific procedures. Taylor was never noted for his humanistic views, but instead was concerned with studying ways to improve productivity among workers. He focused on technical efficiency as an organizational goal. He believed that jobs should be broken down into simple, repetitive activities to increase workplace efficiency. Planning the work should be completely separate from doing the work. Management should control the planning phase, and then simply tell workers what to do.

Although he lacked concern for the human element, some excellent recommendations evolved from Taylor's scientific management principles:

- Work should be studied scientifically.
- Work should be arranged to maximize employee efficiency.
- Employees should be selected carefully and be matched to the demands of the job.
- Employees should be trained to perform work.
- Monetary compensations should be directly tied to performance.

Scientific management had value in that it was the first theoretical attempt to understand management practices, but it also had many drawbacks. The theory assumed that workers would always be motivated by money and they would always act rationally. Both of these factors are not always true. It also failed to recognize the social needs of workers and their need to feel part of a group. Instead employees were isolated, often working alone in a manufacturing environment. The theory is based on repetitive, highly specialized work that can lead to high levels of dissatisfaction among employees. Any gain in efficiency that comes about due to scientific principles may be offset by losses in job satisfaction and the resulting absenteeism and turnover. Finally scientific management cannot be applied to the unpredictable, uncertain, uncontrollable world that we inhabit today. The business world is dynamic and ever changing, making the application of scientific management principles counterproductive.[6]

Many companies still base their organizational practices on principles of scientific management, with tightly controlled work environments where employees are closely supervised. These organizations cling to the outdated belief that employees cannot be trusted and must be pushed and prodded if they are to provide a fair day's work for a fair day's pay. They have not yet entered our current era of evolution characterized by a more humane, knowledge-based workplace.

THE MANAGEMENT REVOLUTION

Eventually theorists realized that scientific management resulted in excessive concern for production at the expense of the workers themselves. This realization brought about the third and current knowledge revolution of **humanistic management** practices. The humanistic school of thought is based on the idea that we are, by nature, motivated creatures who strongly desire to make a contribution at work. Theorists who developed the humanistic management approach include Abraham Maslow, Douglas McGregor, Rensis Likert, Chris Argyris, Robert Blake, and Jane Mouton. They believed that the purpose of leadership was to change the organization to give employees the freedom to fulfill their own needs and to contribute to the attainment of the organization's goals. They argued that organizations should first facilitate the growth of the individual and then seek profits. Their view of human nature, that people are intrinsically good and naturally seek opportunities for growth, provided the basis of the human-potential movement.[7]

HUMANISTIC MANAGEMENT

THE HAWTHORNE STUDIES

Humanistic management is said to evolve from landmark studies that took place at Western Electric in Chicago during the 1920s. Known as the **Hawthorne Studies,** they were the first substantial research projects in human behavior at work. Elton Mayo, dubbed the father of human relations, wanted to examine the effect of the environment on productivity in assembly line workers. During the first study, the level of lighting was varied and working conditions were changed, sometimes improved and sometimes worsened. To the researchers' amazement, production rates started climbing and morale improved with each change. When lighting was bright and working conditions were improved, productivity went up. When lighting was dimmed and working conditions worsened, productivity went up again. The study concluded that the workers were responding the humanistic practices of the researchers and that when people are treated like human beings, not robots, their morale and productivity increase.

The Hawthorne Studies highlighted the need for a more humanistic style of management. Mayo put forth the idea that an organization is a social system, and the worker is the most important element in it. Theorists began developing new ideas that focused on the need for managers to better communicate with their employees, show more concern for their welfare, and see employees as individuals, not parts of the assembly line. Whereas Taylor believed that human problems stood in the way of productivity, Mayo believed that the human element should be the focus of management.

THEORY X AND THEORY Y

Humanistic management gained additional support following World War II. **Theory X** and **Theory Y** was an innovative idea developed by Douglas McGregor to explain why managers behave as they do. It represented an initial attempt to analyze the attitudes and behavior of management and to propose a theory of leadership that has acted as a basis for many of today's thinkers.[8] First, McGregor assumed that management behavior is strongly influenced by their belief system. Some managers believe that employees dislike work, prefer close supervision, want to avoid responsibility, and have little ambition. He called this system of beliefs Theory X. Managers who hold this view use authoritarian approaches to leadership and rely on their power over their employees to get things done. According to McGregor, the Theory X approach to management is ultimately ineffective. If managers want to improve the performance of their employees, they should adopt a more participative style of management. McGregor suggested that leaders put aside the principles of Theory X management and instead adopt the principles he labeled Theory Y which assumes that:

- Employees find work enjoyable and satisfying.
- Employees can exercise self-direction and self-control at work.
- Money is not the only reward. Employees are motivated by their desire to better themselves and to reach organizational objectives.
- Employees can solve problems creatively.
- Only a small portion of the intellectual potential of the employee is being utilized at work.

According to McGregor the underlying assumptions you have about people and about workers will affect the way you lead. See Figure 11.3 for questions that will reveal your assumptions about workers. You can choose how you view your employees. If you perceive them as limited, disinterested, and only working because they have to, you will lead them with bribes, threats, and close surveillance. On the

---

Do you believe that . . .

1. People would prefer not to work than to work?
2. That managers must push the average person to work hard enough?
3. The average person seeks security above all else in her job?
4. Work is as natural as rest or play?
5. People are committed to their work because of the satisfaction it gives them?
6. People have significant untapped potential for creativity?
7. The average person is not ambitious?
8. The average person prefers close supervision?
9. You can trust employees to get things done?
10. Most people enjoy their work?

(*Key*: Questions 1, 2, 3, 7, and 8 refer to Theory X management and Questions 4, 5, 6, 9, and 10 refer to Theory Y management.)

Figure 11.3 Test Your Assumptions

other hand, if you see employees as creative, willing to work hard, highly moti-vated, and responsible, you will emphasize involvement, participation, trust, praise, and recognition as you lead. Your assumptions are communicated by your tone of voice, body language, behavior, and by the words you say.

Although today's leaders generally accept these ideas, back in the 1960s they were considered quite radical. Theory Y opened the door to a new manage-ment philosophy based on improved quality of work life for employees.

PARTICIPATIVE MANAGEMENT

McGregor's Theory Y gave rise to the idea of increased employee involve-ment in the workplace. The philosophy of **participative management,** based on the idea of having individual workers more involved in decisions affecting their work, gained wider acceptance. This principle of management has had a long-term and positive effect upon organizations. In a review of twenty-nine research articles, it was found that employee participation was associated with positive out-comes in productivity in fourteen instances, with ambiguous results in thirteen studies, and with negative outcomes in only two of the twenty nine studies.[9]

A participative environment encourages each person to contribute his or her ideas in a systematic fashion. Participative management is part philosophy and part economy. The creation of an atmosphere of trust where each person feels comfortable expressing his or her ideas openly is a requirement for a participative work environment. There is also an economic component to participative man-agement where employees not only share their ideas with the company; they also share in the organization's wealth. The **Scanlon Plan,** originated by Joseph Scan-lon in 1937 and still used today, contains an element of economic participation. It recommends that employees share directly in additional profits resulting from their costs-cutting suggestions.[10] Typically all employees share in 70 percent of the savings that result from their ideas. If employee ideas save the company $100,000, a total of $70,000 is distributed equally to employees and $30,000 is returned to the company. This system of rewarding employees for their involvement has been highly successful in reducing costs and fostering participation.

QUALITY OF WORK LIFE

With the realization that the work environment had a significant impact on employee satisfaction and productivity, employers became increasingly con-cerned with improving the quality of work life for employees. Companies began making changes to improve the well-being of their employees both by making individual jobs more interesting and by making scheduling concessions for the personal needs of workers. They initiated quality of work life programs in both job enrichment and flexible scheduling to make work more rewarding and to re-duce stress in the environment.

JOB ENRICHMENT

Employees become dissatisfied with highly repetitive, simple tasks. Imagine that you must perform the same task all day every day for the next forty years. You do nothing but load dirty dishes into racks and send them into the dishwasher or answer the telephone with the same greeting and simply transfer calls to other people. It is easy to see how an employee could become burned out from boring, limited job duties. In an attempt to create a more meaningful work environment, two ideas evolved. The first is **job enlargement** or the attempt to make work more interesting by adding additional tasks. The second is **job enrichment,** which involves redesigning jobs in ways that help workers satisfy their needs for growth, recognition, and responsibility. Job enlargement involves making work less repetitive by providing a greater variety of tasks. Buspersons would not only clear dirty dishes from tables, they would also load them into the dishwasher and clean them. They might even be responsible for transporting clean dishes to holding areas, thus having enlarged job duties. As I am sure you realize from reading this description, job enlargement may add more variety to positions, but it certainly doesn't make work more fulfilling.

Job enrichment, on the other hand, not only expands job tasks, but it also provides employees with greater responsibility. Job enrichment provides opportunities for new challenges so that people might learn and develop additional skills and competencies at work. Consider enriching your employees' work by giving them special assignments, new responsibilities, and greater challenge. Let an employee create the week's schedule, calculate food cost percent, lead the department meeting, or develop a new training program. Look for ways to break the established routine at work and relinquish some of your responsibility. Tap into the resources your employees possess by keeping them challenged and engaged at work.

How do you go about enriching boring, repetitive jobs? First examine core job dimensions including:

- **Skills,** or the variety of actives performed in carrying out the work.
- **Tasks,** or the ability of the worker to do the job from beginning to end with a visible outcome.
- **Significance,** or the degree to which the job has an impact on other people or on the organization.
- **Autonomy,** or the amount of freedom and independence that the job brings.
- **Feedback,** or the degree to which workers receive information about performance as they carry out the job.

Develop ways to enrich jobs by expanding these five areas. Create opportunities for the development of new skills, make tasks more challenging, increase the significance of the work, provide greater autonomy or freedom, and provide performance feedback. Give employees responsibility for inspecting their work and maintaining quality control. Encourage each employee to perform as many different jobs as possible. Give work teams responsibility for dividing their work and making decisions regarding performance.[11]

Job enrichment leads to job ownership. Employees need to feel that they are the owners of their work, not management, not the company. As a manager, it is your responsibility to foster job ownership by treating employees in a manner consistent with this philosophy. Think of yourself as a visiting relative. Would you tell your hosts how to decorate their house, mow their grass, or select their clothing? Let's hope not. Just the same, managers who fail to trust the judgment of experienced employees are diminishing their feelings of job ownership. One way to tell if people feel ownership is by listening to their language. Do they talk about "us. our, my, and we" when referring to their department or is it "them, their, or they"? If it's the former, it is likely that the workers feel ownership for their position and their company.

People want independence and responsibility in their work. They need space to make decisions, solve problems, and feel that they are in control of their destiny.[12] Employees need to control:

- **Work processes.** Determine the order in which they complete tasks, decide how they will complete them, and work at their own pace.
- **Work Schedules.** Employees should have the freedom to schedule their lunch breaks, have flexible working hours, and choose the shift and vacation they prefer.
- **Work decisions.** Employees need more control over decisions that affect their workplace. They might be involved in everything from strategic planning to the selection of new uniforms.

WORK FLEXIBILITY

In addition to job enrichment, the quality of work life movement also advanced modifications in the traditional work schedule. Such practices as the compressed, four-day work week and flextime were instituted to give employees more control over their schedules. The four-day work schedule allows employees to work four 10-hour days instead of five 8-hour days, thus giving them an extra day off each week. **Flextime** allows employees to set their start and end times for their workdays within certain guidelines. Employees could choose to begin work each day at 7:00 A.M. and end at 3:30 p.m. or start at 10:00 A.M. and end at 6:30 P.M., depending on their personal needs. Flexible scheduling is a way to give employees more control over their work life and help them better manage family responsibilities.

CONTEMPORARY MANAGEMENT THEORY

Management theory has evolved from its initial stage of scientific management to a more humanistic view by focusing on the psychological needs of the worker. During the 1980s and 1990s, ideas about management have proliferated, resulting in a tremendous body of knowledge referring to organizational leadership. Many of the new ideas you will review were developed in response to changes in our society and in our workforce. Today's workers are much different from those at the turn of the century, making Taylor's scientific management obsolete. Modern-day employees want challenging, fulfilling work. They want to be respected and valued both as individuals and as team members, expecting much more from their jobs than just a paycheck. The principles we will examine in this section were developed to create organizations and leaders who can meet the needs of today's workers. Unique ideas and insights allow companies to manage effectively so they might realize the potential of their human assets.

In this segment you will examine some of the more recent developments in the area of organizational thought. This portion of your text contains an anthology or a brief synopsis of recent organizational theories, some of which are expanded upon in other chapters.

JAPANESE MANAGEMENT

In the 1980s management practices were turned upside down when external pressures such as foreign competition led management to believe that employment conditions must change if American industry was to remain competitive. A new relationship between management and employees evolved that emphasized cooperation rather than conflict. This new relationship was patterned after **Japanese management.** Trust built on mutual respect is the major building block of cooperation between management and employees. Employees must be empowered to control their work and influence the organization if they are to perform at the high levels necessary for continued success.

Historically Japanese management had its beginnings shortly after World War II when Japan literally rebuilt its manufacturing industries by adopting quality principles as set forth by Edwards Deming. Their system is based upon a bottom-up decision-making process where line employees are encouraged to develop ideas and solve problems. Japanese management also followed **just-in-time** (JIT) inventory and delivery systems which consist of limiting storage and production of materials to immediately before they are needed, or just in time, to create a leaner organization. The Japanese also initiated **kaizen,** or the idea of continuous improvement.

Recently, a new management strategy was developed called **4S** where employees and management relationships are guided by the common goal of continuous improvement.[13] In 4S each worker is encouraged to attain the highest level of personal effectiveness by structuring their work life around four basic steps: organization, orderliness, neatness, and cleanliness.

Although there is much to learn from Japanese management, attempts to uniformly apply their systems to our industries have not been entirely successful. Japanese culture and work ethics are much different from ours. Practices that work well in Japan do not always translate well in the United States. In Japan, for the most part, employees have lifetime jobs with their companies, promotions are based on age and seniority, women are a more temporary part of the workforce, and employees feel personally responsible for the success of their organizations.

Another concern with regard to Japanese management principles is the more recent reduction in the profits in their businesses. The Japanese economy was booming during the 1980s, but profits have been off in the 1990s.[14] This has lead experts to question the long-term success of quality circles and empowerment Japanese style. Such weaknesses among Japanese executives as their inability to see their own shortcomings, precede actions with reasoning, think strategically and creatively, and speak the international language of business— English—must be overcome if they are to revitalize their economy.

OPEN-BOOK MANAGEMENT

The concept of **open-book management,** as developed by John Case, involves two practices:[15]

1. Train employees in business and financial data. Make sure line employees understand the financial reports management uses to measure business performance.
2. Use huddles to keep employees informed. This is a system of meetings where the status of the business and its overall performance is presented and discussed.

A unique feature of open-book management is the sharing with line employees of reports and information usually limited to only department heads and managers. Companies that have adopted this practice train their employees to read financial statements, help them to understand company profits and losses, and teach them basic accounting practices.

The premise of open-book management is that if employees fully understand the business aspects of the operation, they will become committed to its success. Companies that adopt this practice find that relationships between managers and workers improve when everyone shares and understands the same information. Employees are also more committed to reducing waste because they can see exactly how it impacts the business. Finally, when employees know how to read financial reports, they know how to keep score. Otherwise working without financial understanding is like trying to make sense out of a baseball game when you have no idea how many runs have been scored. The game has little meaning for those who lack this knowledge.

Open-book management involves actually opening up the financial books, so to speak, to allow employees to see exactly where profits are coming from and where money is going. The sharing of information both upward and downward within the organization takes place during three types of meetings:

- **Prehuddles.** Meetings in which teams gather information about their own performance to pass on to top management. Past performance is compared with current performance to determine whether the department is over or underbudget.
- **Main Huddles.** Performance reports from different departments are sent to a financial team so that all information can be combined into one report. In one company, the main huddle consists of fifty employees and managers who bring the latest numbers from their departments. The numbers are announced one after another and people around the room write them down on scorekeeping forms. Everyone knows how everyone else is doing, and those who show an increase in profits are congratulated.
- **Posthuddles.** Once the main huddle is completed, members return to their areas and share information from other departments with their coworkers.

Open-book management is an effective way to increase employee involvement and commitment through the sharing of knowledge. In the past management horded information, particularly that of a financial nature. This made employees feel like outsiders in their own company, not to be trusted with important data. Open-book management helps equalize management and employees by keeping both groups equally knowledgeable.

THE FEDERAL ORGANIZATION

Some theorists believe that as our knowledge-based society evolves, companies will become decentralized, with responsibility given to smaller units within the organization. Instead of **centralized** organizations, where top-level executives make all decisions, companies will evolve into **federal organizations** where power is distributed to individual units. This notion is guided by the principle that the drive and energy in organizations comes from the outlying parts.[16] In a restaurant chain, drive and energy would come from individual operations that are allowed to create their own unique way of doing things. Each restaurant would operate as an individually owned entity with the same flexibility as a mom and pop operation. If necessary each restaurant could create its own unique menu, décor, and even employee training, to better meet the needs of customers in its locale.

Federalism is based on the following principles:

- **Corporate headquarters is at the center, not the top.** The organization has a small central office found at the center of the company, not at the top. This means that the corporate staff is shrunk and instead of operating like a watchdog, making sure standard procedures are enforced, it researches new ideas and develops new strategies for the individual units to consider.
- **The power of the organization belongs to the units.** Those at the center of the organization, or corporate offices, support the operating units rather than dictate to them.
- **Organizations can be both large and small.** A large chain hotel or restaurant can have the advantage of an independently owned property through federalism. Because individual hotels would have a lot of autonomy and be able to decide things for themselves, they could react quickly to new competition, new ideas, and changing customer needs. Big companies can act like independently owned operations because they have the ability to do whatever it takes to make the customer happy. Imagine walking into McDonald's and asking for provolone cheese on your burger. Of course this request would be impossible to honor because each unit has a standard menu with limited choices. Although standardization is necessary to streamline service, making it as quick and efficient as possible, it doesn't allow for flexibility. In a more federal organization, greater regional variation in menus would be possible.

The employee in a federalist organization would have job duties much different from those found in a traditional centralized company. Here is a snapshot of federalist job elements.

First the employee would be cross trained so that he or she could perform a multitude of tasks. At the front desk, the employee could room guests, answer the switchboard, take reservations, answer any and all questions, take guest's luggage to their rooms, and park cars. The employee would have the authority to provide complete service to the guests when required. Employees would have their own "caseload" of customers to be responsible for. One person could pick guests up at the airport, check them into their room, take their luggage up, and arrange dinner reservations, rather than relying on several employees to perform separate services. The employee would have the authority to spend money to buy products in order to do the job. He or she would monitor his or her own work and performance. The employee could do whatever was necessary to keep customers satisfied during their stay.

Many large restaurant and hotel chains are reluctant to release their corporate power to their individual units. Centralized power and standard operating procedures can make the organization more efficient. It has certainly been responsible for much of the success experienced by McDonald's and Marriott during growth phases of development. It would have been difficult for these companies to provide a high level of quality service and a consistent product without uniform standards. But during periods of decreased growth and greater stability, operating units do not require the close supervision they needed when being developed. Decentralization, or the adoption of a more federal work organization, can lead to much greater flexibility and increased responsiveness to customers. In a decentralized hotel chain, each property would be unique in design, décor, policies, procedures, and products to reflect the needs of the people it employs and the guests it serves. A hotel in New Orleans would be much different in these aspects from one in New York City. Federalism is an interesting idea that may become more widely accepted as both employee groups and guests become increasingly diverse.

THEORY Z

Abraham Maslow developed the motivational theory of self-actualization described in detail in Chapter 7. According to Maslow human needs are arranged according to priority. Physiological needs are at the bottom and must be satisfied before the other higher level needs. Once physiological needs are satisfied, next the need for safety becomes dominant. Following safety are the needs to belong, for self-esteem, and finally, the highest need level, self-actualization, takes over when all lower needs are met.[17] Maslow later built upon McGregor's Theory X and Theory Y by developing **Theory Z** in 1968.[18] In Theory Z he proposed that once people have reached financial security, they would strive for a life driven by values such as creativity and production. Theory Z was further expanded by William Ouchi during the 1980s. It has emerged as a synthesis of both American and Japanese management styles.

Many believe that Maslow was ahead of his time with Theory Z, finding evidence in the new generation of workers who want a job that is fun, cool, and lets them discover who they really are. Richard Barton, head of Microsoft's Expedia, brought Theory Z to life when he said, "Work is not work. It's a hobby you happen to get paid for." Business results cannot be divorced from personal fulfillment. Productivity leaps come from the hearts and minds of people, not from reorganization and automation.[19]

THE SERVANT LEADER

The idea of manager as **servant leader** has great promise in today's decentralized, participative work environments. This theory proposes that managers see employees as equals and act as "servants" or facilitators of their success in the workplace. Managers provide the tools and resources that employees need to do their work rather than direction and control. With the advent of team-based organizations, it is important that managers create high-involvement work teams, not traditionally run departments. Management's role must change to a more supportive, less authoritarian one if employees are to take an active role in the decision-making process.

The idea of the servant leader is drawn from the teachings of Robert Greenleaf, considered to be one of the creators of the modern empowerment movement. According to Greenleaf a servant leader:[20]

- Asks questions of employees to find out how he or she can help, not to check up on them.
- Focuses less on production and more on voluntary action. Employees get things done because they know it's the right thing to do, not because they are coerced.
- Sees himself or herself as first among equals. Employees are colleagues, not underlings.
- Is trusting, accepting, open to new ideas, resilient, wise, insightful, imaginative, positive, and possesses a good sense of humor.
- Makes time for people.
- Accepts employees for who they are and does not attempt to re-create them in his image.
- Asks the following question as the ultimate test of good leadership: "Do those I serve grow as people?"

Although the principles offer many advantages in today's employee-oriented workplace, there are few true servant leaders. It is difficult to find a manager who truly believes that his employees are his equals and that his role is to facilitate their work. More often the opposite is true. Managers expect employees to facilitate their work. Yet the idea of manager as servant leader is gaining recognition with today's leaders who act more like facilitators than like dictators.

The principles of servant leadership require a complete shift in management perspective. To make this shift, managers must see themselves as just one of the boxcars, with the employees acting as the engine that drive the organization. It is based on the rather Zenlike idea that true power comes from the relinquishment of authority. Management gains real power by releasing it to their employees. When workers are highly involved, committed members of the team, both the department and the organization flourish in ways far beyond that possible when managers adopt a traditional role. Servant leaders have real power within their organizations.

YOUR MANAGEMENT PHILOSOPHY

In this chapter you have been introduced to a number of management theories, both historical and contemporary. Throughout history philosophies have changed in reaction to the societal situation of the times. Our current situation requires that managers distribute their power and knowledge to their employees, eliminating the traditional top-down chain of command. As we enter the twenty-first century, new and unique developments in our culture will give rise to innovative ways of dealing with people at work.

Many of the ideas in this book, including those from the past, can be applied to the management of hotels, restaurants, and other hospitality-related businesses. Your task as a leader is to pick and choose ideas that you feel are appropriate for you and your employees and fashion your own unique blend of leadership. You may employ Frederick Taylor's systematic approach to scheduling and organization along with McGregor's Theory Y assumptions and add a bit of Japanese management theory coupled with the ideas of servant leadership to formulate your own brand of management.

As you will realize, the leadership style that you employ is both a function of your personality and the type of employees you manage. Rather than basing your leadership methods on the latest fad ideas, you must find a style that is comfortable for you and your employees. This will be the right management style for you.

CONCLUSION

Management theory has evolved over time to solve the challenges faced during particular eras. Ours has evolved into a knowledge-based society where technology is replacing manual labor. The evolution began with the industrial revolution when early factories were developed. It continued during the second phase, the productivity revolution, when the first attempts were made to use knowledge to improve work methods. Frederick Taylor's theory of scientific management became widely accepted during this time. It was based on the principles that decisions about work should be based on precise, scientific procedures with management controlling the planning and employees simply doing what they are told. The third and current phase of thought is the management revolution brought about by the humanistic movement, suggesting that organizations should first facilitate the growth of the individual and then seek profits.

Humanistic theory originated with the Hawthorne Studies that revealed that concern for employee welfare boosts productivity and morale. This was followed by the development of McGregor's Theory X and Theory Y, which proposed that management's actions are based on their assumptions about people. Theory Y in turn gave rise to the philosophy of participative management which proposed that management should involve workers in the decision-making process by encouraging each person to contribute their ideas in a systematic fashion. Concern for the quality of work life also evolved leading to such programs as job enlargement, job enrichment, and flexible scheduling.

Contemporary management theory was initiated in the 1980s and proliferated during the 1990s in response to increased competition and workplace complexity. Americans began patterning their practices after the Japanese by empowering their employees, adopting quality principles, and decentralizing their organizations. Open-book management has taken employee involvement to a new level by proposing that line employees share in the financial operation of the company. Some predict that as our knowledge-based society evolves organizations will adopt federalist principles where power is further decentralized or distributed to individual units limiting control by corporate headquarters. According to Theory

Z, work is synonymous with personal fulfillment and will become "a hobby you get paid for." Finally the manager of tomorrow will be a servant leader who realizes that true power comes from the relinquishment of authority.

Our current business environment requires that management distribute their power and knowledge to their employees, thus changing or even eliminating the traditional top-down chain of command. Your task as a leader of tomorrow is to recognize this and develop a management philosophy that is both empowering and also is consistent with your personal beliefs and assumptions.

K E Y   T E R M S

Decentralize	Theory Z
Scientific Management	Flextime
Humanistic Management	Japanese Management
Hawthorne Studies	Just-in-time
Theory X	Kaizen
Theory Y	4S
Participative Management	Open-Book Management
Scanlon Plan	Federalist Organizations
Job Enlargement	Centralize
Job Enrichment	Servant Leader

N O T E S

1. P. Drucker, *The Post-Capitalist Society* (New York: Harper Business, 1993), 1–8.

2. P. Drucker, *Managing in a Time of Great Change* (New York: Dutton, Truman Talley Books. 1955), 68–81.

3. Ibid.

4. Ibid.

5. F. Taylor, *Principles of Scientific Management* (New York: Harper and Row, 1912).

6. D. Freedman, "Is Management Still a Science?" *Harvard Business Review* (November/December 1992): 26.

7. R. Zemke, "Maslow for a New Millennium," *Training* (December 1988): 54–58.

8. D. McGregor, *The Human Side of Enterprise* (New York: McGraw-Hill Book Company, 1960), 33–35.

9. High Performance Work Practices and Firm Performance. Washington, D.C.: U.S. Department of Labor, 1993, i.

10. S. Markham, K. Dow, and W. Cox Jr., "The Evolutionary Development of a Scanlon Plan," *Compensation and Benefits Review* (March-April 1992) 50–56.

11. R. Woodmand and J. Sherwood, "A Comprehensive Look at Job Design," *Personnel Journal* 56, no. 8 (August 1977): 388.

12. P. Perreive and F. Vickory, "Combating Job Stress," *Training and Development Journal* (April 1988): 51–53.

13. I. Abramovitch, "Beyond Kaizen," *Success* (February 1994): 85.

14. "What's Killing Japanese Business? Japanese Management Style," *Tokyo Business Today* (July 1993): 24.

15. J. Case, *Open-Book Management* (New York: Harper Business, 1995), 73.

16. C. Handy, *The Age of Unreason* (Boston: Harvard Business School Press, 1994), 134–141.

17. A. Maslow, *Motivation and Personality*, 2nd ed. (New York: Harper & Brothers, 1970).

18. A. Maslow, D. Stephens, and G. Heil, *Maslow on Management* (New York: John Wiley & Sons, 1998), 72.

19. F. Rose, "A New Age for Business?" *Fortune* (1990): 157.

20. A. Fraker, "Robert K Greenleaf and Business Ethics: There is No Code," *Reflections on Leadership: How Robert Greenleaf's Theory of Servant Leadership Influenced Today's Top Management Thinkers*, Edited by Larry Spears (New York: Wiley, 1995): 153.

CASE 11.1: PHILOSOPHY OF MANAGEMENT

Melissa is very excited. She just learned that she is being considered for a promotion from front desk supervisor to assistant front office manager. The new job would expand her supervisory responsibilities to the entire front office, including reservations, the bellstand, and concierge. Next week Melissa will be interviewed by the hotel general manager as part of the selection process. Her supervisor has warned her that Harriet Roth, the G.M., is very big on management style. She always asks interviewees to describe their philosophy of management.

Although Melissa did study management theory back in college, she never really gave much thought to her own philosophy of management. After careful thought and consideration, Melissa decides that her management style is guided by three principles:

- Employee empowerment.

- Treat employees with respect.

- Support employees so they will be successful.

She feels that this response might be too simple and wants to be able to describe her management philosophy in terms of various theories. She goes to her mentor for help with this.

1. Based on the three principles that guide Melissa's supervisory style, empowerment, respect, and support, what management theory or theories described in this chapter best support her views?

2. Using your knowledge of management theory and Melissa's three guiding principles, write a statement that Melissa might use during her interview to best describe her philosophy of management.

R E V I E W   Q U E S T I O N S

1. Name three developments both within the hospitality industry and in other fields that indicate our movement toward a knowledge-based society.
2. Draw a timeline and plot the evolution of management, beginning with the industrial revolution. Organize your timeline by listing years on the bottom events and theories on top, beginning with the Industrial Revolution.

Ind. Rev.

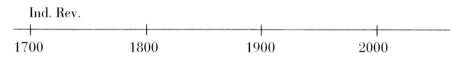

1700   1800   1900   2000

3. Most people agree that there were both positive and negative aspects of Scientific Management. Analyze these by using a T diagram and listing the pros and cons of Taylor's Scientific Management theory:

Pros	Cons

4. Although the Hawthorne study failed to demonstrate the expected results, what did we learn from this experiment?
5. How does job enrichment differ from job enlargement?
6. What job duties might a restaurant server have in a federalist organization?

Match the following statements to the corresponding theory:

7. Servant leadership   a. Allow employees to see how money is used.
8. Theory Z   b. Synthesis of American and Japanese manage-
9. Theory X   ment
10. Scientific Management   c. Managers see employees as equals
11. Open Book   d. Power is distributed to individual units
12. Federalism   e. Managers believe employees dislike work
     f. Focuses on technical efficiency

C R I T I C A L   T H I N K I N G   E X E R C I S E S

1. Now that you have reviewed the various management theories, which one appeals to you the most? Why?
2. Take the quiz in Figure 11.3 to test your assumptions. What were your results—are you more Theory X or Theory Y? Were you surprised by the results?
3. Review the various theories described in the chapter and answer the following questions about your own views on management style:
   a. McGregor's Theory X and Theory Y were based on a number of assumptions about people. What are your assumptions about employees?

    b. What degree of employee participation would you be comfortable with?

    c. What will you do to create a satisfying quality of work life in your deparatment?

    d. What might you do to be a "servant leader"?

    e. How you will assure that your employees are fully committed to the organization?

4. Historically larger organizations in the hospitality industry have been very centralized. What factors have prevented such companies as Marriott and McDonald's from adopting a more decentralized, federalist style of operation?

5. As you found in this chapter, management theory has evolved over time. Recently many new ideas about leadership have been set forth at a fairly rapid rate. Think about the changes you expect to occur in the work place during the next five to ten years and try to predict a new management theory that might evolve.

O N - L I N E   L I N K

Our particular personality type often determines the leadership style that we are most comfortable with. In fact many organizations are providing their managers with customized training and support based on the results of a personality assessment tool called the Myers-Briggs Type Indicator. Those taking the survey answer a series of questions and then identify their "type" or personality style. Although the Myers-Briggs inventory is not available on line, there is a similar inventory that you can take and score right on your computer for a $3 fee. Go to www.personalitypage.com and complete the survey that is available at the site. Once it is scored, read the information provided about your personality type and answer the following questions:

    1. Do the results seem accurate—does the description of your identified personality type seem like you?

    2. How might your personality type affect your work habits? What aspects of management might come easy to you (creativity, organization, relations with people) and what aspects of management might you have to work harder at based on your personality type?

P O R T F O L I O   E X E R C I S E

Companies today hire and promote individuals who can inspire workers to do their best. Add to your portfolio a statement that describes your personal philosophy of management. This will communicate to employers the attitudes and beliefs that you bring to the job that will make you a successful leader. As you summarize your philosophy, base it on your answers to question 3 in the Critical Thinking Exercises.

Strategic Management

12

ADVANCED ORGANIZER

As we enter the twenty-first century, the lodging industry must overcome a number of challenges. New brands created during the 1990 expansion resulted in a narrower market, making it more difficult for hotel chains to differentiate their products and services. Many chains have experienced stock price weakness, providing reduced return on investment to its holders. This can be attributed to a weakened market in resort areas such as Hawaii and a fall off in convention and group business in such major cities as New York and Chicago. To complicate matters customers want greater value for their dollar and are more demanding than ever before.

To remain viable in the uncertain future, hospitality organizations must address these issues by continually reinventing themselves through strategic management, keeping an eye to the role of their human assets. Supervisors are key players in the development and implementation of strategy. They are the "front-line" workers in the quest for success.

BEHAVIORAL OBJECTIVES

- Describe the important role of strategic management in assuring organizational success.

- Identify outcomes experienced by organizations when they fail to address the needs of customers, owners, and employees.

The Mansion on Turtle Creek Main Dining Room

- Demonstrate understanding of core competencies.

- Differentiate between internal and external scanning.

- Describe organizational practices including balanced scorecard, reengineering, learning organization, and systems thinking.

- Apply the principles of systems thinking to organizational practices.

CREATING VALUE

Success in the hospitality industry is determined by a company's ability to create value for its customers, employees, and owners. In order to sustain growth, companies must constantly increase customer satisfaction, reduce costs, and increase human resources effectiveness. To be successful organizations must address the needs of each group in a balanced manner. Companies that meet the needs of employees and owners, but fail to meet customer needs will lack customer retention. On the other hand, when companies meet the needs of owners and customers, but not those of employees, they will experience high levels of turnover and low motivation. Organizations that meet the needs of customers and employees, but not owners, will experience falling stock prices and lack financial resources. Only those organizations that consistently meet the needs of all three factions, employees, customers, and owners, will experience sustained success and profitability.

To achieve this goal, organizations must carefully plan, manage, and measure results. In the past, strategic management took place at the top of the organization chart, but today organizations realize that planning and implementation are ineffective if employees at all levels are not made part of the process. It is up to supervisors and managers to get employees involved in strategic management.

The purpose of **strategic management** is to structure the organization so that resources can be targeted to achieve corporate goals. This process takes place at different levels within the organization.

- **Corporate.** Company owners, or the corporate headquarters, manage the development of the overall strategic plan that outlines the company's mission, vision, and goals that are to be achieved.
- **Departmental.** Each department in the organization also creates a plan to identify specific steps to be taken to help the company achieve its overall goals.
- **Individual.** Strategic planning occurs at the individual level where managers, supervisors, and line employees identify the ways they help the organization meet its goals.

Successful organizations integrate corporate, departmental, and individual plans to coordinate goals. The cornerstone of strategic management is **strategic planning,** which is the process of determining what your organization intends to accomplish and how to direct resources toward accomplishing goals in the coming months and years.[1] It involves developing a corporate vision, creating a mission, identifying current and potential customers, and defining the products you will offer. Finally you must assess your resources—human, financial, and knowledge based—and determine where they should be allocated or directed for future success.

Strategic planning is receiving newfound interest among organizations today. A recent survey by the Association of Management Consulting Firms found that strategic planning is the number one management issue now, and is likely to be for the next five years. In the past, its importance was questioned because companies found that it was too difficult to develop long-range plans when the marketplace was constantly shifting. It was impossible to plan for the future when everything kept changing overnight. Today change is even more evident, but companies are developing new attitudes toward strategic planning. They no longer see their strategic plan as set in stone, or something that must be followed exactly. Instead it is an ever-evolving guide that provides flexible direction for the future. According to Harry Mintzberg, strategic planning is like molding a clay pot over time. The design gets clearer and better after you begin shaping the organization's future and determining what is possible.[2] Many organizations create a long-term strategic plan, but update it annually or semiannually as needed.

CORE COMPETENCIES

The essence of strategy is found in a company's ability to distinguish itself from its competition. Choosing to perform different activities than your competition, or choosing to perform them in a unique manner does this. It means developing your company's **core competencies,** or the special knowledge and skills that distinguish your business from its competition. For example Starbucks distinguished itself from its competition by developing a distinctive product, delivering it differently than its competition, and managing growth in a unique manner. They were the first company to serve European coffees in the United States in a big way; they offer customized service to their customers, and through their avoidance of franchising, Starbucks keeps tight control over product quality and growth.

PEOPLE DRIVE SUCCESS

Of particular importance in the future is planning as it applies to human resources. Management guru Peter Drucker predicts that in the near future, businesses will evolve from an emphasis on **physical capital** such as equipment, supplies, and products, to an emphasis on **human capital** or the value of the people that work there.[3] Organizations will become knowledge based, focusing on the expertise, skills, education, and training of their workers. Companies who fail to shift their focus will be left in dust of those who optimize the value of their employees. Customers today are very demanding, and they have many choices in our marketplace. We must do more for less, and the best way to accomplish this is by getting the most from every employee.

Strategic planning will reflect this trend by focusing on the management of people in the organization. New systems must be identified and planned to foster employee self-management and commitment. Employees must know that it's their commitment, their ideas, and their work ethic that will drive your company's success. As a supervisor, you must focus on basic issues like getting the right people in the right jobs, giving them proper training, and maximizing the benefits of a diverse workforce. You need to create a work environment where employees can be successful by finding ways to help your employees develop the capabilities they need to succeed now and in the future.

Thus strategic planning, as it applies both the organization as a whole and the people who work there, will play a key role in the success of both the company and its workforce. It reflects both the organization's and its members' commitment to those who come after them. Those who create and follow a long-range plan are demonstrating their desire to build an enduring institution that will leave behind a legacy for those that come after them. Thus the long view must be a shared view that reaches in two directions: embodying wisdom and values from the past as well as hopes and dreams for the future.[4]

ROLES AND RESPONSIBILITIES

The chief executive officer (CEO) is ultimately responsible for developing the strategic plan and for implementing it. Well-known corporate leaders such as Ray Kroc, Walt Disney, Bill Marriott, and Horst Schulze have given their organizations direction and meaning. They have modeled high standards and have provided the inspired vision that drives the strategic plan to reality.

Although the CEO is the major player in strategic planning, it takes a team effort to develop the plan and oversee its execution. Teams produce better strategic plans because they bring a wealth of ideas to the process, and through their participation, they generate ownership of the vision. The planning team typically consists of top-level executives within the organization. The strategic planning team depends on the rest of the organization to provide information and implement the plan. People support what they help create. The more people in the organization at all levels that help plan and implement strategic goals, the more likely that the company will achieve success.

Today companies realize that people are the link between a strategy and its success and try to keep everyone involved throughout the sequence of events.

BEST PRACTICES

At Ritz-Carlton goals include providing quick, efficient check-in, and making certain that guest rooms that receive total maintenance every ninety days. Employees put these goals into action by developing the following strategies:

- Hotel Engineers develop a system called CARE (Clean and Repair Everything) to create defect free guestrooms. Housekeeping and engineering combine forces to deep clean each room and provide preventive maintenance every nintey days.

- At the Ritz-Carlton, Buckhead, business travelers are checked in quickly and efficiently, and leisure guests are given the option of a more pampered check-in.

One planning process that gets everyone in the organization involved is called "future search" and involves finding common ground for plan development.[5] In this procedure a large group of stakeholders. which might include management, employees, and perhaps even customers, assemble for a marathon session to examine the past, present, and future of their organization. They then formulate strategic goals based on the vision of the future they have created. They must identify core capabilities that will create value for customers, employees, and stockholders.

THE STRATEGIC PLANNING PROCESS

The goal of strategic planning is to provide a blueprint for the future. This blueprint or plan is subject to change and revision as new opportunities and threats develop. Although business owners or the corporate headquarters initiate the planning process, ideally all employees will be involved from dishwasher to general manager. See Figure 12.1 to learn about the practices of the best strategic planners. Without support throughout the organization, it will be difficult for the company to realize its goals.

THE COMPANY MISSION

A company mission statement is a brief description of the organization's major goals and values. All hospitality organization share the mission of creating value for the customer, but differ in specifically how they accomplish this goal. As they create their statement of mission, companies must ask themselves such fundamental questions as:

- What is the purpose of our company?
- Who is the customer?
- What is important us?

- Think out of the box. Develop ideas and plans that shift your business to new arenas. Don't just stay with the same old practices.
- Use continuous improvement as your guide. Create plans that are flexible and keep trying to make them better.
- Communicate your strategic plan throughout the organization.
- Emphasize action plans and measurable objectives.
- Identify and build core competencies that make your business unique.
- Don't mistake improvements to operational efficiency for strategic planning. It's not just about increasing productivity, but developing new ideas that will increase future success.
- Make strategy implementation part of everyone's job.

*P. Galagan. "Strategic Planning Is Back." *Training & Development* (April 1997): 32–38.

Figure 12.1 Ten Practices of the Best Strategic Planners*

- What will our business be in the future?
- How can we increase the value we give customers?

The answers to these questions will help the organization identify its current status and develop a overall plan for the future. For example, MHOA, McDonald's Hispanic Operator's Association, a self-help organization focused on serving as a resource to Hispanic owner/operators and the entire McDonald's system, has identified its mission as:[6]

- Representing owner operators.
- Supporting the economic growth of its members.
- Providing a forum for the exchange of information and services.
- Recognizing the achievements and contributors of its members.
- Supporting the development of the Hispanic consumer.
- Supporting McDonald's corporate goals.

The organization's mission statement should be exciting and motivating. It should include the major goals the organization wants to achieve and the values that drive it. The mission is publicized to customers, owners, employees, and to the general public so it should be concise, well-written, and accurate.

VISION

The mission statement is often based on the corporate vision. A compelling vision in and of itself is a force to be reckoned with. It builds commitment and drives people to take action they might otherwise not support. Several years ago Ritz-Carlton Hotels had the vision of winning the coveted Malcolm Baldridge National Quality award. They transformed this vision into action and made major changes in their organization. Not only did they win it the first time, they also have become the first and only service company to win the award two times in a row. Horst Schulze, president and chief operating officer, recognized the important role that employees have played in the company's success when he said, "This award belongs to the 17,000 ladies and gentlemen at 36 Ritz-Carlton Hotels and Resorts worldwide who are committed to providing the very best experience for our guests."[7]

Companies must have a clear idea of where they want to go in the future. In the past involvement in the planning process was limited to the corporate elite—only those at the top were involved. Today most companies realize that getting everyone involved means greater innovation and higher levels of employee commitment to corporate goals.

SCANNING

Another important step in strategic planning is scanning which allows you to gain a better understanding of how factors inside and outside your organization affect it. Factors that are important to the future of the company are strengths, weaknesses, opportunities, and threats. Strengths and weakness are found within the organization itself whereas opportunities and threats are outside the company. All four factors are then considered as the strategic plan is formulated.

ENVIRONMENTAL SCANNING

Environmental scanning identifies the external parameters of the environment that your department or your organization operates within. The external environment consists of opportunities and threats that are outside the organization and cannot be controlled. The external environment has two parts, the task environment or those factors directly affected by the organization such as suppliers, competitors, and customers, and the societal environment, including politics, technology, and population changes.

External scanning at the task level includes investigating other hotels and restaurants that are near your location or have the potential of reducing your customer base in order to find out specifically what they are doing to be successful. Scanning related to human resources areas might involve finding out what competing hotels or restaurants pay their employees, what benefits they offer, and the types of training they provide. Not only are you competing with these hotels for customers, you are also competing to attract the best employees. When you scan the environment for opportunities and threats, you must also consider the societal level by examining external trends in business and society in general to assess the effect these might have on your department or organization. Some of these factors might include increased diversity, our aging society, and low unemployment rates. All these factors contribute to changes in the way you must recruit and hire employees.

Environmental scanning is done by collecting information through observation, written questionnaires, focus groups, and also by doing library or online research. Your goal is to identify key economic, political, social, and technological trends that might affect your business.

INTERNAL SCANNING

The internal environment consists of the strengths and weakness that are part of the organization itself. These might include the organization's culture (see Chapter 14), the skill level of its employees, and the financial assets the company holds. Internal scanning involves assessing whether your department or organization has the ability to achieve its vision. From a human resources standpoint, you would consider the abilities and skill level of your employees. Are they motivated and able to provide the level of service you propose?

BENCHMARKING

In addition to examining the internal environment and competition, strategic planners often look outside their own industry or markets to try to anticipate the next winning move. For example hotels might consider some of the innovative practices found in patient care in hospitals today and apply those principles to their organization. This is a total quality management principle known as **benchmarking.** If a restaurant is seeking to improve food production efficiency, they might look to the manufacturing industry for ideas on how to increase speed and quality in their kitchens. See Figure 12.2 for additional examples of benchmarking.

Remember that benchmarking is the enthusiastic borrowing of ideas from other companies and other industries. Here are a few good ideas relating to strategic management that the hospitality industry might want to borrow.*

Six-Step Problem Solving
All employees at Xerox have been trained in small group activities and problem solving techniques. The company teaches them a series of six steps for solving problems: (1) identifying and selecting problems, (2) analyzing problems, (3) generating solutions, (4) select and plan the solution, (5) implement the solution, and (6) evaluate the solution. Employees learn and practice these tools during training sessions that last for several days. Training is presented in "family groups" or by department and then applied back on the job.

Boundaries
Boundaries limit the flow of information and keep individuals and groups isolated from each other. General Electric has opened up boundaries by bringing various departments together at meetings, conferences, and workshops to keep ideas flowing. Opening up the organization so that everyone can share ideas fosters innovation.

ANet
Anderson Consulting has developed a system known as ANet that links its 82,000 employees worldwide. The network connects people so they can share information via data, voice, and video. When problems with customers occur, they are posted on-line and others within the network can suggest solutions.

*D. Garvin, "Building a Learning Organization, 47–80.

Figure 12.2 Benchmarking Examples

FORMULATE THE STRATEGIC PLAN

The next step is to formulate the critical success factors that the organization must achieve to reach its vision. This phase begins with the development of a series of core strategies that bridge the gap between where the company is now and where it wants to be in the future. It is the specific actions that the organization will take to achieve its corporate vision.

CORE STRATEGIES

The strategic plan is based on a series of core strategies that guide the specific actions that will be taken throughout the organization. They provide a framework to everyone in the company as they set department, team, and individual goals. Core strategies might include:

- Empowerment of employees.
- Self-directed work teams.
- Value-added products.
- Revitalize image.
- Cost reduction.

Each core strategy must be defined so that everyone knows exactly what is meant by the goal and how they can contribute to it. If the organization's core strategy is to empower employees. it must define what it means by empowerment, how much control will be given to employees, and how it will be monitored.

STRATEGIC ACTIONS

To ensure that all departments and teams are organized under the same core strategies, a series of specific action steps are identified by each department or area in the company. In a hotel the front desk, housekeeping, sales, restaurants, and so on each identify the specific actions they will take during the next year to support the corporate plan. Only when all areas of the organization are adhering to the same core strategies and have identified actions they will take to achieve these strategies, will the company successfully achieve its goals.

Once each department has identified its strategies, a review meeting consisting of representatives from each area must be called to collectively share, critique, and refine the unit plans. If the sales department hopes to increase return customers and housekeeping plans to adopt cost-cutting practices that may affect the cleanliness of guest rooms, the two departments must carefully review these actions to make certain that housekeeping's goals do not conflict with those of sales.

MEASURING PERFORMANCE

An important component of strategic planning is the ability to measure organizational performance. If you don't know how well you are doing, you won't know if you have achieved your goals. Planning without the follow up of evaluation is like judging the long jump without measuring the distance of the leap. Officials would have to "guesstimate" how far each person jumped, never really knowing who won. Translating strategy into measurable objectives is the next challenge in the strategic planning process.

THE BALANCED SCORECARD

The **balanced scorecard** takes the company's mission and translates it into measurable objectives so that critical success factors can be evaluated and compared. In other words the scorecard highlights the questions that good business managers would normally ask about performance and communicates the importance of these measures throughout the whole company.[8]

The balanced scorecard approach translates a company's strategy into objectives with regard to four areas of performance: financial indicators, customer satisfaction, internal process, and innovation and improvement. Figure 12.3 describes some of the factors that might be included on a balanced scorecard. It is a sophisticated business model that helps a company understand what's really driving its success.[9]

The balanced scorecard provides answers to four basic questions about corporate performance:[10]

1. How do customers perceive us?
2. What must we do to be excellent?
3. What must we do to add value to overall operations?

Financial Information

- Cash flow.
- Ability to meet budget.
- Gross profits.
- Cost factors.

Customer Measures

- Results of satisfaction measures.
- Percentage of complaints.
- Percentage of return customers.

Internal Processes

- Training programs.
- Turnover rate.
- Employee satisfaction.
- Employee accident ratio.

Growth and Development

- New products developed.
- New markets entered.
- Organizational improvements: TQM, empowerment, staff diversity.

Figure 12.3 Balanced Scorecard

4. What are the shareholders' expectations in terms of financial returns and long-term viability?

The balanced scorecard is like the control panel on an airplane in that it keeps track of many measures of corporate performance at once—everything from customer satisfaction to financial profit.

An important intent of the balanced scorecard approach is to link strategic objectives so people can understand how their actions affect company success. Most companies using this practice incorporate special software that tracks the measurement of different factors. Scorecard software can be distributed throughout a company's computer network so managers across the entire organization can access it. For example, if a hotel is experiencing a drop in occupancy, the front desk manager, director of marketing, and housekeeping manager will all see the same information and be able to solve the problem together.

According to a recent study by the Institute of Management Accountants, 64 percent of U.S. companies are experimenting with some sort of new performance measurement system.[11] Hilton Hotels recently adopted a balanced scorecard system to overcome performance discrepancies among its hotels and to ensure consistent products and service at all properties.[12] Read more about Hilton's new approach in Insight 12.1.

How do you decide what to include on your scorecard? Typically there are five aspects of business that are addressed:

- **Financial measures:** Profit and loss, return on investment.

INSIGHT 12.1

BALANCED SCORECARD AT HILTON

In an effort to ensure greater consistency in service and product quality among its properties, Hilton Hotels adopted a balanced scorecard system to measure the creation of value.* The company initiated this system to integrate all aspects of the organization and to change the company's culture to achieve the desired results. The balanced scorecard allowed Hilton to translate its strategy into operations by measurement and communication throughout the organization.

The process began with the development of the Hilton Value Chain to link long-term objectives to short-term practices. The components of the value chain are five stakeholders that Hilton serves: customers, team members or employees, owners and shareholders, vendors, and the community as a whole. Value drivers are the factors that contribute to successfully serving value chain members and include service delivery, revenue maximization, operational effectiveness, and loyalty.

Next Hilton developed eight measurements to assess the organization's present and future performance. The achievement of property goals is linked to incentive bonuses, performance reviews, salary increases, and stock-option grants. This allows for the alignment of action with goals. People throughout the corporation from line employees to top management know what is expected of them and how they are doing. Results are communicated in a simple manner with the green zone indicating that the property is meeting or exceeding goals, yellow designating results below goal, and red identifying performance far below the goal. Team members can easily see how their hotel is performing and make necessary adjustments.

*D. Huckstein, and R. Duboff, "Hilton Hotels: A Comprehensive Approach to Delivering Value for All Stakeholders," *Cornell Hotel & Restaurant Administration Quarterly* 40, no. 4 (August 1999): 1–15.

- **Operational measures:** Food cost, labor cost, productivity per man-hours.
- **Customer data:** Measures of service performance, including product quality, speed of delivery.
- **Soft measures:** Customer complaints and employee errors.
- **Employee measures:** Including staff turnover, morale, training, innovation, and learning.

Begin the process of selecting factors by surveying your customers to find out what is important to them. Identify both the financial measures such as budgets, forecasts, and profit and loss reports that indicate how well your business is doing. Also consider the nonfinancial measures that you will track. These might include guest satisfaction with room cleanliness, speed of service at the front desk, amenities, and a myriad of other factors that affect their stay. Next measurements of customer satisfaction are linked to financial indicators. For example you might measure the percentage of sales of new menu items in a restaurant. Or, you might link new guest service training programs to increases in guest satisfaction and revenue. Marriott considers an additional important component of overall operational health, employee satisfaction. Each year the company surveys all associates and includes a measure of employee satisfaction in their scorecard.

STRATEGIC PLAN ROLL OUT

Once the company has developed a shared vision and translated it into measurable objectives, the next step in the process is to assure buy-in, or the commitment of everyone in the organization to the plan. If your company has truly gotten everyone involved in the planning process and the company vision is based on personal vision, commitment should logically follow because the plan is one that not only addresses the company's concerns, but also addresses the concerns of the individuals that work there.

The goal of this step in the planning process is to get everyone excited about the new direction the company will be taking, and to translate this excitement into commitment and hard work. Here are ways that companies communicate their strategic plan:

- Distribute a summary of the plan to all employees.
- Hold an organizationwide manager's meeting.
- Organize departmental meetings for employees.
- Hold workshops to discuss the process and build supporting plans at the departmental and individual levels.
- Display posters with planning themes.
- Distribute cards, buttons, or name tags with the mission printed on them.
- Produce a motivational videotape featuring the CEO explaining the vision.
- Publish internal and external articles to promote the plan.

KEEPING THE PLAN RELEVANT

Most plans are designed to project goals for the next five years, but you can't expect everything to remain static in today's volatile marketplace. The strategic plan is an organic document, meaning that it must react quickly to changes in the environment. Ideally the strategic plan will be reviewed and updated annually. In times of crisis or increased competition, companies may need to change their goals more frequently. New competitors or changes in the political situation may require drastic change to the strategic plan. During the Gulf War, concern about terrorism was rampant, and convention and meeting travel nearly came to a standstill for several months. Hotels had to revamp their financial goals to reflect this sudden and extreme situation.

DEPARTMENTAL STRATEGIC PLANNING

Now that you understand the broad principles of strategic planning at the organizational level—developing the corporate mission, creating a vision, formulating, implementing, and measuring results—it is time to examine these principles to the planning process at the departmental level. The old adage, the whole is only as good as its parts, applies here. The organization can only be as successful as the departments and work groups that comprise it. In this section we will examine some planning principles that you can use with your work group to increase their involvement and commitment to your organization's goals.

As a supervisor or manager, you may not be part of the strategic planning team, but you still play a key role in the process. Typically each department in an organization will develop its own plan that takes its direction from the strategic focus of the overall operation. At the departmental level you must develop goals that:

- **Support corporate strategy.** Identify the priorities that are addressed in the corporate plan and develop specific departmental goals that will make your area instrumental in helping the organization achieve its mission. For example, if your restaurant chain's goal is to develop a menu strategy that is based on the regional preferences of its customers, your store might contribute to this by first conducting research to examine dining preferences of those who live in your region. Next, you might create and test a series of new menu items and then incorporate these into your existing selections.

- **Support the plans of other departments.** If the catering department plans to market its services to more local groups, the kitchen might support this by developing recipes for some lower cost items that would appeal to those having weddings, family reunions, or small functions.

- **Make employees accountable.** Incorporate strategic objectives into your selection process, training programs, and performance appraisal systems. If your goals are to have a friendlier, more helpful staff, make sure you focus on these qualities when you hire and train employees. When you assess performance, be sure to evaluate specific behaviors that demonstrate friendliness and helpfulness.

CREATE SHARED VISION

The first step in getting your employees involved in planning is to create a shared vision for your area or work group that will help your organization reach its overall vision of the future. Before developing a group vision, we must take a step back to focus on the individual. Shared vision begins with the personal visions of the individuals who comprise the organization.[13] Shared or team vision is built on the dreams and desires of its members. This differs from the traditional approach to visioning which involves a top-down process whereby managers identify the vision and tell the employees to buy into it. How much more effective this process will be if leaders first asked employees, "What do you want our department to become?" and then crafted a shared vision meshing the ideas and dreams of employees into the corporate vision to create the final product.

Some companies seek to get employees involved in the overall visioning process right from the beginning. They realize that employees who feel like they are part of the planning process will be more committed to achieving the organization's vision. Companies that seek to create a shared vision typically follow this process:

1. Gain top management support for shared vision. Without this, all effort will be futile.
2. Form a steering committee consisting of employees and managers who are committed to the vision process.
3. Communicate the process to all employees in the company.
4. Hold meetings at the departmental level to identify members' visions for both the company as a whole and each department.
5. Form cross-functional teams or small groups consisting of representatives from various departments to refine the process and develop an overall vision of the future.
6. Communicate the vision throughout the organization, generate feedback, and revise.
7. A final shared vision evolves that provides a direction that ensures the future success of the organization.

Even if your company is not committed to this organizationwide process, you can use many of the same principles outlined earlier to develop a shared vision for your work team.

- Sit down with employees individually and in groups and ask them to identify those factors that would make both themselves and the department successful.
- Ask employees what they want for themselves and for the department. Of course, many of the dreams will be impossible to accomplish, but perhaps the essence of the desire will not be.
- Incorporate personal visions into departmental goals. An employee who dreams of owning a hotel one day may find that there is much that he or she can do right now, in his or her current job, to help prepare for the employee's dream. One component or skill set the employee will need to realize his or her dream is current department and overall hotel operations knowledge. By allowing the employee to pursue extra departmental training and to cross train in other areas of the hotel, you might help the employee to work toward his or her own personal vision while upgrading skills and making a more motivated and valuable employee now. So a personal vision of knowledge acquisition can be incorporated into a departmental vision of developing a highly skilled work group.

DEVELOPMENTS IN MANAGEMENT STRATEGY

In this next section, you will learn about some new developments in the field of strategic management. These newer practices are being tested in many organizations, some of them in the hospitality industry. By understanding such principles as reengineering, systems thinking, and knowledge-based management as they related to planning and leading in the hospitality industry, you will have a clearer understanding of important organizational practices.

REENGINEERING

Reengineering is one of the most popular strategic management tools of the past decade. To many reengineering has become synonymous with downsizing, although that certainly wasn't the intent of those who coined this term. **Reengineering** is defined as the fundamental rethinking and radical redesign of business processes to achieve dramatic improvements in performance, including cost, quality, service, and speed.[14]

There are five basic stages to reengineering:

1. **Identify your case for action.** This is a statement of what you need to do. The reengineering process begins with the recognition by corporate executives of the need for restructuring the organization. Goals are established by breakthrough thinking, by looking beyond established goals and procedures and developing new ways of doing things. Companies must develop a change plan that will serve as a guide for the reengineering team.

2. **Identify the organization's core processes.** How does your organization get things done at this time? When identifying the model, focus on process and strategies that are of value to the customer. In a hotel this would include check-in, checkout, room cleanliness, and how well the hotel solves problems as they arise.

3. **Build the business operating model.** This is accomplished by identifying your vision for the future. How should the organization operate for optimal performance and guest service?

4. **Process redesign.** This involves coming up with a better way to deliver your products to your customers.

5. **Implementation of the new design.** Putting the vision of your new organization into practice. This might necessitate evaluating and retraining existing personnel.

THE HUMAN ASPECTS OF REENGINEERING

Companies must focus their attention on the human aspects of organizational performance during reengineering if they expect employees to support the endeavor. Reengineering isn't just about making structural changes to the organization; it is also about increasing worker performance. The following tasks related to people in the organization must be completed as part of reengineering to create outcomes that increase human capital:[15]

- Empower customer contact employees.
- Perform job analysis.

- Prepare job descriptions for both employees and teams.
- Identify the skill needs of the organization and staffing requirements that correspond to those needs.
- Create a management structure.
- Redesign organizational boundaries. Some departments such as bell stand, front desk, and concierge might be combined, and employees in each area cross trained.
- Design career paths for employees.
- Develop incentives for optimal performance.
- Plan the implementation of the changes.

Reengineering is similar to the total quality management (TQM) process in that it involves organizational change and is initiated and carried out by top management (see Chapter 14 for more on TQM). The two differ in that reengineering involves radical change over a short period of time whereas TQM involves less dramatic continuous improvement. Reengineering is something that you do once and do right. One expert describes it as similar to losing weight. You don't keep losing the same twenty pounds every year. You lose it once and then maintain that weight loss.[16]

Some organizations have had great success following reengineering, although many have failed. It is estimated that as many as 50 percent to 70 percent of reengineering efforts fail to achieve the goals set for them.[17] Failure is often due to unclear definitions of the process, setting unrealistic expectations, having inadequate resources, taking too long to complete, and lack of top management support. Read about a company that has found an innovative alternative to downsizing during slow periods in Insight 12.2.

> *Business reengineering means putting aside much of the received wisdom of two hundred years of industrial management. It means forgetting how work was done in the age of the mass market and deciding how it can be done now. In business reengineering, old job titles and old organizational arrangements—departments, divisions, groups, and so on—cease to matter. They are artifacts of another age. What matters in reengineering is how we want to organize work today, given the demands of today's markets and the power of today's technologies.*
>
> —Michael Hammer and James Champy,
> *Reengineering the Corporation*

THE NEW ORGANIZATION

Peter Drucker, an expert in the field of strategic management, predicts that twenty years from now, the typical large business will be information based and consist of groups of specialists brought together in task forces that will cut across traditional departments.[18] At the heart of the new organization will be the knowledge possessed by these groups of specialists. According to Drucker, to remain competitive, perhaps even to survive, businesses will have to transform

INSIGHT 12.2

AN ALTERNATIVE TO DOWNSIZING

Utell International, the hotel reservation and marketing giant, has found a way to avoid downsizing a layoff by keeping its employees working during slow periods. Utell introduced the "8,000 Hour Program," their proactive approach to staffing that allows them to keep employees working on alternative projects during November and December each year.*

The 8,000 hours refers to the estimated number of surplus hours during which reservationists are not taking calls. Utell fills these hours with the following activities:

- Philanthropy: Utell donates 500 to 1,000 hours of work to local chapters of United Way, the American Heart Association, and the National Kidney Foundation.

- Training: Reservationists increase their knowledge of products and sales techniques and also cross train in other departments.

- Interdepartmental assistance: Reservationists who have cross trained in other areas can provide assistance.

- Employee sharing: Reservationists move to other companies for brief periods of time but remain on Utell's payroll.

In the past Utell lost good employees when lags in business required layoffs. Now they are able to hold on to experienced workers.

*B. Gillette, "Company Finds Alternative to Downsizing," *Hotel & Motel Management* (January 3, 1997): 10.

themselves into organizations of knowledgeable specialists. Hotels might have guest service specialists or a team of line employees and managers who really understand the meaning of guest service. It might consist of college-educated managers or supervisors and several long-term line employees from different departments who have reputations for providing exemplary service. This team would be given the task of developing service standards for the hotel, monitoring guest satisfaction, dealing with customer complaints, and developing new ways to improve performance.

If knowledge-based organizations are to be successful, they must develop the ability to learn from their mistakes. They must be able to improve their actions through better knowledge and understanding. See Chapter 9 for more on Drucker's knowledge-based organization.

THE LEARNING ORGANIZATION

> *Those who cannot remember the past are condemned to repeat it.*
>
> —George Santayana

Today we hear much talk about optimizing the value of our employees by creating learning organizations. It sounds great, but what does it really entail? A **learning organization** is defined as one that skillfully creates, acquires, and transfers knowledge while modifying its practices to reflect new insight.[19] These organizations have the ability to detect and correct errors in order to ensure continuous success. Learning organizations engage the whole worker, not just their hands, but also their minds. These organizations are skilled in five important activities:[20]

1. **Problem solving.** Employees look beyond the obvious to identify and solve problems.
2. **Experimenting.** These companies constantly look for new and better ways to do things, then implement them and measure their success.
3. **Learning from past experience.** Organizations systematically review what worked and what didn't. They recognize that knowledge gained from mistakes is necessary for success and view failure as their ultimate teacher.
4. **Benchmarking.** This is an ongoing investigation that uncovers best industry practices, analyzes them, and develops ways that the company might adopt them. It's a nice way of saying—look for good ideas in other businesses and industries and implement all or parts of them in your organization. See Figure 12.2 for benchmarking ideas.
5. **Transferring knowledge.** Developing ways to spread ideas throughout the organization.

CREATING THE LEARNING ORGANIZATION

Peter Senge, author of the book *The Fifth Discipline: The Art and Practice of the Learning Organization*, describes the learning organization as "a group of people working together to collectively enhance their capacities to create results that they truly care about. Learning is the ability to enhance one's capacity to accomplish something one really cares about."[21] Companies that have achieved learning are made up of knowledge communities that create tools, human capability, and practical know-how to continuously improve themselves.

THE FIVE DISCIPLINES

There are four components that innovate learning organizations.[22] These include:

• **Building Shared Vision.** This is the practice of creating a shared picture of the future that fosters genuine commitment.
• **Personal Mastery.** The skill of continually clarifying and deepening your personal vision. See Chapter 4 for more on personal mastery.

- **Mental Models.** The ability to unearth our views of the world, examine them, and revise them as necessary.
- **Systems Thinking.** This is a way of making patterns in the organization clearer so that we might change them.

Perhaps the most important process with regard to strategic management is systems thinking. It allows organizations to diagnose concern and identify the heart of the problem so it can be solved properly.

SYSTEMS THINKING

Guiding the development of the learning organization is the concept of **systems thinking.** To better understand this term, let's apply it to a system we are all familiar with, the human body. The food that we consume is used to create new cells and fuels bodily functions. Our body then operates healthily—our hearts beat regularly, respiration brings in necessary oxygen, and waste is expelled. We can only understand how the human body functions by considering the system as a whole. Each component is interdependent. Without water we quickly become dehydrated, and the lack of fluids results in an irregular heartbeat and a shutdown of our kidneys, which can lead to death. Just as the human body is a system, so is the organization. An **organizational system** consists of a series of interrelated components that all affect one another. Companies fail to solve their deepest problems because they view only small parts of the organization when seeking causes of problems. Instead they must consider patterns that occur within the entire organization. We cannot diagnose a problem with room cleanliness in a hotel without considering the front desk, reservations, and sales. Room attendants may be forced to rush through cleaning because guests are promised early check-ins or front desk staff are not careful about only sending guests to rooms that have been inspected. What happens in one area of the property affects other departments.

Systems thinking is a conceptual framework that was developed over the past fifty years to make patterns clearer and to help us see how to change them.[23] It is easy to understand systems thinking when we apply it to a restaurant. A restaurant owner might wonder why his profits are 10 percent less than they were last year. When the owner considers the problem in a superficial manner, he or she might conclude that revenue is down because not enough was done to market the business. To solve the problem, the owner just needs to run some advertisements and increase his or her traffic. So the owner runs a series of ads. More customers do come in and try the restaurant, but they don't return. Another year passes, and profit is down an additional 7 percent for a total loss of 17 percent of revenue over two years. Were the owner to take a systems approach to solving the problem, he or she would consider all components of the restaurant when diagnosing the problem. The owner might look at the kitchen and analyze such cost factors as portion control, waste, theft, and scheduling, or the owner might look at the front of the house and consider customer satisfaction, service quality, and speed of service. Certainly marketing would be a systems area to explore, but in a more thorough fashion. The owner might hold focus groups with customers or interview customers to gather their opinions. I think you get the idea. Systems thinking involves looking at the whole operation to solve problems. Most likely the restaurant owner would discover that no single practice was causing his or her revenue loss, but that several components were contributing to it. By making systemswide changes to menus, marketing, and cost control, the owner would be likely to turn business around and realize greater profit.

The key to successfully implementing systems thinking lies within the people in the organization. A company's ability to identify and solve organizational problems is dependent on the knowledge, skills, and abilities of its employees, the human capital that comprise the business.

INTELLECTUAL CAPITAL

The sum of a company's intangible assets is its intellectual or human capital. Converting human intelligence into useful products and services is one of the most important capabilities a company can have today and in the future. Human intelligence creates most of the value in our organizations and in our society. The key to developing and nurturing human capital or intelligence is to create environments that nurture self-motivated creativity. Organizations that nurture this characteristic among its work groups outperform those where employees are simply punching a time card and putting in their hours without really becoming involved in the work they are doing.

How do you go about getting the most from your employees and maximizing the potential of your workers? Here are some best practices for managing intellect:[24]

- **Hire the best people.** The Four Seasons Hotels often interview fifty candidates to make one hire. Not all hotels and restaurants can be that choosy, but don't just settle for a "warm body" when you hire. Try to find and retain the best people you can.
- **Focus on early development.** Knowledge is developed by repeated exposure to real problems. Those who have lots of opportunity to interact with customers early on, learn the importance of service quickly. Put new employees in contact with customers under the watchful eye of an experienced coach.
- **Constantly increase challenges.** Set challenging goals for employees so they will have something to work toward.
- **Evaluate and weed out deadwood.** Assess employees objectively and provide frequent performance appraisal and feedback. If necessary get rid of employees who do not perform well.

CONCLUSION

Organizations practice strategic management to align practices with goals. They must identify, implement, measure, and control goals that meet the needs of customers, employees, and owners. Strategic planning identifies specifically what the organization needs to accomplish and decides how resources will be directed toward reaching these ideals. Strategic management as applied to human resources is particularly important today as emphasis shifts from physical capital to human capital.

The strategic planning process begins with the development of a corporate vision or mission based on the ideas and dreams of the employees that comprise the company. Next companies must scan their environment to identify key economic, political, social, and technological trends that might affect the business. The strategic plan is formulated and goals that will create value for customers, employees, and stockholders are identified. When implementing the plan, companies must generate excitement among employees to assure their commitment to the plan. Finally the resulting performance must be measured to assess the success of the plan.

One method of measuring strategic success that is gaining popularity is the balanced scorecard. It takes the company's mission and translates it into measurable objectives, making evaluation possible. The balanced scorecard links strategic objectives so people can clearly understand how their actions affect company success.

Reengineering is a strategic management tool that involves rethinking and redesigning organizations to achieve dramatic improvements in performance. Companies must also focus on the human aspects of organizational performance during reengineering to assure employee support.

Companies can strategically optimize the value of their employees by creating learning organizations where knowledge is created, acquired, and transferred to modify practices and create new insight. Organizations learn to detect and correct errors to ensure continuous success by problem solving, experimenting, learning from the past, benchmarking, and transferring knowledge. Learning organizations have four components: building shared vision, the personal mastery of its constituents, use of mental models, and systems thinking.

The successful organization of tomorrow will learn to maximize the benefit of its human capital by converting intelligence into useful products and services. Companies must create environments that nurture self-motivated creativity by hiring the best people, developing them, increasing their challenges, and evaluating their performance.

K E Y   T E R M S

Strategic Management	Balanced Scorecard
Strategic Planning	Reengineering
Core Competencies	Learning Organization
Physical Capital	Benchmarking
Human Capital	Systems Thinking
Vision	Organizational System
Environmental Scanning	

<u>N O T E S</u>

1. B. Barry, "A Beginners Guide to Strategic Planning," *Futurist* (April, 1998): 33–37.

2. Ibid.

3. P. Drucker, "The Coming of the New Organization," *Harvard Business Review* (January-February 1988): 45.

4. R. Kanter, "Managing for Long-Term Success," *Futurist* (August-September 1998): 43–46.

5. P. Galagan, "Strategic Planning Is Back," *Training & Development* (April 1997): 32–38.

6. McDonald's, *www.mcdonalds.com/corporate/ourpeople/mhoa/mission/mission.html*

7. Ritz-Carlton Hotels, *www.ritzcarlton.com/corporate/ritz_award.htm.*

8. A. Campbell. "Keeping the Engine Humming," *Business Quarterly* (Summer 1997): 40–47.

9. J. Kurtzman, "Is Your Company Off Course? Now You Can Find Out Why," *Fortune* (February 17, 1997): 128–131.

10. Ibid.

11. Ibid.

12. D. Huckstein and R. Duboff, "Hilton Hotels: A Comprehensive Approach to Delivering Value for All Stakeholders," *Cornell Hotel & Restaurant Administration Quarterly* 40, no. 4, (August 1999): 1–15.

13. Ibid.

14. M. Hammer and J. Champy, *Reengineering the Corporation: A Manifesto for Business Revolution* (New York: Harper Business, 1993): 31.

15. B. Smith, "Business Process Reengineering," *HR Focus* (January 1994): 17–18.

16. Ibid.

17. T. Steward, "Reengineering: The Hot New Management Tool," *Fortune* (August 23. 1998): 40.

18. P. Drucker, "The Coming of the New Organization," in *Harvard Business Review on Knowledge Management* (Boston, Mass.: Harvard Business School Publishing, 1998), 1–19.

19. D. Garvin, "Building a Learning Organization, in *Harvard Business Review on Knowledge Management* (Boston, Mass.: Harvard Business School Publishing, 1998), 47–80.

20. R. Fulmer and J. Bernard, "A Conversation with Peter Senge," *Organizational Dynamics* (Autumn 1998): 33–42.

21. P. Senge, *The Fifth Discipline: The Art and Practice of the Learning Organization* (New York: Doubleday, 1990).

22. Ibid., 7.

23. J. Quinn, P. Anderson, and S. Finkelstein, "Managing Professional Intellect," in *Harvard Business Review on Knowledge Management* (Boston, Mass.: Harvard Business School Publishing, 1998), 181–205.

CASE 12.1: STRATEGIC GOALS

Al Houghton, the owner of the restaurant where James works, recently called a meeting. In attendance were all managers and supervisors from the three restaurants that were part of the same small chain that he owned. Houghton opened the meeting by saying, "Business is not what it should be. Sales are dropping and repeat business is declining. I am very concerned about the future of these restaurants. If business doesn't improve, we may have to consider scaling down." Although this was not a surprise to James, hearing about the possibility of layoffs or even closing made him anxious.

Houghton continued by saying that, "Although our mission is clear, I just don't believe that it is being followed consistently. If it were, we wouldn't be having these problems. Let me restate it for you:

1. To provide courteous service, quality food, and value at conveniently located restaurants.

2. To provide a work environment where employees are treated with respect, dignity, and honesty and where high performance is expected and rewarded.

3. To operate in a cost effective manner."

Houghton ended by asking each restaurant to develop a set of specific actions they would take to put the mission into action.

James's boss, Sam Williams, immediately gave James the task of developing a series of goals the restaurant could accomplish that would correspond to the objectives stated in the mission. James began by thinking about each point in the mission and relating it to how things are really being done in his restaurant:

Point 1: *To provide courteous service, quality food, and value at conveniently located restaurants.* The restaurants were conveniently located, but that was about it. Service was courteous when servers felt like it and when they thought they would get a generous tip. Otherwise workers could be down right rude. Food quality was also inconsistent. Different ingredients were being used—depending on what the supplier was pushing, and no set measurements were used.

Point 2: *To provide a work environment where employees are treated with respect, dignity, and honesty and where high performance is expected and rewarded.* Sam Williams, the new general manager, was a nice guy and he did treat employees well, but James didn't feel that he really expected a lot from people. He seemed willing to overlook poor work and often ignored it when employees arrived late.

Point 3: *To operate in a cost-effective manner.* James knew there was a lot of waste. Lots of produce was tossed because it had gone bad. Part of the problem was the decrease in business. Although there weren't as many customers, the chef was still placing a standing order with the purveyor without using all the food he bought.

Williams asked James to identify actions that will help solve some of these problems and that can be readily implemented. James realizes that this is his chance to really make a contribution to the restaurant. Williams has given him the opportunity to show what he can do. James comes to you, his mentor, for help.

1. How would you suggest that James go about identifying strategic goals?

2. Specifically what are some actions that James might suggest to overcome some of the problems the restaurant is facing and to help it achieve its mission?

3. How can James make sure that employees accept the plan?

R E V I E W   Q U E S T I O N S

1. Give an example of how a hospitality organization might fail to meet the needs of its:
   a. Customers.
   b. Employees.
   c. Owners.
2. What is the purpose of strategic management? What might occur in companies that do not plan strategically?
3. What are core competencies? Give an example of a core competency possessed by McDonald's and Marriott.

   Indicate whether the following are examples of:
   a. internal scanning   b. external scanning
4. Dining in competing restaurants.
5. Assessing training provided by competitors.
6. Conducting an employee opinion survey.
7. Assessing the menu mix—which items on menu are most popular and profitable.
8. Imagine that a friend has asked you to tell her what the following management practices involve. How would you describe each of the following to your friend?
   a. Balanced scorecard.
   b. Reengineering.
   c. The learning organization.
   d. Systems thinking.
9. How does a company's mission differ from its vision?
10. As a manager or supervisor, what might your role be in the strategic planning process?
11. How does shared visioning differ from the typical methods of developing corporate vision?
12. What is human capital and how might companies go about maximizing its benefit?

C R I T I C A L   T H I N K I N G   E X E R C I S E S

1. Identify benchmarks (in addition to those mentioned in the text) that companies outside our industry practice which might be applied to the hospitality industry.
2. As a manager or supervisor, how would you go about making sure that the employees you supervise were working in ways that would help the company achieve its mission?
3. What are some innovative strategies that hospitality organizations might adopt to better meet the needs of their employees specifically with regard to:

a. Helping employees to meet their family responsibilities—caring for children or aging parents.

b. Better utilizing older workers. How might companies make them feel more comfortable and benefit from their knowledge?

c. Encouraging employees to continue their education by attending a community college or university.

4. Apply systems thinking to a hotel situation. Review each action below and describe how other departments will be affected by these events:

a. The restaurant will no longer serve breakfast and lunch—only dinner.

b. All guests will use an automated check-in system allowing them to completely bypass the front desk and go straight to their rooms.

c. The human resources department will no longer provide employee orientation—it will be done at the department level.

5. What might happen in a company that fails to consider the human aspects of reengineering as they make major changes?

ON-LINE LINK

Visit web sites for several major hospitality organizations such as McDonald's, Marriott, Hyatt, or Burger King. Which of the web sites, if any, describe the company's:

1. Strategic plan.
2. Mission statement.
3. Corporate vision.
4. Core competencies.
5. Core strategies.

PORTFOLIO EXERCISE

A company's mission statement is a brief description of the organization's major goals and values. Create your own personal mission statement that describes your purpose, what is important to you, and what you hope to achieve in the future. Having a specified mission tells prospective employers that you have values and have given careful thought to who you are, what is important to you, and what you hope to accomplish. Add a section to your portfolio and include your "Personal Mission Statement."

The Diversity Advantage

13

ADVANCED ORGANIZER

Imagine that you are interviewing for your first supervisory position in the hospitality industry. The position requires that you manage a restaurant located in a major city. The very diverse staff consists of twelve women, seven minority group members, three gays and lesbians, two people with physical disabilities, and ten white males. The owner tells you that the reason the last manager failed was because he could not supervise such a diverse work group. She first asks what you know about multiculturalism and then delves further by asking you how you would maximize the benefits of diversity and minimize the difficulties that can arise.

If you're not sure how you would respond to this difficult question, you're not alone. Although diversity is a hot issue today, it is often misunderstood and misrepresented. The following will introduce you to the timely topic of multicultural management and help you develop the leadership skills you will need to manage today's diverse workforce.

BEHAVIORAL OBJECTIVES

- Identify those corporate actions that maximize the benefits of diversity.

- Differentiate between practices that promote multiculturalism and those that hinder it.

- Describe how your cultural background has affected your life.

- Assess the cost of turnover. an outcome of mismanaged diversity.

- Evaluate the accuracy of common stereotypes.

- Describe the importance of multiculturalism to organizational success.

Loews Miami Beach Hotel

DIVERSITY: A CURRENT AND FUTURE TREND

As hospitality-related businesses position themselves as leading competitors in the emerging global marketplace, the key to their success is their ability to develop a diverse workforce. Over the past twenty-five years, the American workforce has changed from predominately all white, male constituencies to a tremendously diverse array of men and women of different races, nationalities, and ethnic origins. **Cultural diversity**, defined by Cox as the representation, in one social system, of people with distinctly different group affiliations of cultural significance,[1] has become a common buzzword in today's society. This new focus is not without justification. Our workplace is being reshaped with respect to race, ethnicity, gender, national origin, and age. Multiculturalism is readily evident in the hospitality industry. Take a walk through a large hotel in a major city and you are likely to encounter employees from as many as seventy different countries who speak forty-seven different languages (see Insight 13.1 for more about diversity in hotels). The diversity we see today is likely to become even more evident in the future. Consider the following statistics:

INSIGHT 13.1

HOW ONE HOTEL MANAGES STAFF'S DIVERSITY

With employees representing seventy different countries and speaking forty-seven languages, the Marriott Marquis in New York's Time Square is certainly a model of diversity. Although the hotel can certainly benefit from its multicultural environment when serving their diverse clientele, managing people from such a wide range of backgrounds presents a constant challenge. In fact just maintaining a basic level of civility can be a daily struggle. Housekeeping quality assurance manager Jessica Brown, who is of both Jamaican and Honduran descent, refuses to lower her standards for anyone. Yet she is unfazed by difficulties that arise in her dealings with her racially diverse staff. When she rewards African American housekeepers, she is chided by Latin Americans for favoring her own people. When she commends Hispanics, black housekeepers grumble.

Marriott works hard to achieve cultural harmony in its hotels. All employees can partake of their "guarantee of fair treatment" policy by appealing grievances all the way to the company chairman. Their recently introduced "peer review" procedure allows workers to review disciplinary action. Diversity training is required of all managers and they are taught that the best way to cope with diversity-related conflict is to focus only on performance—not gender, race, or culture.

The result is a management team that will "bend over backward" in an attempt to respect cultural differences among employees. For example, when a guest with an overflowing bathtub needed help immediately, Manager Victor Aragona fixed it himself rather than interrupt a room attendant's daily Islamic prayers. The employee was laying on a towel in a housekeeper's closet, bowing to Mecca. "It wasn't fair or efficient to have him fix the problem," recalls Aragona. "My problem was a flood, his was God."

Marriott actively recruits minorities for management positions. Individuals who are bilingual in English and Spanish are particularly attractive management applicants because employees who speak English as a second language are more comfortable with them.

Source: Information from *The Wall Street Journal*, (November 20, 1996): B1. "How One Hotel Manages Staff's Diversity."

- Roughly 45 percent of all additions to the labor force through the year 2000 will be nonwhite, with half of this number representing immigrants from Asian and Latin countries.[2]
- Sixty-five percent of new jobs created during the 1990s will be filled by women and by the year 2000, nearly half of all civilian workers will be women.[3]
- By the year 2000, the majority of public school-age children in the United States will be nonwhite.[4]

A NEW PARADIGM FOR MANAGING DIVERSITY

Many organizations assume they have achieved multiculturalism because they employ a large number of minority group members. They display their diverse workforce in company photographs and publications, but, in fact, they have created only the superficial appearance of diversity. Hiring and retaining women, minorities, and persons with disabilities is an important beginning to diversity management, but by no means its conclusion. True multiculturalism goes way beyond increasing cultural group representation on the payroll. It involves creating an organizational culture where all employees are respected and valued for the unique knowledge they bring to the job.

Often companies are spurred on to add African Americans or Hispanics to their sales staff by their desire to increase market share in racioethnic communities. For example a hotel may want to increase sales among Hispanic groups in the community and hire representative managers to handle these clients. Although the employment of minority managers is certainly a progressive step, the company is limiting their potential development by assuming that the main contribution these employees can make is restricted to their knowledge of their own people. This assumption, which implies tokenism, is limiting and detrimental to diversity efforts.

Women, Hispanic Americans, Asian Americans, African Americans, and Native Americans all bring much more to the workplace than just their racial or gender identity. They bring unique knowledge and perspectives about designing work, reaching goals, creating effective teams, communication, and leadership that can help companies improve their performance. Companies must think about diversity more holistically—as providing fresh and meaningful approaches to work—and stop viewing diversity in terms of appearance or group membership if they are to reap full reward from their efforts.[5] Ideally members of the organization can say, "We are all on the same team, with our differences—not despite them."

VALUING DIVERSITY

In recent years, the most astute business leaders have recognized the diversity of their workforce as a preeminent business issue. Often the presence of qualified women, African Americans, Hispanics, gays and lesbians, or disabled individuals is not just the result of compliance with federal law, it is a matter of competitive necessity. Companies striving to succeed in today's competitive markets and in international business ventures must assemble the best talent regardless of race, gender, ethnic origin, or other cultural factors. They must be able to elicit highly creative ideas, and a broad spectrum of views from managers and employees.

Although the diversity drum is being beaten loudly, few U.S. companies are diversifying their workforce effectively. A 1992 survey conducted by the Hay Group showed that only 5 percent of the 1,405 participating companies thought they were doing a "very good job" of managing diversity in their workforces.[6] A homogenous corporate culture is no longer an advantage, but can be a limiting factor in corporate growth and development. For example, in 1991, the number of complaints of racial discrimination drastically increased among Denny's restaurants.[7] Some black customers charged that they were forced to prepay for food when white customers were not. Flagstar CEO Jerry Richardson immediately took action and fired managers who had discriminated, officially apologized to customers, and instituted a corporatewide diversity awareness program. Recognizing the economic impact of racism, Richardson said, "It makes no sense that we condone racism. Denny's needs all the customers it can get." Denny's efforts to promote diversity have had positive results. Recently the company was listed on Fortune's inaugural list of the fifty best companies for Asians, blacks, and Hispanics.[8] Minorities now own 35 percent of the company's 737 franchised restaurants, up from only one African American franchisee in 1993.

This dramatic example highlights the importance of addressing diversity issues quickly, decisively, and sincerely. Companies that work to create a cohesive, multicultural workplace will be much stronger contenders in tomorrow's market than those who seek to ignore the importance of this issue.

ASSET OR LIABILITY?

Before buying into the need to address cultural differences, many managers question its effect on bottom-line profitability and performance. Is a diverse organization more profitable or more competitive? Research suggests a good news–bad news scenario, with diversity having the potential for both positive and negative effects on organizational performance.

INCREASED TURNOVER

Let's start with the bad news. On the negative side, turnover and absenteeism among women and nonwhite men can be double that of white men.[9] With the rising cost of selection and training, turnover can be an extremely serious and costly obstacle to profitability and high performance. To find out just how costly turnover can be, check out Calculating the High Cost of Turnover in the Critical Thinking Exercises at the end of the chapter. If turnovers among women and minorities are to be reduced to the level experienced by white males, companies must give these employees the same degree of respect and opportunity as white males, and, at the same time, be willing to address some of their unique concerns and issues. For example women have the primary responsibility for child care and are more likely to leave companies that require long hours, an inflexible schedule, and offer no provision for time off when children are ill. Companies that want to retain highly qualified female employees must be sensitive to the work-family conflict that they are more likely to experience.

THE SKILL AND LANGUAGE BARRIER

Another downside to diversity is the erratic nature of job skills among immigrant employees. Statistics indicate that immigrants fall into one of two extremes with regard to education and skills. More male immigrants are college educated than native-born males (26.6 percent versus 25.1 percent, respectively), but at the same time, 33.1 percent of immigrants are high school dropouts while only 12.2 percent of native-born males are in this category.[10] Unskilled workers have a staggering effect on American business, costing nearly $225 billion each year in lost productivity, unrealized tax revenue, welfare payments, and social problems.[11] Finally critical management functions are more difficult, more time-consuming, and less accurate due to the language barriers that often characterize a diverse work group in the hotel industry.[12] Language barriers can also lead to strained relationships between supervisors and employees due to misunderstandings. Supervisors or managers may unwittingly create barriers with their employees if they are not sensitive to cultural and language barriers. For example, when a housekeeping inspector chastised a room attendant for leaving a piece of paper on the floor in a guest room by saying, "Any woman off the street could see this is garbage," due to her limited understanding of the English language, the room attendant interpreted the comment as meaning that she was a prostitute or "street-walker".[13] The room attendant was highly offended by the misinterpreted insult, and it took a great deal of time to heal the relationship between employee and supervisor.

Skill and language barriers are a serious issue in the hospitality industry, well known as an employer of large numbers of new immigrants and unskilled workers. Companies can overcome this limitation by offering employees the opportunity to expand their language proficiency and to learn new skills either on-site or at a local college. Marriott Management Services is addressing this need by offering an English As a Second Language program called "At Your Service." Hotels and restaurants that invest in their employees will benefit from a more qualified work staff.

Now for the good news. Cultural diversity in the United States has been viewed as a dark cloud, but the results of empirical studies show that it also has a silver lining.[14] A diverse workforce can lead to improved communication, creativity, and problem solving.[15] This is particularly important in light of today's trend toward team decision making and problem solving. Ethnically diverse groups

BEST PRACTICES

When DAKA, a $164 million foodservice company, learned that several of its employees had AIDS, they approached the issue proactively and instituted polices and procedures to help their employees.* They offered flexible sick leave, disability benefits, opened an AIDS counseling office, started an AIDS hotline, and required all employees and managers to attend AIDS education seminary. They actively fought panic and prejudice with facts and have largely defused AIDS as a workplace issue in their company. As a result the company has been able to attract and retain loyal, motivated employees and has increased its productivity.

*David Bollier, *Aiming Higher: 25 Stories of How Companies Prosper by Combining Sound Management and Social Vision* (New York, AMACOM, 1997), 151–153.

have been found to generate ideas higher in overall effectiveness and feasibility[16] and to produce higher quality solutions than homogenous groups.[17] Companies that value multiculturalism are also better able to meet the needs of diverse customers, have reduced turnovers, fewer lawsuits, increased productivity, and are better able to attract and retain higher quality employees and managers.[18]

The "right" company for minorities is one that appreciates and uses the contributions of all of its people and provides opportunities for workers to succeed and grow. It provides well-trodden career paths, special assignments, participation on teams both within and outside the department, decision-making

INSIGHT 13.2

THE BEST COMPANIES FOR MINORITIES

Lawrence Graham, in his book *The Best Companies for Minorities* (1993), profiled eighty five companies with outstanding diversity practices. Those identified from the restaurant and hotel industry include:

- **Burger King Corporation:** Actively recruits applicants and successfully moved minorities into high-ranking management positions with a total of 565 minority-owned restaurants in 1991. The company has formed a Diversity Resource Group to provide a forum for discussing minority issues. It also has a minority vendor program to build entrepreneurship. Burger King has succeeded in creating an environment in which minorities feel free to express their culture. According to Terri Giles, manager of consumer relations. "Once I get to the door, I can still be a black woman at work."

- **General Mills, Inc.:** As the owner and operator of Red Lobster Restaurants and the Olive Garden chain, General Mills has an impressive record of promoting minorities and working with the community. In 1992, 31 percent of all marketing hires and 42 percent of all sales hires were minorities. General Mills offers companywide diversity training, which teaches managers how to support diverse employees. The company actively recruits at minority career fairs and places emphasis on identifying and hiring minority vendors.

- **McDonald's Corporation:** The largest restaurant company in the world was also a pioneer in diversity management. With 70 percent of restaurant management employees consisting of minorities and women, McDonald's began offering career development seminars tailored to their needs in 1970s. It sponsors a number of employee networking groups, including The McDonald's Black Employee Network created in 1980. McDonald's utilizes minority-owned marketing firms and has a program that develops minority entrepreneurs.

- **Marriott Corporation:** As a leader in the hotel industry, Marriott is also aggressively committed to minority recruiting and retention. The company recruits at colleges with large minority enrollments and serves on their advisory boards. Marriott has initiated several programs to promote diversity and enhance cross-cultural communication. Its Valuing Diversity Committee makes recommendations to senior management. Marriott was recognized as Corporation of the Year in 1991 by the Washington, D.C., chapter of the National Black MBA Association.

- **PepsiCo, Inc.:** Owner of several successful restaurant chains including Taco Bell, Pizza Hut and Kentucky Fried Chicken. PepsiCo was the first Fortune 500 company to have a black vice president in 1962. It actively recruits minority professionals and offers diversity training to management employees. PepsiCo sponsors a number of minority support groups and associations. The company also has a minority business enterprise program that awards contracts to minority suppliers.

power, formal education, and informal training. To learn more about hospitality-related companies that have been recognized for diversity management, review Insight 13.2, The Best Companies for Minorities.

MULTICULTURAL TOURISM

A diverse workforce is a particular advantage in the hospitality industry. Multicultural tourism, which effects every aspect of our field, is a rapidly growing sector of the travel industry. The Clinton administration is promoting international tourism as a means of achieving minority economic development. It is expected that multicultural tourism will bring more dollars to minority entrepreneurs and communities. To meet this new challenge, it is important that guest contact employees have proficiency in foreign language and understand guests' cultural expectations. What better way to assure that international guests feel comfortable than to have someone of their ethnic origin in charge of their service experience?

Organizations that embrace diversity can minimize the negative effects of high turnover and skill and language barriers and maximize the positive effects of increased creativity and problem solving. Those that attempt to block or hinder multiculturalism will find it increasingly difficult to remain competitive in today's global environment. When managed effectively diversity in the workforce can be a source of strength. When organizations support diversity, minorities report high levels of satisfaction with their jobs, careers, and the organization as a whole.[19] In contrast, when organizations fail to support diversity, minorities are isolated from key information and networks, feel that others underestimate their abilities, and sense a lack of sponsorship or support.[20]

THE DIVERSITY MATRIX

Organizations that seek to optimize diversity must do so at both the organizational and individual level. Individual employees must be sophisticated and experienced enough to accept those who are different. They must have adequate skills to communicate and work with employees and managers from diverse backgrounds. At the same time, organizations must set policy and be willing to make financial and leadership decisions that foster an environment of equal opportunity and fair treatment for all employees. Figure 13.1 presents a matrix that describes four possible conditions that can result from varying degrees of individual and organization support of diversity.

DORMANCY

In the least desirable situation, dormancy results when both the organization and the individual employees fail to effectively address diversity issues. In this condition the organization cares little for its minority members and sets policies that limit their opportunity. Individual employees and managers are polarized by race, gender, or other group membership and do not seek to understand or work with those who are different. Majority group members are way

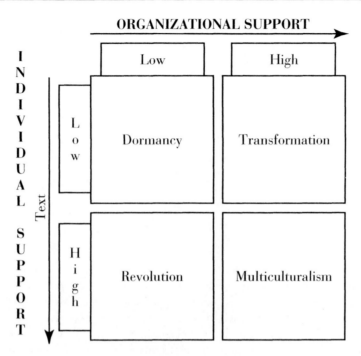

Figure 13.1 The Diversity Matrix

ahead with regard to power and income. Although minority group members may be aware of the inequities, their sense of helplessness prohibits their taking action to rectify the situation. This is an extreme example, but represents a historically traditional type of organizational structure that still exists today. Organizations overcome this dormant state when either individual employees attempt to revolutionize practices or the organization seeks culture transformation.

REVOLUTION

When there is high individual support for diversity but low organizational support, employees may attempt to drive change in policy and practices. If management is unwilling to acknowledge the rapid increase in workforce diversity or the differences in managerial thinking they require, it may be up to employees to drive change. They may seek to do this through legal efforts in the form of class-action lawsuits, or they may instead choose more collaborative methods by forming committees and discussing concerns with top management. In either case the organization must either move forward and create a more supportive environment for minority members, or experience significant legal expense and high turnover.

TRANSFORMATION

Responding to social conscience or pressures from our legal environment, many organizations seek to transform their traditional, polarized work environment into a true multicultural organization where diversity is embraced, not shunned. In transformation there is high support at the organizational level for diversity, but low support from individual employees and managers. Majority group members may feel threatened by new practices and work to stave off change. The organization may have policies and practices in place that promise equal treatment for all, but due to individual attitudes and prejudices, these cannot be implemented properly. The organization drives change from the top and seeks to transform itself and its employees from an immobilized environment to a highly effective multicultural workplace. There may be resistance from employees and managers who prefer an organization that caters to the majority at the expense of the minority. Change in this situation takes time, but through careful selection, training, and group intervention, organizations can create a culture of respect.

MULTICULTURALISM

In the multicultural environment, both individuals and the organization seek to create a workplace where persons from all cultural environments are valued equally. The organization has adopted affirmative action programs, training for employees and managers, audits of compensation programs to ensure equity for all, and carefully selects employees who embrace this culture. At the same time, employees and managers respect diversity, are encouraged to express their cultural differences in dress and practice, and benefit from the new ideas and views of those who are different. These organizations attract and retain the best employees, both minority and majority, and are often touted as "best places to work." Known for innovation and creativity, multicultural organizations are able to react quickly to environmental challenges and maintain profitability and market share.

The scope of this chapter is to specifically describe the situations that contribute to the four components of the matrix. You will learn about the causes and characteristics of the "dormant" environment, and, more importantly, how organizations and individuals can overcome these limitations to achieve multiculturalism. You will preview the latest tools of organizational change that can be employed to transform a culturally impaired workplace into one where difference is celebrated.

BARRIERS TO MULTICULTURALISM

There are a number of practices and beliefs at both the individual level and the organizational level that hinder the creation of a true multicultural workplace. In this section you will learn about such forms of individual bias as prejudice and stereotyping and organizational bias in the form of discrimination. In addition you will discover proven methods and practices for overcoming bias and achieving both diversity and equality in the workplace.

INDIVIDUAL BIAS

We all bring baggage in the form of beliefs and attitudes resulting from past experience to our places of work. If our upbringing and experience leads us to view those who are different with interest and high regard, we can do much to foster an atmosphere of multiculturalism in our workplace. In opposition, if our baggage consists of negative feelings and emotions about those who differ from us, it can tarnish our relationships with coworkers. But this baggage in the form of negative feelings and attitudes toward diversity can be set aside. The first step in achieving attitudinal change is knowledge. In this section, you will learn about important individual factors that affect multiculturalism.

GROUP IDENTITY

A **group identity** is a personal affiliation with other people which whom one shares certain things in common.[21] Your group identity has a tremendous effect on how you feel about and interact with others who both share your affiliation or are different. According to social identity theory, our self-concept is partly defined by our group affiliations.[22] We form group identities based on phenotypes and cultural identities.

Phenotype Identity Groups: These groups are formed based on the physical, visually observable differences in people. Members of different racioethnic groups are often identified by such characteristics as hair color, skin color, and facial features. We use visible cues to categorize people as men, women, black, white, Asian, Hispanic, gay, and so on.[23] **Phenotype identity** then effects the way we interact with others. The closer a person's visual appearance is to our own, the more we identify with that person. For example, historically, "whiter" ethnic minorities reported less racism than respondents whose skin color was less Euro-American.[24] Phenotype, or visual appearance, can have a significant effect on our relationships with others.

Cultural Identity Groups: Members of the same **cultural identity** group share a particular subjective culture or typical pattern of viewing the environment.[25] A culture group consists of individuals who share norms, values, and goal priorities that distinguish one culture group from another.[26] Identity groups can be based on gender, race, religion, sexual preference, age, or many other attributes. Cultural identity is an organic characteristic, or one that changes over time. Helms[27] has documented a stage model of identity development that begins with a complete lack of understanding and acceptance of racioethnic identity of self and others and progresses to a final stage of autonomy or complete awareness and acceptance of one's own identity, as well as that of others. When we reach this final autonomous stage, we are interested in learning from members of other groups that differ from our own, and we are able to transcend prejudice.

PREJUDICE

In a cultural sense, prejudice is defined as negative attitudes toward certain groups and their members.[28] **Discrimination** is the behavioral manifestation of prejudice and is defined as actions carried out by members of dominant groups that have a differential and harmful effect on members of subordinate groups.[29] When a dominant group of male executives feel that women do not have the decision-making skills needed for top management positions, this is prejudice. When the same majority group blocks the promotion of women, this is discrimination.

Why are some people prejudiced while others are not? The answer may lie in differences in personality type. Individuals with authoritarian personalities are less tolerant toward members of minority groups.[30] Also past history has much to do with our beliefs about others. If we are raised in families with racist views, our outlook toward those who are different may be affected. In addition, if we grow up in a community that lacks diversity, we may have difficulty understanding the concerns of various groups.

STEREOTYPING

According to Cox,[31] **stereotyping** is a process by which individuals are viewed as members of groups, and the information we have stored in our minds about the particular group is applied to the individual. Stereotypes are easier to remedy than prejudice and will normally decline as our association with a particular group member lengthens.[32] Stereotypes are common and can be based on age, gender, race, weight, physical ability, or a wide variety of other attributes. A black woman who is taunted by whites may generalize her negative feelings to all white people based on their group identity. She may assume that all whites cannot be trusted and create a barrier that limits their access to her ideas and feelings. If she later has positive experiences with this group, her stereotype may begin to dissolve.

Stereotyping may be responsible for much of the inequity in the workplace. It has been linked to differences in status, role conflict, career mobility, performance appraisal, distribution of power, opportunity for training, performance feedback, and job segregation.[33] Reduction of stereotyping is a critical component in developing successful multicultural work environments.

RESEARCH BRIEF 13.1

A LESSON IN DISCRIMINATION

A landmark experiment from 1970 dramatically demonstrates how discrimination can be created very swiftly. Jane Elliot, a third-grade teacher in Riceville, Iowa, decided to teach her class a lesson on discrimination. On the first day of her experiment, blue-eyed children were given special privileges like seconds at lunch and extra time at recess. At the same time, brown-eyed children were made to wear large collars, denied privileges, and told that they were not as smart and not as well behaved as blue-eyed children. Within just half an hour, the blue-eyed children began calling the brown-eyed children names and treated them as if they were inferior. The next day the teacher switched roles and brown-eyed children received the privileges, and blue-eyed children wore the collars and were described as inferior. On each day the children that were the out-group, those who wore the collars and were described as inferior, seemed to wilt. They become depressed, they fought, and they performed at a much lower level than usual.

The experiences of these children can be quickly applied to the workplace. If we allow stereotypes, prejudice, and discrimination to make others feel inferior, we will create dissent, dissatisfaction, and poor morale.

ORGANIZATIONAL BIAS

Institutional or organizational bias refers to the preference patterns inherent in the business setting that create barriers to full participation by minority group members.[34] Historically most organizations were created and populated by white males, so the norms, expectations, and ways of doing business are a natural consequence of organizational history.[35]

FORMAL ORGANIZATIONAL BIAS

Organizational bias can either be formal or informal in nature. Formal bias is the more familiar of the two and consists of practices that directly discriminate against groups of employees with regard to hiring, promotion, and wages. A series of legal actions protect our individual rights and have greatly reduced the frequency of formal organizational bias. For a synopsis of the various laws affecting human rights that have been passed since 1960, please refer to Figure 9.2 in Chapter 9, Protecting Employee Rights.

Companies may also be biased in the manner that their organization has structurally integrated minority and majority group members. **Structural integration** refers to the proportion of members of various cultural groups in the workforce of an organization. In biased organizations majority members will cluster in positions of status and authority whereas minority group members hold low status and low-pay positions in the hierarchy. In the majority of hotels during the 1970s, men held virtually all management positions, and women and minorities were relegated to housekeeping, the front desk, and PBX. Today we still see structural bias in the hotel industry, particularly in top management where women and minorities are underrepresented. Structural bias can have a detrimental effect on the work climate in an organization. When workgroups are diverse and the power distribution is heavily skewed in favor of certain groups, it is more difficult for members of different culture groups to work harmoniously together, hampering organizational performance.[36]

INFORMAL ORGANIZATIONAL BIAS

Although blatant discrimination in public or business life tends to be rare these days, many subtle yet pernicious stereotypes are quietly condoned. Many managers cling to myths that women cannot be aggressive, gutsy managers; that gay employees are likely to be difficult to manage; or that racioethnic minorities cannot perform as senior managers. Such informal organizational bias is perhaps even more difficult to overcome than its formal cousin due to its hidden, insidious nature. Even when companies are adhering to legal guidelines and seeking out and hiring minority group candidates, informal bias can still prevail. Informal bias consists of any policies or practices that make it difficult for minority members to succeed and do their best in their jobs. Examples include policies that require employed mothers to work evenings, weekends, or long, inflexible hours, limiting their ability to both meet family responsibilities and have a successful career. Other policies that have potential for informal bias are those that do not allow "extreme dress" of a cultural or religious nature. Indian men who practice religious beliefs by wearing beards and turbans are often frowned upon by management for their unusual practices. Also those who are extremely overweight are often denied employment and promotion due to their difference.

Informal bias is couched within the organization's culture. To fully grasp measures to overcome this barrier to multiculturalism, you must first understand the components of organizational culture.

ORGANIZATIONAL CULTURE

The culture of an organization refers to its mystique or credo. Culture consists of the underlying values, beliefs, and principles that serve as a foundation for the way an organization is managed.[37] Just as people have characteristics that set them apart from others, so do organizations.

FLEXIBILITY

Some organizations are more flexible, have fewer rigid rules and standards, and are better able to deal with ambiguity or uncertainty. Flexible organization may be better able to handle the conflict that sometimes occurs when a diverse work group is brought together. By openly acknowledging dissent, the flexible organization can better resolve it. Inflexible organizations focus on avoiding conflict and try to gain control of the situation. They may allow work groups to polarize, or separate by culture, instead of attempting to assimilate them.

VALUE STRUCTURE

Organizations can also differ in their value structure. Those that do not place a high value on diversity may pressure its members to conform to a single set of organization values or norms and do not allow free cultural exchange.[38] Organizations that value diversity will allow each employee to bring his or her beliefs to the workplace and they will accept that there is no single correct attitude toward work, but that many different outlooks can have positive results.

STRENGTH

Organization culture can differ in strength. Strength is defined as a combination of the extent to which norms and values are defined and reinforced.[39] In companies with strong cultures, there are more cues regarding how to behave, dress, and interact. For example the Ritz-Carlton Hotels have a very strong culture. Employee behavior, appearance, and communication style is strongly dictated. Everyone must behave like "ladies and gentlemen" at all times. When culture is weak, there is less direction regarding behavior, and fewer negative ramifications resulting from divergence from the norm. An example of a weak culture would be Hard Rock Cafe. Employees are freer to dress, talk, and behave in line with their own cultural norms. Organizations with weak culture allow employees to express their norms and values more readily. On the other hand, low enforcement of culture may mean that essential values are not shared by members, resulting in chaos.[40]

CONTROL

Organization culture can also vary in the amount of formal structure and control imposed on employees. When an organization is centralized, with most decisions made at the top, this is a mechanistic organization system. Organizations that have a very formal, bureaucratic control system do not foster multiculturalism. Their mechanistic system, created and imposed by the majority group, demands conformity from employees. This limits their ability to explore and benefit from cultural difference. Because there is little need for group cohesiveness and communication, work groups and departments can polarize without seriously limiting organizational function.

On the other hand, an organic organization characterized by loose, free-flowing, and adaptive management structure tends to foster diversity. Decision making is decentralized with responsibility and control shifted from top management to lower levels. Employees are encouraged to address and resolve problems by working directly with one another. Various cultural groups must work together on a regular basis to develop new ideas and resolve difficulties as they arise. Due to the requirement that work groups and departments collaborate, there is little opportunity for polarization. When differences relating to culture do arise, they must be addressed and resolved or the organization will be unable to function effectively within its framework. Organizational culture can do much to either facilitate or hinder multiculturalism. Figure 13.2 describes characteristics of organizational culture that fosters diversity.

CREATING A MULTICULTURAL WORK ENVIRONMENT

An organization that contains a large proportion of diverse employees is a plural organization, but not necessarily a multicultural one. It is multicultural only if it values this diversity. There is a definite distinction between simply tol-

---

- Employees and managers are allowed leeway in how they get things done. There is no one way to complete a job or task, and employees are given the opportunity to define their work style.
- Errors and mistakes are viewed as opportunities for learning and growth. Employees are not penalized for honest mistakes, but instead guided to learn from them.
- Managers act as facilitators and coaches and do not seek to control the work environment.
- Employees are empowered to make decisions and allowed to think for themselves.
- Employees are encouraged and rewarded for developing new ideas and better ways of doing things.
- Rigid, standard operating procedures do not exist.
- Employees communicate freely and openly with each other and with top management.

Figure 13.2 Organization Culture That Fosters Diversity

erating diversity and valuing it. A multicultural organization has the following characteristics:

- Seeks to diversify both management and line staff by attracting well-qualified majority and nonmajority member candidates.
- An absence of both formal and informal bias within the organization.
- A proactive management style that minimizes conflict.
- Relies upon all employees, including majority and nonmajority group members, for planning, goal setting, decision making, and day-to-day operation of the organization.
- The diverse ideas and views of the multicultural staff are sought out and valued.

The organizational transformation to multiculturalism is not a fast or easy road. It is a long-term process that requires a high level of commitment from top management. There will be many roadblocks along the way in the form of resistance to change, fear, and conflict. Human nature dictates that we value the familiar and fear uncertainty. For many a diverse, highly involved work group creates a high degree of anxiety and animosity. Old ways of doing things must be abandoned. Power structures, particularly the "old boy network," no longer control the organization. The success of multiculturalism depends on management. They must be willing to adapt to a new company culture, have a desire to increase their own level of cultural awareness, and be willing to guide employees through the change process with patience and understanding. Supervisors must change the way they interact with staff and be willing to spend extra time training existing and new employees in diversity awareness. But as difficult as cultural transformation may seem, it is an inevitable part of the future of organizations that strive for high performance in tomorrow's diverse environment.

BEST PRACTICES

Industry leaders such as McDonald's Corporation prove that diversity and success go hand and hand. Organizations that have effectively managed multiculturalism will benefit from reduced turnover, less conflict, and greater work-group cohesiveness. Such organizations will also attract top minority candidates based on their reputation of multiculturalism. McDonald's Corporation has been practicing diversity training since the 1970s. According to company executive Robert M. Beavers, "If a company is going to really provide opportunities for blacks, Hispanics, and women, it must be willing to take risks." McDonald's offers career development, operations training, and "Fast Track" programs developed specifically for minorities. As a result, 25.9 percent of the company's employees and 15.8% of its managers are black.* The company has adopted multicultural training workshops, aggressive recruiting efforts, management sponsorship in community networks, and a mentoring program for minorities.

*J. E. Peters, "Bridging the Gap." *Restaurant Business* (September 1, 1989): 86–91.

DIVERSITY STRATEGY

Organizations can adopt several different approaches to handling diversity depending on their varying needs and resources in the form of time and money. Efforts can range from "not doing anything" to a full-blown cultural transformation. Middle ground can consist of diversity awareness training, the formation of special interest groups, or affirmative action efforts. First let's examine two strategies to reduce formal organizational bias: Equal Employment Opportunity (EEO) and affirmative action efforts.

EQUAL EMPLOYMENT OPPORTUNITY

The Civil Rights Act of 1964 and the Equal Employment Opportunity Act of 1972 contributed to major changes in the makeup of the workforce by opening doors for minorities that were once closed. Both guarantee individual rights in the form of equal employment opportunity and have had long-standing consequences in diversity management. According to their statutes, individuals have the right to employment without regard to race, color, national origin, religion, or gender.

As additional forms of discrimination became evident, subsequent laws were passed to extend protection to the handicapped employees of companies with federal contracts or financial assistance (The Vocational Rehabilitation Act of 1973), individuals between the ages of forty and seventy (Age Discrimination Act of 1981), and persons with disabilities of both public and private sector companies (Americans with Disabilities Act of 1990). Organizations are required by law to adhere to EEO guidelines in hiring, selection, promotion, and dismissal. For a more thorough description of legal issues effecting the human resource function, see Chapter 9.

AFFIRMATIVE ACTION

Another example of legal action taken to rectify formal institutional bias is affirmative action programs. Designed to increase employment opportunities for women, minorities, veterans, and the handicapped, affirmative action resulted from two Executive Orders originated by President Johnson. In practice, **affirmative action** means the explicit use of a person's group identity as a criterion in making selection decisions.[41] The purpose of affirmative action is to assure that women, minorities, and other groups are represented in the workforce in proportion to their actual availability in the labor market. The guidelines apply to all organizations that do business with the federal government. Should these organizations fail to meet their quota of employees from protected groups, they must either increase their recruiting and hiring of these individuals or lose federal funding and contracts.

Many private sector organizations have voluntarily adopted affirmative action programs to create a more diverse, representative workforce. For example, if a hotel is located in a city with a 30 percent African American population, according to affirmative action guidelines, the hotel not only should employ the same proportion of line employees, but also managers.

There are two strategies that guide the implementation of affirmative action programs.[42] The first is the good faith effort strategy which strives to change practices that contribute to unfair hiring practices and might include placing ads in papers that reach minorities, supporting day care services, flexible working hours, and skills training programs. The second is the quota strategy which restricts hiring and promotion, so that the organization can achieve a quota or a numerical mix of minority and majority employees.

The quota system, which requires that a specific number and class of job positions be filled by minority rather than majority group members, has been linked to reverse discrimination, or the nonselection of a majority candidate who is equally qualified due to race. A number of legal cases have addressed the issue of quotas and discrimination, but no uniform rulings have emerged. In *United Steelworkers v Weber* (1979) the court rejected the complaint of a white employee who claimed that the company was practicing reverse discrimination when it allotted 50 percent of training positions to minority members. In other cases such as *Firefighters Local No 1784 v Stotts* (1984) and *Wagant v Jackson Board of Education* (1986), the courts have prohibited racial preference.

There are two opposing views with regard to affirmative action. One view suggests that instead of reducing bias, affirmative action serves to create it in the form of reverse discrimination. Others believe that our society has a history of discriminating against women, minorities, and persons with disabilities in hiring and promotion and that some means of regulatory action must take place to create equity in the workplace. There is no question that affirmative action has a downside for both majority and nonmajority group members. Majority group members must have qualifications that not only match, but also surpass nonmajority group applicants. Perhaps even more difficult, nonmajority group members must overcome the stigmatism attached to being selected as part of affirmative action.

DIVERSITY AWARENESS TRAINING

EEO and affirmative action programs may reduce or eliminate formal organizational bias, but they may have little or no effect on informal or individual bias. Many organizations have chosen to expand their efforts to manage diversity by adopting diversity awareness programs. Unfortunately many so-called diversity efforts are doomed to fail. Companies rarely pursue diversity strategies with the same commitment as those that directly effect the bottom line. A diver-

BEST PRACTICES

In addition to the avoidance of bias in hiring and promotion, companies must also adopt fair practices during periods of layoff. Burger King, which has had several major cutbacks in recent years, keeps close track of who's being let go. Their diversity representative carefully monitors this process to make sure there is no discrimination due to age, gender, or ethnic group. When there is a 5 percent companywide reduction in force, Burger King assures that the number of women and minorities is not overly represented.*

*Rice, "How to Make Diversity Pay," 78.

sity effort might only consist of a one-time presentation by a visiting expert, or the purchase of off-the shelf videos.

Diversity training, a widely used, and sometimes misused tool, is growing in popularity. Although many claim expertise in this topic, skilled trainers are difficult to find. Diversity training usually consists of several days of programming designed to teach managers and employees skills to build effective, culturally diverse teams. They may focus on such topics as gender differences, communication style, legal issues, and overcoming stereotypes and prejudices.

Diversity is potentially an inflammatory topic, and if objectives are not clear and the consultant conducting the training program is not skilled, it can actually do more harm than good. This occurred in a major government agency when they brought in a diversity consultant to conduct sessions. In one session men were asked to walk through a gauntlet of women who looked at and touched the men and then rated their masculinity on a scale of one to ten. In other sessions workers discussed personal traumas and viewed and reacted to sexually explicit materials. Later the agency had to settle unfair labor practice complaints made by offended workers.

Just like other forms of successful training, diversity programs must be carefully planned, based on measured needs, effectively delivered, and must be ongoing, not "single shot" training. Training that focuses on better understanding of real cultural differences, not "white male bashing," is a far more effective process. Rather than focusing on past injustices, instead, attend to changing unproductive behavior. Diversity training has the greatest impact when employees who work together are trained together. Another important component of diversity training is transfer, or the assurance that skills and ideas learned in training will be applied back in the workplace. Follow-up and reinforcement differentiate effective diversity training from short-lived, feel-good programs. Ray Hood–Phillips, former vice president of diversity affairs at Burger King, recommends programs that are tailor-made for a particular organization because every culture is unique. She avoids programs that are combative, guilt-driven, or contemptuous of white males.[43]

CULTURAL CHANGE

Organizations seeking to create a true multicultural environment will most likely need to undergo a major change process to achieve this. They must commit significant resources in time and money to this process. The most effective diversity strategies are those generated or championed by top management but also supported and accepted by employees at all levels of the organization. If a true multicultural organization is to be created, training and education must be extensive and coupled with vigorous CEO-backed efforts to measure change, hold managers accountable for implementation, and reward practitioners through compensation. An institutional framework must be in place that will guide the effort to make a long-lasting change in corporate culture. Let's examine the steps involved in effecting cultural change.

Step 1: Create Shared Vision

The first step in a comprehensive diversity strategy is the development of a **shared vision** that specifies in broad terms the objectives of the change process. Leadership must come not only from top management, but also from other significant members of the organization who are deeply committed to creating multiculturalism. These idea champions, typically line managers, can persuade, coerce, and sell others on the change process. Many organizations begin this process by creating a vision task force who painstakingly gathers the ideas and opinions of employees from all levels of the company. This is an excellent time to move toward an organic management system that fosters participation at all levels.

Step 2: **Diagnosis of the Problem**

A careful evaluation of the existing situation with regard to both formal and informal diversity practices follows the creation of a shared vision. Typically, this process is managed by a professional organization development consultant who specializes in diversity issues. Tools for diagnosis may include interviews, surveys, focus groups (group discussion), and observation. It is also important to evaluate potential language barriers at this time. If employees are not able to communicate well in English, information and programs must be offered in their native tongue if they are to be part of the process.

The results of the assessment are then communicated to all members of the organization in a manner that they can understand, so they are aware of the need for change. Everyone must clearly see the problem if they are to be convinced of the need to unfreeze and commit the time and energy necessary to adopt new ways of doing things.

Step 3: **Strategic Planning**

The best way to generate the energy and resources needed to make change happen is to get everyone involved in the process. Change teams are formed to plan and implement the process. These high-involvement teams are made up of cross-sectional groups consisting of managers, supervisors, and line employees from a variety of departments. It is important that the teams are representative of all constituencies and are diverse in terms of race, gender, lifestyle, and culture. These teams must be given the authority to make decisions, get others involved, and maintain open lines of communication at all levels. They must be allotted the time and resources to successfully drive the change process.

Next the teams work to generate a clear plan of attack. Ideas flow freely up the organizational chart with top management commitment still an integral component of the process. A number of effective tools can be built into the master plan for cultural change. These include a wide array of practices, including an affirmative action plan designed to attract and develop a high-quality, diverse work group, effective training programs, and the development of special interest groups.

Step 4: **Implementation**

Rather than implementing a multimillion dollar corporate diversity program, only to have it fail, incremental implementation is a far more effective strategy. A large hotel or restaurant chain might "test drive" the program by instituting it at a single property. This allows designers to carefully measure and assess the results and debug the program before corporatewide implementation. This significantly reduces the cost of failure as fewer resources are expended on a bad idea.

Step 5: **Measurement**

A critical and often overlooked aspect of change is measurement. The success of diversity training can be measured by surveying employees before, during, and after participation in various programs. It is also critical to track training transfer, or the degree to which new skills are practiced in the work place. This can be accomplished by periodic assessment following program participation in the form of self-evaluation, peer evaluation, and supervisory assessment.

Diversity training is an expensive endeavor, with costs running from $1,500 to $4,000 per day, and companies spending millions of dollars a year on such programs. To continue to justify such expenditures, careful measurement of the effect of diversity programs must be undertaken.

Step 6: **Continuous Improvement**

Finally, as in all quality efforts, continuous improvement must occur if the diversity program is to have long-reaching effects. A one-time, one-month diversity effort is unlikely to have much effect on cultural relationships a year later. Like a garden, multiculturalism requires constant attention if it is to maintain life and grow. Companies that have a permanent diversity officer in place, have cross-sectional teams that continuously measure and assess diversity awareness, and make diversity part of their daily business, just as quality service is, are much more likely to reap long-term benefits from diversity programs.

SUPERVISING A DIVERSE WORK TEAM

As a manager in the hospitality industry, it is very likely that you will have the opportunity to supervise a diverse work team. To a large degree, your reputation as a manager and your future with your organization will depend on how well you guide your work group. Consider the experiences of two white male restaurant managers employed by a major hotel chain. Both were called upon to supervise a diverse employee group consisting of women, minorities, and persons with disabilities. The first manager lacked the ability to view his diverse population as individuals and was unable to understand the various cultural norms of those he supervised. Morale and productivity were extremely low, and eventually this manager was reassigned to a less desirable, but less diverse property. He was replaced by a second white male, but this time, the new manager was much more effective in leading the same diverse group of employees. He encouraged all employees to do their best, not just other white males. He allowed workers greater flexibility in scheduling, and he planned small celebrations around ethnic holidays. Perhaps the most important change in practice was the respect and concern he showed for all employees. Productivity increased, and employees who once just went through the motions took new interest and new pride in their jobs. After a year in the position, the manager was considered "fast track" material and rapidly moved up the corporate ladder.

The management practices that you will learn about in this text are certainly prerequisites for leading a diverse work group, but additional skills are needed.

INTERPERSONAL COMMUNICATION

You may be called upon to lead employees who have limited English proficiency, heavy accents, or different ways of expressing themselves. Perhaps the best preparation for this challenge is to study a foreign language. If you are conversationally proficient in Spanish, you will have a tremendous advantage in both your ability to communicate effectively and your appeal in the job market. Other techniques that will help you improve communication in a multicultural environment are:

1. Listen carefully for both meaning and feeling. Be aware of body language and facial expression. Visual cues can help you understand meaning even when you can't understand what is said verbally.

2. Speak slowly and clearly. Americans typically speak at a much faster rate than those from other countries.

3. Exchange polite conversation prior to getting down to business. This is particularly important if you are interacting with people from a Latin culture where pleasant conversation precedes business transactions.

4. Adjust your level of eye contact. In most cultures, eye contact during conversation displays interest, but in some Asian cultures, it is considered polite to avert one's eyes when speaking. Also white listeners in conversation typically maintain more eye contact than the speaker, although the opposite has been found to be true among blacks.[44]

5. Use reflection to verify your understanding. Speakers may be annoyed if you constantly ask them to repeat what they said because you aren't sure you heard correctly. Instead reflect or repeat the main message back for clarification. Say, "So you would like to have. . ." or "I hear you saying that. . ." rather than "Could you repeat what you just said" or "I can't understand you." If

you must ask the person to repeat what they have said, do so politely and calmly.

6.   Avoid interrupting the speaker. You may be confused by the first part of the conversation, but if you allow the speaker to continue on, his or her meaning may become clear.

7.   Avoid physical contact with employees. Employees from some cultures may appreciate a pat on the back or even a hug, whereas others would be extremely uncomfortable with such physical contact. Be on the safe side and avoid any contact other than a handshake.

Fortunately the more we communicate with people from other cultures, the easier it becomes. We develop an understanding of speech patterns and rhythms and can become quite adept at understanding even those with the heaviest accents.

RESPECT DIFFERENCES

Another prerequisite for successful management in a multicultural environment is the development of a sincere attitude of respect for others who are different. Comments in the workplace regarding the abilities or characteristics of those culturally different are not just inappropriate, they are illegal. If you have prejudices, seek out their root cause and work hard to change the attitudes that have created any bias you may harbor. Watch movies such as *Malcolm X*, *The Joy Luck Club*, or *A Color Purple* to develop an understanding of racioethnic relations in the United States. Seek out friendships with those who are different. Look for opportunities to prove old stereotypes wrong. For example, if you believe women have poorer math skills than men, look for exceptions to this rule. Ultimately changes in individual bias must come from within each of us. Diversity awareness programs will not be successful if we ourselves resist change.

CONCLUSION

The effects of cultural diversity on organizational effectiveness are highly complex and very powerful. Understanding and managing diversity issues must be a high priority for industry leaders today and tomorrow. Our knowledge of diversity issues is in its infancy and continues to evolve over time. Initially companies hoped to create a "melting pot" where everyone adopted similar cultural values and beliefs. Today's progressive companies instead strive to create a salad bowl of cultures where differences not only are accepted, but also create a more pleasing whole. If employers and employees can work together to expand their understanding, they will be much better prepared to meet one of the greatest challenges to be faced by hospitality managers in the twenty-first century.

K   E   Y   T   E   R   M   S

Cultural Diversity   Stereotyping
Group Identity   Structural Integration
Phenotype Identity   Affirmative Action
Cultural Identity   Shared Vision
Discrimination

N   O   T   E   S

1. T. H. Cox, *Cultural Diversity in Organizations: Theory, Research & Practice* (San Francisco: Berrett-Koehler), 1993.

2. H. N. Fullerton, "Labor Force Projections: 1986–2000," *Monthly Labor Review* (September 1987): 19–29; and W. Johnson, "Global Work Force 2000: The New World Labor Market," *Harvard Business Review* (1991): 115–127.

3. J. P. Fernandez, *Managing a Diverse Workforce* (Lexington, Mass. Lexington Books, 1991).

4. Cox, *Cultural Diversity in Organizations.* p 7.

5. David Thomas and Robin Ely, "Making Differences Matter: A New Paradigm for Managing Diversity," *Harvard Business Review* (September October 1996): 79.

6. F. Rice, "How to Make Diversity Pay," *Fortune*, 130 (1994): 78.

7. A.E Serwer, "What to Do When Race Charges Fly," *Fortune* (July 12, 1993): 95.

8. A. Faircloth, "Guess Who's Coming to Denny's," *Fortune* 138 (August 3, 1998): 108–110.

9. C. Hymowitz, "One Firm's Bid to Keep Blacks, Women," *Wall Street Journal*, February 16, 1997 p. B1.

10. M. Farrell, Mandel, C. Young, D. J. Lau, G. C. Del Valle, and S. L.Walker, "The Immigrants: How They're Helping to Revitalize the US Economy," *Business Week* (July 13, 1992): 114–122.

11. M. Sherer, "If You Don't Have a Literacy Program: Read This Now," *Restaurants & Institutions* (October 31, 1990): 75–92.

12. Julia Christensen-Hughes, "Cultural Diversity: The Lesson of Toronto's Hotels," *The Cornell Hotel and Restaurant Administration Quarterly* (1992): 78–87.

13. Ibid.

14. Rice, "How to Make Diversity Pay," 78.

15. Cox, *Cultural Diversity in Organizations*, 17.

16. P. S. McLeod, S. A. Lobel, and T. Cox, "Cultural Diversity and Creativity in Small Groups," Unpublished working paper, University of Michigan, Ann Arbor, 1993.

17. L. R. Hoffman and N. R. Maier, "Quality and Acceptance of Problem Solutions by Members of Homogeneous and Heterogeneous Groups," *Journal of Abnormal and Social Psychology* (1961): 401–407.

18. E. Mighty, "Valuing Work for Diversity," *Canadian Journal of Administrative Sciences*, 8 (1991): 64–70; and A. M. Morrison, *The New Leaders* (San Francisco: Jossey-Bass, 1992).

19. Christensen-Hughes, "Cultural Diversity," 78–87.

20. C. P. Alderfer, "Diagnosing Race Relations in Management," *Journal of Applied Behavioral Sciences* 16 (1980): 135–165.

21. Cox, *Cultural Diversity in Organizations*, 43.

22. B. Ashforth and F. Mael, "Social Identity Theory and the Organization," *Academy of Management Review* 14 (1989): 20–39.

23. Cox, *Cultural Diversity in Organizations*, 45.

24. Fernandez, *Managing a Diverse Workforce*, p. 72

25. H. C. Triandis, "The Future of Pluralism Revisited," *Journal of Social Issues*, 32 (1976): 179–208.

26. Cox, *Cultural Diversity in Organizations*, 48.

27. J. E. Helms, *Black and White Racial Identity* (New York: Greenwood Press, 1990).

28. T. F. Pettigrew, "Prejudice" in S. Thernstrom, A. Onou, and O. Handlin, eds., *Dimensions of Ethnicity: Prejudice* (Cambridge: Harvard University Press, 1982).

29. J. Feagin and C. Feagin, *Racial and Ethnic Relations* (Englewood Cliffs, N.J.: Prentice Hall, 1993).

30. M. H. Ijzendoorn, "Moral Judgement, Authoritarianism, and Ethnocentrism," *Journal of Social Psychology* 129 (1989): 37–45.

31. Cox, *Cultural Diversity in Organizations*, 48.

32. A. H. Eagly, "Gender and Social Influence: A Social Psychological Analysis," *American Psychologist* 38, no. 9 (1983): 971–981.

33. A. Gregory, "Are Women Different and Why Are Women Thought to Be Different?" *Journal of Business Ethics*, 9 (1990): 257–266.

34. Cox, *Cultural Diversity in Organizations*, 90.

35. M. Loden and J. B. Rosener, *Workforce America! Managing Employee Diversity as a Vital Resource* (Homewood, Ill: Irwin, 1991).

36. Cox, *Cultural Diversity in Organizations*, 189.

37. D. Denison, *Corporate Culture and Organizational Effectiveness* (New York: Wiley, 1990).

38. T. H.Cox, and J. Finley-Nickelson, "Models of Acculturation for Intraoriganizational Cultural Diversity," *Canadian Journal of Administrative Sciences* 8 (1991): 90–100.

39. D. Denison, *Corporate Culture and Organizational Effectiveness* (New York: Wiley, 1990).

40. Cox, *Cultural Diversity in Organizations*, 189.

41. Cox, *Cultural Diversity in Organizations*, p. 196

42. K. Marino, "Conducting an Internal Compliance Review of Affirmative Action," *Personnel* 59 (March-April 1980): 24–34.

43. Rice, "How to Make Diversity Pay," 78.

44. P. Watts, "Bias Busting: Diversity Training in the Workplace."
     Management Review (December 1987): 53–54.

CASE 13.1: BREAKING THE LANGUAGE BARRIER

The majority of kitchen workers in James Moore's restaurant are Hispanic/Latinos. While they are working in the back of the house, they prefer to communicate with each other in Spanish. Recently several of the servers have complained about this practice and say that it's not right that back of the house employees are not required to communicate in English at all times. They took their complaint to Barry Rogers, the general manager of the restaurant, who in turn asked James to look into the matter. First James is bilingual so it was fairly easy for him to communicate with both parties involved. He began by gathering relevant information:

- The kitchen manager, Xavier Ortega, is Hispanic and can communicate with his employees in both languages.

- While most of the servers are not Hispanic and do not speak Spanish, virtually all the kitchen staff are Hispanic and have limited English-speaking ability.

- Due to the new automated ordering system, back and front of the house employees do not interact often as they serve customers.

Initially James thought this issue wasn't really a big deal. But as he gathered facts and talked with both back and front of the house employees, he found that serious cultural differences were underlying this issue. The Hispanic employees really felt that they had the right to use their own language among themselves. The Anglo servers also felt strongly that all employees should speak English at work. James decides to visit his mentor before making recommendations about solving this problem. James asks you the following questions:

1. What do you think will happen if we crack down and say that only English can be spoken by all restaurant employees at work?

2. What might happen if the other alternative is chosen and the kitchen workers are allowed to continue speaking Spanish?

3. Is there a win-win solution to this problem that might satisfy both groups?

R E V I E W   Q U E S T I O N S

1. What are the assets and liabilities that diversity brings to the work place? List them in a T diagram like the one below.

Assets	Liabilities

2. Specifically what actions might companies take to overcome the liabilities listed above?

3. What are some common practices with regard to diversity shared by the companies listed in Insight 13.2, The Best Companies for Minorities?

Complete the following sentences with the correct level from the Diversity Matrix:

4. When _____ exists, employees try to improve diversity efforts through legal efforts or internally with committees and talks with top management.

5. The organization dives change from the top with little support from employees and managers in _____.

6. In _____ the organization cares little for the needs of its minority members, and employees do not seek to understand or work with those who are different.

7. When the organization has adopted practices to promote diversity and employees and managers appreciate and express cultural differences, _____ exists.

Match the following terms with their correct definitions:

8. Phenotype group
9. Prejudice
10. Discrimination
11. Cultural identity group
12. Stereotyping
13. Organizational bias

a. Actions carried out by members of dominant groups that have a harmful effect on members of subgroups.

b. Individuals are viewed as members of groups and we apply preconceived notions to individuals in the group.

c. Preference patterns in organizations that create barriers for minority group members.

d. Identity groups formed on the basis of physical observable differences in people.

e. Group membership based on norms, values, and goal priorities.

f. Negative attitudes toward certain groups and their members.

CRITICAL THINKING EXERCISES

1. Diagram your cultural identity. Draw a large circle on a sheet of paper. Next, construct a pie chart by drawing slices of pie to indicate the group affiliations that effect your self-concept and make you who you are. The size of the slices should reflect the importance of each identity factor as a component of your total self. In the example on the next page, the woman of Hispanic origin identifies with being an American, her Hispanic descent, being an employee, followed by student, and finally, her athletic ability.

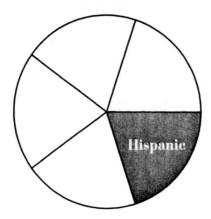

When you are finished, compare your identity affiliation with those of others. How are they the same? How do they differ? Try to develop explanations for the differences.

2. To further explore the effect culture has had on your life, imagine that you were born as the opposite gender. If you are male, imagine you were born female, and if you are female, imagine you were instead born male. Describe how your life would now be different in the following areas:

- Your friends.
- The car you drive.
- Your career aspirations.
- Your hobbies and interests.
- The sports you are interested in.
- Where you live.
- How others see you.

When finished, consider the overall effect gender has had on your life. If lots of differences are evident, this indicates that your gender has had a large effect on your life; few differences indicate a lesser effect. Share the results with your classmates.

3. Calculating the Cost of Turnover. Organizations that fail to successfully manage their diverse workforce are more likely to experience high turnovers. But what is the actual cost of turnover? Consider the following example:

A major hotel chain has forty properties and 20,000 employees. Half the workforce consists of women and nonwhites with a turnover rate of 10 percent, whereas turnover among the other half, white men, is only 5 percent.

- Each year, the company loses 500 white males and 1,000 women and nonwhite males.
- Conservatively, each replacement costs the hotel $15,000.
  a. What would be the annual cost of turnover among white males?
  b. What is the annual cost for women and nonwhites?
  c. What would the company save in dollars if they could achieve the same turnover rate among minorities and women as they have among white males?

4. List at least three common stereotypes that you are familiar with such as, "Blondes have more fun," "Men make better leaders," or "Teenagers are irresponsible."

    Are these stereotypes accurate? Why or why not?

O N - L I N E   L I N K

Which hospitality companies are best for women and minorities? To answer this question, search several corporate web sites, noting statements and information they provide regarding such issues as equal employment, flexible schedules, and concern for family issues. Print the information from the best sites and share it with your classmates. As a group, develop your own list of "Best Companies for Women & Minorities."

P O R T F O L I O   E X E R C I S E

At some point in your supervisory career in the hospitality industry, it is a given fact that you will be called upon to manage a diverse work group. It is important to anticipate in advance how you will meet this challenge. Review the Advanced Organizer presented at the beginning of this chapter. Imagine that you are that job applicant and your interviewer has asked you how you would supervise a very diverse workforce. Based on what you have learned in this chapter, formulate answers to the following interview questions:

1. Why is multiculturalism important to organizational success?
2. How would you maximize the benefits of a diverse work group and minimize the difficulties that can arise?

The Quality Movement

14

ADVANCED ORGANIZER

You are a supervisor with a large chain operation and quite happy with the way the organization is currently managed. One day, the company president announces that if your organization is to remain competitive, some changes must be made. The company will adopt a quality management approach and will empower all its employees to make decisions and solve guest problems. The president goes on to say that supervisors and manages will have new roles in the organization. Rather than directly overseeing their employees' work, they will coach and facilitate them to higher levels of performance.

Such an announcement is sure to generate lots of concern, particularly among managers and supervisors. What new roles might you take on in an empowered, quality-oriented company? What do you think it would be like to work in such an origination? In this chapter we will explore new practices, including quality management, teams, empowerment, and self-direction. You will understand the important issues that arise when organizations choose a less traditional way of doing things.

BEHAVIORAL OBJECTIVES

- Understand why organizations adopt total quality management and empowerment practices.

- Identify the components of TQM and its implementation process.

- Develop knowledge of the role of corporate culture in creating a successful organization.

- Know the dimension of empowerment and implementation strategy.

- Identify the benefits of a team work environment.

- Understand the evolutionary process of self-managed teams.

- Identify the skills needed by managers in a team environment.

The Peabody Orlando Ducks in their marble fountain. Our VIPs or Very Important Poultry, our MVPs, "Most Venerated Personnel."

THE QUALITY MOVEMENT

The quintessential example of poor service quality is the scene in the movie, *Five Easy Pieces*, where the server refuses to bring Jack Nicholson a simple order of toast because it isn't on the menu. We have all experienced service glitches of varying magnitude, ranging from incorrect orders to downright rudeness. At last companies have heeded customers' pleas for better products and services by implementing quality improvement processes.

During the past decade, the quality movement has taken American business by storm. With its roots in the Quality Circles process initiated in Japan by American W. Edwards Deming, total quality management (TQM) practices were first adopted by manufacturing and more recently applied in the service industry. In 1992 The Ritz-Carlton Hotel Company did what many people assumed no hospitality-related organization could accomplish: it became the first hotel company to win the coveted Malcolm Baldridge National Quality Award. The award is considered by many to be the equivalent of the "Nobel Prize" for quality, and by winning it, Ritz-Carlton established itself as much more than just a luxury hotel chain.

Below are some critical organizational problems that have spurred organizations to seek solutions through quality management principles:

INSIGHT 14.1

MALCOLM BALDRIDGE AWARD

The Ritz-Carlton is the only hotel chain to receive a Malcolm Baldridge National Quality Award. To win this coveted award, the company drastically changed the way they managed their organization.* In addition to empowering their employees, Ritz-Carlton adopted quality processes to carefully monitor the way work is completed and guests are served. For example the company requires that each hotel compile daily reports covering 720 work-related tasks. Managers measure the amount of time it takes to clean a guest room, seeking employee input in finding more efficient ways to perform this task. When employees overhear guest's complaints about service problems, they report this information immediately to a supervisor who responds to the problem. Finally the hotel is committed to providing each guest with customized service. A database consisting of the names and preferences of each customer is constantly updated with new information. All employees carry a notebook in which they record customer preferences and complaints that are later entered into the company's database for monitoring and future reference. When John Smith reserves a room for his next stay, the database will be consulted and will indicate that he prefers a nonsmoking room, requires extra assistance due to a disability, and orders breakfast from room service each day.

Other nonhospitality-related companies have come to Ritz-Carlton for advice in improving customer service. Mobil Oil managers attended employee training session conducted by Ritz-Carlton and came away with ideas for developing a service culture that led to major changes in the way Mobil hired and trained their staff.

*R. Hiebeler, T. B. Kelly, and C. Ketteman, *Best Practices: Building Your Business with Customer-Focused Solutions* (New York: Simon & Schuster, 1998).

- The need to reduce cost and improve service.
- The need to become more customer focused by listening to customers, meeting their expectations, and responding instantly to their problems.
- The need to fully utilize the knowledge and experience of front-line workers.
- The need to improve service without increasing labor cost.

WHAT EXACTLY IS TQM?

Total quality management is a set of practices that focus on meeting and often exceeding customer expectations and significantly reducing the cost of defects and errors by shaping a new management system and corporate culture.[1] Let's examine this definition more closely. TQM is a way of defining organization culture by placing customer satisfaction at the forefront. The process focuses on continuous improvement of products and services. Existing ways of doing business are constantly evaluated, and new, better ways are sought. One never achieves perfection in TQM, but constantly seeks improvement. When companies adopt a corporatewide quality improvement program, they:

- Commit themselves to satisfying the customer.
- Involve employees at all levels to determine the best practices and performance standards.
- Constantly search for new and better ways to do things.
- Communicate openly with all employees at all levels.

To accomplish these lofty goals, companies must implement a significant change process. They often begin by examining their corporate culture, or the very personality of their organization. They typically adopt a team-based system of management that involves employees at all levels in decision making and problem solving. Quality-focused companies must also empower their employees to do whatever it takes to make the guest happy. Finally they must develop a system of measurement that allows them to track their progress.

IMPLEMENTING TQM

Total quality management is not a quick fix or simple solution. The implementation process is costly and can take years to complete. Companies that adopt this process literally turn themselves upside down, placing customers and employees at the top of the hierarchy instead of at the bottom. When new systems are in place, companies often find it all worthwhile due to increased customer satisfaction, employee loyalty, and product quality.

Let's examine a series of steps that must be taken to implement total quality management principles:

Step 1: **Top Level Involvement:** Although TQM is based on bottom-up management where decisions made at the top are based on information supplied by front-line employees and managers, TQM cannot be successful without complete commitment from top management. Successful quality movements are initiated and championed by top management.

Step 2: **Create a Blue-Ribbon Study Group:** Once top management commits to implementing TQM, the next step is to form a study group to assess organizational readiness. Led by top management, the study group typically consists of an internal or external consultant and key department heads. Their charge is to assess the culture of the organization and evaluate its compatibility to TQM. This group will decide whether the company should proceed with the adoption of quality practices.

Step 3: **Establish an Action Task Force:** If all systems are go and the study group recommends processing with TQM, the next step is to form an internal **task force** or quality council. This group consists of representative members from various departments and includes both line employees and managers. The task force works together to create a clear vision or philosophy for the organization and to develop a specific plan for implementing TQM. They will also identify the areas where employee and management training is needed due to expanded skill requirements.

Step 4: **Implementation:** The successful implementation of TQM demands involvement at all levels of the organization. Although the process is driven by top management, it is implemented from the bottom up. This means that line employees and middle managers are completely engaged in the process and work together to tackle problems relating to service and customer satisfaction. These teams then report to the task force and top management. Additional training may be needed to fine-tune decision-making skills and to teach employees how to function as part of a team. The TQM process is ongoing, and evaluation and assessment must take place at each step. Thus, continuous improvement is made throughout the implementation process.

Both the initial and long-term success of TQM processes depend on three important organizational components:

1. An organizational culture that supports quality management principles.
2. A team-based organizational structure.
3. The involvement and empowerment of employees at all levels.

We will examine these three important components of TQM processes in greater detail. You will learn about the importance of assessing, and, if necessary, transforming organizational culture prior to the implementation of TQM. You will learn about the various types of team environments in organizations and how individuals and managers work together. Finally, we will explore the principles of empowerment and how empowered employees can keep customers coming back again and again.

ORGANIZATIONAL CULTURE

Corporate culture refers to the environment or the personality of the organization. In its simplest form, it is "the way things are done around here" based on the values, behaviors, management styles, and written and unwritten laws and policies. Prior to implementing a new corporatewide process, it is important to assess the culture of the organization to assure that it is consistent with the proposed change. To be successful TQM requires that the organization have a culture that supports team planning and decision making, employee empowerment, and customer-driven practices. For example historically the culture at Marriott Hotels was based on top-down management directive with strict adherence to standard operating procedures. Over the years, its culture has changed to allow for increased employee involvement and greater emphasis on creativity, leading to the corporatewide implementation of employee empowerment practices.

CULTURE SHOCK

To help you better understand the impact of corporate culture, let's compare two very diverse cultures, that of the Hard Rock Cafe versus Ritz-Carlton Hotels. Both companies are very successful and highly regarded by both customers and employees, yet obviously have very different ways of doing things. The Hard Rock Cafe is young, funky, a little wild, and strictly informal. The people working there embrace this culture and expound it in the way they talk, dress, and interact with customers. At the other extreme, Ritz-Carlton Hotels are lavish, formal, and of course, "Ritzy." The core of the company's philosophy or culture is their credo.

INSIGHT 14.2

STARBUCK'S CULTURE

A great deal of the success experienced by Starbucks coffee comes from its powerful corporate culture.* Starbucks's employees have a strong spirit of teamwork that is readily visible in their philosophy of treating each other and customers with respect and dignity. Employees quote "Howardisms" or wise words from their CEO Howard Schultz like, "If we serve the best coffee in the world, how we treat people should be the same." Starbucks's culture is also based on the need to contribute to the common good. They donate to CARE and fund projects to help coffee-producing countries.

To date Howard Schultze is the driving force behind Starbucks and is credited with creating and supporting their strong culture. With dramatic and rapid growth, Starbucks is faced with the challenge of maintaining their strong culture and disseminating it to the more than 2000 stores they expect to operate by the year 2,000. It will be impossible for Schultze to directly influence each employee to perpetuate the desired culture. Instead the company must plan to nurture their culture as they expand.

*J. Sherriton and J. L. Stern, "Corporate Culture Team Culture: Removing the Hidden Barriers to Team Success. 62–63. New York: Amacom 1997.

"We Are Ladies and Gentlemen Serving Ladies and Gentlemen." This motto is printed on cards and carried by employees at all times.

It is critical to the success of the organization that employees buy into and exemplify the corporate culture. Can you imagine what might happen if Ritz-Carlton employees were replaced with Hard Rock Cafe employees for a day? If the Hard Rock employees maintained their original culture at the Ritz, customers would be shocked, outraged, and very confused. This is an extreme example of a poor cultural match.

THE ACCULTURATION PROCESS

How do we become acculturated? It all starts when we are children. We learn to adopt the beliefs of our parents, peers, churches, and societies. Culture is a learned characteristic. Five-star Ritz-Carlton employees are not necessarily born "ladies and gentlemen," they have learned the skills and attitudes needed to work in a luxury hotel. Organizations maintain their culture by having the right person–company fit. When important values in the organization are also the values of its employees, such as innovation or team orientation, there is a good person–company fit. How well do employee values match those of the organization? If it's a close match, the employee is likely to be successful. If not, success is difficult to achieve. Could you imagine a Hard Rock Cafe employee who hates rock music enjoying his job? Or an individual who likes to dress and behave in a new wave style (body piercing, shaved head, very long, bright nails, etc.) being a happy, successful employee of a conservative, luxury hotel? Not a chance.

BUILDING CULTURE

Successful companies work hard to foster a unified culture where all members share similar beliefs and values. In the past companies accomplished this goal by hiring a certain type of employee who looked, dressed, and behaved like everyone else in the company. IBM was famous for their clones in the navy power suits with dark red ties. In today's society, it is unlikely that employees in any company will fit neatly into a mold, or that rapidly changing organizations would want such a homogenous workforce. Instead it is more important that all employees share important beliefs in the value of service, honesty, creativity, hard work, and team spirit than mere superficial characteristics. Organizations

BEST PRACTICES

Visitors to Disney theme parks quickly become aware of the strong culture among employees, or as they are known in the company, "cast members." How did Disney build such a strong culture? They did so by committing fully to the following:

- Special uniforms for employees.

- A common language: Customers are guests, rides are attractions, and employees are cast members.

- Thorough new employee orientation, including "Traditions" which includes Disney history and lore.

that are most effective at socializing or helping newcomers adapt to their corporate culture begin by creating a shared cultural environment.

CREATE*ing* A WINNING CULTURE

Seeking a congruent or shared organizational culture is well worth the effort. In a recent study, companies that focus on their employees and seek to create a shared culture experience a significant increase in profitability.[2] At Ritz-Carlton, Disney, McDonald's, and other highly successful companies, the culture and values that drive the behavior of employees is in harmony with the goals and strategies of the companies.

The process of managing culture begins with identifying the type of culture desired and determining to what degree our existing culture differs from our ideal. This first step is the same whether the business is a hot dog stand or a multimillion dollar corporation. To improve their level of effectiveness, corporations must:

- *Create a shared vision.* Employees and management groups work together to decide where the company should direct its resources and energy in the future.
- *Develop a model for change.* This model may come from top management, as was the case with Ritz-Carlton, but champions of change may also be found among midlevel managers or line employees. Pioneers who implement new procedures with regard to hiring, training, or feedback may create a spark that leads the entire organization toward change.
- *Reward desired behavior.* People do what they are rewarded for doing. Make sure the new management systems reward new desired behaviors, not old undesirable ones. Reward employees for great new ideas, empowered acts, and team spirit, not just for following the old rules and procedures.

Total quality Management

When necessary adjustments have been made to an organization's culture, the TQM practice that most companies move toward is employee empowerment and a team-based management system. Employee empowerment is considered to be the chief mechanism for ensuring the steady quality improvement required by those seeking to win the Baldridge Award as did Ritz-Carlton.[3] In the next section, you will learn about empowerment in conjunction with the new team orientation.

EMPOWERMENT

In their quest for service quality, hospitality organizations are empowering their front-line employees to solve problems and provide added value to guests. **Empowerment** involves restructuring the traditional top-down, control-oriented management model by distributing power, information, knowledge, and rewards throughout the organization. **Empowerment** is not a set of prescribed techniques. Instead it is a philosophical shift of responsibility and control from management to the people doing the core work of the organization, line employees. Empowerment involves taking some of the authority typically held only by managers and passing it on to employees. Empowerment brings many benefits to both the company and its employees. It has been linked to improved service, increased job satisfaction, loyalty, concern for others, and decreased turnover intention.[4]

In the past traditional management has revolved around supervisors and managers planning, organizing, and controlling the employees that work for them. Management made all the important decisions and employees did what they were told. During the past decade, companies began noticing problems with this system. It became more and more difficult to motivate employees to meet the rising needs of customer's in today's competitive environment. Organizations have realized that tighter controls, clearly defined jobs, and direct supervision have run their course and can no longer support the high level of productivity and quality today's competitive markets require. There is a distinct need for employees to take personal responsibility for the success of the companies they work for. Customers expect more extensive and higher quality service than ever before. At the same time, they are downsizing to cut costs and protect their narrowing profit margins. Businesses must do more with less. They must increase the quality of their service, but do so with fewer employees. The only way organizations can accomplish this seemingly insurmountable task is to get 100 percent from each employee all the time. Hotels and restaurants must have a well-trained, highly skilled workforce committed to meet organizational goals. An empowered workforce provides a way to accomplish this challenging goal.

THE EMPOWERING MANAGER

It is up to you as a manager to create an environment that supports the empowerment of others. How do you go about empowering your employees? Most experts agree that you really cannot empower another person, but you can create a work environment that allows others to make decisions and take responsibility.

During implementation companies gradually give employees greater responsibility and move from a traditional management systems to one of empowerment. Empowered employees have more authority to conduct the business at hand. When guests have problems, empowered employees have the power to solve them. They also have the authority to take initiative, anticipate guest needs, and provide extra service to "wow" their customers. When an empowered bellstand member overheard a guest complain to another guest that the gift shop did not have his favorite over-the-counter remedy for an upset stomach, the employee hopped in his car, went to the nearest drug store, and promptly delivered the medication to the guest in his room. Was this guest surprised! He had no idea that the employee had overhead his complaint and certainly wasn't expecting such service. Empowerment allowed this employees to use his own judgment without first locating his supervisor, asking permission, and finally heading out to do his good deed. Thus empowerment is not just another word for delegation, but a permanent transfer of both responsibility and authority to those in front-line positions.[5]

In many organizations, empowerment is considered the best way to lead and motivate employees. When given a choice, most of us would prefer working in an environment that granted us more authority. Why do employees prefer empowerment?

- People are usually smarter and more capable than we assume they are.
- Everyone wants to be treated as an adult.
- We all want to be consulted before decisions that affect us.
- Nearly everyone wants to do an outstanding job and is proud of their work.
- We want to be trusted and have greater authority and freedom at work.

DIMENSIONS OF EMPOWERMENT

In itself, empowerment is a rather esoteric term that can mean different things to different people. What does it really mean to be empowered? Researchers have been working to clearly define empowerment and its components. Four dimensions or characteristics of empowerment have been identified:[6]

1. *Meaning:* The fit between the requirements of a work role and a person's beliefs, values, and behaviors. It is the value of an activity's goal or purpose in relation to your own ideals or standards. Empowered employees believe in and care about what they do.
2. *Competence:* Self-efficacy or beliefs in one's capability to perform work activities with skill. Empowered employees believe they are capable of solving problems on their own.
3. *Self-determination:* A sense of choice in initiating and regulating actions. Empowered employees feel that they control the decision-making process and have the power to make their own choices.
4. *Impact:* The degree to which a person can influence strategic, administrative or operating outcomes at work. Empowered employees believe the success or failure of their organization lies with them. What they do has direct effect on whether their organization will achieve its goals.

If employees are to be truly empowered, they must experience meaning, competence, self-determination, and impact in their work. Without these four feelings about their work, true employee empowerment will be difficult to achieve. Companies that merely give lip service to empowerment may fail to address these four areas. In such organizations employees are simply told that they are "empowered" and to go for it, without being given any real authority to make a difference. When they take risks and use their initiative, they are reprimanded. Eventually employees will cling to past practices, fearing failure or believing that they have no real power to make choices.

MAXIMIZING THE BENEFITS OF EMPOWERMENT

Companies that want to maximize their employee's sense of empowerment must commit to the following practices:

- *Get employees involved in goal setting at all levels.* Employees must be involved in setting goals for themselves, their department, and the organization.
- *Clearly define roles.* Empowered employees must understand their new roles in the company, the roles of their coworkers, and, most importantly, new roles that management is taking on.
- *Become a coach and facilitator.* As a manager you may have to release some of your control and authority and take on new roles in the organization. You must learn to lead through others and facilitate the success of your department and your employees.
- *Make sure top management support is felt.* Empowered employees must feel that they not only have support from their supervisors, but also from top management.
- *Create a participative climate.* This is why the assessment and possible adjustment of organizational climate is so important to empowerment. If the climate does not encourage involvement at all levels, empowerment will not be successful.

EMPOWERMENT STRATEGY

Companies that commit to adopting an empowered work environment must choose between a structured and flexible system of participation.[7] In **structured empowerment** employees are given specific guidelines for making decisions with regard to guest recovery when problems occur. These guidelines might be specific dollar amounts they can spend in certain situations or specific actions they can take. On the positive side, this system gives employees guidelines and limits to work within. Companies that choose the structured system are still clinging to a traditional management practices, often afraid to release real power to their employees. In **flexible empowerment** employees are given broad guidelines and limits to work within. For example, at Ritz-Carlton employees at all levels are empowered to spend up to $2,000 to satisfy a guest. Employees decide when and how to spend a sum they feel appropriate to please a dissatisfied guest or to wow an important client.

Empowerment may also take place at either the individual or team level. In **individual empowerment,** employees are given authority along with responsibility. In **team empowerment,** ad hoc teams are formed to solve problems, improve processes, or take on a challenge. At the highest level of group participation, **self-directed work teams** manage themselves and their work. Employees take on responsibilities normally reserved for management such as hiring, scheduling, and evaluation. In this situation the principles of empowerment are applied to the work team. In the next section you will learn about the important role of the work team in organizations and how some innovative companies are moving toward higher employee involvement with self-directed or empowered teams.

THE NEW TEAM ENVIRONMENT

Teams have been a part of the work environment since the beginning of time. Groups of people have worked together to perform similar tasks and achieve common goals for as long as civilization has existed. In past organizational settings, the team's function has been pretty much left to chance. Typically an informal leader would emerge, and some teams would perform highly whereas others became bogged down in conflict and failed to achieve their potential. Today's organizations are seeking to optimize the benefits of teams in improved service, creativity, and productivity by creating new systems of team management and design. Katzenbach and Smith[8] identify several phenomena that are responsible for the high performance of teams.

- *The sum of the whole is greater than any of its parts.*
  Teams bring together skills and experience that when

INSIGHT 14.3

CARE PAIRS

There is a new approach to providing outstanding, customer focused service in health care where overspecialization is rampant. Specialists and technicians wouldn't dream of doing any thing but their own narrow duties, even if they are idle most of the time. To combat this several hospitals have adopted a patient focused path by organizing bedside care around teams of multi-skilled practitioners.* These consist of a registered nurse and a cross-trained technician backed by a unit-based pharmacist, a unit clerk, and a support aide. The care pairs handle the majority of care for four to seven patients. The care pairs admit, process records, chart, charge, pass trays, transport patients, clean, and administer diagnostic tests and therapy. Nurses at Lakeland Regional Medical Center in Lakeland, Florida, say they actually prefer this system. The dramatic results of the Lakeland Pilot study include:

- Turnaround time for tests dropped from 157 to forty-eight minutes.

- Care pairs more than doubled the time they spend with patients.

- Fewer patient falls.

- The average patient encountered only thirteen hospital personnel rather than the usual thirty-eight.

Most importantly patient satisfaction levels soared. Their perceptions of quality, responsiveness, and empathy were far above average. Patient costs also fell significantly. As a result Lakeland plans to shift entirely to patient-focused care during the next five years.

*T.Peters, *Liberation Management*, (New York: Alfred A. Knopf, 1992), 229–232.

combined, exceed those of any one individual. This allows teams to respond to complex problems like innovation, quality, and customer service.

- *Teams support real-time problem solving and initiative.* As new information becomes available, teams can adjust their approach with greater speed, accuracy, and efficiency than individuals.
- *Teams socially enhance the job.* Teams work together to overcome barriers to high-level performance. Team members learn to trust each other and have confidence in the team's ability. Teams are trained extensively in communication, listening, and feedback and are more like to interact effectively with each other and with other teams.
- *Teams have more fun.* Working together to achieve common goals is enjoyable. The authors hear that the deepest and most satisfying source of enjoyment is from team members "having been part of something larger than myself."[9]

TYPES OF TEAMS

Many companies today are reorganizing to a team-based structure, but not all teams are alike. There are three basic types of teams commonly found in organizations.

- ***Functional teams*** *or work teams.* The functional team (Bold) consist of those members of a department who work together to perform a specific function. Groups of room attendants responsible for cleaning a particular floor, servers in a particular dinning room, and reservationists at a hotel are all members of functional teams.

BEST PRACTICES

Housekeeping is the largest and one of the most complicated departments to operate in hotels. Many employees find the work itself less than satisfying, but clean rooms are the key to success in the hotel industry. Team interventions were introduced to room attendants in a luxury property in Miami. They listed a series of fifteen problems in the department that have a negative effect on guest service. Team members discussed the problems, developed solutions, and took responsibility for implementation. A major problem in the department was lack of adequate linen supply. Causes of the problem ranged from disorganization in the laundry to room attendants hoarding linens. Room attendants met with the laundry staff and developed a series of interventions to assure that adequate linen supplies were available. The interventions led to the elimination of the linen supply problem at the hotel. This may sound like a small step, but each room now had an adequate towel supply, and productivity was increased because room attendants no longer had to search out linens before starting to clean.

- *Cross-functional teams* In cross-functional teams (Bold), individuals from several different departments brought together to solve specific problems, develop new products, or to implement new strategies. A good example of a cross-functional team is the in-house safety team that most larger hotels support consisting of a diverse group of members representing each department. This team meets weekly or monthly to review accidents, identify safety hazards, and plan future incentive campaigns.
- *Self-directed work teams* can either be functional or cross-functional in nature, but have the added benefit of self-management or empowerment. Team members take on duties normally reserved for supervisors. They are cross-trained in a variety of work skills, share and rotate leadership, set their own goals, create their own schedules, and may even hire, reward, and appraise team members.

INSIGHT 14.4

QUALITY IN LAS VEGAS

Las Vegas is bombarded by competitors on all fronts with the development of riverboat gambling, video gaming, and the threat of casino development in other cities. Several visionary properties have adopted quality assurance and employee involvement to become more strategically focused on customer service. MGM's Cindy Kiser describes how employee involvement (EI) teams at the operating and executive levels are given the training and tools needed to make valuable contributions to strategic planning and day-to-day problem solving.* A steering team of top executives head the program with each executive serving as a coach to an EI team. Each team also has a group leader and a facilitator. Kiser offered the following examples of how EI teams have improved service or saved money:

- At the Sands a team of room attendants developed a solution to excessive tearing of bed sheets. By installing a $12 hook on laundry carts, the casino saved $60,000 per year.

- A safety team came up with a reward plan for accident prevention that saved $200,000 and reduced grievances from 6,200 to one.

- A front desk team at the Mirage redesigned and computerized the check-in–check-out process and eliminated long lines.

- A team of cocktail servers developed employee guidelines in the sensitive area of personal grooming.

Employee involvement teams at the MGM Grand will also be involved in employee selection, the development of training manuals, and skills development and training at the "University of OZ," its internal training facility.

*B. C. Reimann, "The Newest Game in Vegas Is Strategic Management." *Planning Review* (January\February 1993): 38–49.

MOVING TOWARD SELF-MANAGEMENT

Teams have become an important business strategy in today's competitive environment. Organizations must capture the creative, innovative spirit of their employees if they are to become high-performance companies. Hospitality-related businesses must tap the energy of everyone involved, from dishwasher to CEO. One way of incorporating knowledge-work into the front lines, or making sure that everyone's thoughts are heard and valued, is through teams.

SELF-DIRECTED TEAMS ARE MORE EFFECTIVE

Transforming an organization from top to bottom into a self-directed work team environment takes time, money, and tremendous commitment. Why do companies choose such radical change? Companies that change to a self-directed team environment are seeking:[10]

- *Improved quality, productivity and service.* Team members feel more ownership for their job and company. They emphasize continuous quality improvement which has led to tremendous increase in quality, productivity, and service.
- *Greater flexibility.* Companies must find ways to increase responsiveness to customers. They must adapt quickly and teams help them do this.
- *Reduced Operating Costs*. When decision making occurs at lower levels, fewer layers of management and supervision are required. Empowered teams allow employees to take responsibility once reserved for managers and supervisors.
- *Ability to attract and retain the best people.* Organizations are finding it increasingly difficult to attract employees who have the high skill level they need. Employees value freedom, accomplishment, participation, and challenge as much as fair. Workers enjoy the challenge of self-managed teams and are more likely to stay with a company that respects their abilities. For example the Ritz-Carlton Hotel located in Tysons Corner reported that their turnover rate fell from 57 percent to 36 percent after their first year of self-directed work teams.[11] After the second year, turnover fell

BEST PRACTICES

Ritz-Carlton Hotel Company contends that self-directed work teams have reduced employee turnover and increased satisfaction. Management's role has shifted from control to coaching and their new "shared leadership" approach has been implemented in all but two of their thirty-one properties. Productivity is up, employee satisfaction is at 90 percent, and turnover has fallen. Prior to implementation employees received training. Employees then make decisions about what products to purchase, promotions that should be run, and whom to hire. Team decisions must stay within the philosophy of the company.

further to 32 percent, and the hotel expects to have a turnover rate of less that 25 percent after their third year.

Organizations that are in a competitive, changing market where customer expectation is high are particularly ripe for reorganizing into a team-based management system. Teams increase collaboration, communication, and bring problems to the forefront. They give groups of employees the opportunity to identify guest problems and solve them. When the system is effective, guest satisfaction increases, and satisfied guests are more likely to return.

SELF-DIRECTED TEAMS ATTRACT THE BEST EMPLOYEES

Empowered team members have greater responsibility. They are required to do more than simply know their jobs and perform the required duties. These individuals participate in creating their jobs, adding and deleting duties as needed to better serve their customers. Notice the difference between the excerpts from the job description of a traditional front desk clerk and that of an empowered member of a front office team:

Front Desk Clerk

The front desk clerk is responsible for all procedures involved in rooming guests. This requires knowledge of the front office computer system and the ability to communicate with guests effectively. Employees practice suggestive selling techniques to upgrade guests when possible. The front desk clerk must also interact effectively with coworkers and supervisors and perform all job duties as assigned.

Front Office Team Member

The team member must have knowledge of all procedures involved in rooming guests, including the front office computer system, and be able to teach other team members these skills. This individual must be able to communicate effectively with individuals and groups, solve problems, and take initiative. Team members work together in hiring, scheduling, performance appraisal, quality improvement, developing standards, and budgeting.

Which job would you prefer? The traditional, more routine desk clerk position or the team position that would require more skills and commitment? In the first position, learning is limited to job duties offering little understanding of the overall function of the department or hotel. The second position sounds more like a manager's job description. That is the purpose of empowered teams, assigning responsibilities typically held by a manager or supervisor to the entire team. This creates a more interesting, exciting, challenging position. Employees are no longer required to simply "perform all job duties as assigned" but are required to be intelligent, skilled, resourceful members of a dynamic work team.

WHICH ORGANIZATIONS BENEFIT FROM SELF-DIRECTED TEAMS?

Typically the need for team intervention arises from the strategic planning process. As management and employees develop the organization's vision, they realize that the goals cannot be achieved without shared leadership. Management alone cannot assure that guests' needs are met 100 percent of the time. They must have total commitment from employees to achieve this. Getting such a buy-in is impossible if employees are not involved in setting and implementing policy changes.

Organizations that might benefit from self-managed teams may be experiencing one or more of the following problems:

- Lack of interdepartmental communication
- High turnover rate.
- Lack of employee-manager communication.
- Dissention and conflict among employees.
- Guest problems that reoccur over and over again.
- Lack of consistency in meeting customer expectations.
- Managers are overburdened with day-to-day operations.
- Managers are frequently called in to "put out fires."

Self-managed teams will not miraculously solve all of these problems, but many companies adopt this system when faced with these and other challenges.

THE EVOLUTION OF SELF-MANAGED TEAMS

Self-managed teams are developed over a period of time. Organizations begin to move toward empowered teams by making some basic changes in the way they are structured, the language they use, and the practices they follow. Here are a few stepping-stones leading to change:

- Revamping the names typically used to denote position and authority. Employees become associates or team members and managers and supervisors become group leaders or coordinators.
- Begin awareness training that focuses on the establishment of new roles and identities for employees and manager. Deal with concerns and fears of managers and employees. Eventually fewer people are needed to perform traditional management duties, but there is a greater need for trainers, team facilitators, and technical experts.

After these basic needs are addressed, the organization may choose to continue the evolutionary process by reorganizing into a team based structure. Typically a planning committee or design team consisting of top management, department heads, supervisors, and employees work together to develop, implement, and monitor the team process.

Issues this group might deal with include:

- The training needs of team leaders, facilitators, and members.
- The size and organization of teams.
- Team goal setting and monitoring of progress.
- Overall assessment of the success of the team effort.
- The changing role of supervisors and managers.
- Compensation and team incentives.
- Selection and performance appraisal of team members.

When the planning team has thoroughly explored these and other issues related to team implementation, they will often begin with a pilot project. One particular department will be redesigned in a team function. Employees, leaders, and facilitators will be trained and the process implemented. Difficulties are ironed out, results are assessed, and a decision can then be made to either slowly phase in teams or immediately implement them throughout the organization.

Ideally team size is limited to ten to twelve employees. Large departments such as housekeeping can be divided into many work teams. Perhaps housekeepers from each floor would be a team with the traditional supervisor acting as group leader or facilitator.

Next team meetings are initiated. The group meetings do not have to be lengthy or involved. Many companies feel that teams would actually decrease productivity because so much time is spent talking. If done effectively teams not only will increase productivity but also certainly increase work quality. After initial training for team leaders and members, meetings need only be held once each week. The same time typically set aside for traditional department meetings can be used for team meetings. The goal of self-directed work teams is not to have people engaging in lengthy conversation and discussion, but to have work groups collaborate to solve organizational problems, improve the product, and increase guest satisfaction.

Another important step in the change process is **cross-training.** Each team member develops expertise in tasks normally carried out by members of other teams by receiving training in areas outside their department. A front desk clerk would be cross-trained to also do the job of a cashier, telephone operator, guest attendant (bell staff), and concierge. Multiskilling enables the desk clerk to work more effectively with members of other areas and increases the department's flexibility.

Throughout the transition open lines of continuous communication are critical for team success. Information once passed on only to managers and supervisors must be communicated to all team members. Restaurant employees must be given sales data and operating costs so they know exactly how the business is doing. If employees are to run a business as though it was their own, they must be given adequate information.

THE SKILLS TEAM MEMBERS NEED

Members of empowered teams need all the skills of traditional employees and more. They must have a high degree of technical knowledge about their own jobs and the jobs held by other teams they work with. Cooks must be highly skilled in food preparation, and also know what it's like to be a server. Cooks will then have a better understanding of their role in guest service and how their performance can effect guest satisfaction.

Team members work together to identify and solve problems. This is a new role for most employees, and skill in communication, decision making, and negotiation must be developed. Training in conflict management, meeting leadership, and customer service must be given before the team system is implemented. Team members also become quality-control specialists. Effective teams members are part of a continuous quality improvement loop. They identify problems, develop solutions, implement them, and assess the results. If the results are not 100 percent successful, the team starts the process again.

THE SKILLS TEAM LEADERS NEED

A team leader is not separate from the self-directed work team, but is also a team member. The leader is typically a department employee, and the responsibility can be rotated among the team members. The group leader, sometimes called facilitator, coach, or manager, is external to the team and differs from the team leader position in that the group leader has responsibilities in addition to the team function. A group leader in the front office might be a front desk manager who is responsible for several teams consisting of front desk clerks, guest attendants, cashiers, and telephone operators.

Where managers once controlled, organized, planned, and supervised, team leaders now coach, facilitate, empower, train, and support team members. New team leaders will require special training to develop these skills. As a team leader, power and control are two words that you must almost totally eliminate from your job description. As a team leader, you will not give direction and instructions to team members, but facilitate their identification of goals and development of standards and procedures. You must be the ultimate delegator, but you must also be skilled in recognizing when members are ready to take on additional responsibilities. You must provide members with the training and support they need to develop their skills.

HIGH-INVOLVEMENT TEAMS

There are few limits to what empowered teams can accomplish once they achieve an advanced level of functioning. It can take years of commitment to become fully self-directional. Here are just a few of the functions that highly involved self-managed teams might tackle:

- Teams go beyond identifying and solving department problems and begin to anticipate trends that lead to new guest needs.

- They identify and take responsibility for their own training. Individual team members may decide to return to college to learn more about computers or communication.
- Team members may become more involved in the overall
operation of the organization. They may give presentations to top management and take leadership roles.
- High-involvement teams are totally committed to the organization and actually act as though they were the owners.
- The team process of identifying and solving problems is
no longer separate from the job, but an integral part of it.
Members automatically take action as difficulties arise.
- Team members may also take responsibility for selecting
new members. When a position is open, rather than management interviewing and hiring a new person, the team
will interview and make a decision about who to hire.
- Team members also monitor the performance of individual members and the team itself. They appraise each
other, recommend areas for improvement, and may also
allocate financial rewards.

When we consider the traditional structure of the typical hospitality operation, all of this may sound pretty far-fetched. As customer expectation and
demand for high-quality service continue to increase, companies must take a
more proactive approach if they are to survive. High-quality service demands
high quality employees; leaders not followers. Organizations are finding that
work teams work.

CONCLUSION

To improve the quality and delivery of service, many hospitality organizations are seeking to adopt new systems of management to reduce cost and become more customer focused. Total quality management is one of these systems.
It consists of reducing defects and service glitches and increasing customer satisfaction. Before implementing corporatewide change, companies must first assess
their culture to assure that it supports the desired outcomes. Companies must
achieve a winning culture by creating shared vision, developing a model for
change, and rewarding desired behavior.

Empowerment is another contemporary practice that is being widely
adopted by hospitality-related companies. Employees are become empowered or
given added responsibility to solve guest problems and increase guest satisfaction. Other companies are also seeking to increase team effectiveness by making
work groups increasingly more self-directed. Self-managed teams have been
found to increase quality, reduce operating costs, and attract better employees.
As corporations change, so does the role of management. Rather than planning
and controlling the work of others, today's managers must learn to facilitate employee and team decision making and problem solving.

K E Y   T E R M S

Total Quality Management   Flexible Empowerment
Task Force   Structured Empowerment
Corporate Culture   Individual Empowerment
Shared Culture   Team Empowerment
Empowerment   Self-directed Work Teams
Meaning   Functional Teams
Competence   Cross-functional Teams
Self-determination   Cross-training
Impact

N O T E S

1. T. Berry, *Managing the Total Quality Transformation* (New York: McGraw-Hill, 1991), 1.
2. F. Schuster, D. Morden, T. Baker, I. McKay, K. Dunnins, and C. Hasan, "Management Practice, Organization Climate, and Performance, an Exploratory Study, *Journal of Applied Behavioral Science*, 33, 2, June 1997, 209 (18).
3 C. G. Partlow, "How Ritz-Carlton Applies TQM," *Cornell Hotel and Restaurant Administration Quarterly* 34, 16–24. August 1993.
4. R.T. Sparrowe, "Empowerment in the Hospitality Industry: An Exploration of Antecedents and Outcomes," *Hospitality Research Journal* 17 (1994): 51–73; M. D. Fulford and C. A. Enz, "The Impact of Empowerment on Service Employees," *Journal of Managerial Issues* 7 (1995): 161–175.
5. C. E. Whiting Jr. and N. E. Gilbert, "Reaching Hidden Stakeholders: TQM and Empowerment for Professionals, *Journal for Quality and Participation* (June 1993): 61.
6. K. W. Thomas and B. A. Velthouse, "Cognitive Elements of Empowerment: An Interpretive Model of Intrinsic Task Motivation," *Academy of Management Review* 15 (1990): 666–681.
7. R. Brymer, "Employee Empowerment: A Guest-driven Leadership Strategy," *Cornell Hotel and Restaurant Administration Quarterly* 32 (1991): 58–68.
8. J. R. Katzenback and D. K. Smith, *The Wisdom of Teams* (Boston, Mass. Harvard Business School Press, 1993): 12.
9. Ibid., 19.
10. R. S. Wellins, W. J. Katz, A. J. Laughlin, and C. R. Day Jr. "Self-Directed Teams: A Study of Current Practice," in *Survey Report* (Pittsburgh, Pa. Development Dimensions, 1990).
11. R. Leiser, "Ritz Reduces Turnover with Self-directed Work Teams," *Hotel & Motel Management*, 211, no. 4 (March 4, 1996): 27.

CASE **14.1**: TRANSITION TO EMPOWERMENT

The parent company of Melissa's hotel has just issued an announcement of a major organizational change. The company has adopted a new system of employee empowerment, giving individual workers responsibility for solving guest problems and developing strategies to improve the company's functioning. The general manger of Melissa's property, Irma Turner, has appointed Melissa to a special implementation committee that will be responsible for seeing that the transition to this new way of managing will be a smooth one. The committee will be meeting with Turner next week, and she wants to hear about possible problems that might arise from this change and how they should be dealt with.

Melissa wants to make a significant contribution to the committee so she can demonstrate her leadership ability. Give Melissa some mentoring advice so she will be well prepared for her first committee meeting next week.

1. Describe some of the possible problems that an organization might encounter when it moves from a traditional management system to one where employees are empowered.

2. How might employees react to the new system? What concerns might management have about their new role in an empowered organization?

3. What additional training might both managers and employees need to take on their new responsibilities?

R E V I E W   Q U E S T I O N S

1. If someone were to ask you, "What is TQM?" what would you say?
2. What type of culture must an organization have if it is to successfully implement TQM principles?
3. What are the benefits of a congruent culture?
4. What are the benefits of empowering employees? Why has it become so important in recent years?
5. Would you prefer to be an hourly employee in an empowered work environment or in a traditional environment where managers make all decisions? Why?
6. Would you prefer to be a manager in an empowered work environment rather than a traditional one? Why or why not?
7. List and define the four dimensions of empowerment.
8. How does structured empowerment differ from flexible empowerment?

Indicate whether the following statements refer to:

    a. Functional team b. Cross-functional team   c. Self-directed team

9. Team members conduct interviews and select new team members.
10. Servers who all work in a restaurant together.
11. Employee of the month committee—a group of employees from different departments who meet to select the employee who will be recognized each month.
12. Review the two sample ads for front desk employees included in your Chapter. Which position would you prefer? Why?

C R I T I C A L   T H I N K I N G   E X E R C I S E S

1. Select two hospitality organizations (other than those described in your text) that have very different cultures. Describe in detail the cultural practices of each and how these practices have effected the organizations' success.

2. Lists three additional activities (not included in the chapter) that might be accomplished by self-managed teams.

3. Imagine that you had the ability to decide how much control to pass on to empowered employees. Rate your comfort level with having your employees perform the following tasks on a scale of 1 to 7 with 1 being "No way you'd give them that power" and 7 being "I'd be very comfortable giving employees this responsibility." You can assume they all have the knowledge, skills, and ability to complete the tasks.

No way					Very Comfortable	
1	2	3	4	5	6	7

   _____ a. Decide which of three job applicants should be hired.

   _____ b. Develop their own work schedules.

   _____ c. Select the new department uniforms.

   _____ d. Solve guest problems without assistance.

   _____ e. Decide when each team member should take their breaks.

   _____ f. Conduct peer evaluations—do performance evaluations for other hourly employees.

   _____ g. Decide how the annual salary increase should be distributed among employees.

   _____ h. Develop performance goals for the department for the next year.

   _____ i. Meet as a group and develop solutions to department problems.

   _____ j. Schedule and lead department meetings.

   Scoring:
   Total your score: _____ (10 to 70 pts.)

   Traditional manager score = 10 to 30 pts.: You have a more traditional way of operating your department and prefer maintaining control of most aspects of its functioning yourself.

   Empowered but not self-directed score = 31-50 pts.: You are comfortable with giving your employees greater responsibility but not with managing a self-directed work team.

   Totally self-directed score = 51 to 70 pts.: You are very comfortable in a self-directed work environment and would seek out ways to empower your employees as extensively as possible.

4. Think of an organization in which you have worked or completed an internship. To what degree were employees empowered to make decisions and control their work environment? Do you think the company should have increased the amount of responsibility they gave to employees? Why or why not?

O N - L I N E   L I N K

Learn more about the quality movement by visiting the web site for the National Institute of Standards and Technology at www.quality.nist.gov, the organization that is responsible for setting quality standards and selecting winners of the Malcolm Baldridge Award. While you are there, learn about the history of the quality movement by visiting "Our Story" and the winners of the Baldridge award by visiting "Winner's Showcase." Select several other pages to view and when you have finished exploring this site, write several paragraphs to summarize what you have learned about the quality movement and the Baldridge Award.

P O R T F O L I O   E X E R C I S E

Your ability to both act as a team member and to provide leadership to work groups is very important in today's organizations. Document your team-based experiences in your portfolio by including the following:

1. Describe those qualities that make you an effective team member and team leader.
2. Describe non work-related team experiences you have had and what you did to contribute to your team's success. These experiences might be in sports, educational settings, clubs, or organizations.
3. Finally describe team experiences you have had at work, either in the hospitality industry or in other fields. Once again provide detail of specific actions you took to contribute to your team's success.

I N D E X

658 - 407-208

A

Acculturation, 325
Active instruction, 142–145
Adult learner, 130–131
Advertising, 110
Affirmative action, 307–308
Age Discrimination Act, 207
Alternative dispute resolution, 240
American Federation of Labor, 231
Americans with Disabilities Act, 209
Andragogy, 130
Apathy, 40
Appearance standards, 210
Arbitration, 238
Assertiveness, 33–34
Authorization cards, 235

B

Balanced scorecard, 275–277
Behavior modeling, 12–13
Behavior modification, 162–163
Behavior, 150
Behavioral interviewing, 117–118
Behavioral simulation, 116–117
Behaviorally anchored rating scale, 189
Benchmarking, 273
Bonafide occupational qualification, 102
Boycott, 238
Brainstorming, 63
Business agent, 230

C

Career days, 110–111
Career development, employee, 196–197
    Multilayered job categories, 197
    Succession planning, 197

Career development, personal, 82–89
    Advancement, 89–91
    Interviews, 83–84, 87–89
    Job hunt, 85–87
    Portfolio, 82–83
    Resume, 84–85
Case study, 116–117
Centralized, 259
Certification vote, 235
Challenging feedback, 38–40
Civil Rights Act, 100–101, 206
Closed shop, 232
Coaching, 181–188
    Coachable moments, 186
    Peak performers, 182–183
    Performance improvement, 183–185
    Respect, 187
Coachable moments, 186
Coaching with respect, 187
Collective bargaining, 236
Communication, 312–339
    Feedback, 38–40
    Interpersonal effectiveness, 32–34
    Leadership, 28–32
    Nonverbal, 36
    Physical attending, 35–36
    Poor habits, 30–32
    Relationships, 28–30
Competence, 328
Competency modeling, 171–172
Computer based training, 147–148
Conflict management 40–45
    Resolution, 42–44
    Style, 41–42
Conflict resolution, 61–63
    Compromise, 62
    Imposed solution, 61
    Mutual agreement, 62
    Win-win, 62–63
Conflict style, 41